AF323670

SHARP NIGEL PARRY

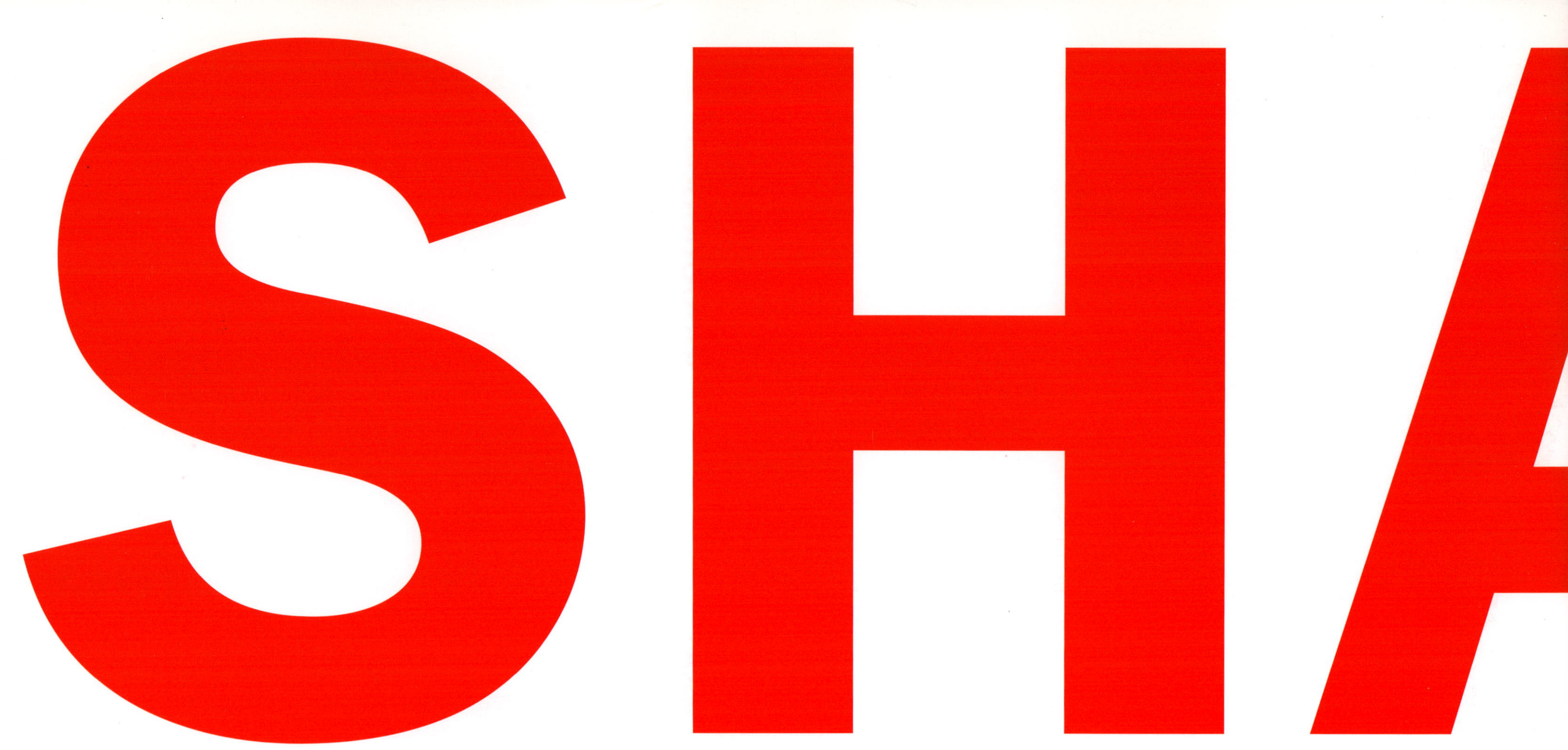

powerHouse Books   New York, NY

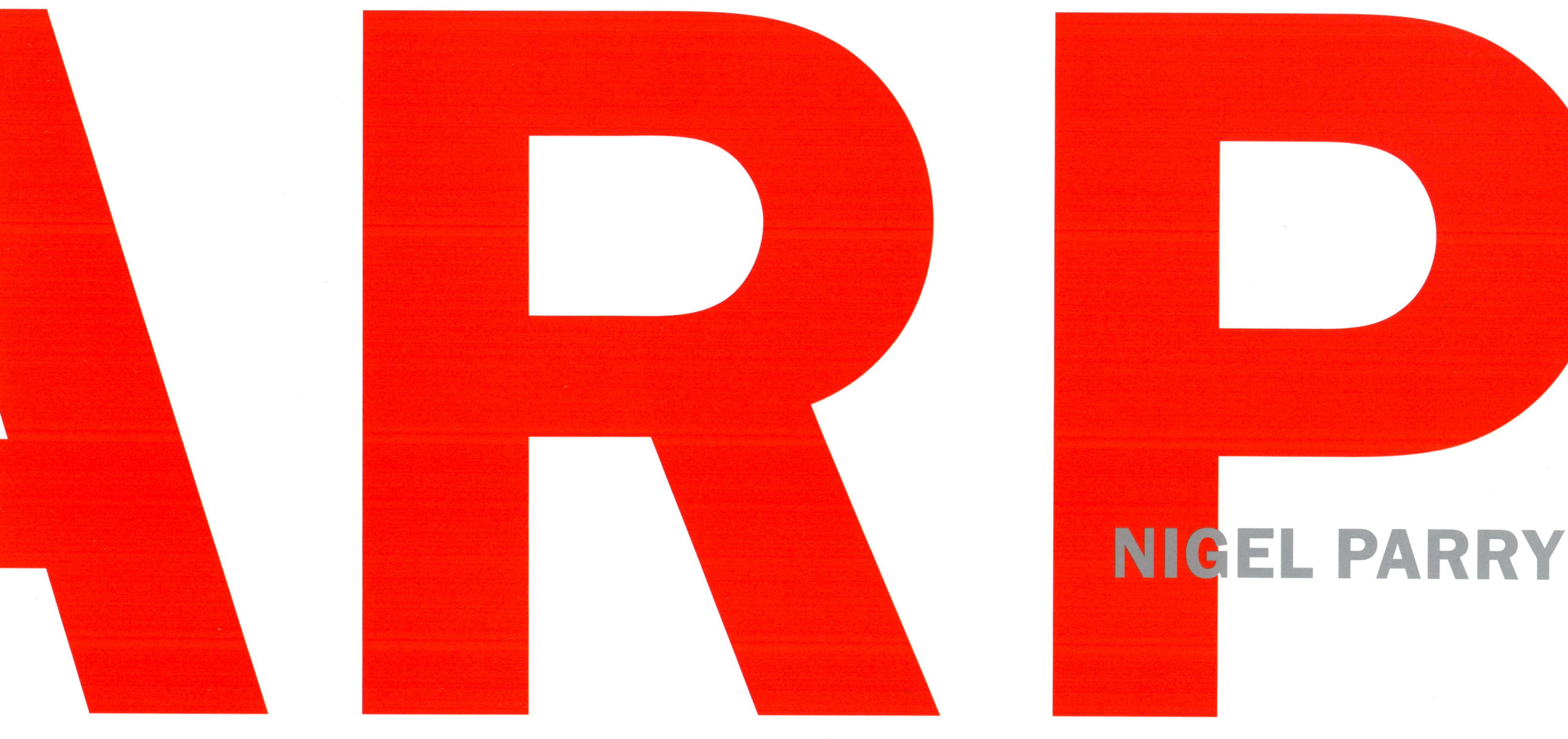

ARP

NIGEL PARRY

INTRODUCTION BY LIAM NEESON

DEDICATED

TO EMMA AND JACK

...I HONESTLY DON'T KNOW. MY FIRST EXPERIENCE WITH **BEING PHOTOGRAPHED** GOES BACK TO WHEN I WAS A SIXTEEN-YEAR-OLD BOY IN NORTHERN IRELAND. I WAS AN AMATEUR BOXING CHAMPION. I POSED PROUDLY IN FRONT OF A RELATIVE'S NEWLY-INVENTED POLAROID CAMERA DRESSED IN MY BOXING CLUB'S COLOURS. MY BODY WAS FAIRLY WELL HONED AND I FLEXED EVERY MUSCLE, HOLDING UP MY FISTS TRYING TO LOOK MEAN AND TOUGH. FIVE MINUTES LATER A WET STICKY PICTURE SLITHERED OUT OF THE CAMERA. INSTEAD OF A GREEK ADONIS, I WAS VERY **SURPRISED** TO SEE A RATHER INTENSE, SHY, INTROVERTED, GAWKY TEENAGER.

SINCE BECOMING AN ACTOR I HAVE BEEN PHOTOGRAPHED MORE TIMES THAN I CARE TO REMEMBER. THIS USUALLY REQUIRES POSING FOR A PHOTOGRAPHER FOR UP TO A FULL WORKING DAY IN VARIOUS STAGES OF DRESS OR UNDRESS. **THE PHOTO SHOOT INVOLVES QUITE A FEW PEOPLE**: THE PHOTOGRAPHER'S IMMEDIATE CREW (TWO-TO-FOUR PEOPLE); MAKEUP AND HAIRDRESSING ARTISTS; ONE'S PUBLICIST TO ENSURE ONE'S HAPPINESS; AND SOMEONE FROM THE MAGAZINE. ALTOGETHER IT IS QUITE A CROWD, AND VERY **INTIMIDATING**.

DURING A SHOOT I HAVE **VERY MIXED FEELINGS**; THEY CAN BE **EXTREME**, DEPENDING TO A GREAT EXTENT ON WHO THE PHOTOGRAPHER IS. WHAT YOU WANT IS SOMEONE WHO MAKES YOU FEEL AT EASE AND MAKES THE WHOLE THING RELAXED AND EFFORTLESS. THAT IS THE EXPERIENCE I HAVE HAD WITH NIGEL PARRY. NIGEL HAS **SHOT ME SEVERAL TIMES**, AND THE PHOTOS KEEP GETTING BETTER. I GUESS WE HAVE A **CHEMISTRY** THAT WORKS; WE KNOW IT AND DON'T ANALYZE IT. (IF THE DOOR DOESN'T CREAK, DON'T OIL IT!) DURING A SHOOT I CAN SENSE WHAT NIGEL WANTS AND WHY. WE USUALLY HIT THE "MEAT" OF THE SESSION DURING THE LAST HOUR—WE'RE IN A GROOVE, WE'RE CONNECTING—AND IT IS EXHILARATING AND VERY SATISFYING. HE IS A WONDERFUL PORTRAITIST, AND HE HAS TAKEN SOME SHOTS OF ME THAT I'M PROUD OF AND THAT HAVE WON INTERNATIONAL AWARDS. WE DID A SESSION AT THE RELEASE OF *STAR WARS* WHERE I WAS IN FULL COSTUME AS A JEDI MASTER. THE PHOTOGRAPHS ARE **POWERFUL, INTENSE, AND INTIMATE**. THEY HAVE A SENSE OF MYSTERY AND MYTHOLOGY ABOUT THEM, AS WELL AS A SENSE OF FUN. THAT'S THE DIFFERENCE BETWEEN FEELING EXPOSED BEFORE A WONDERFUL PHOTOGRAPHER OR BEFORE SOMEONE YOU'RE NOT CONNECTING WITH.

WHEN NIGEL SHOOTS WE ALWAYS HAVE A GOOD TIME, AND I ALWAYS ASK FOR HIM WHEN I AM PROMOTING A MOVIE. HE ALSO MANAGES TO MAKE ME LOOK GOOD— WHICH IS NO MEAN FEAT!

INTRODUCTION

BY LIAM NEESON

WHAT PEO
REALIZE IS
IT'S THE S
THAT COU
NOT THE

PHILIP JOHNSON SHOWS SOME SHREWD INSIGHT LOOKING AT A POLAROID OF HIMSELF.

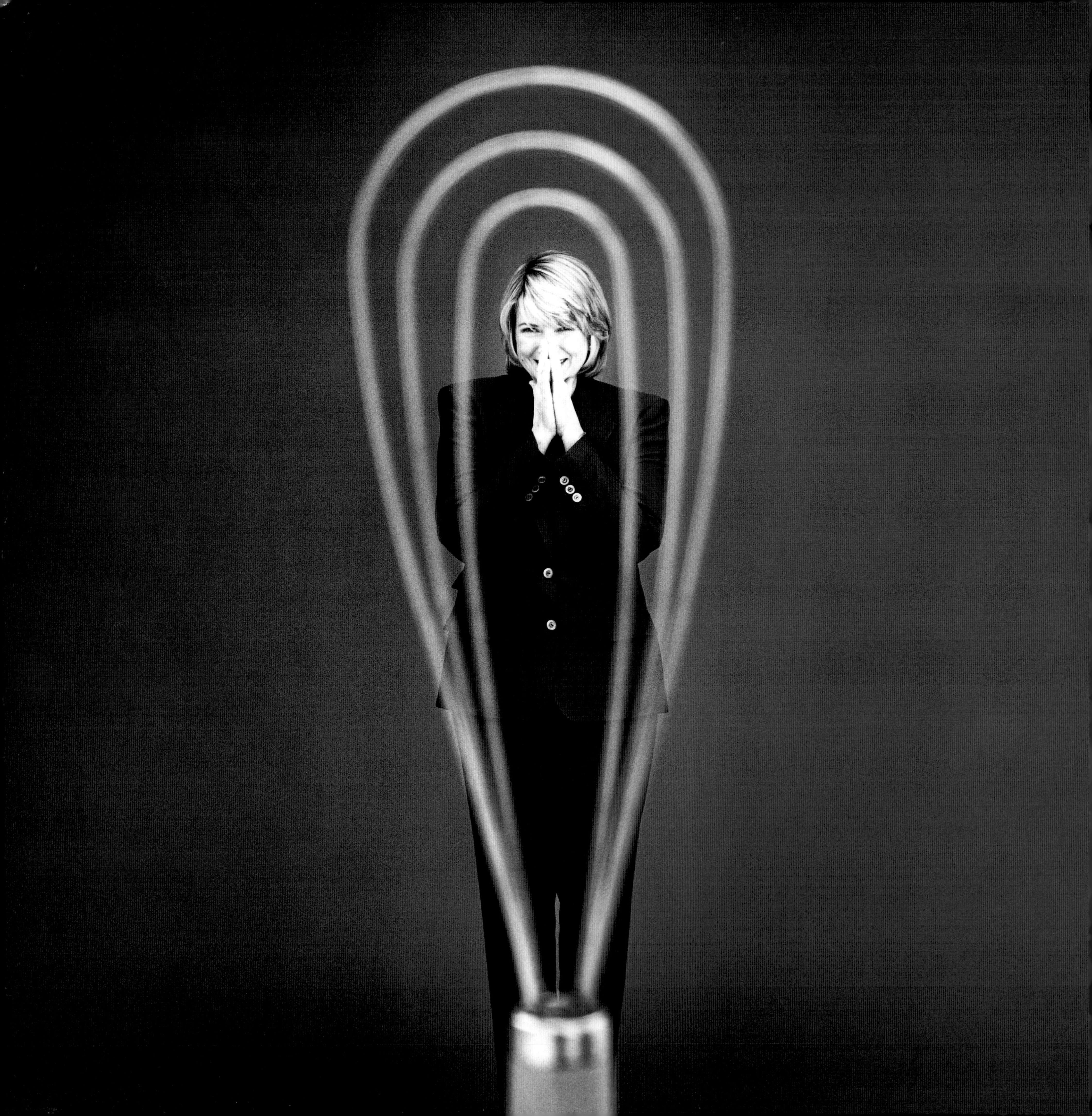

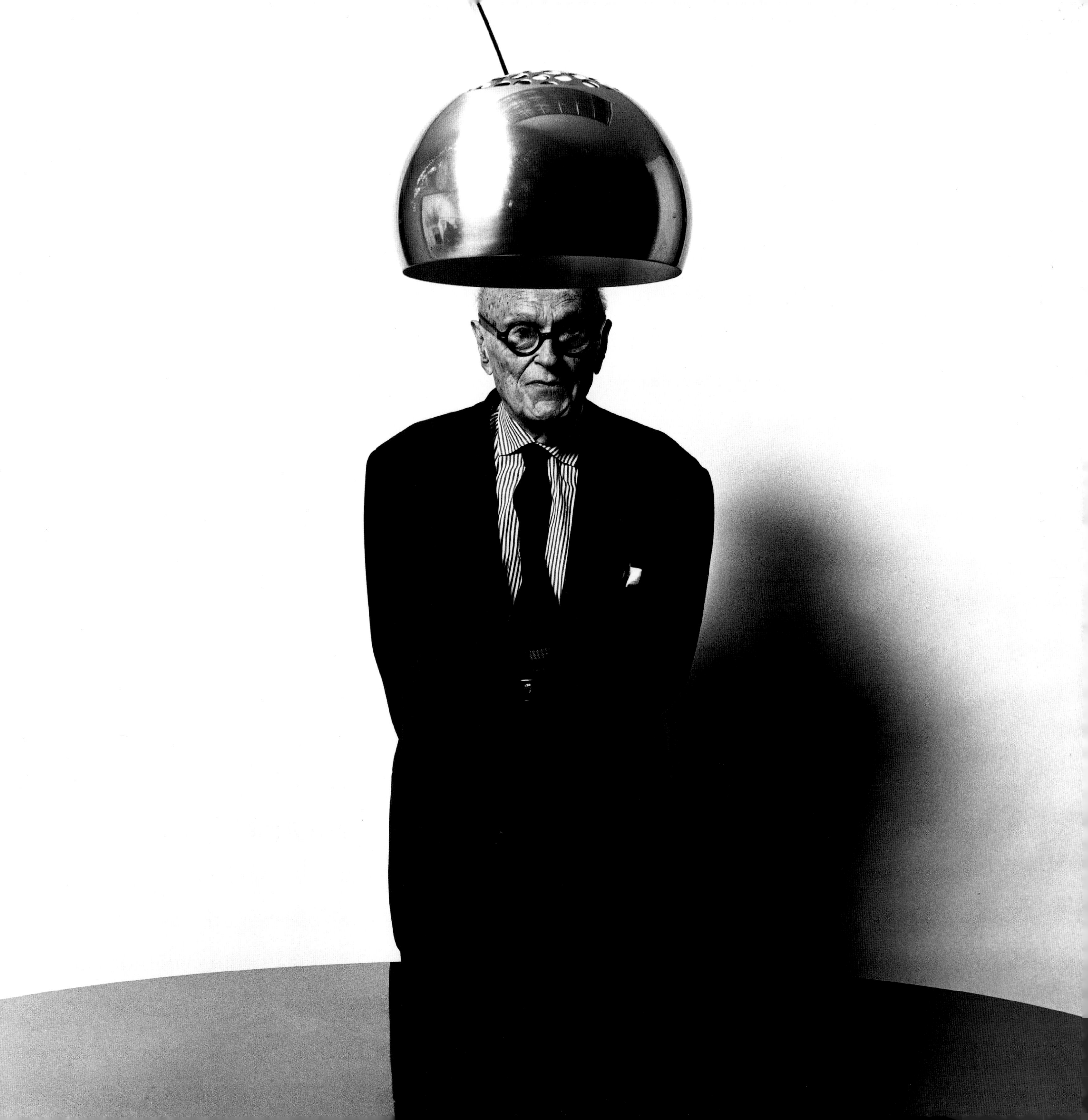

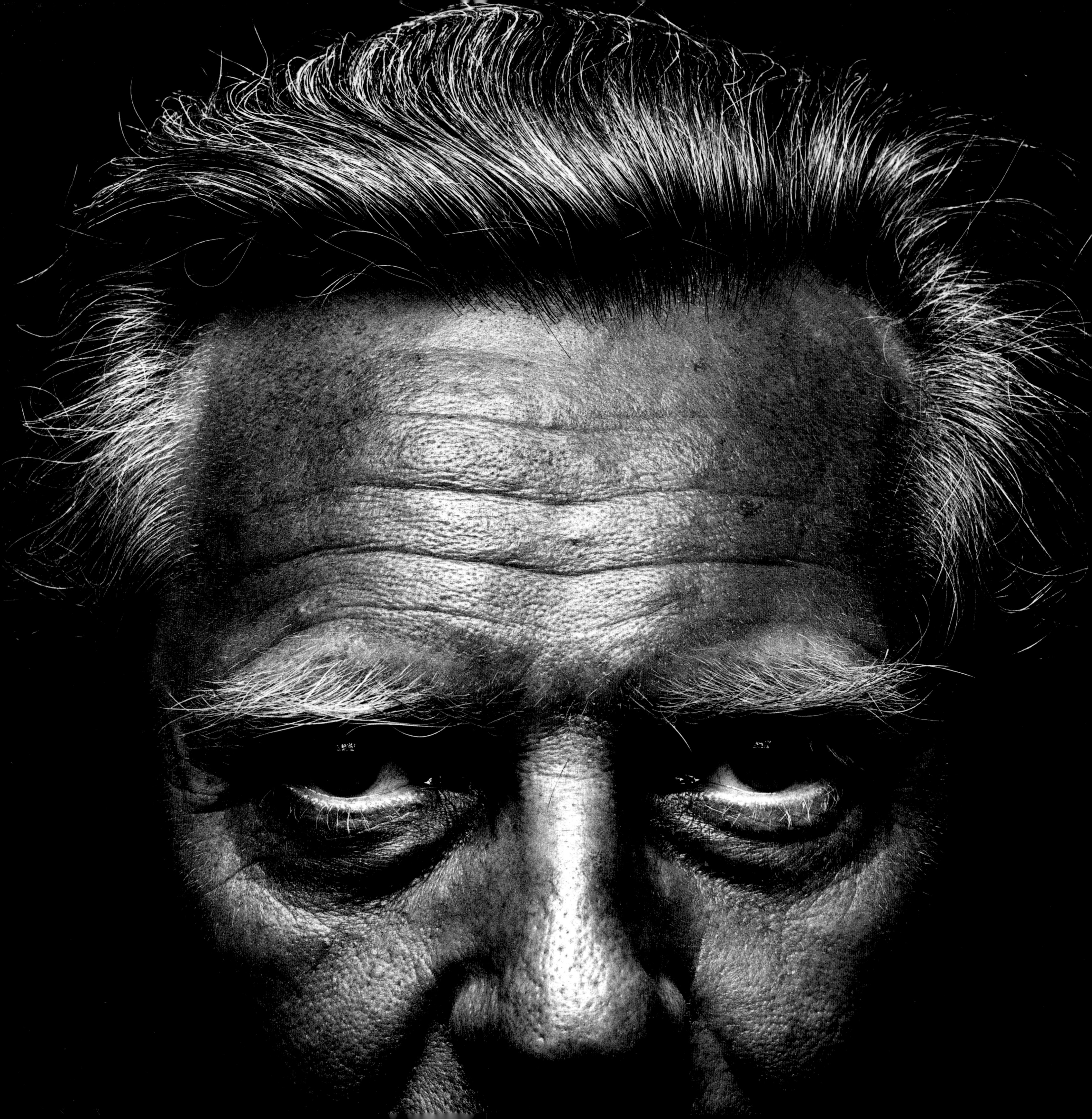

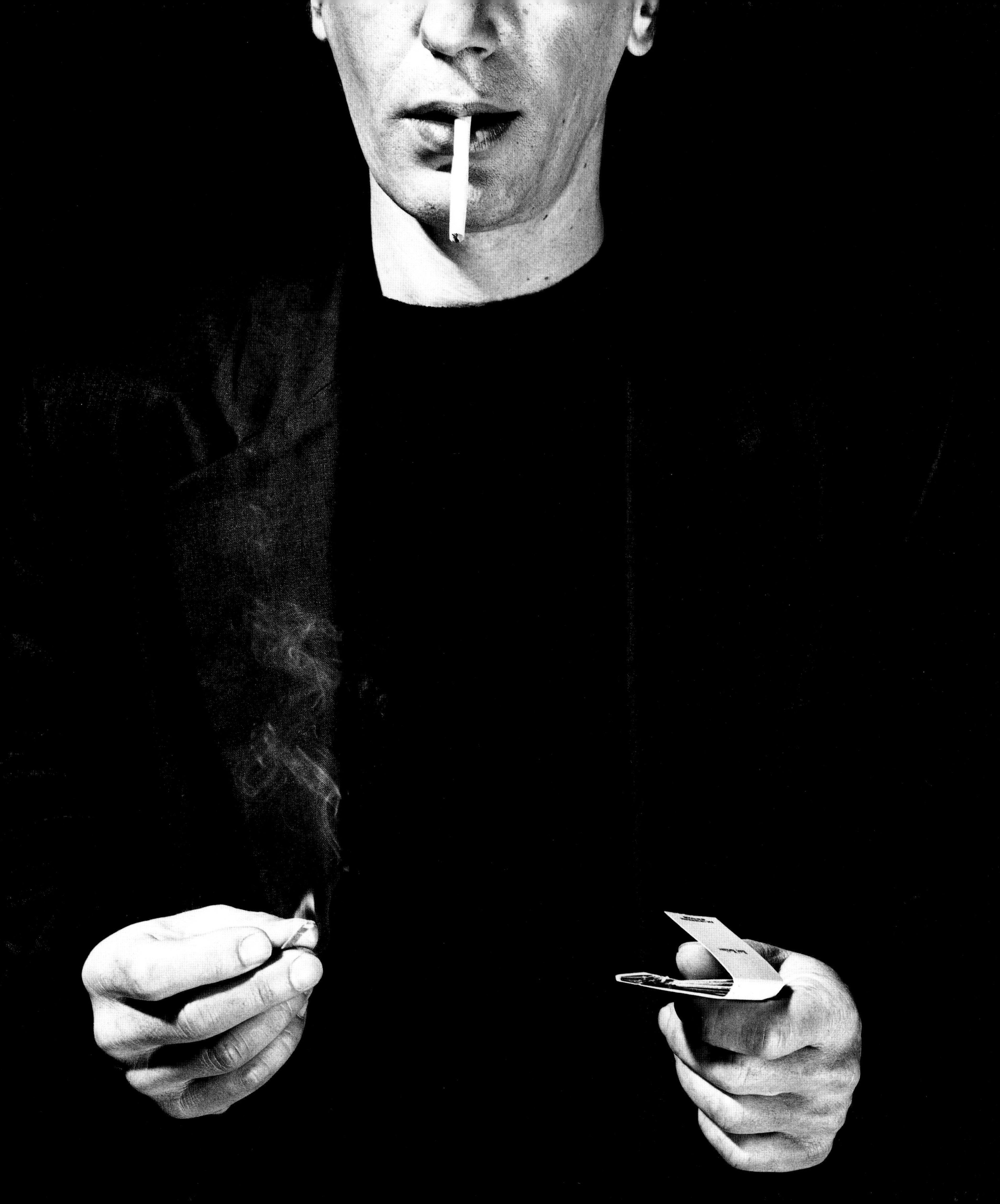

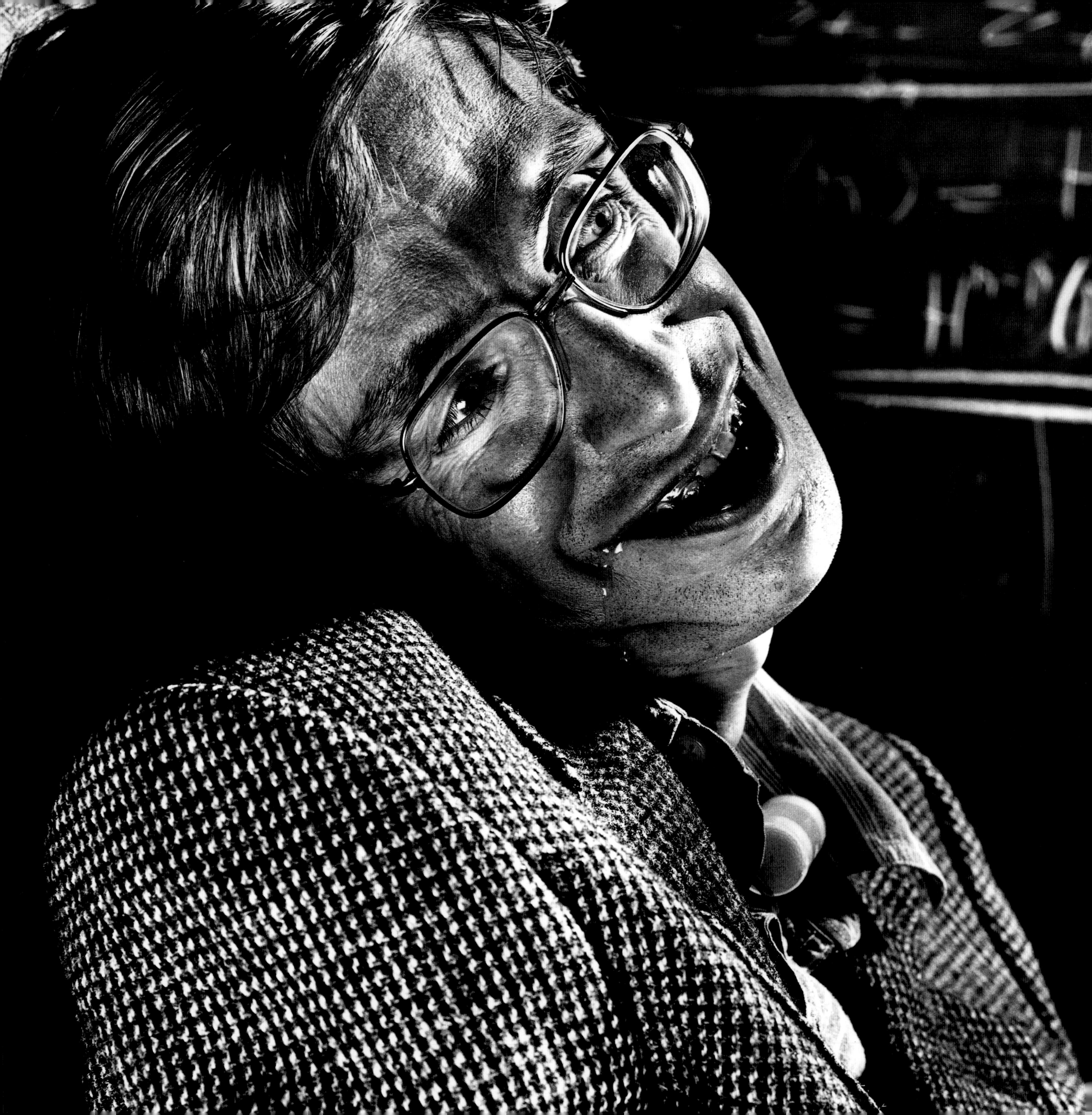

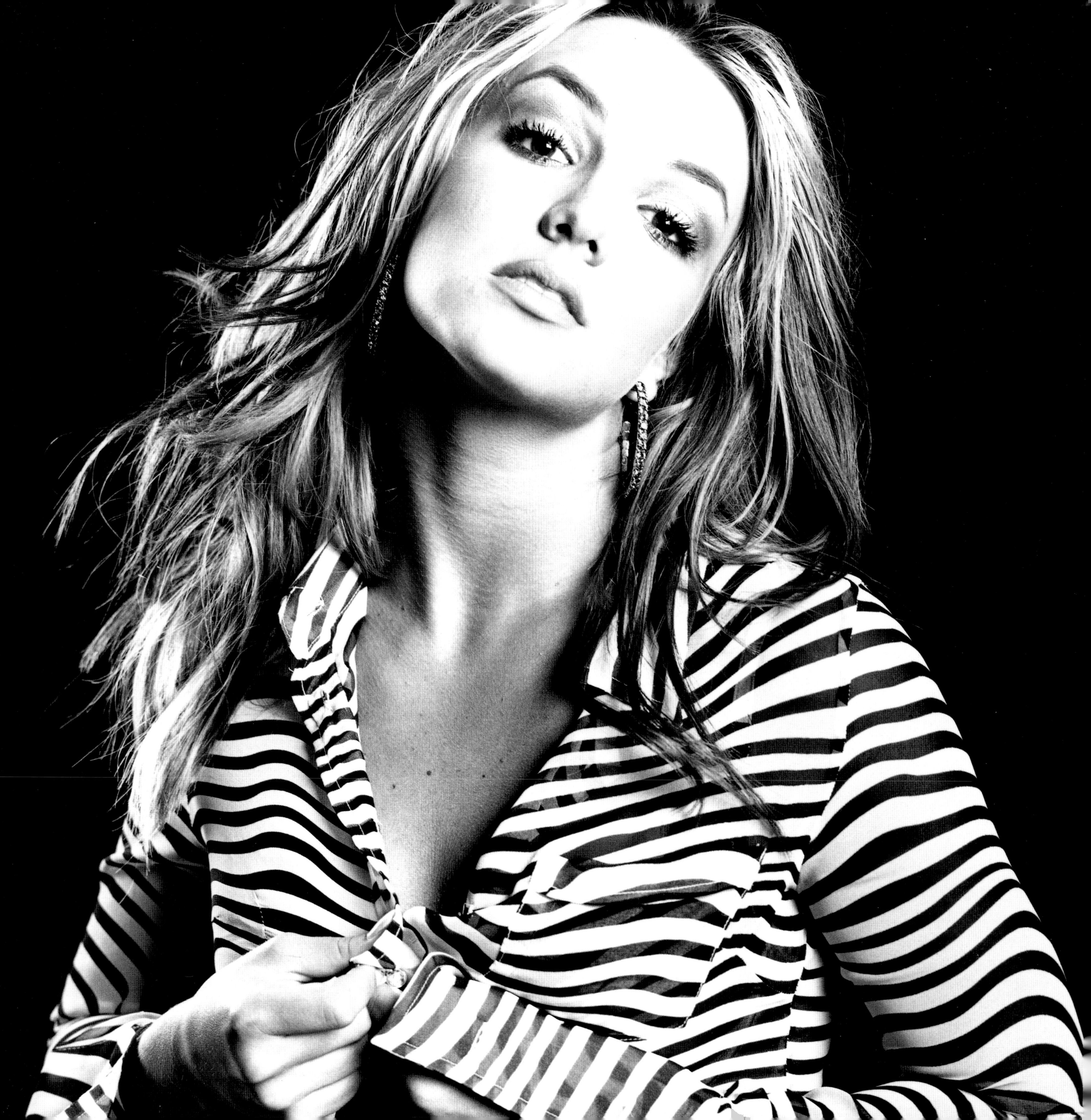

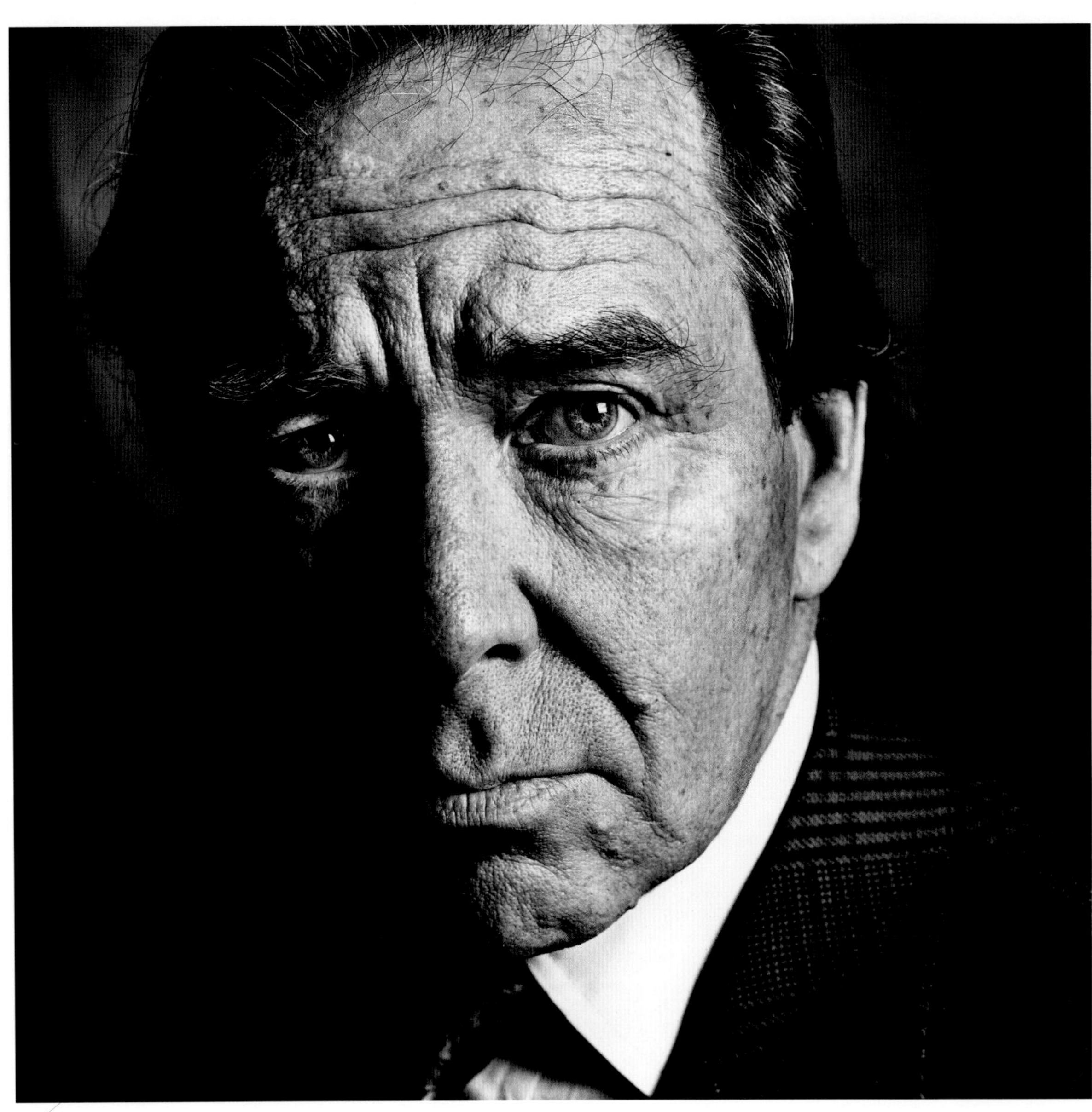

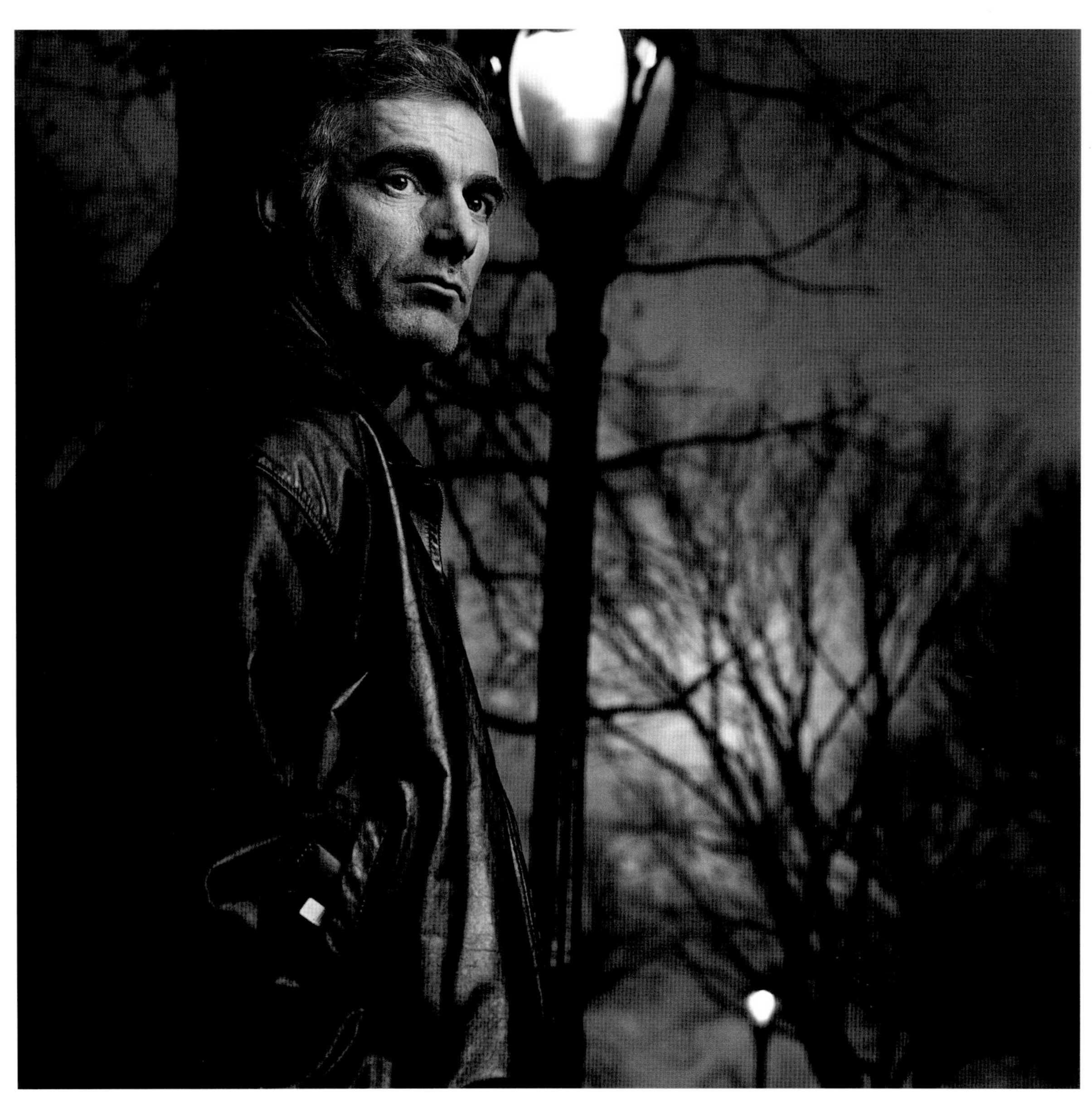

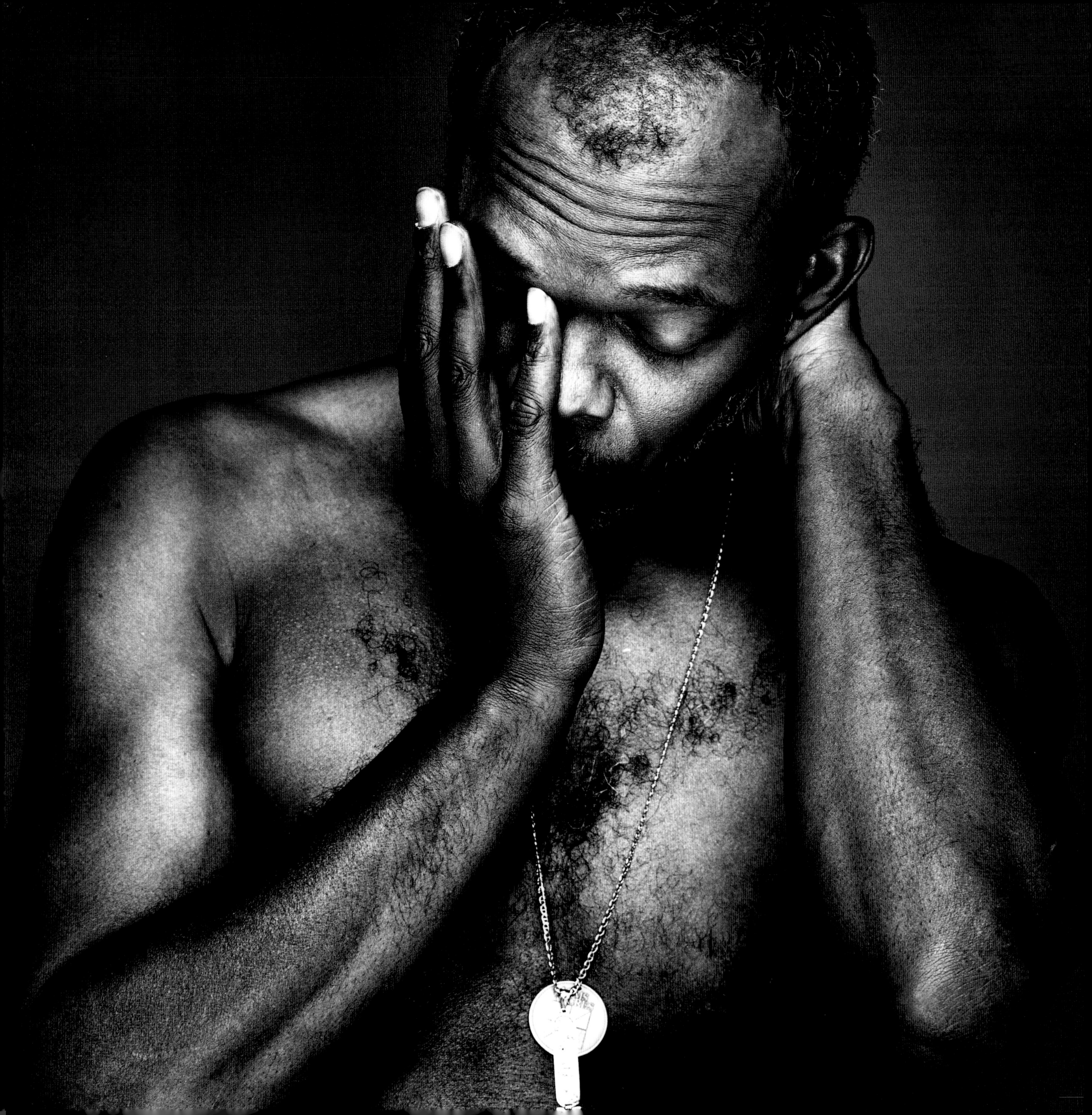

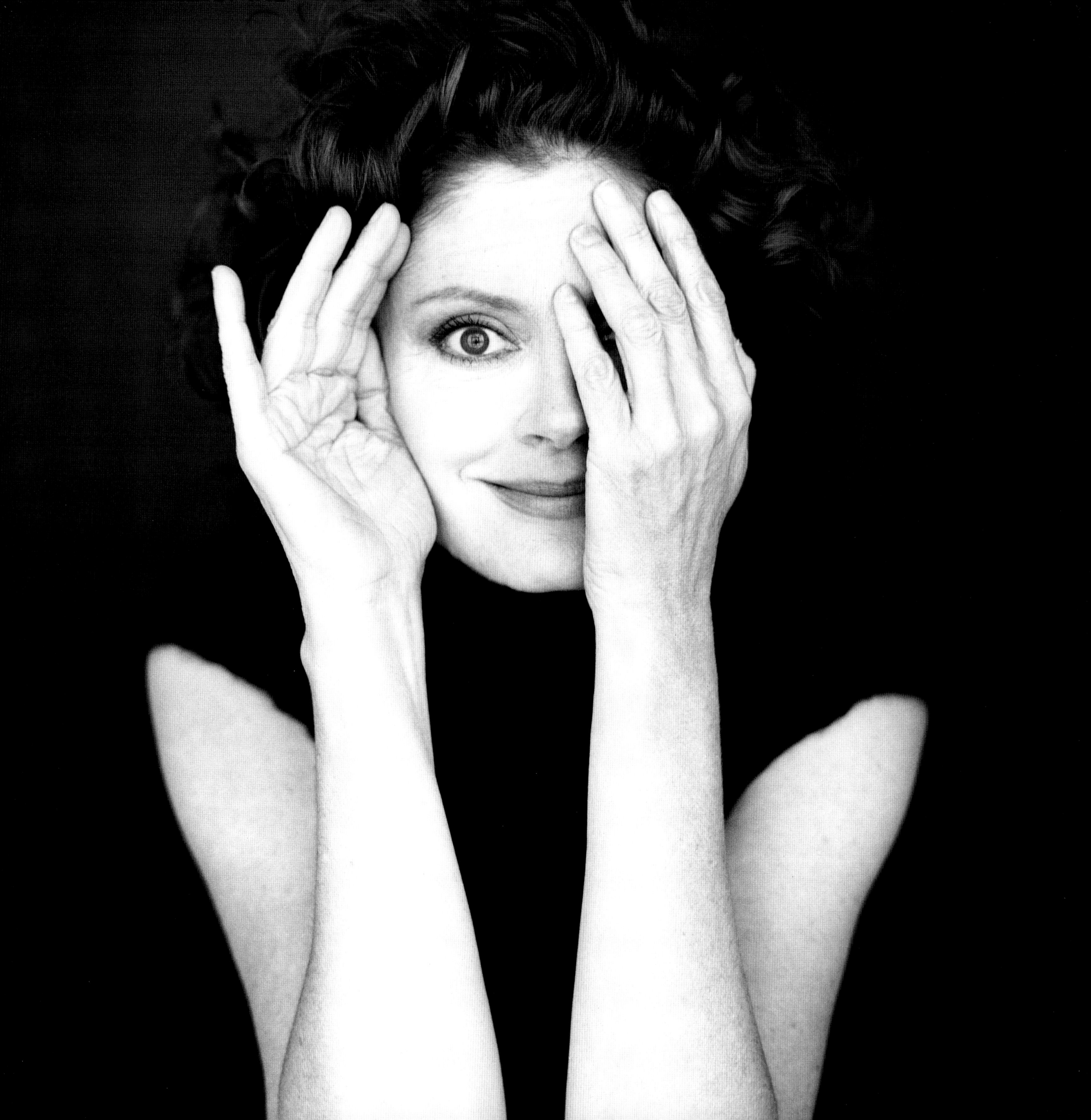

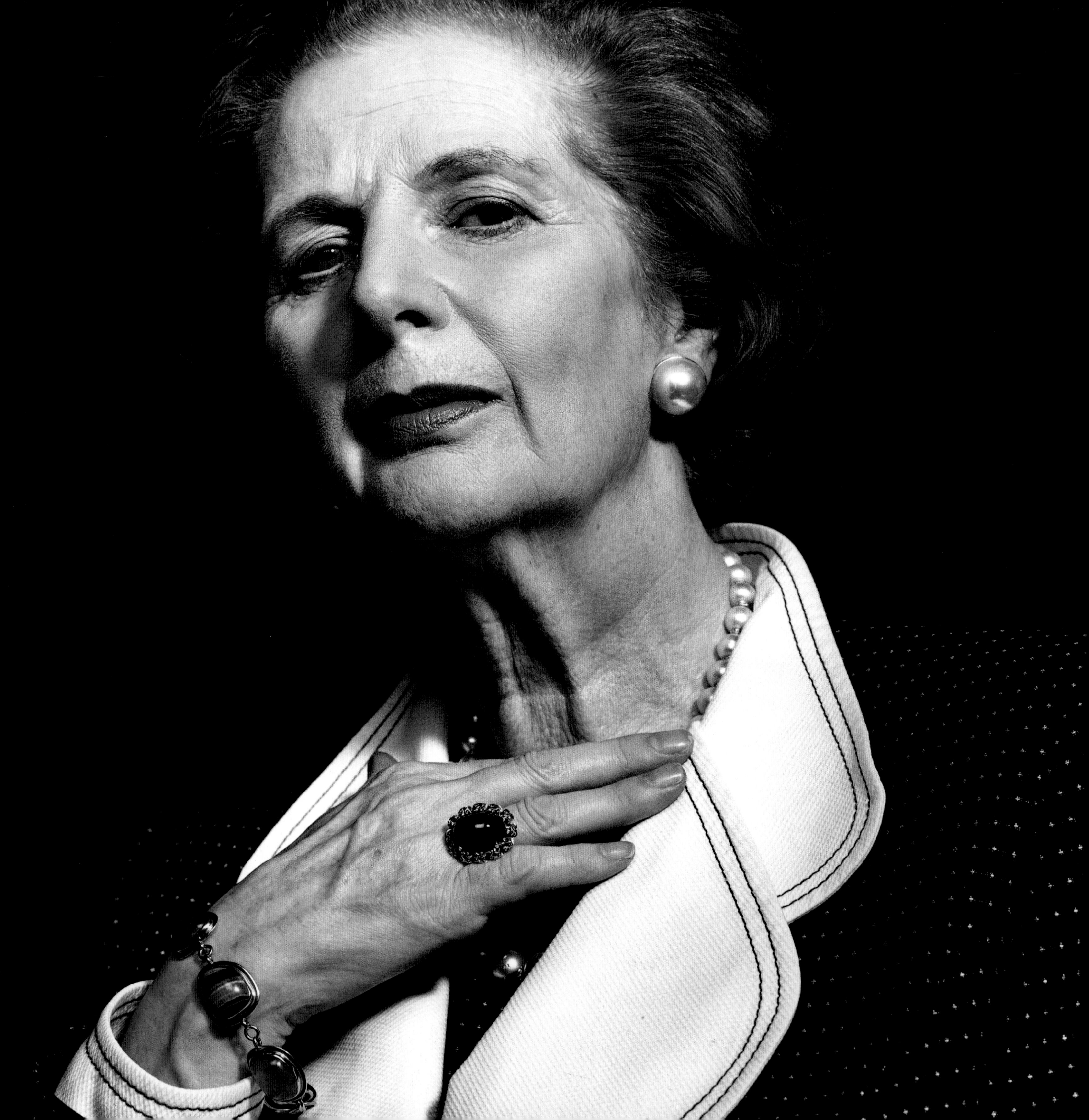

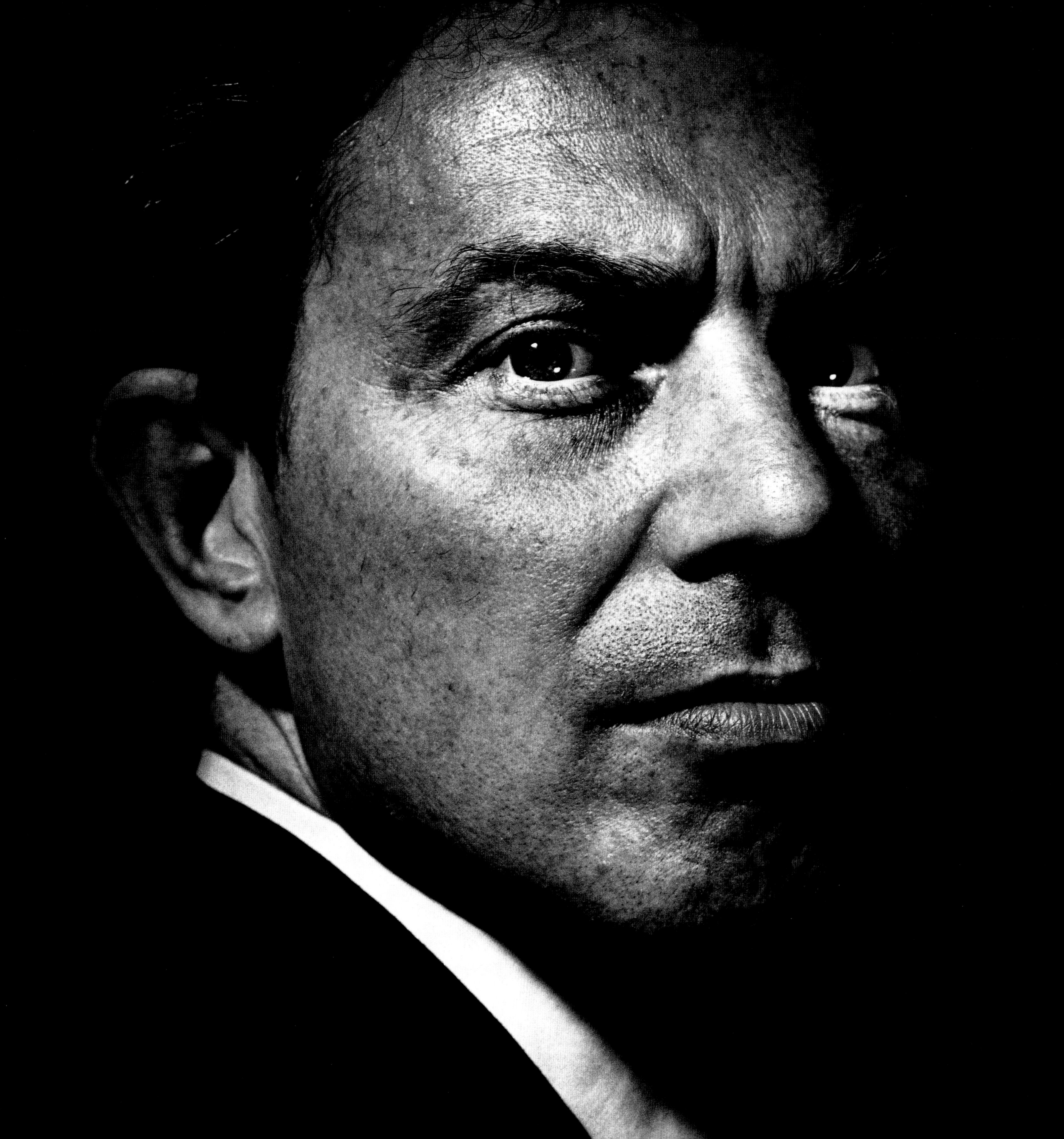

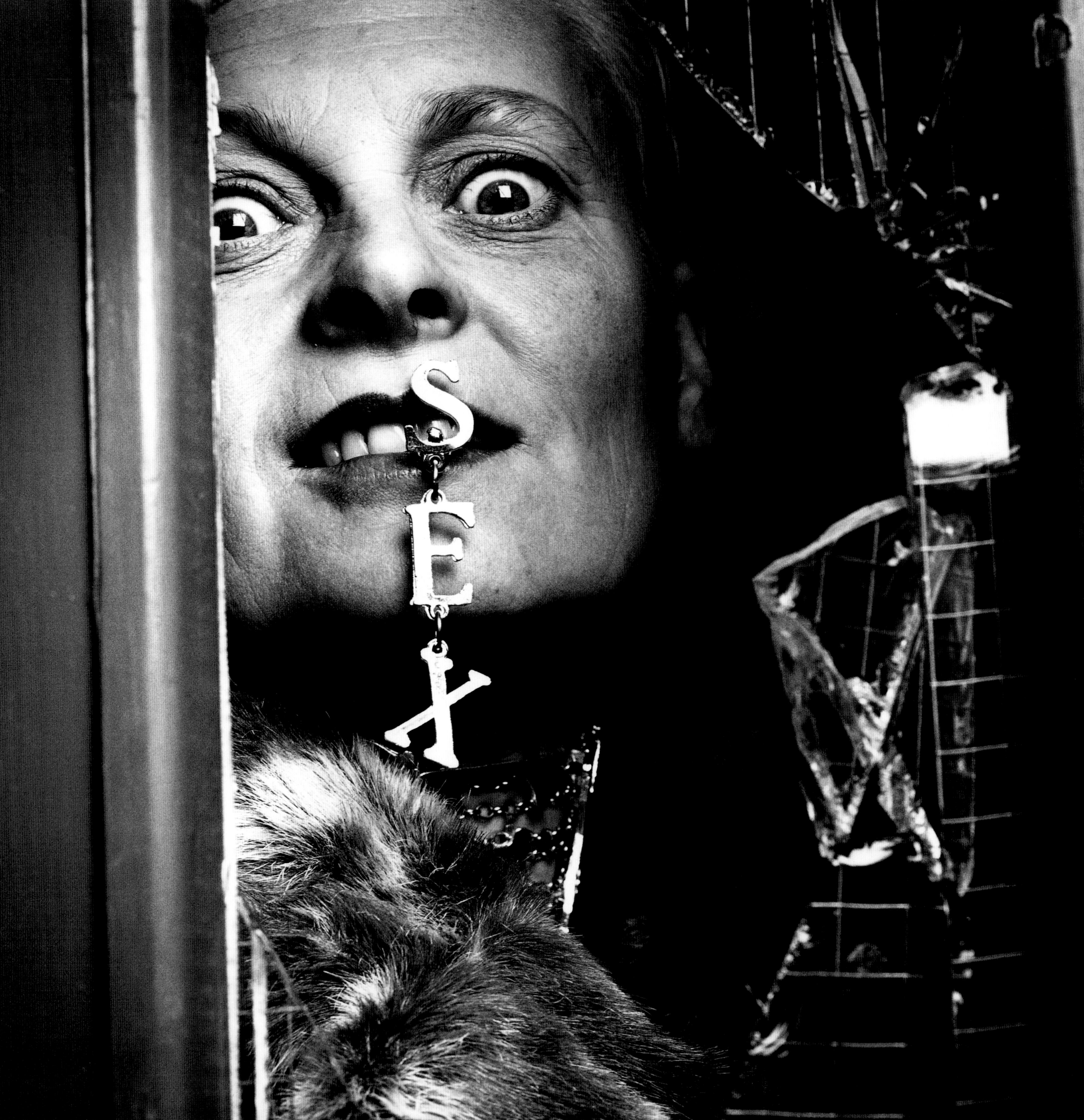
S
E
X

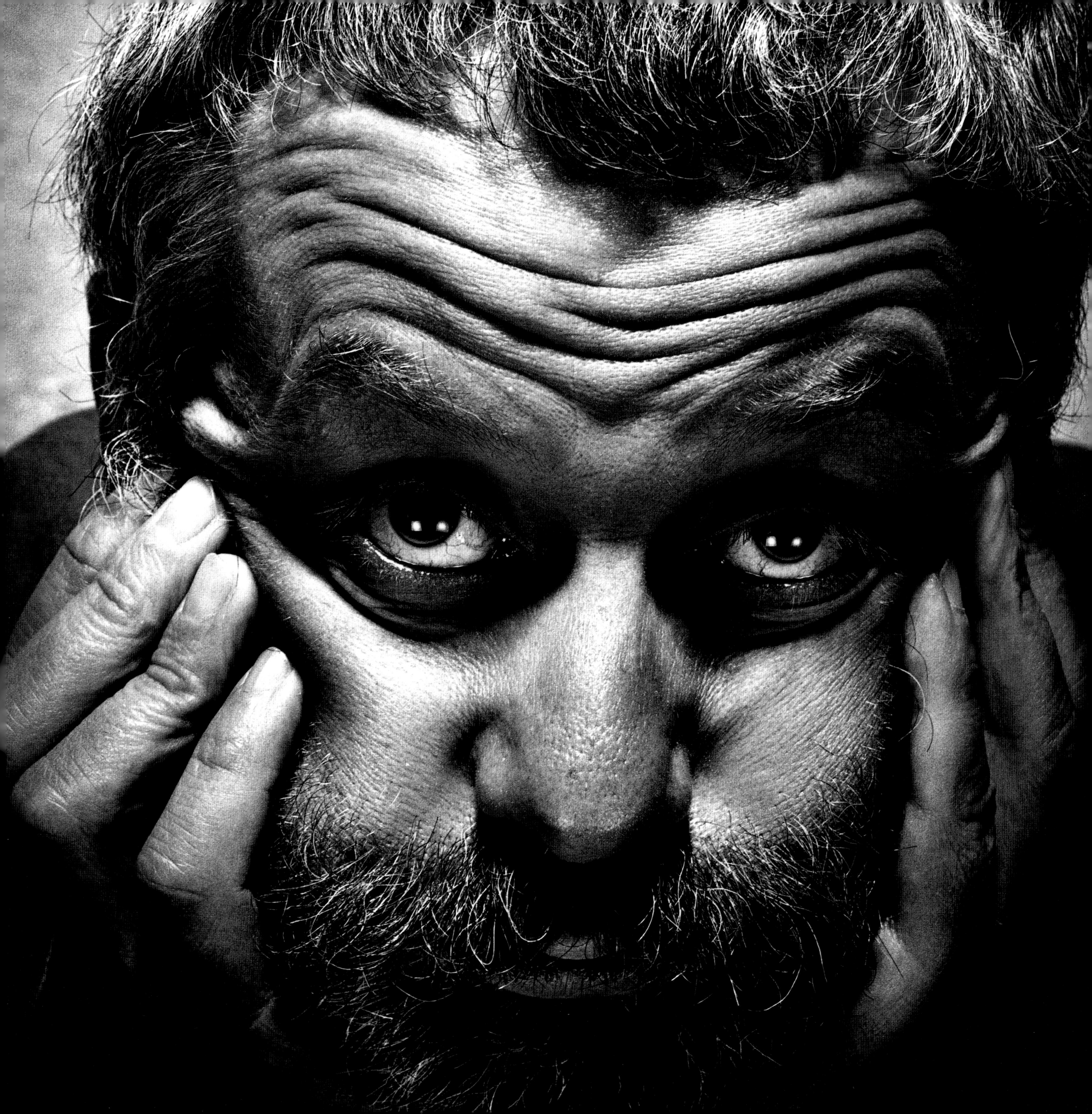

HELLO, NIC

I'VE A GRE

WE'RE DO

THE SHOO

BE READY

ONE HOUR

EL....

AT IDEA:

NG

NOW!

IN

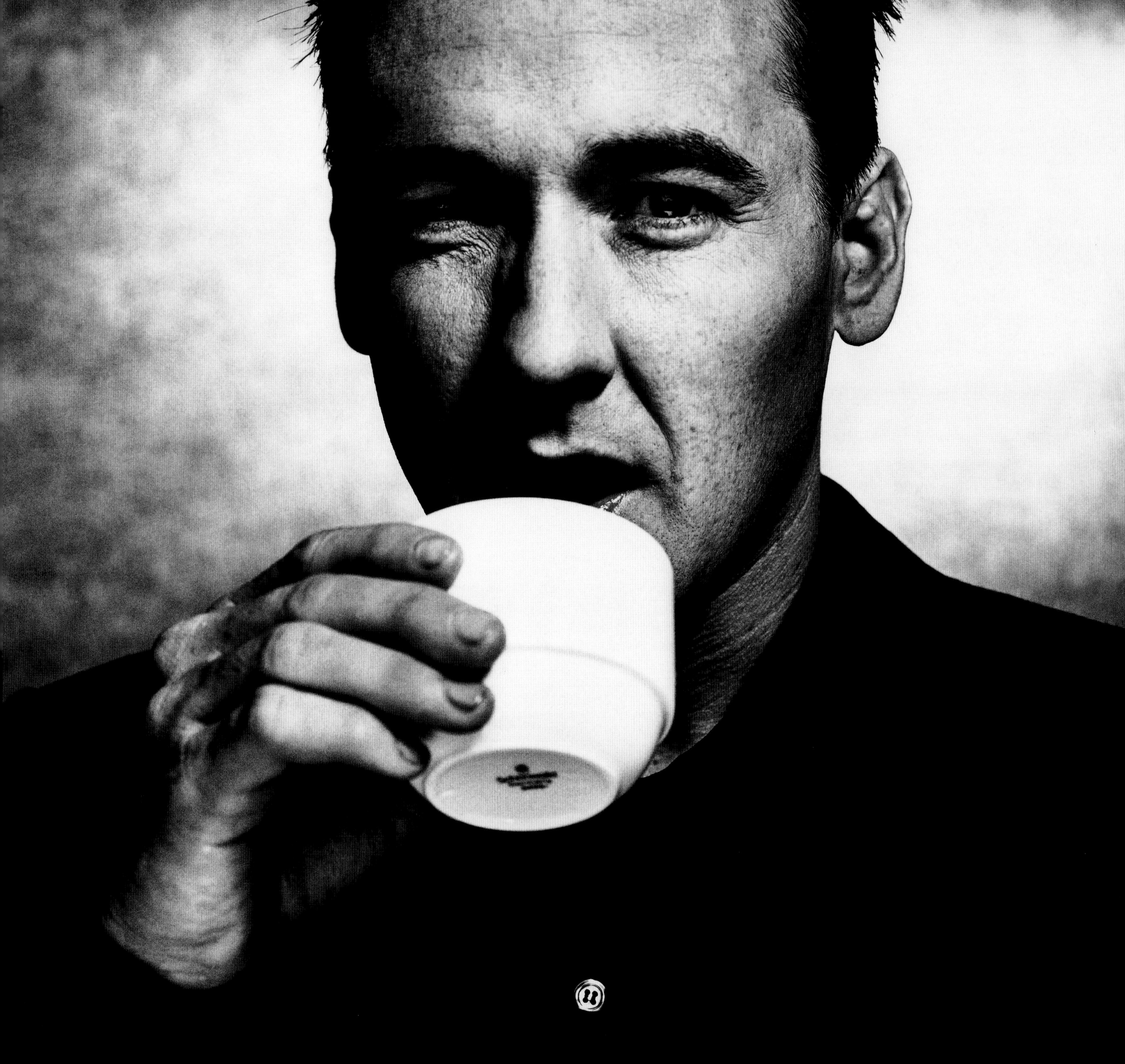

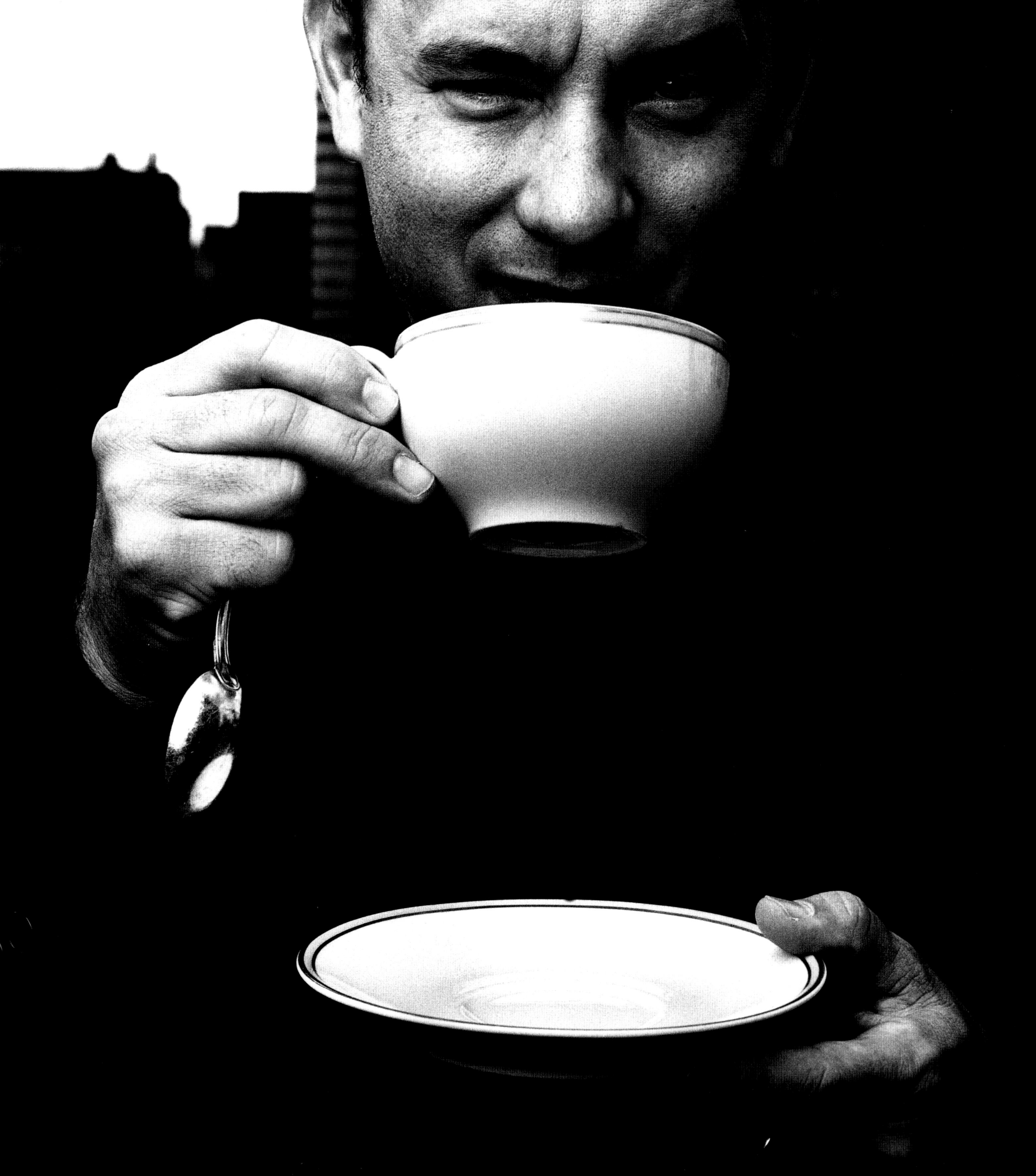

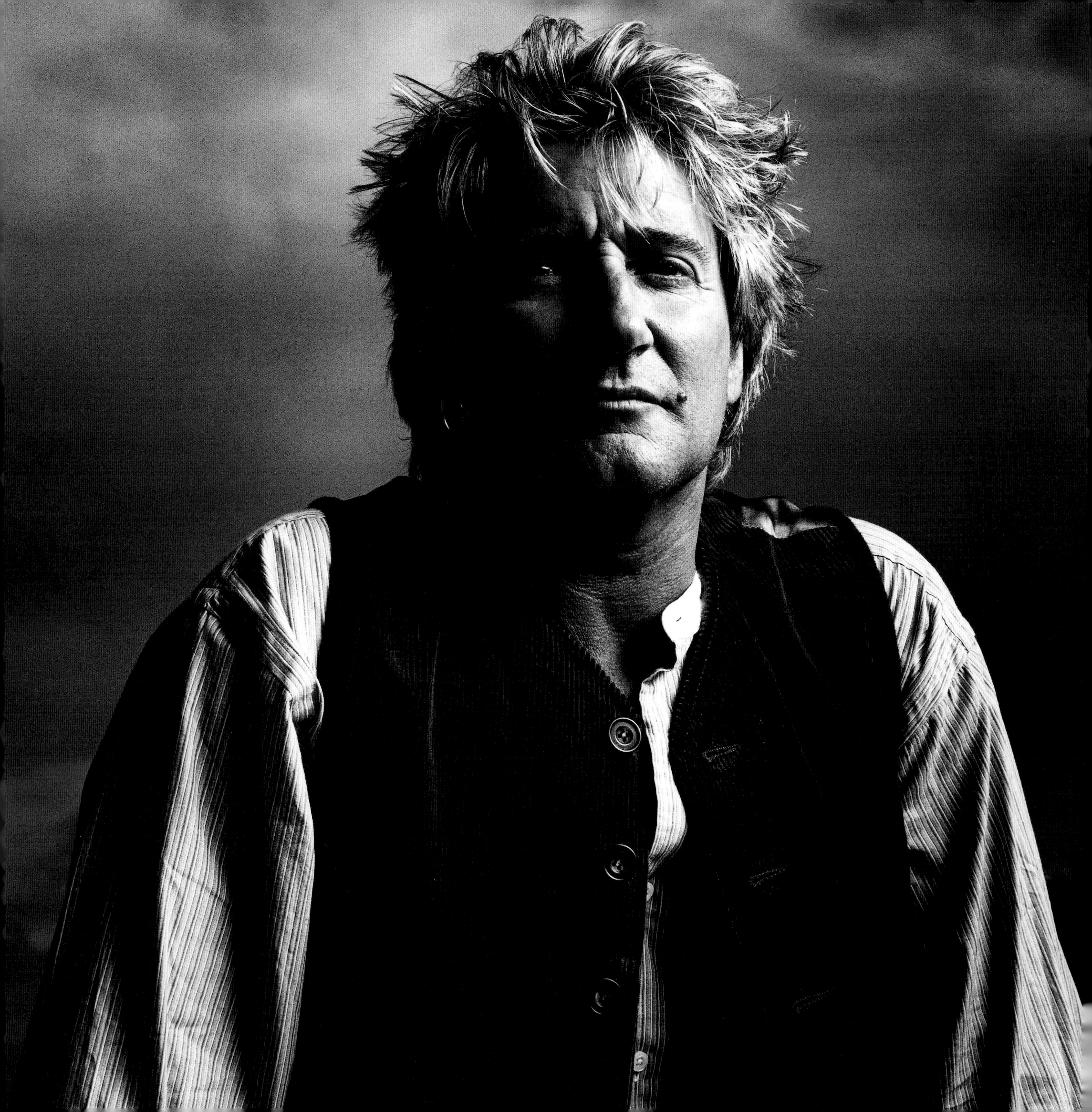

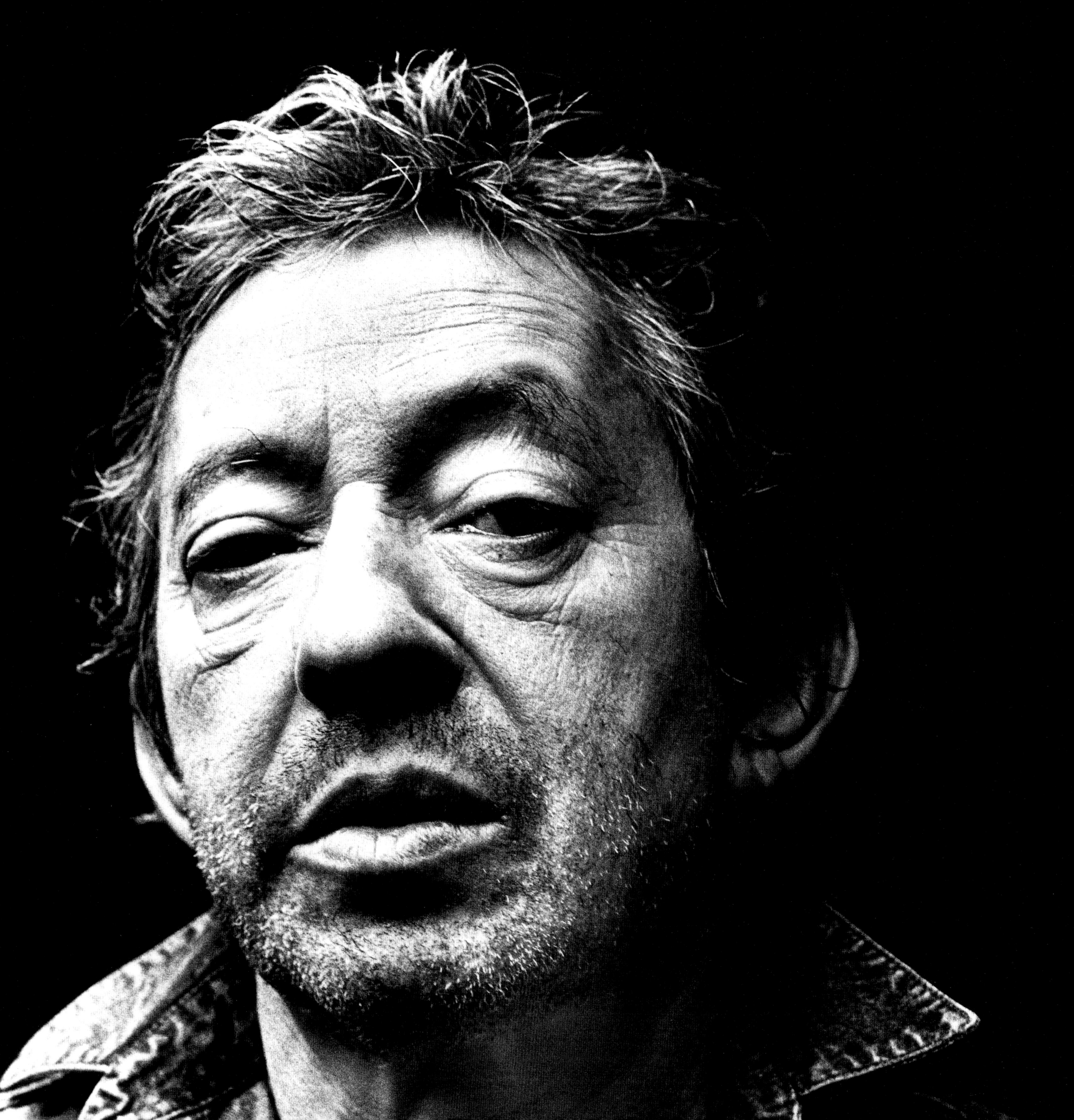

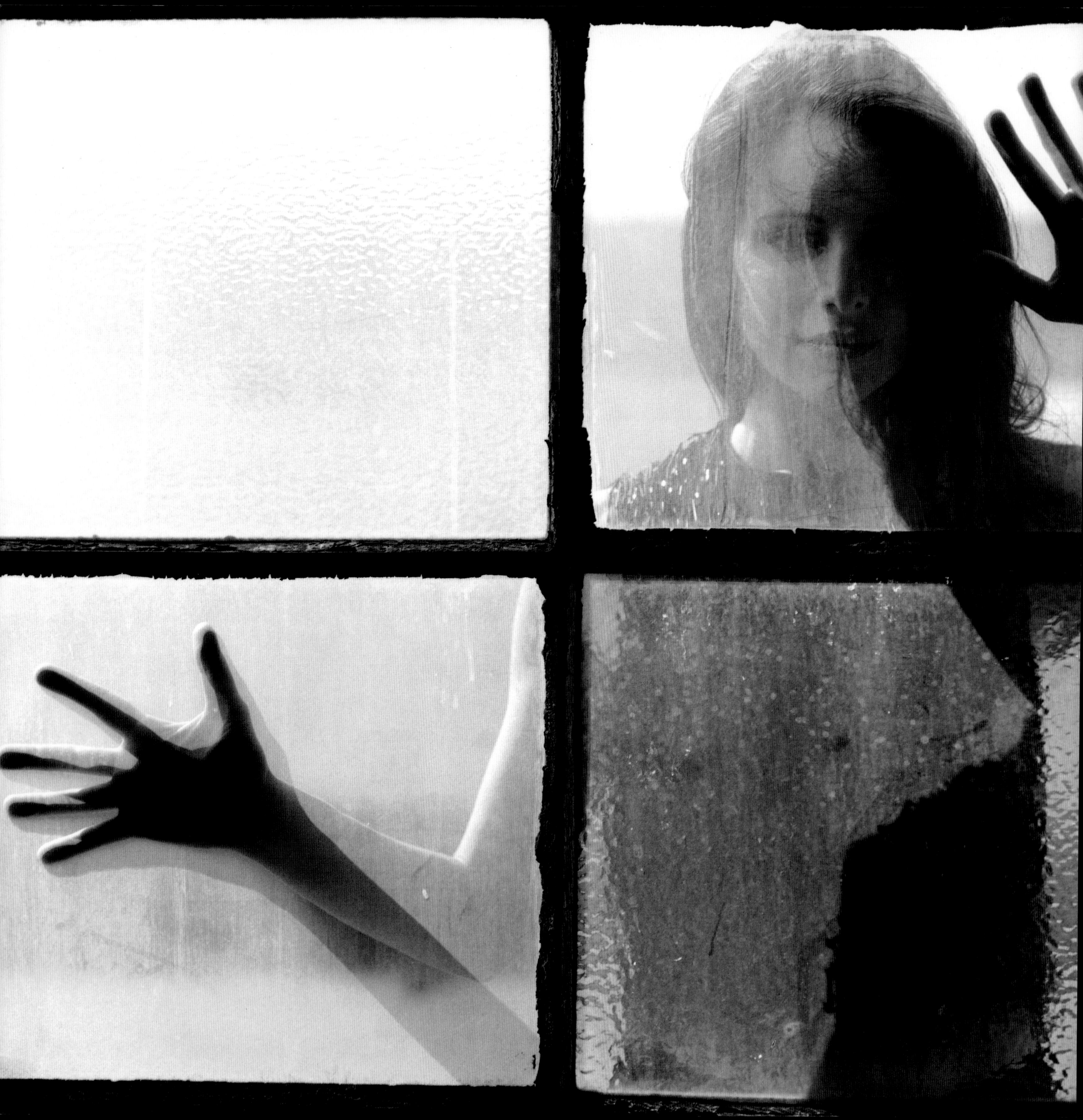

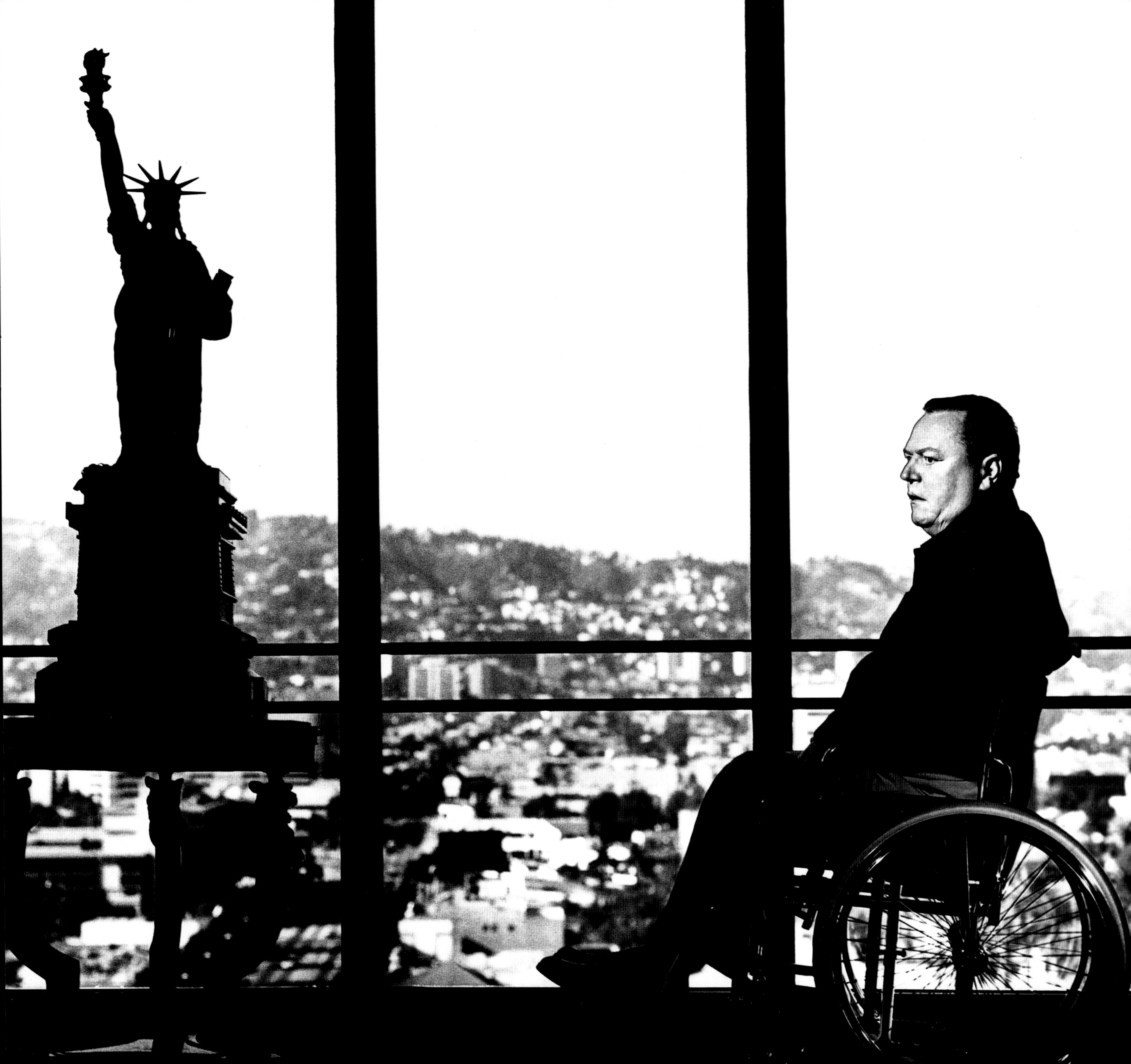

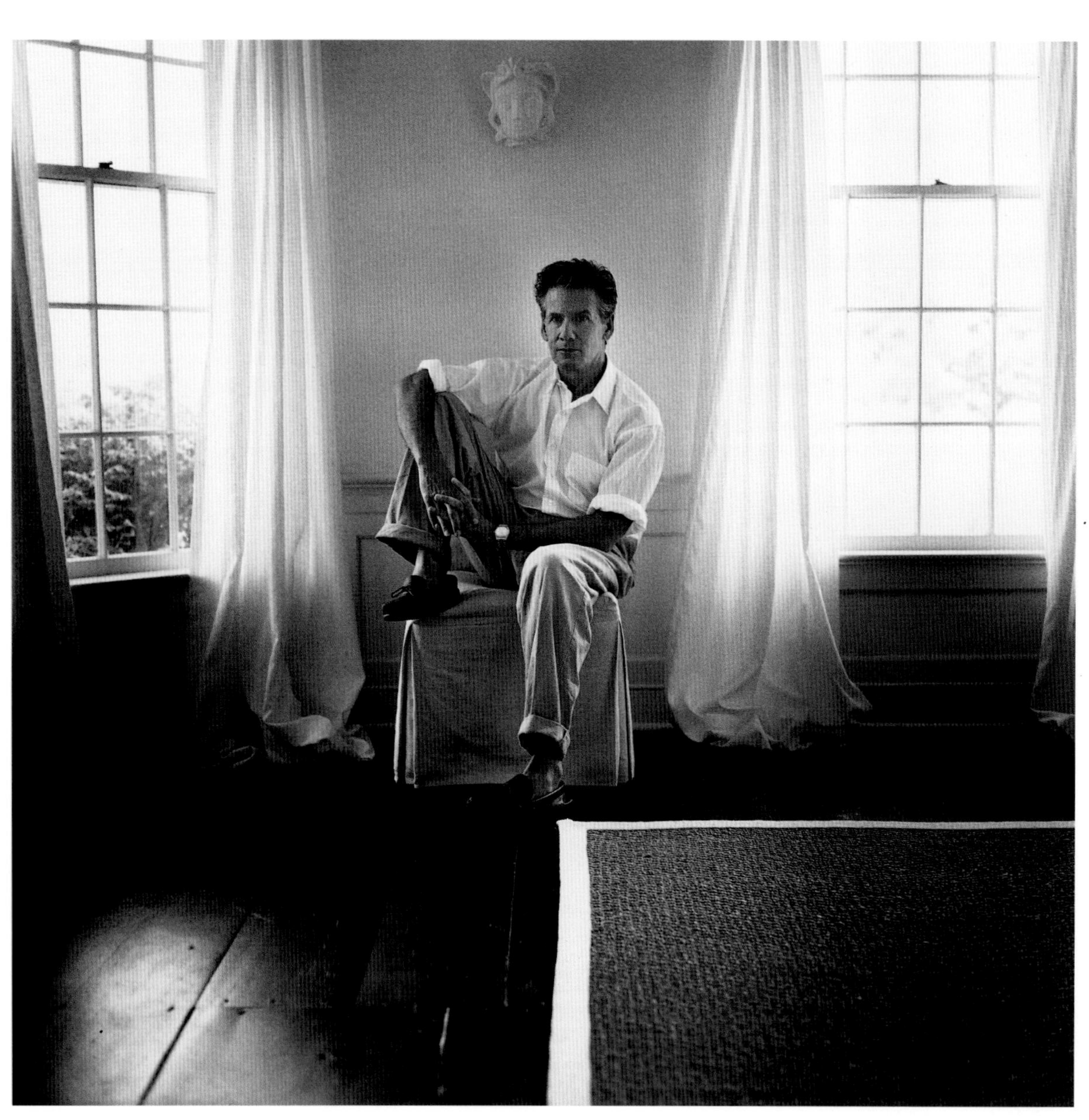

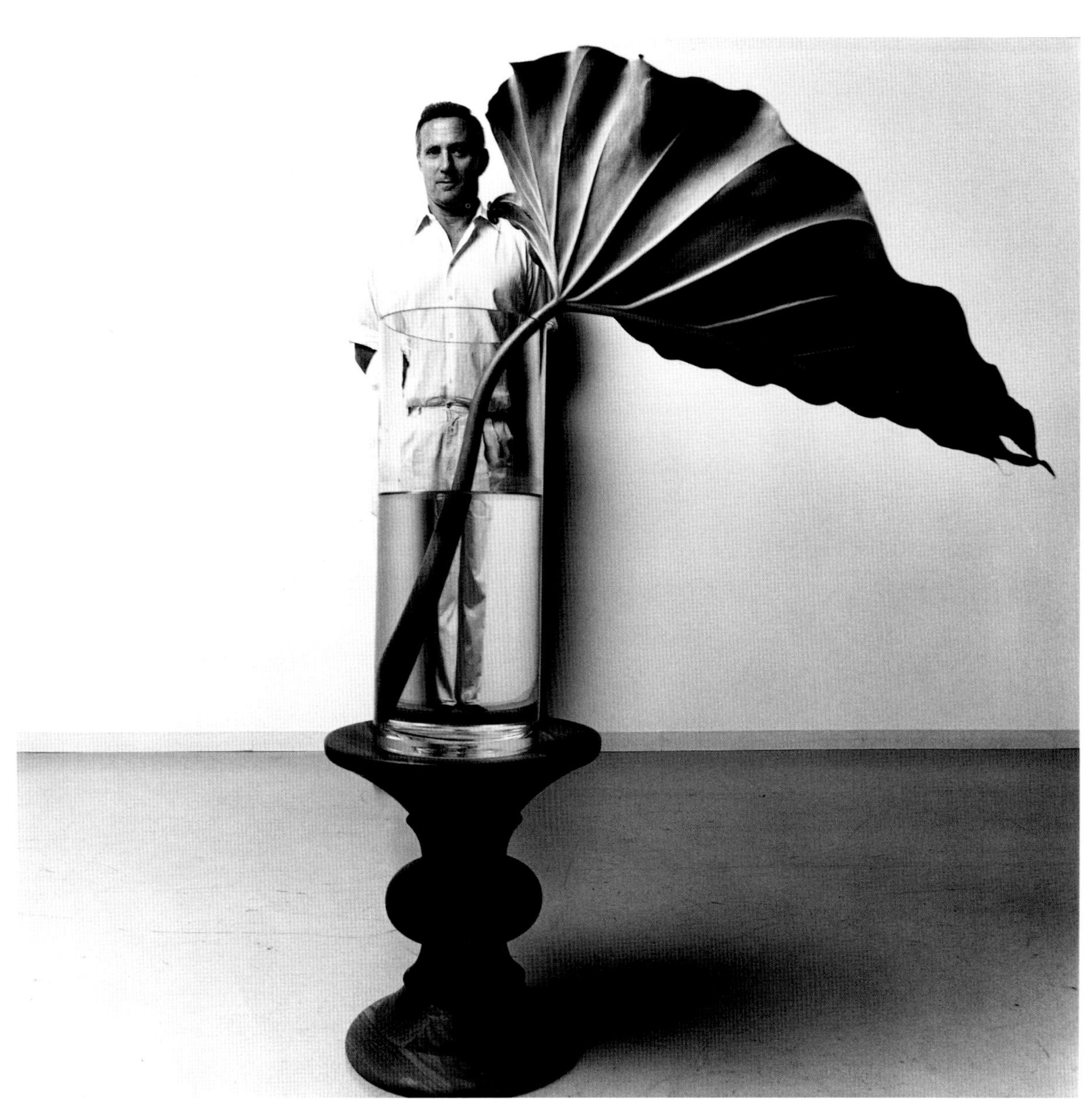

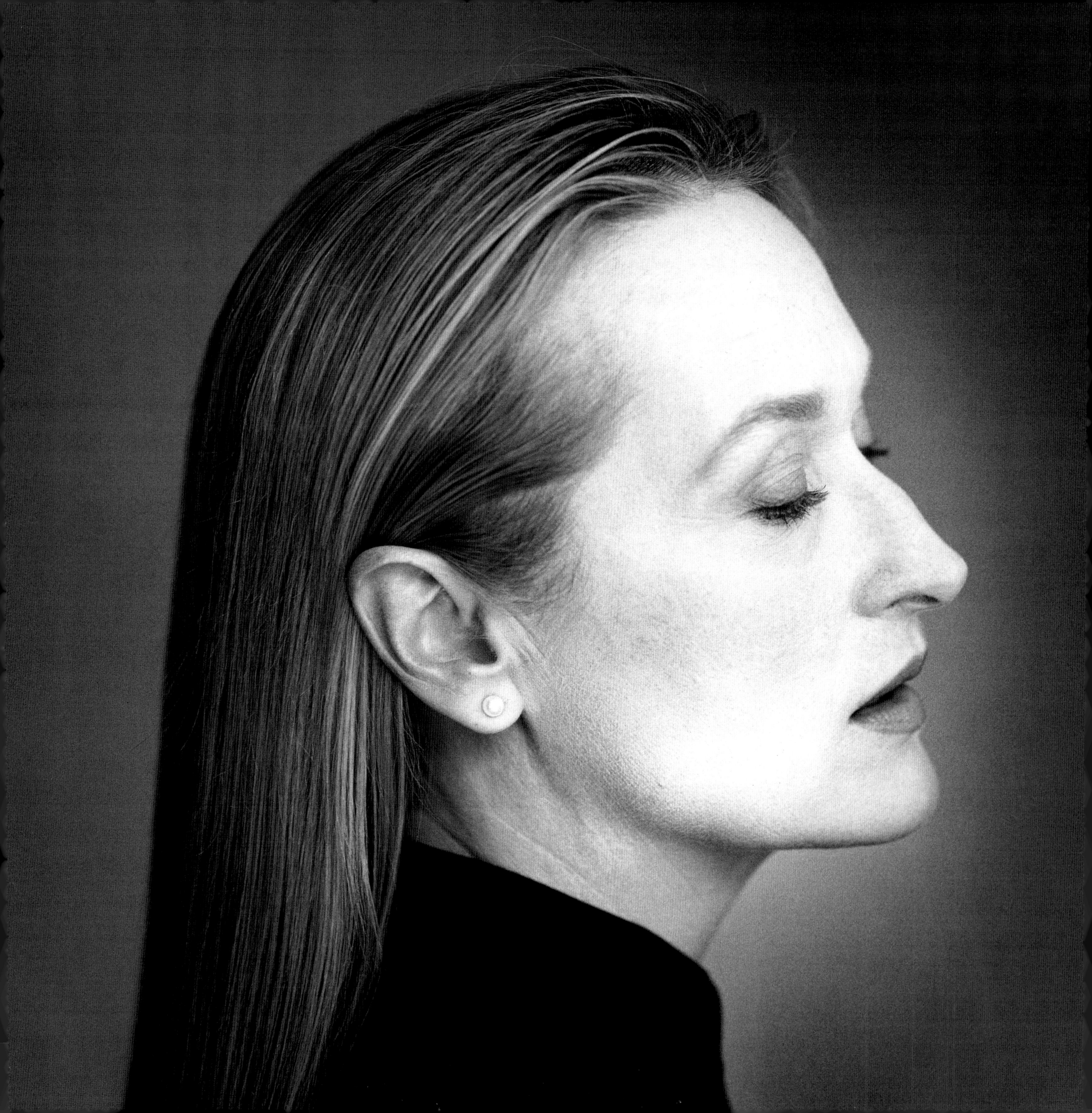

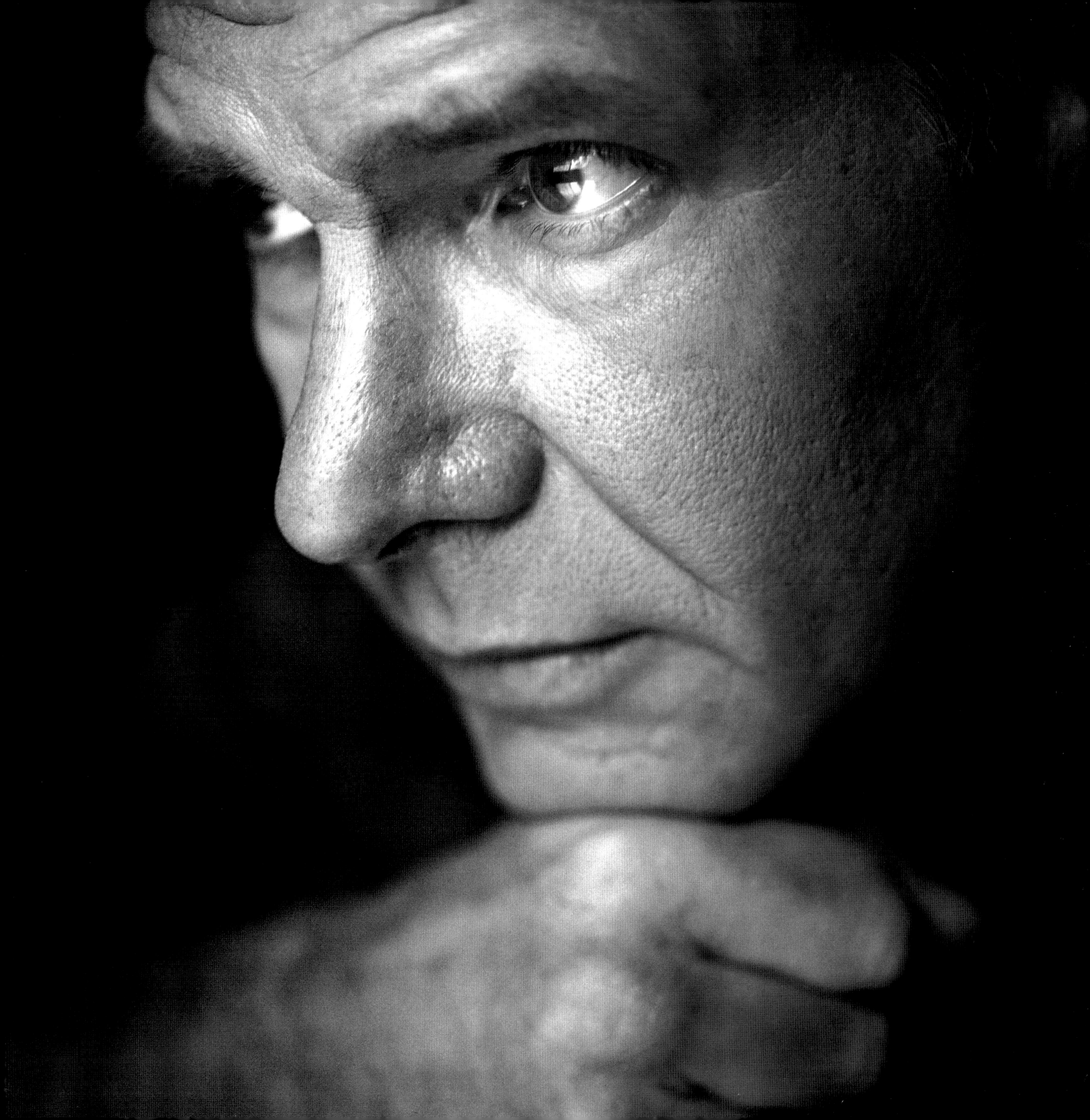

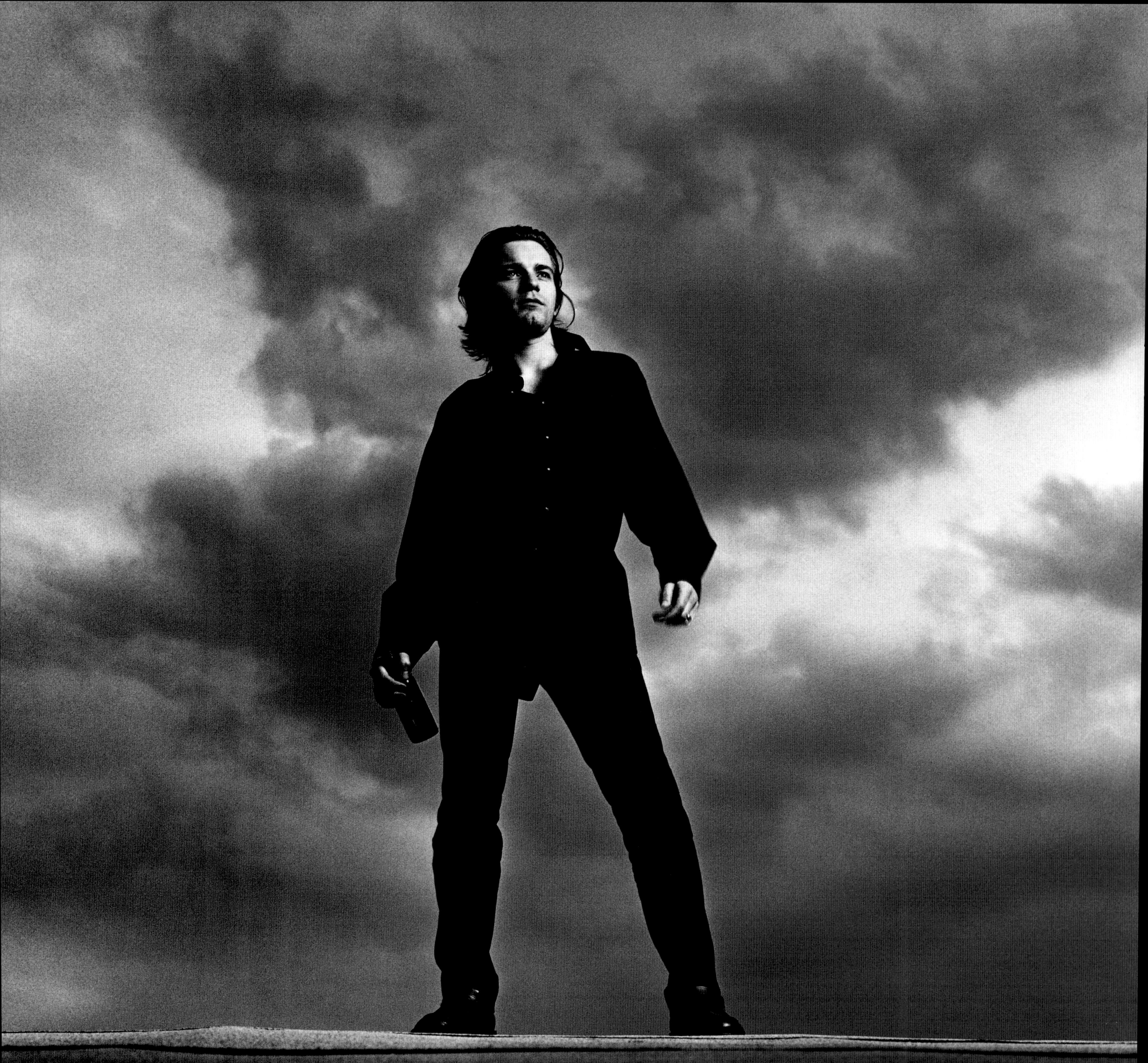

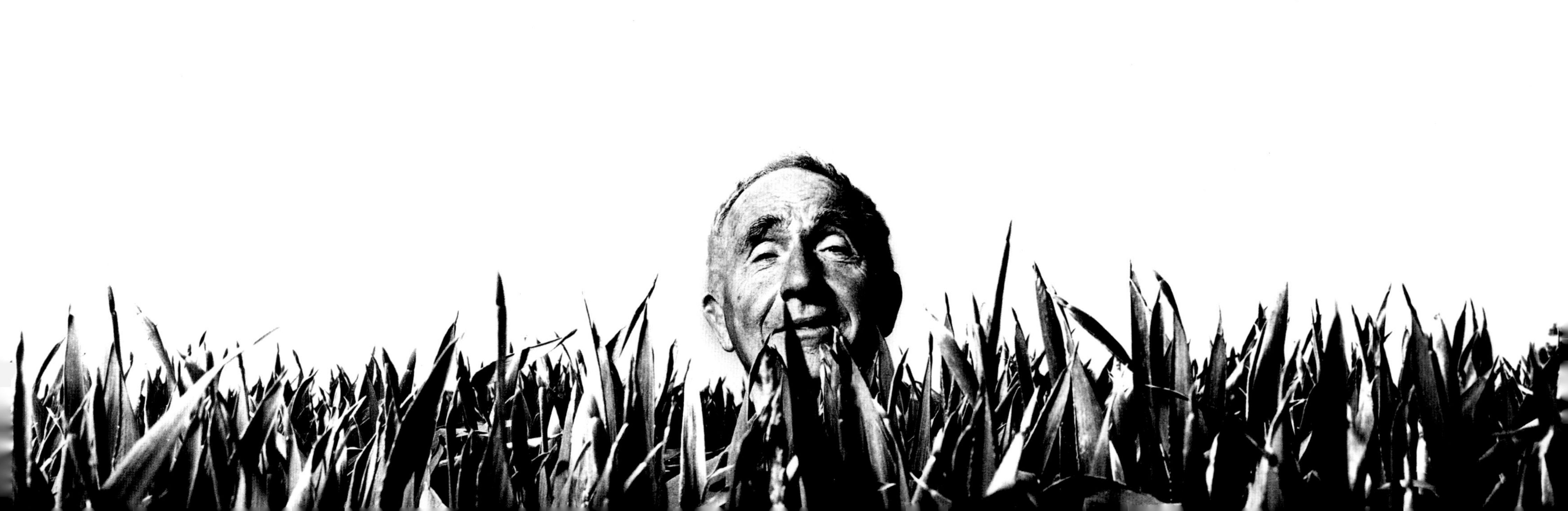

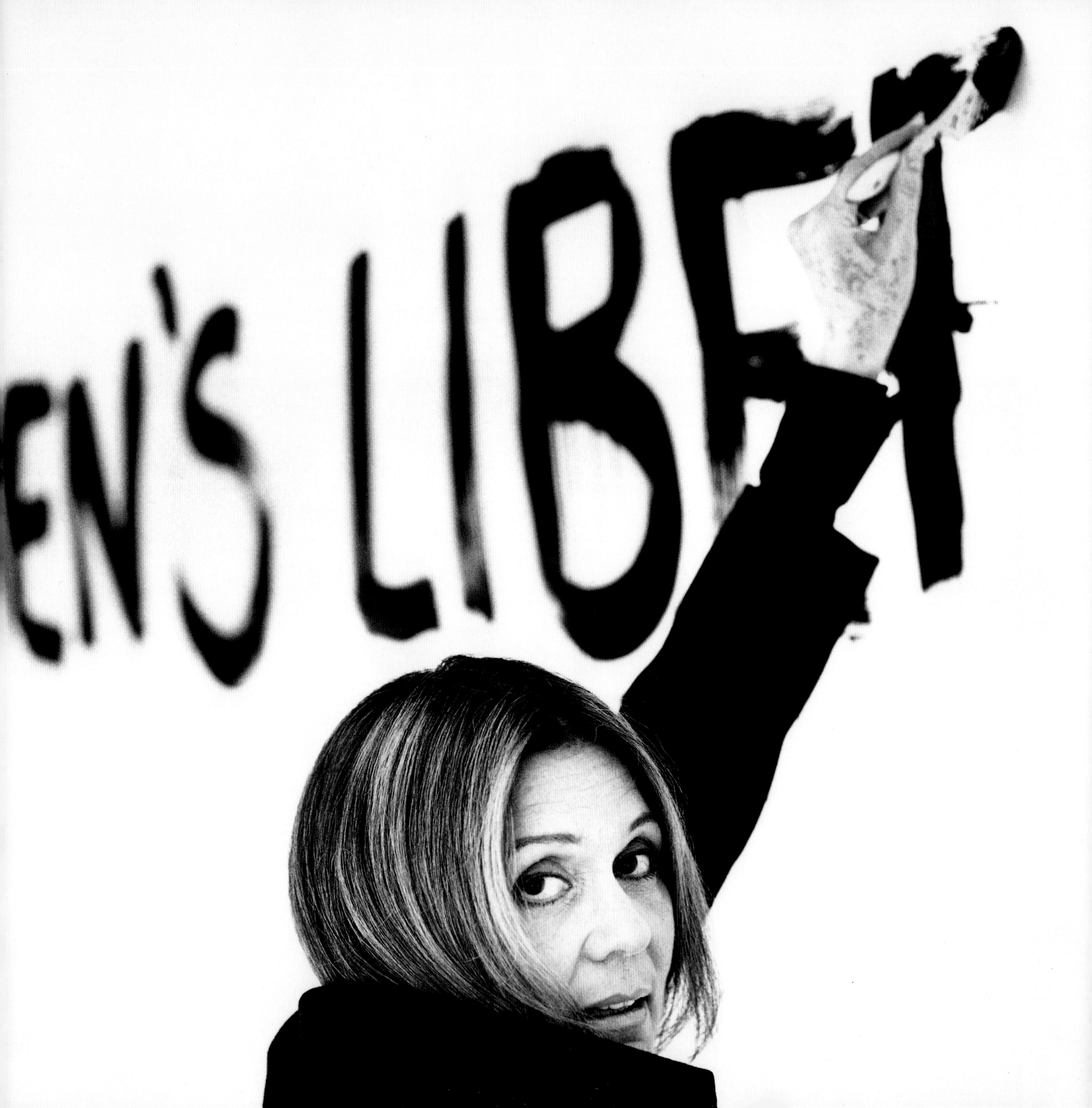
EN'S LIB

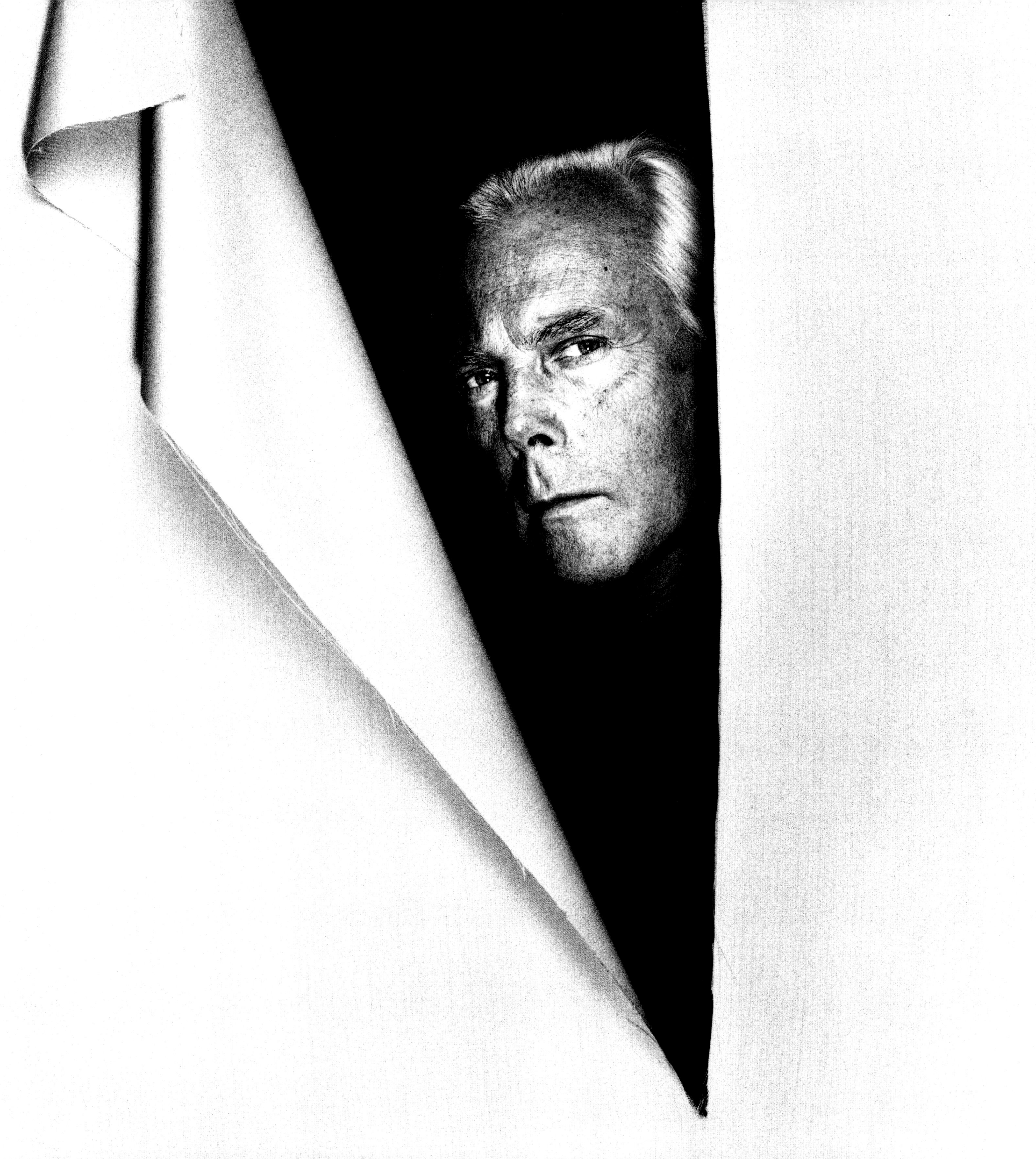

OK NIGEL,
YOU HAVE
MINUTES..
NO LIGHTS
NO BACKD

FIVE

ROP!

THE WHITE HOUSE PRESS OFFICER'S
IDEA OF BEING HELPFUL WHEN WE
ARRIVED TO PHOTOGRAPH
PRESIDENT BILL CLINTON IN THE
OVAL OFFICE.

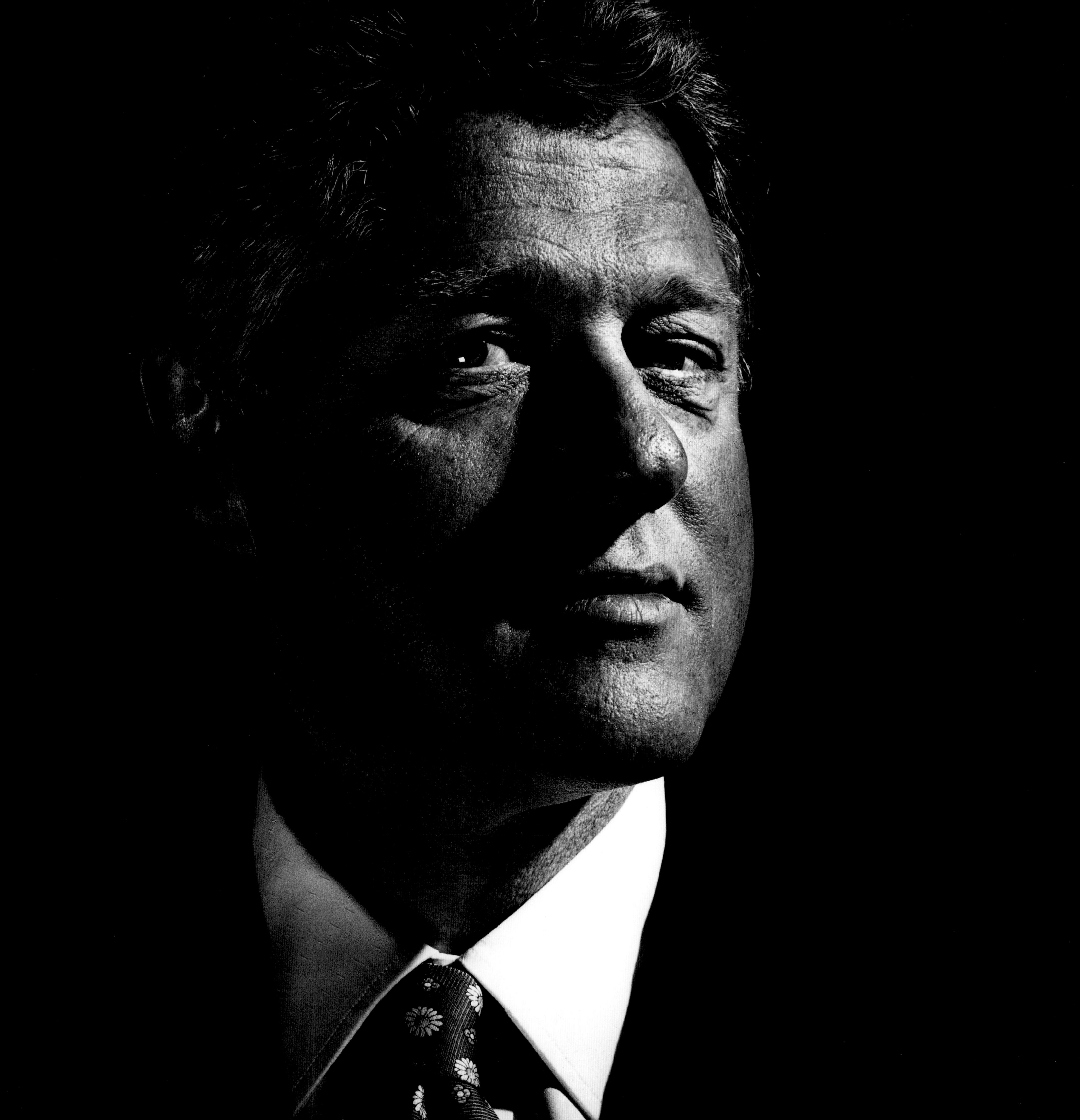

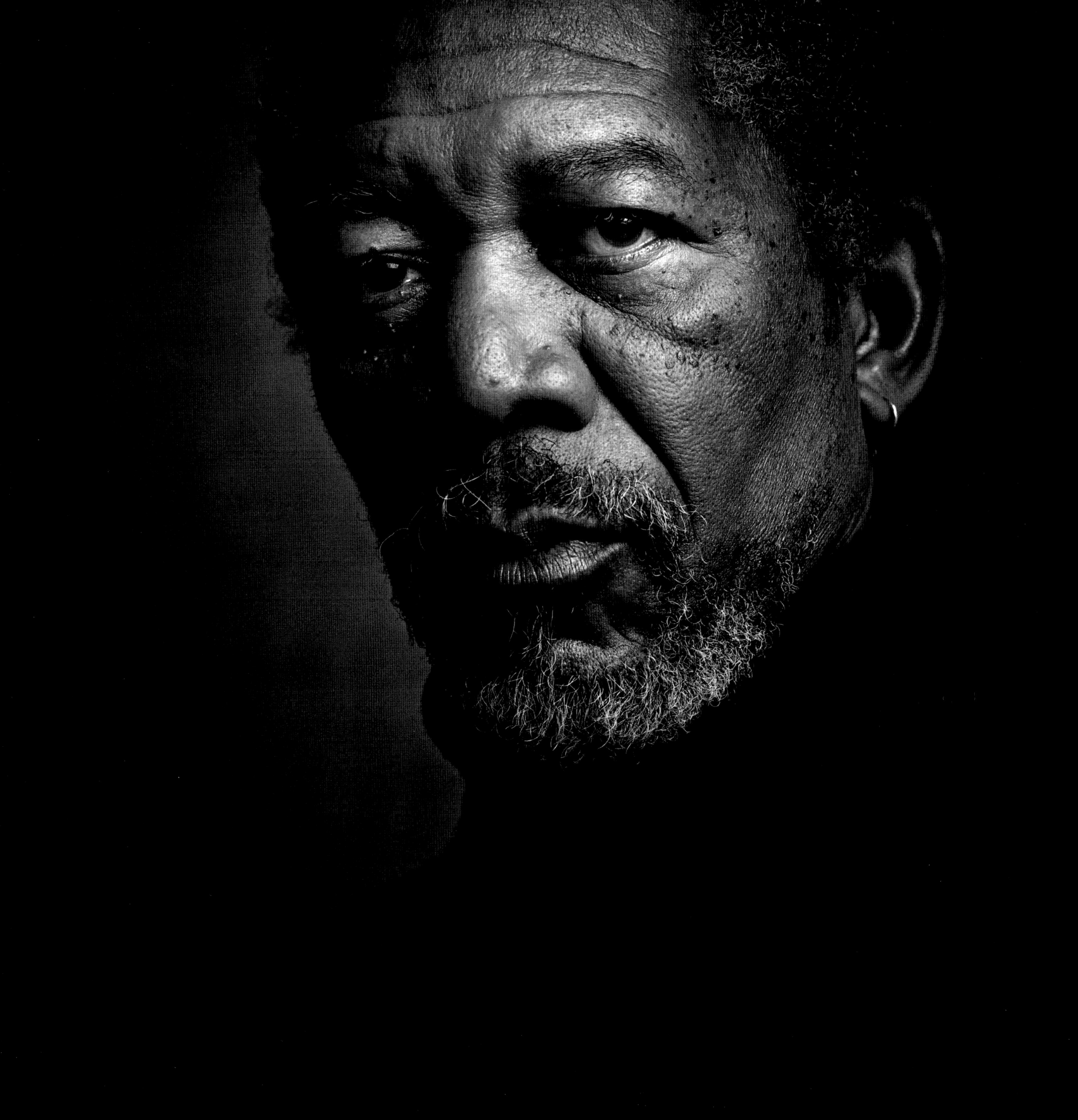

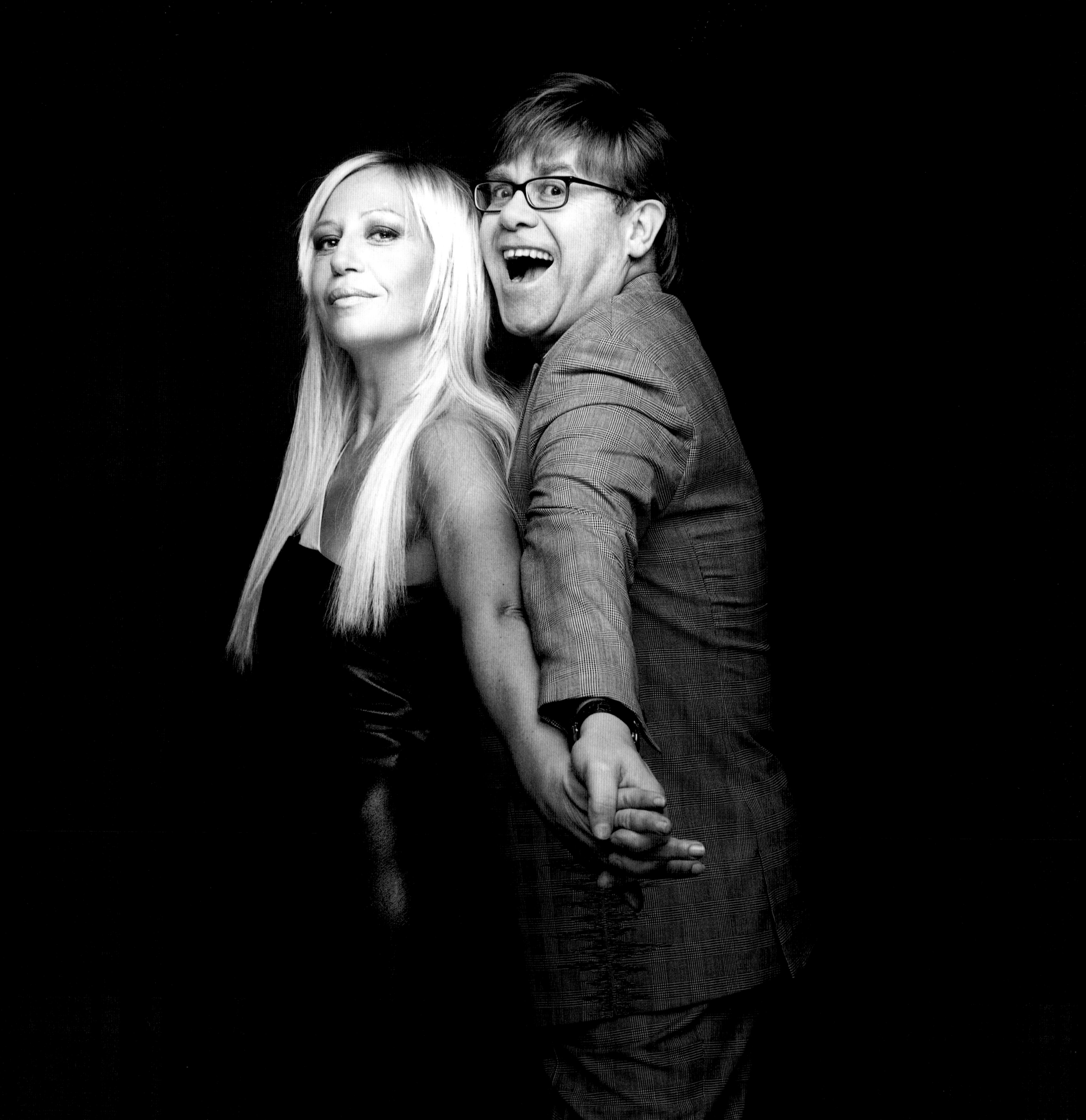

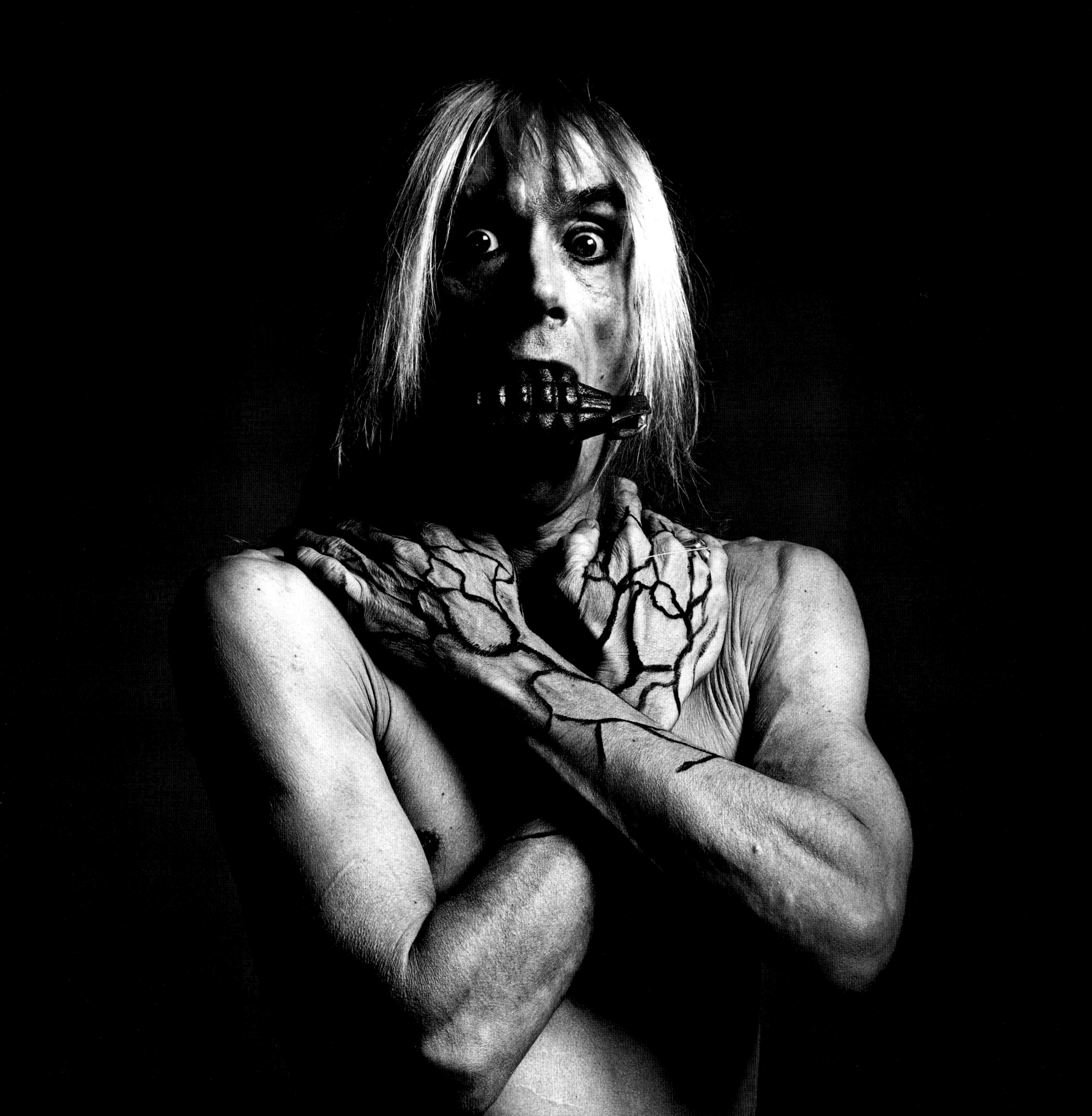

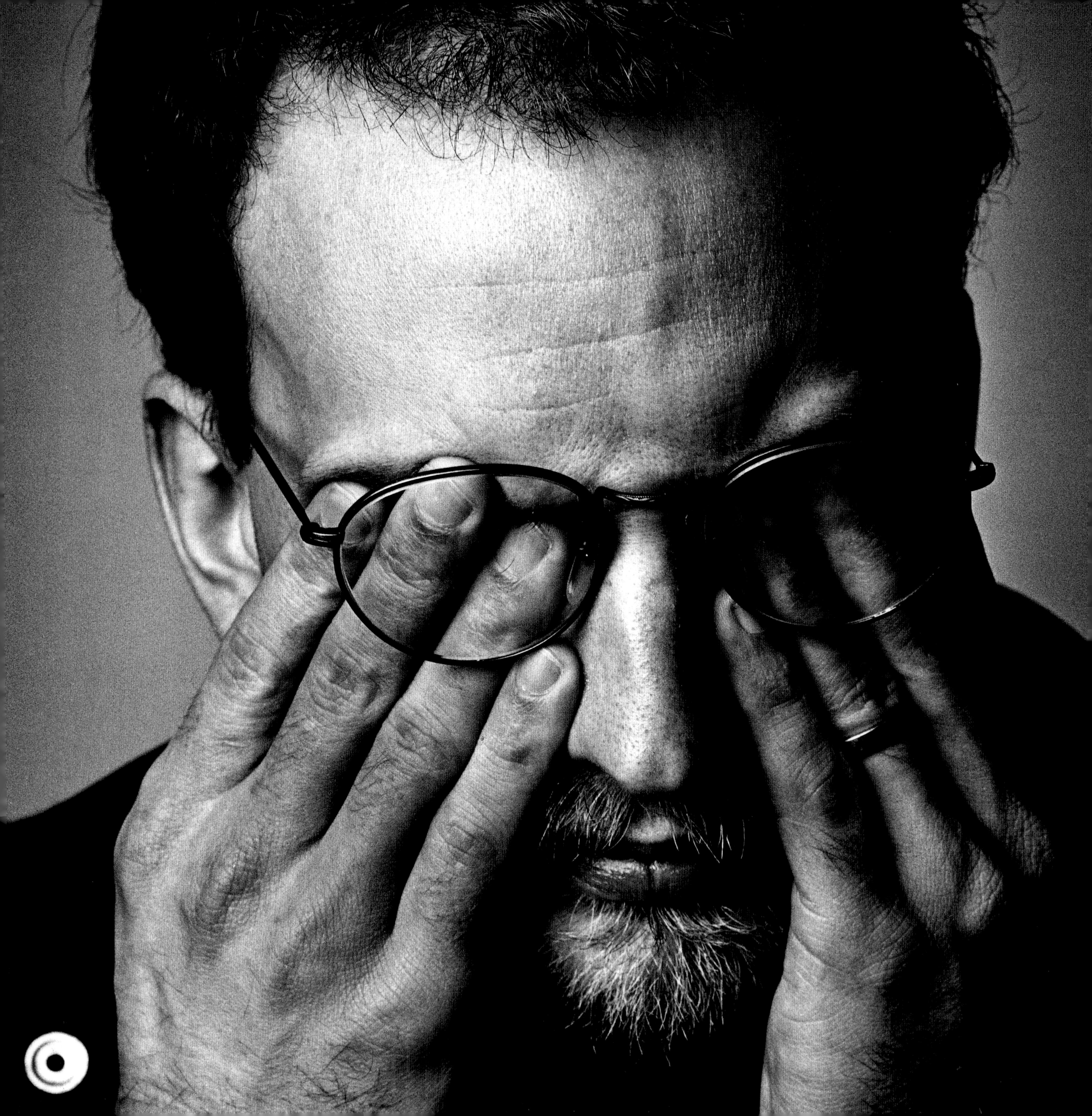

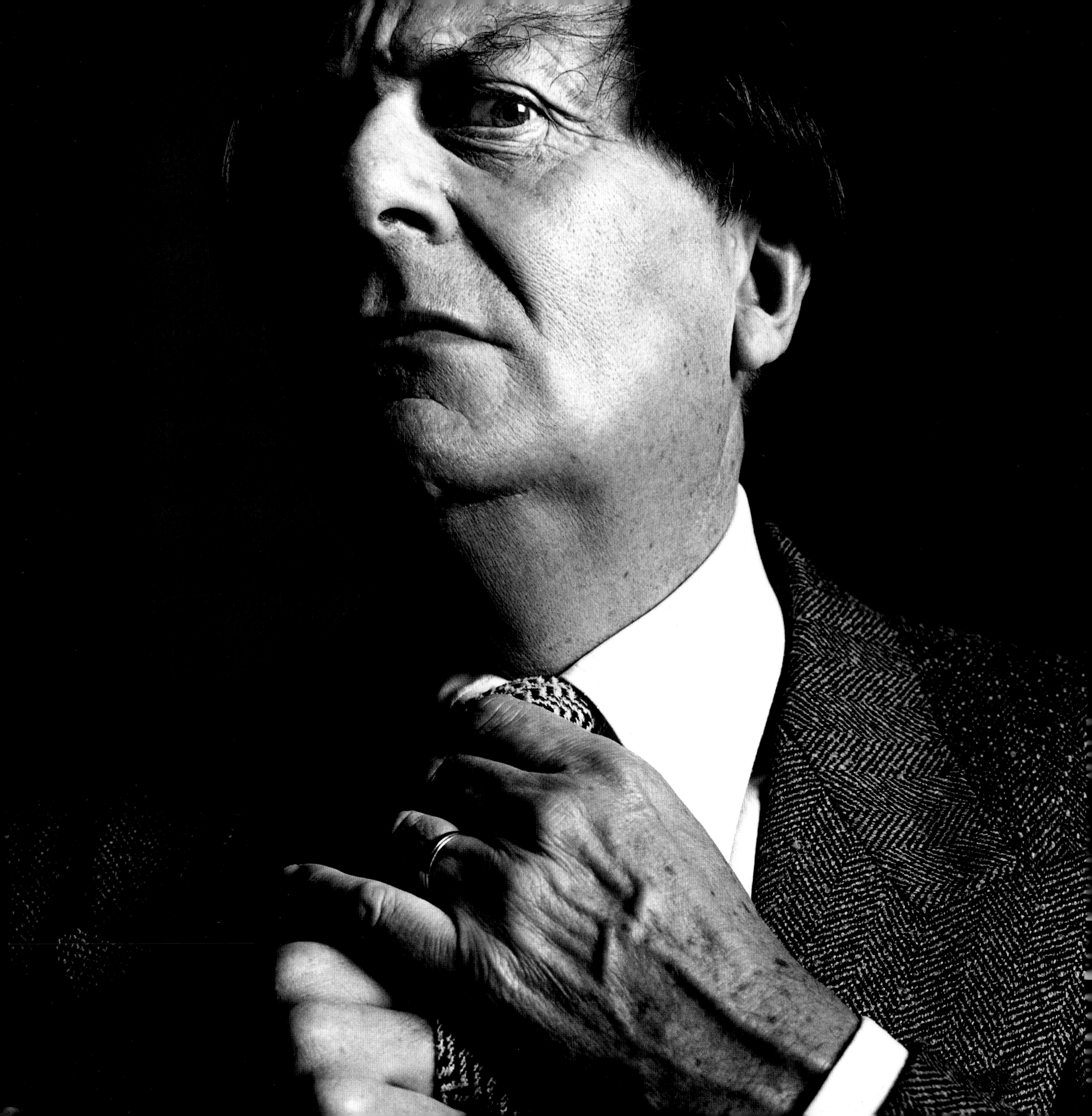

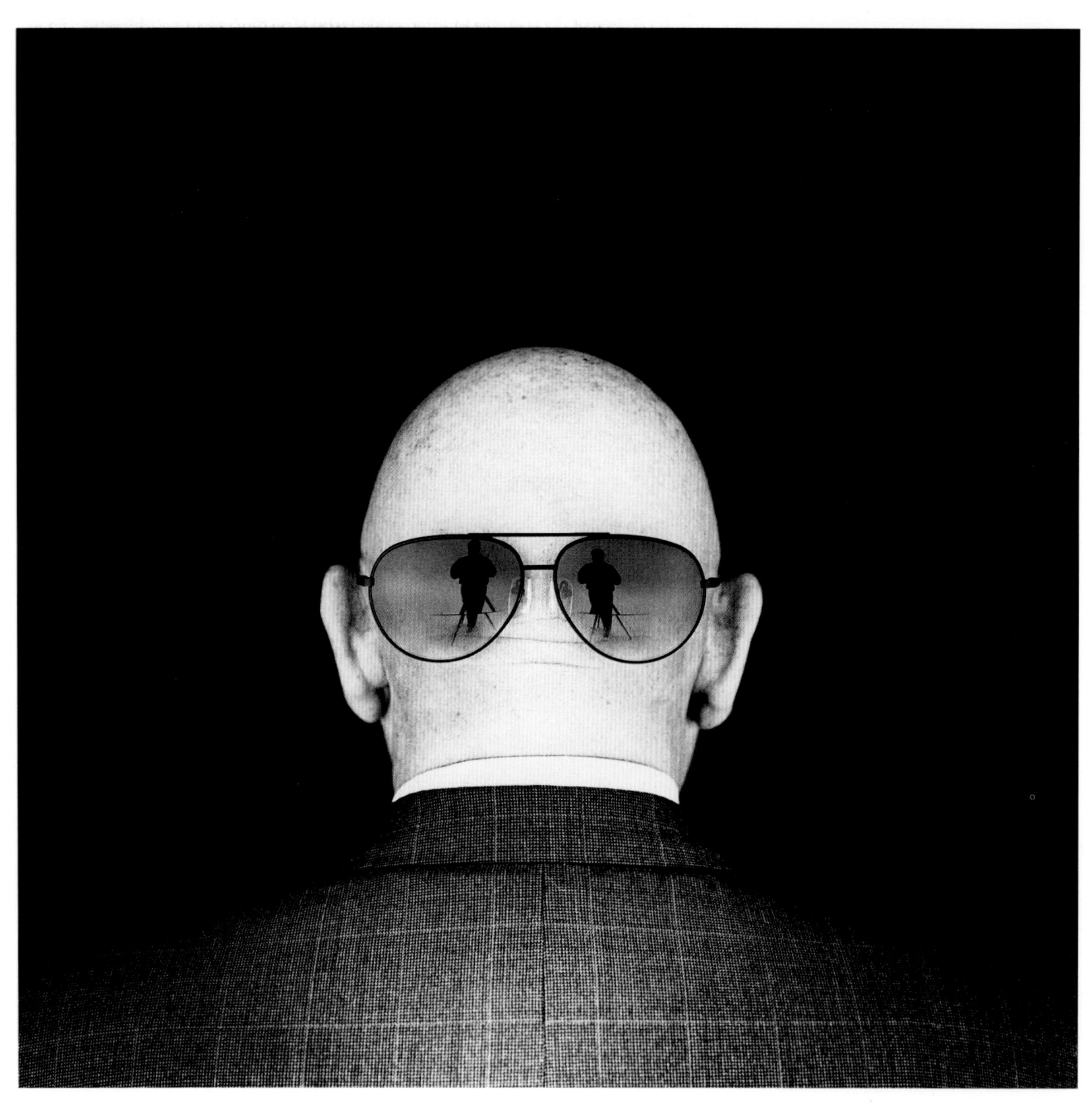

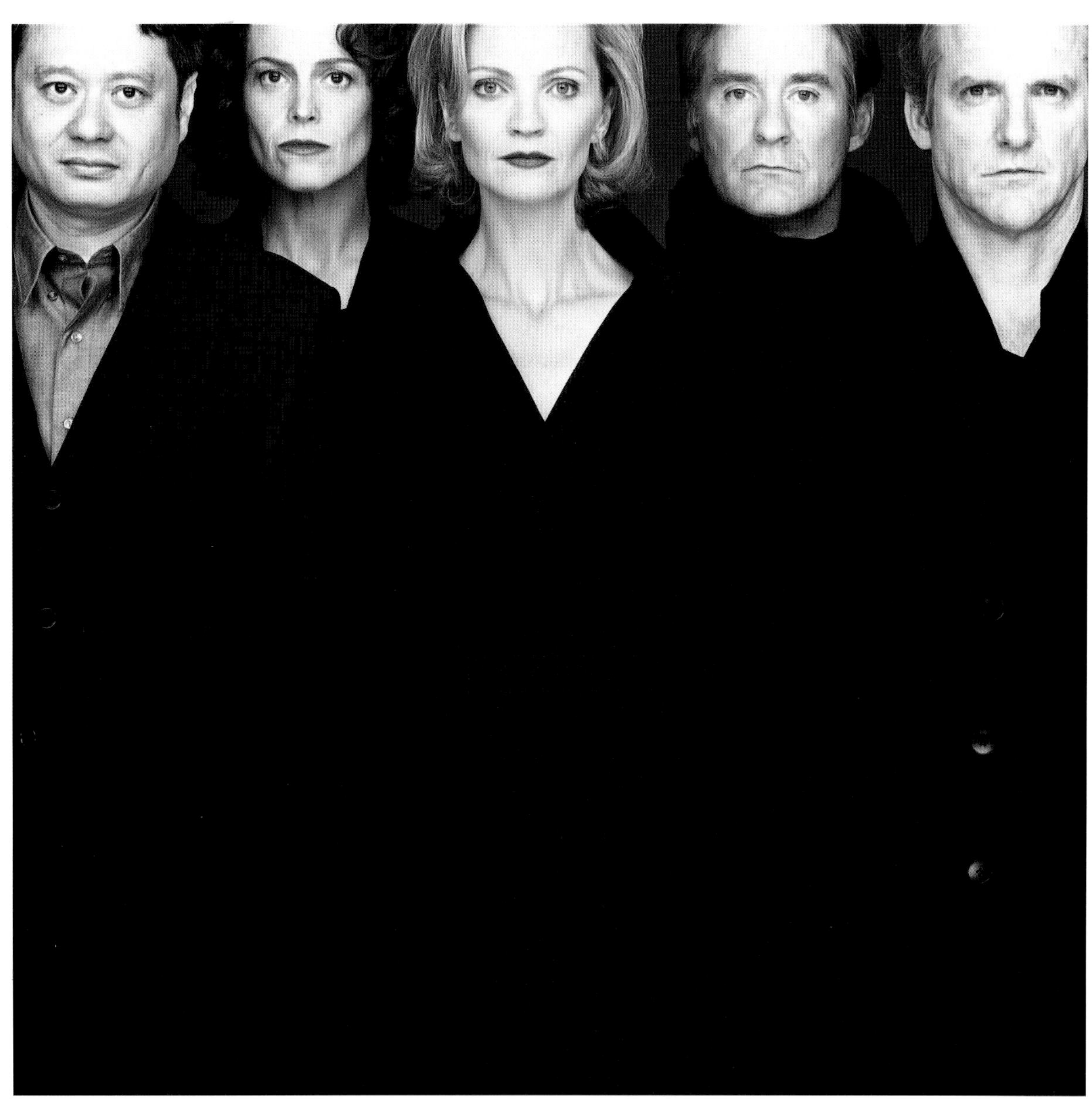

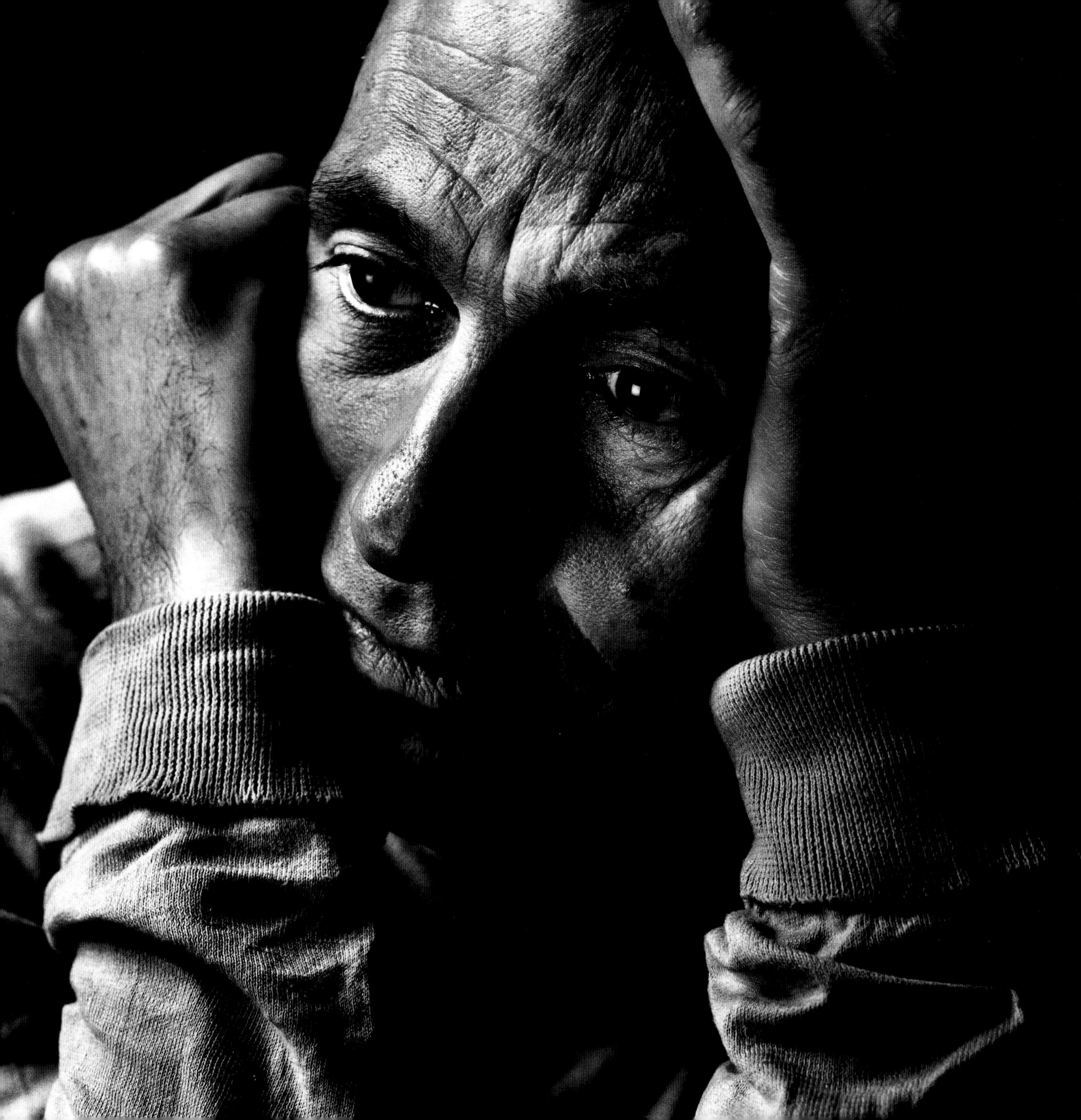

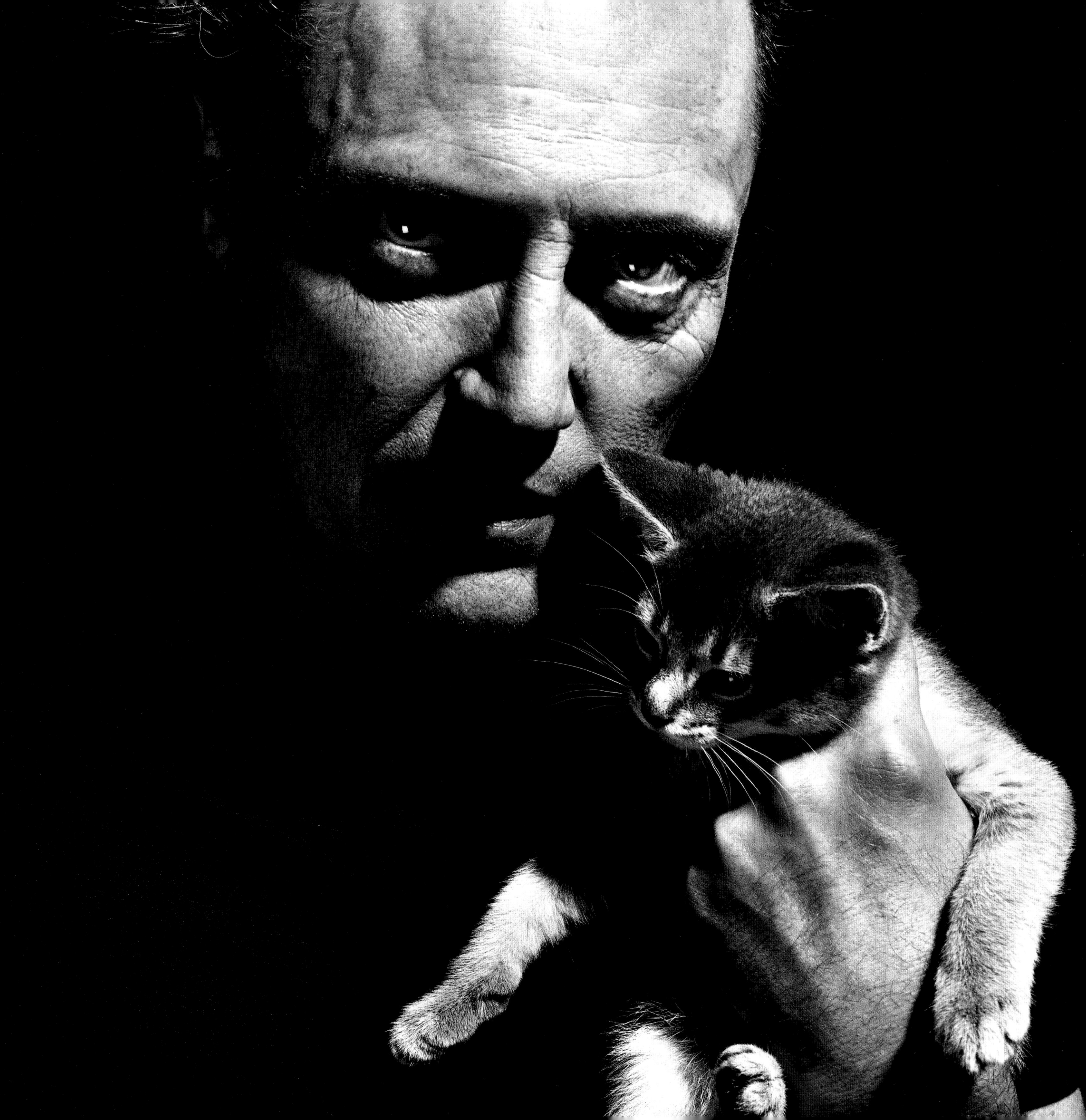

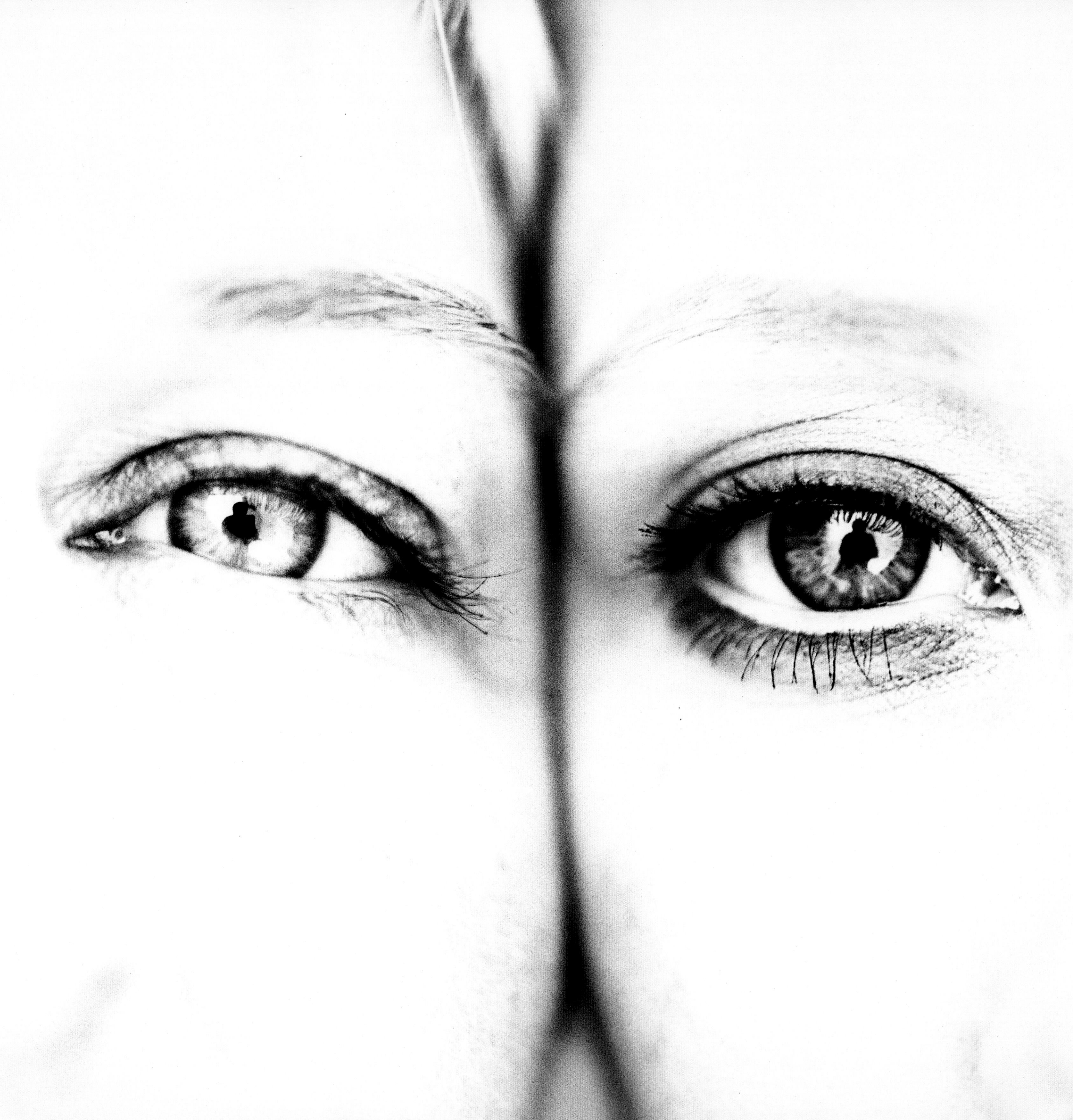

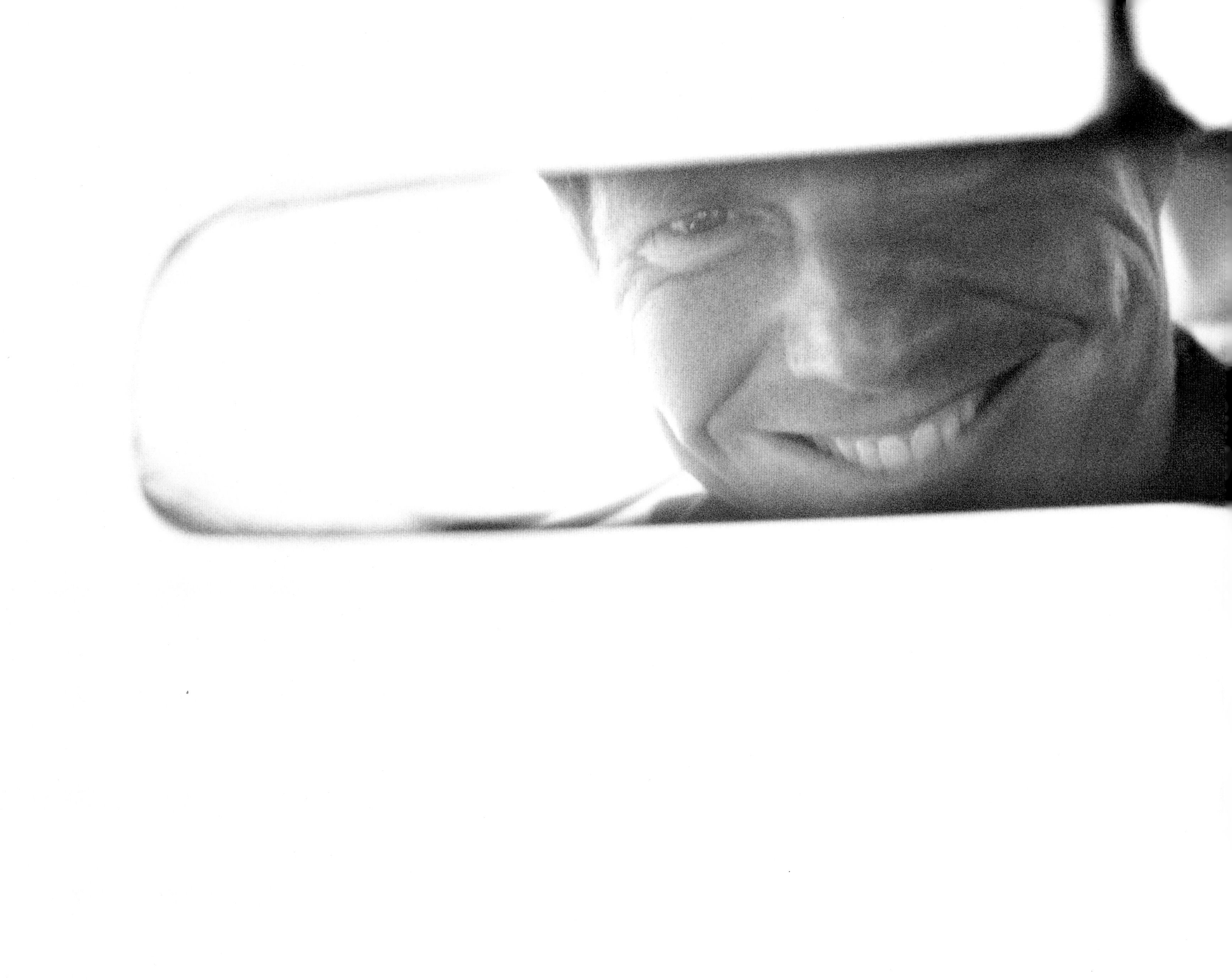

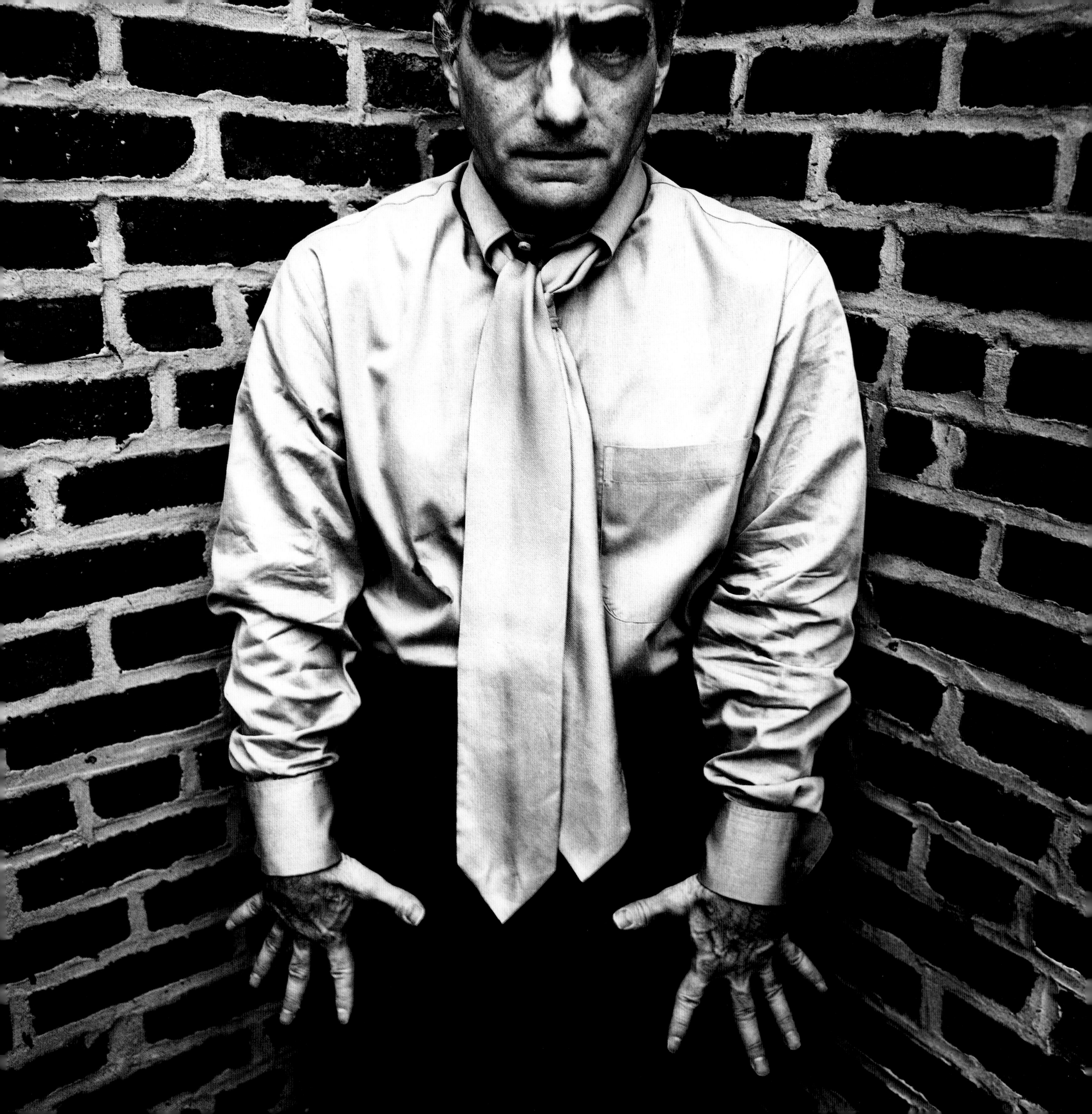

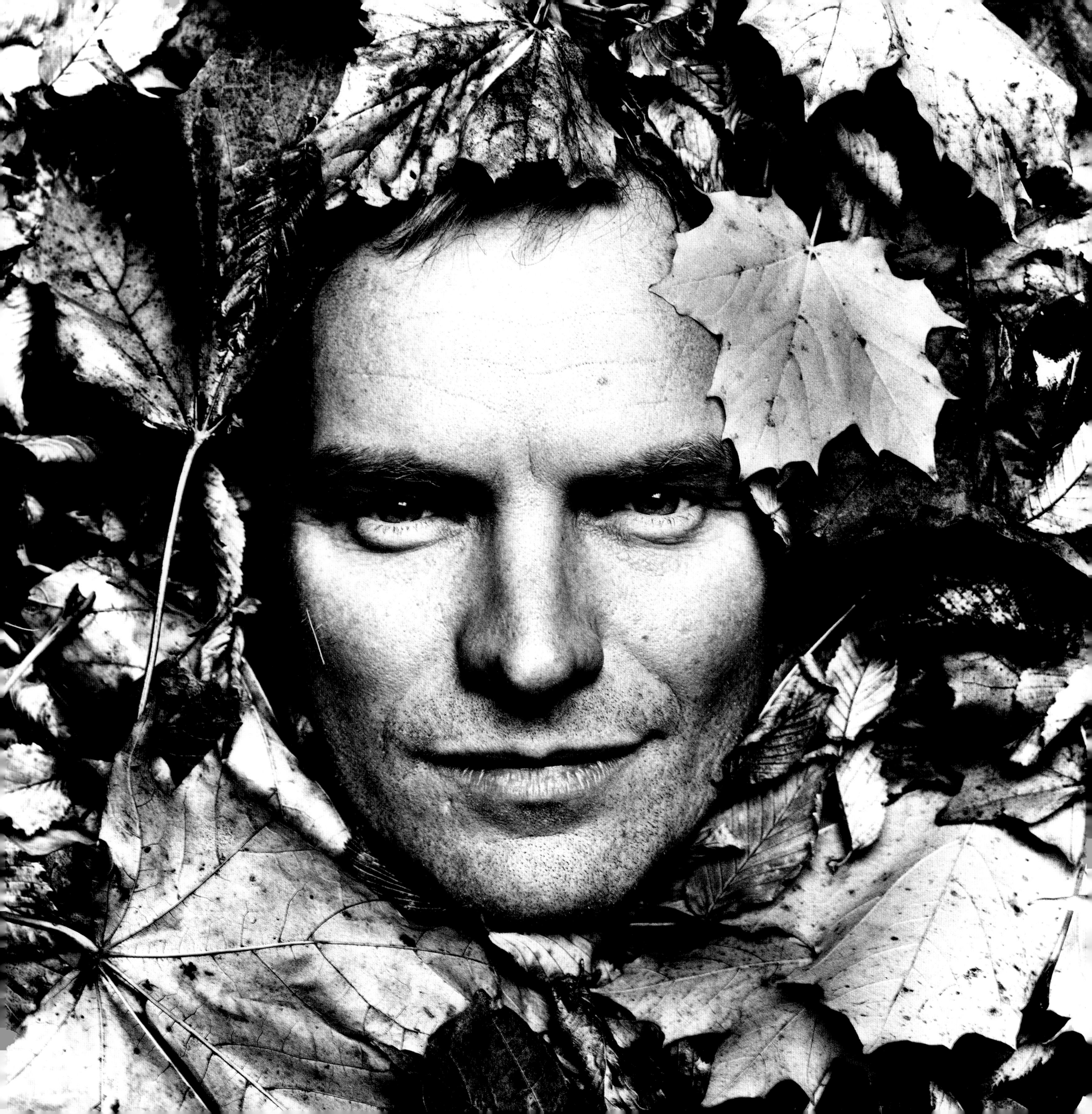

PLEASE SH

NIGEL...

YOU SOUN

SOME DEM

DAVID HEN

FROM *BLO*

UT UP,

D LIKE
ENTED
MINGS
WUP.

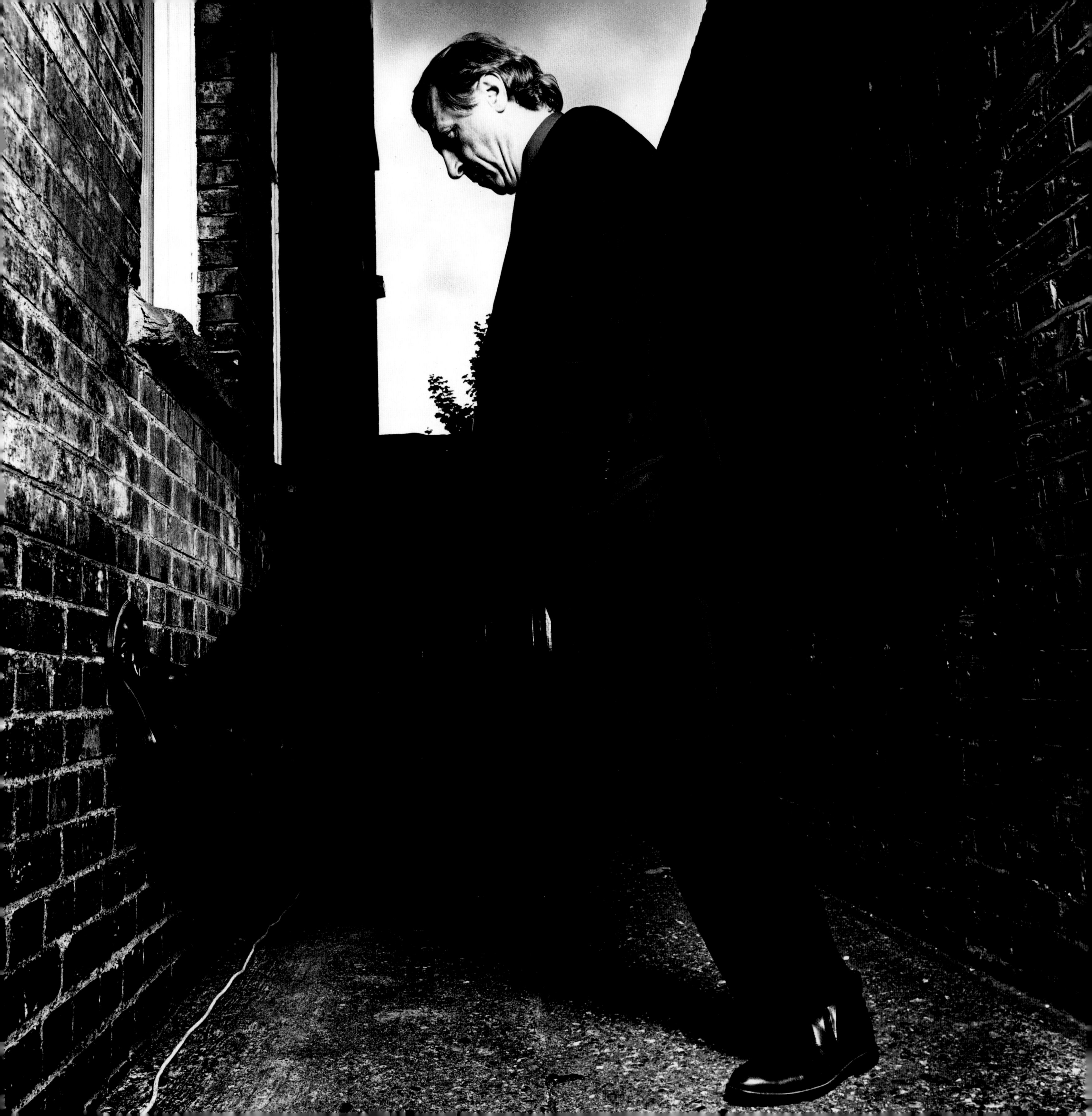

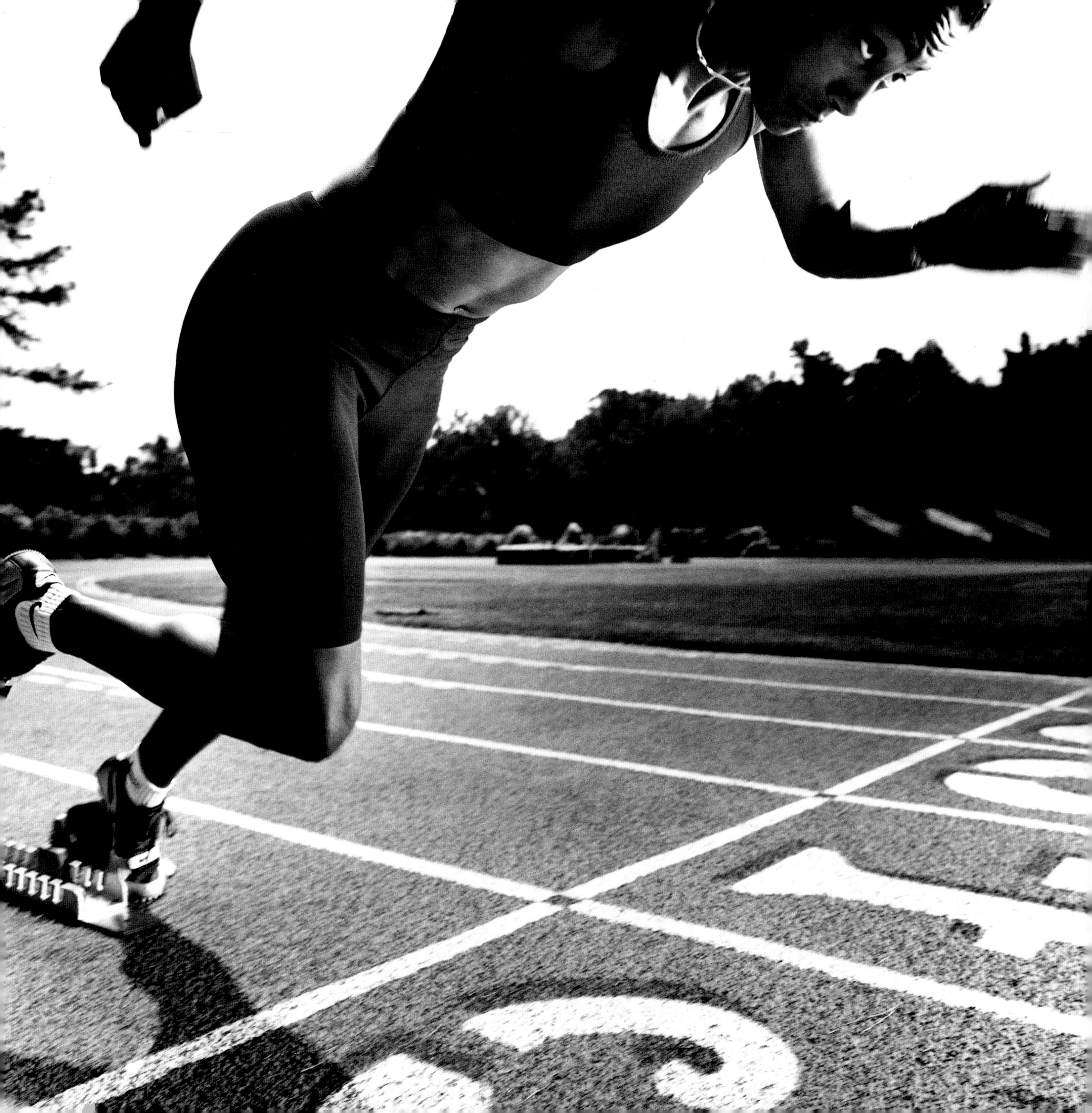

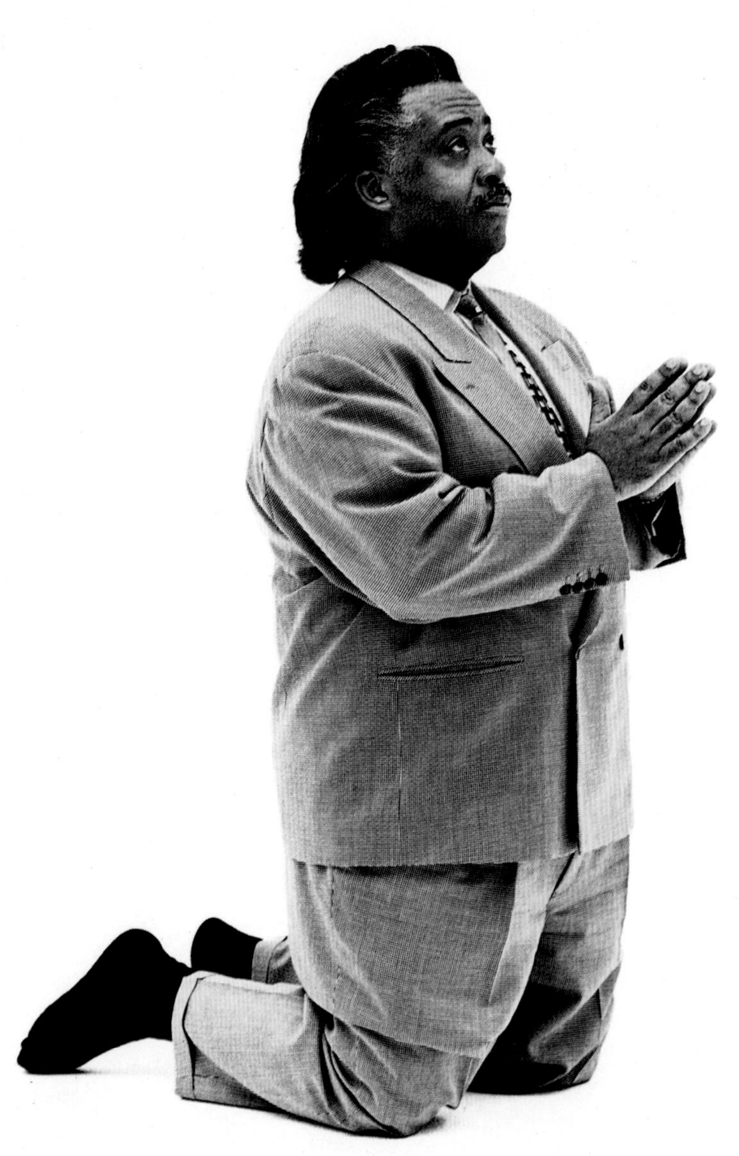

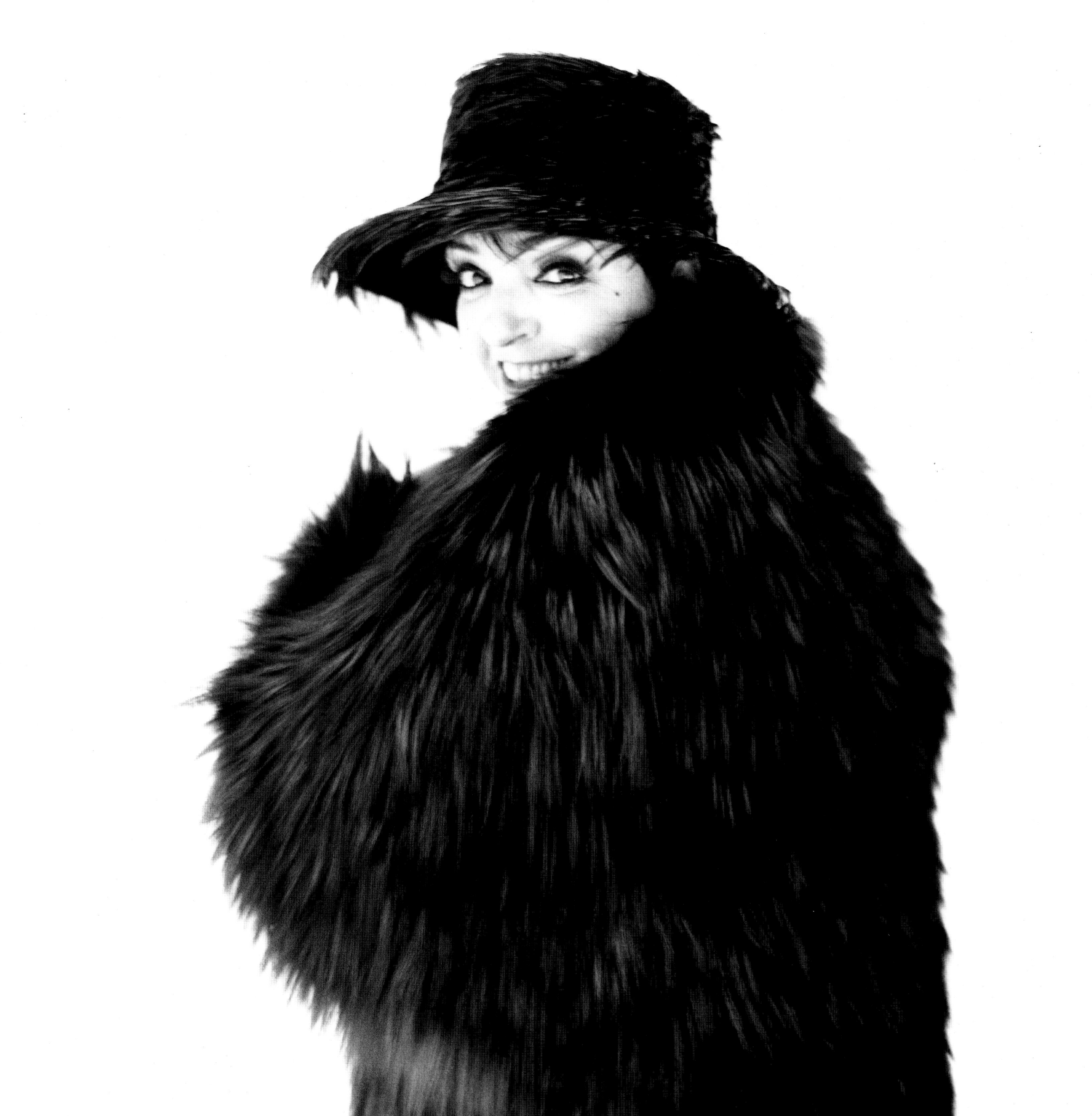

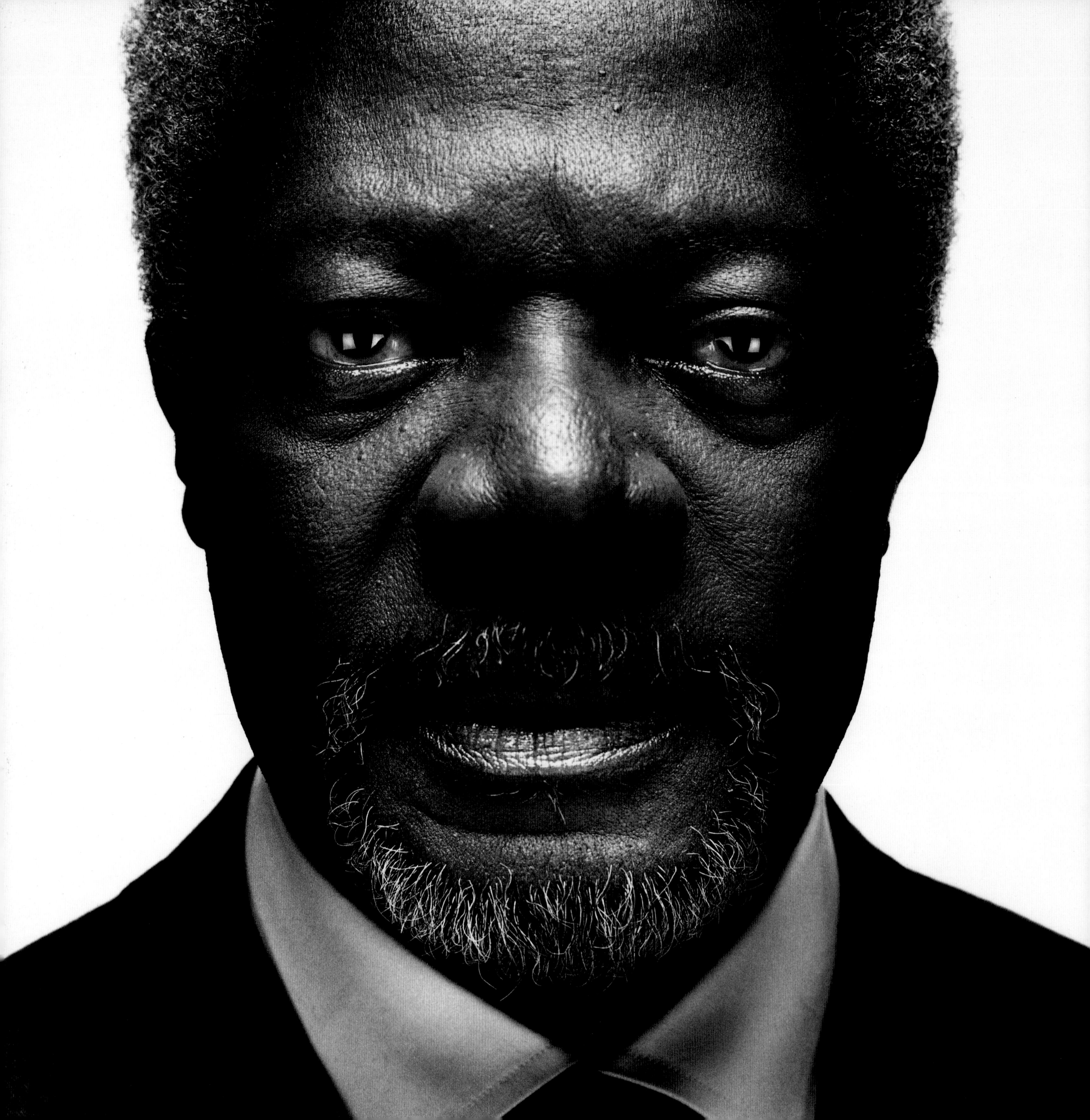

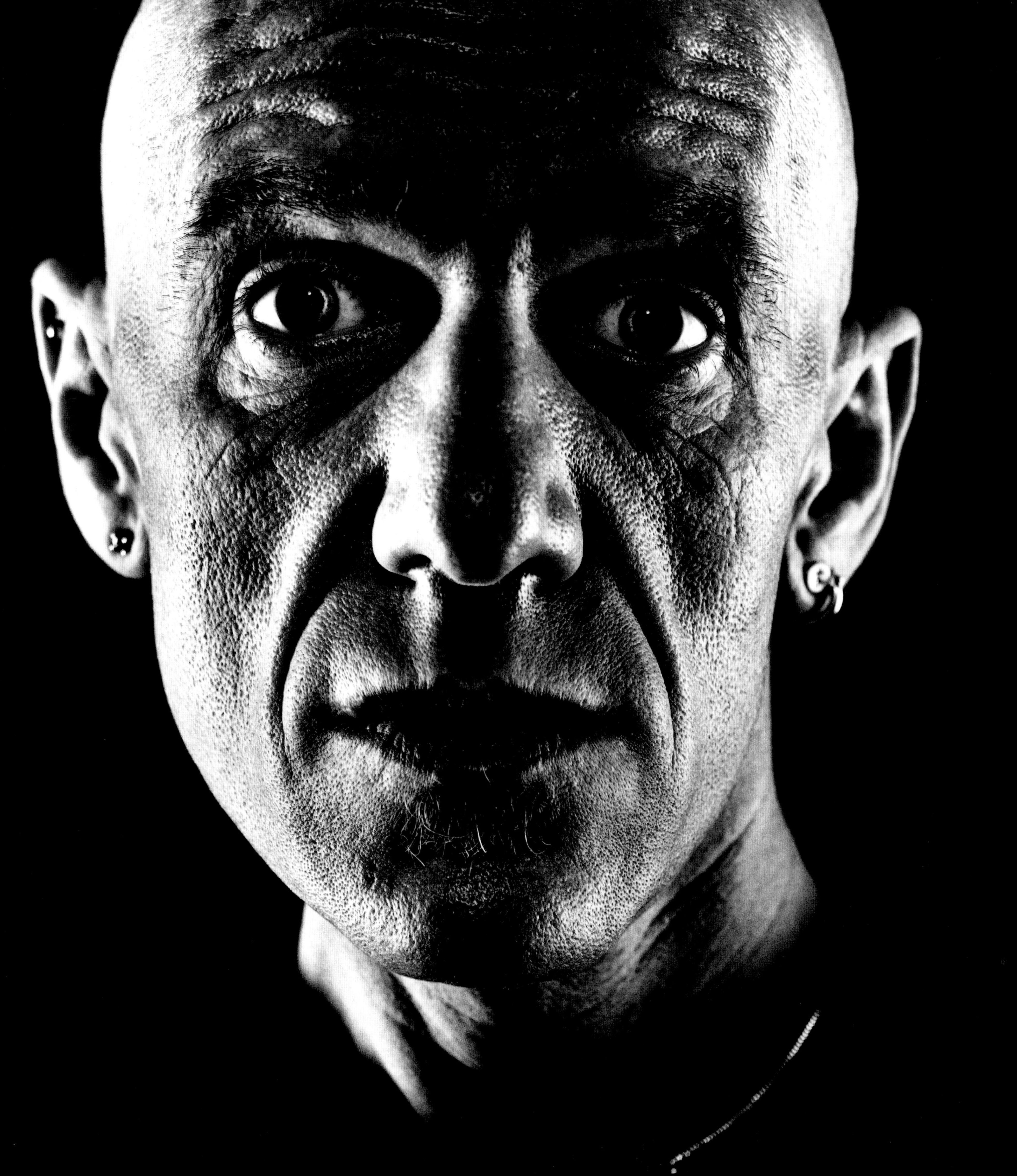

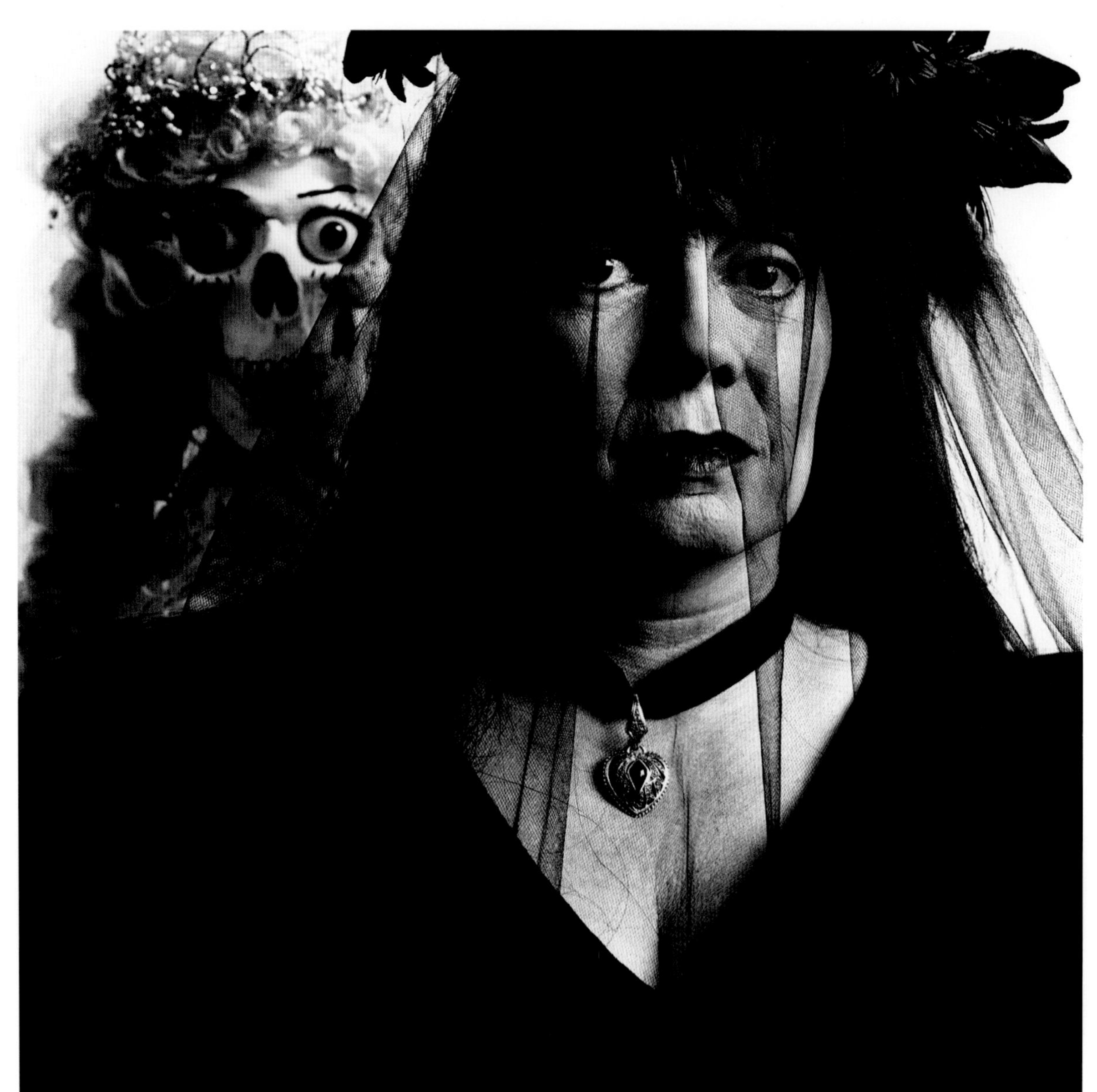

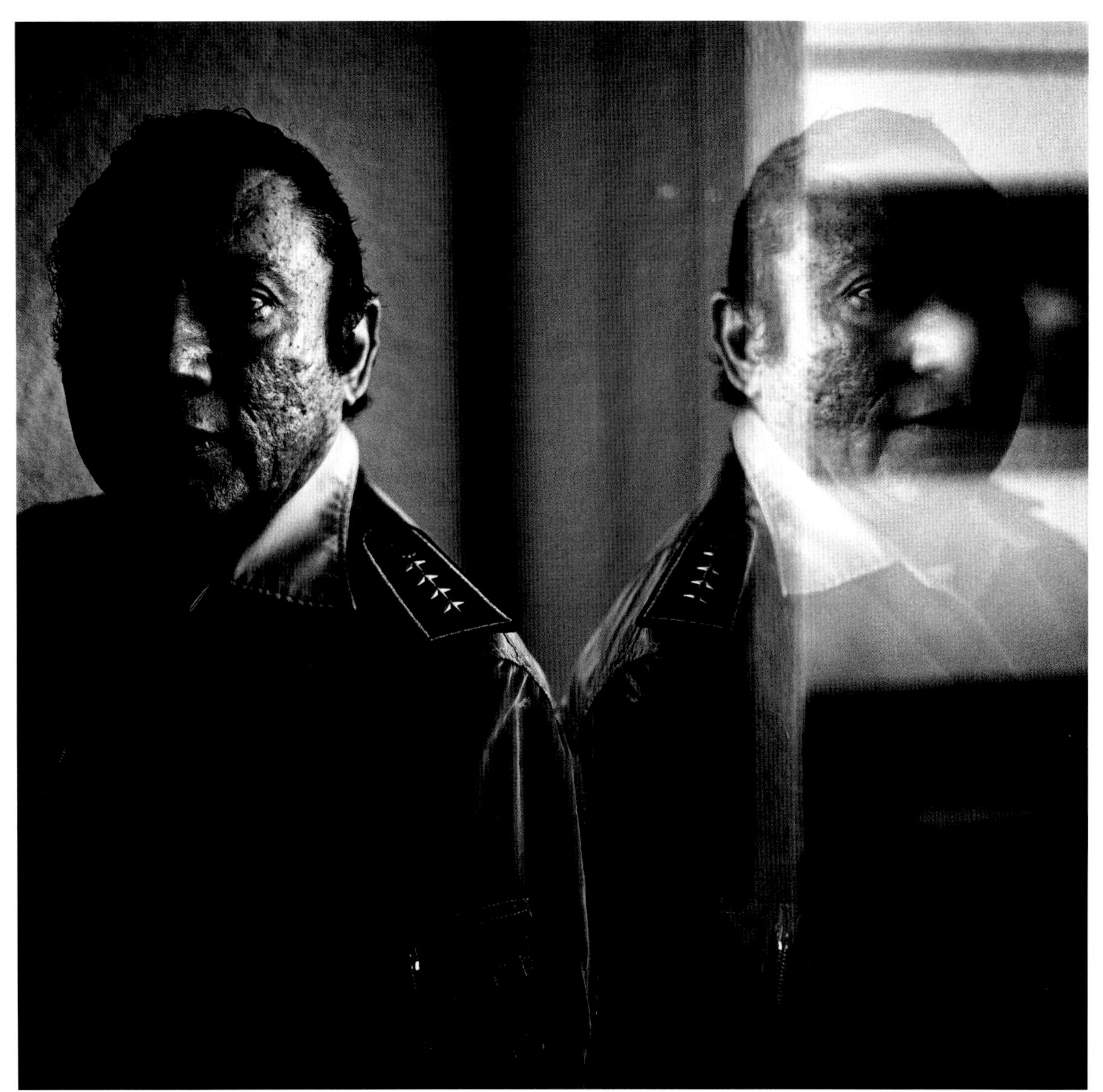

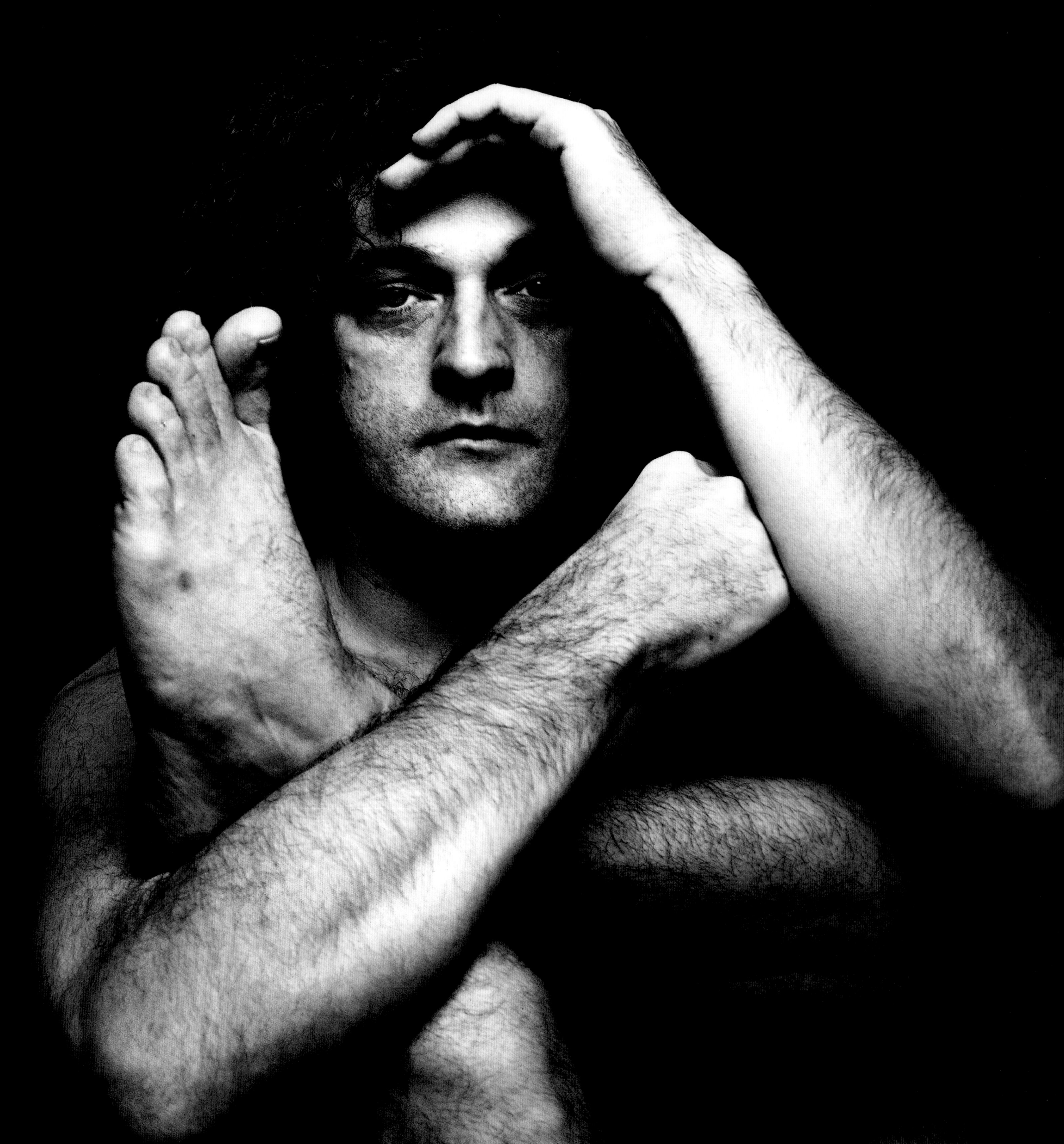

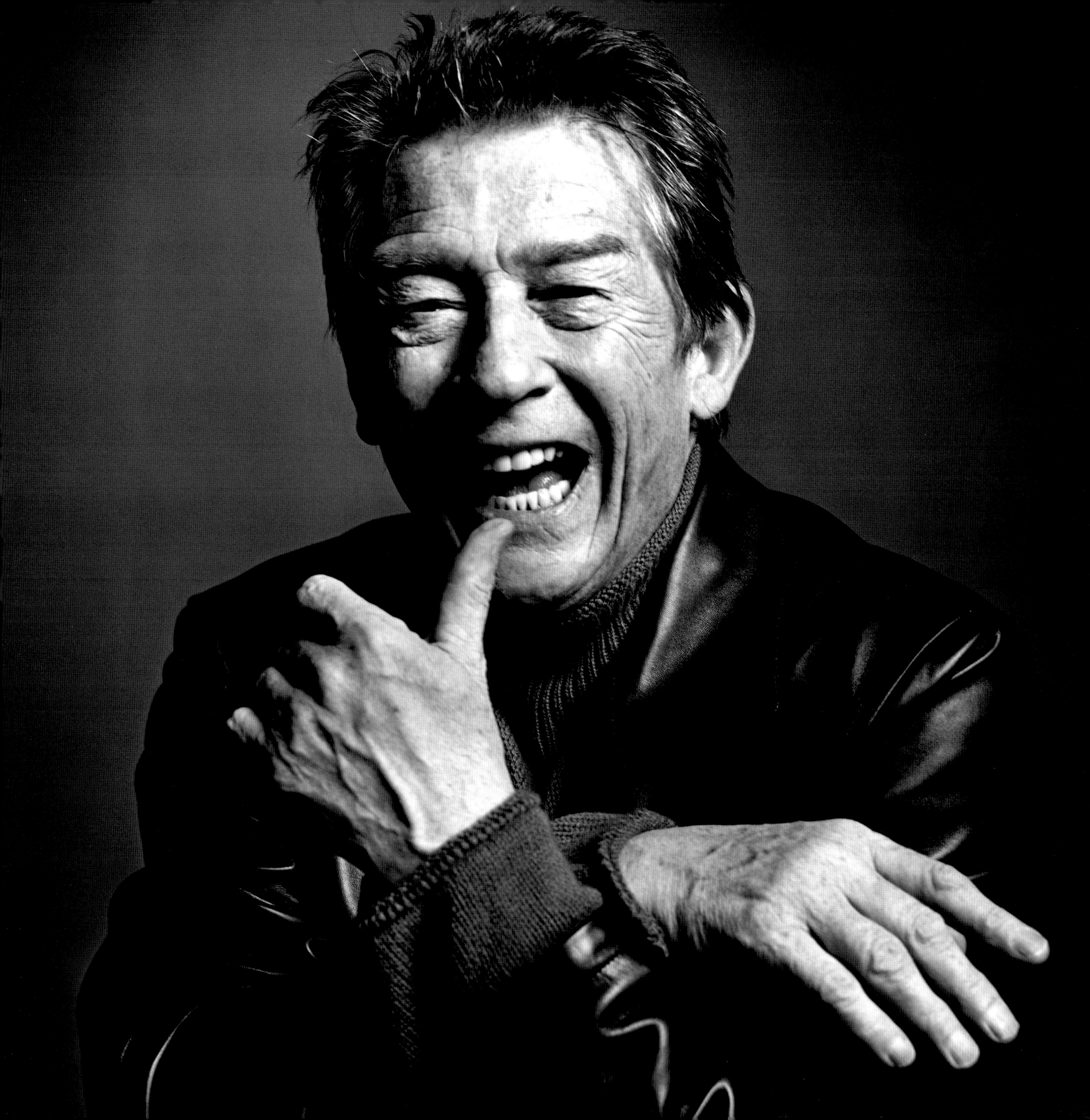

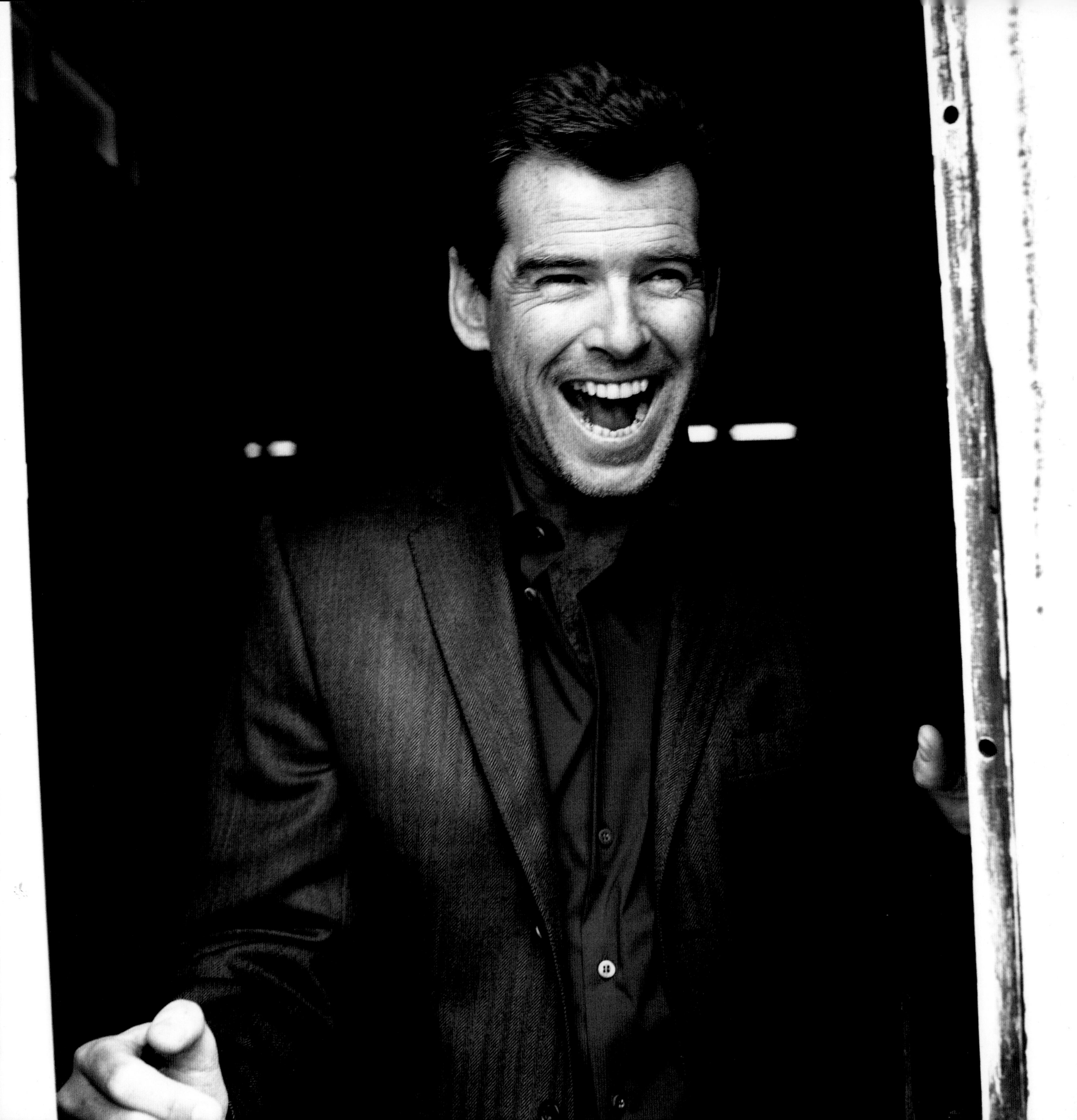

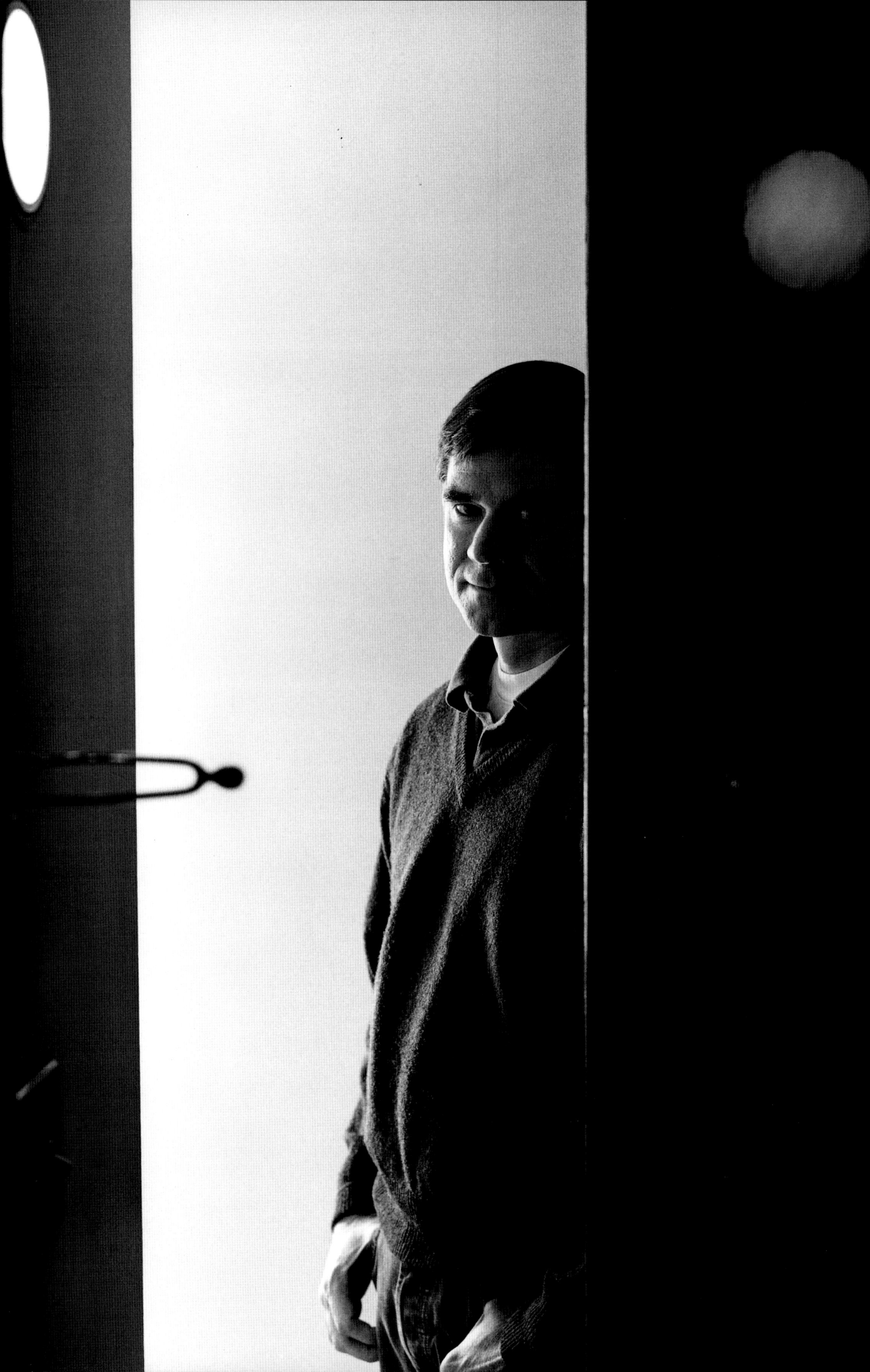

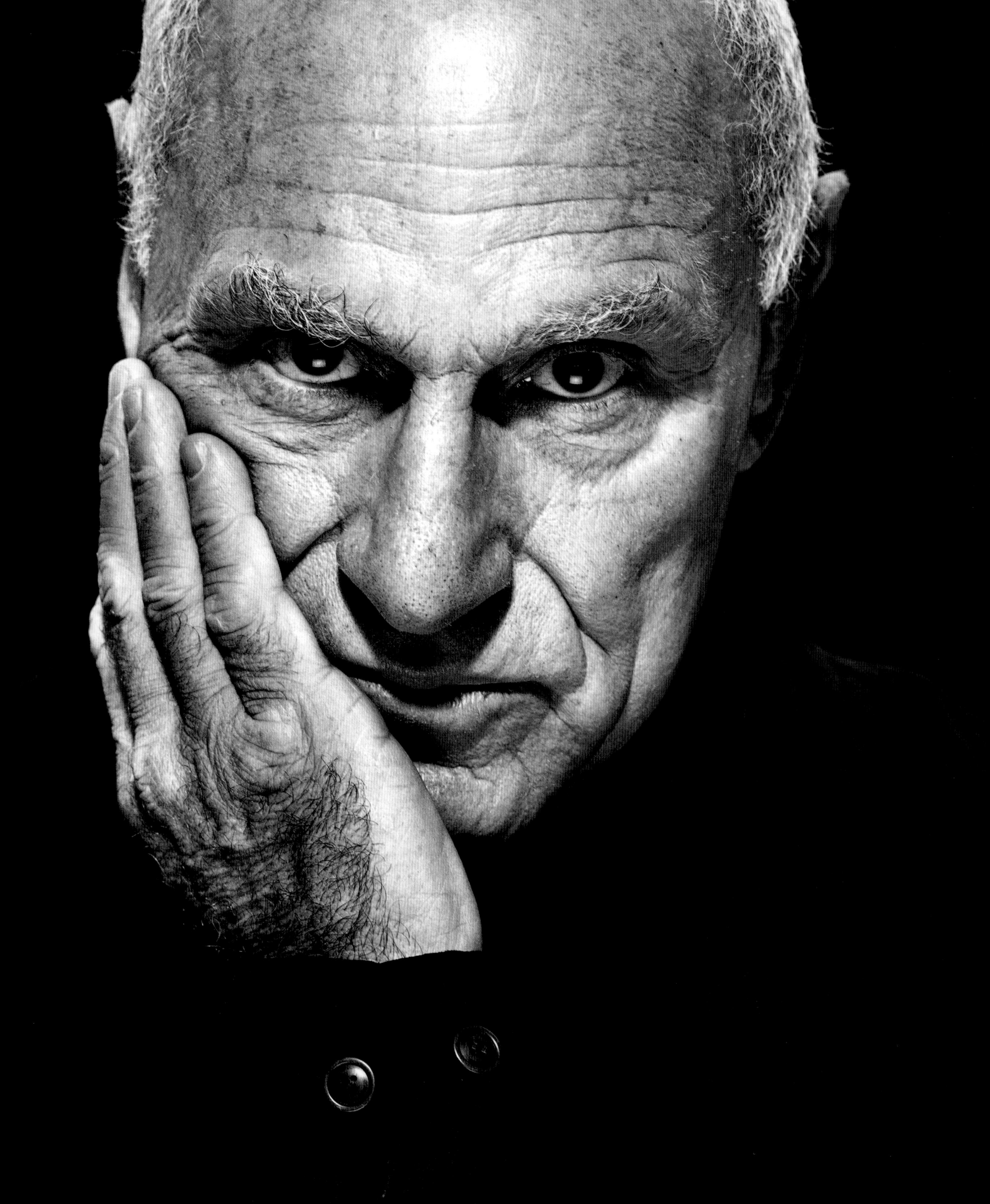

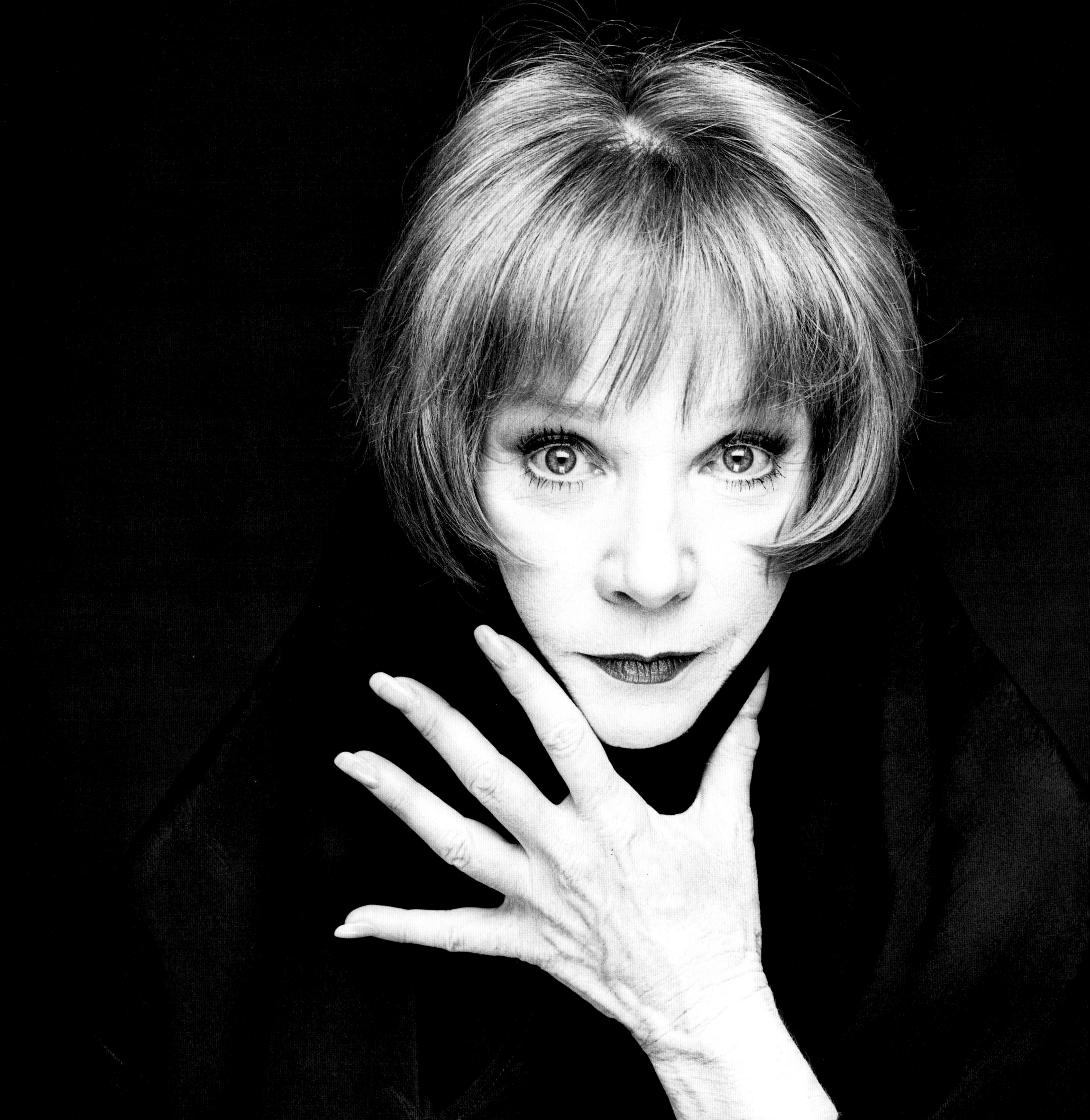

YES IT DID
AND GUES
HER FEET

HURT....
WHERE
GO!

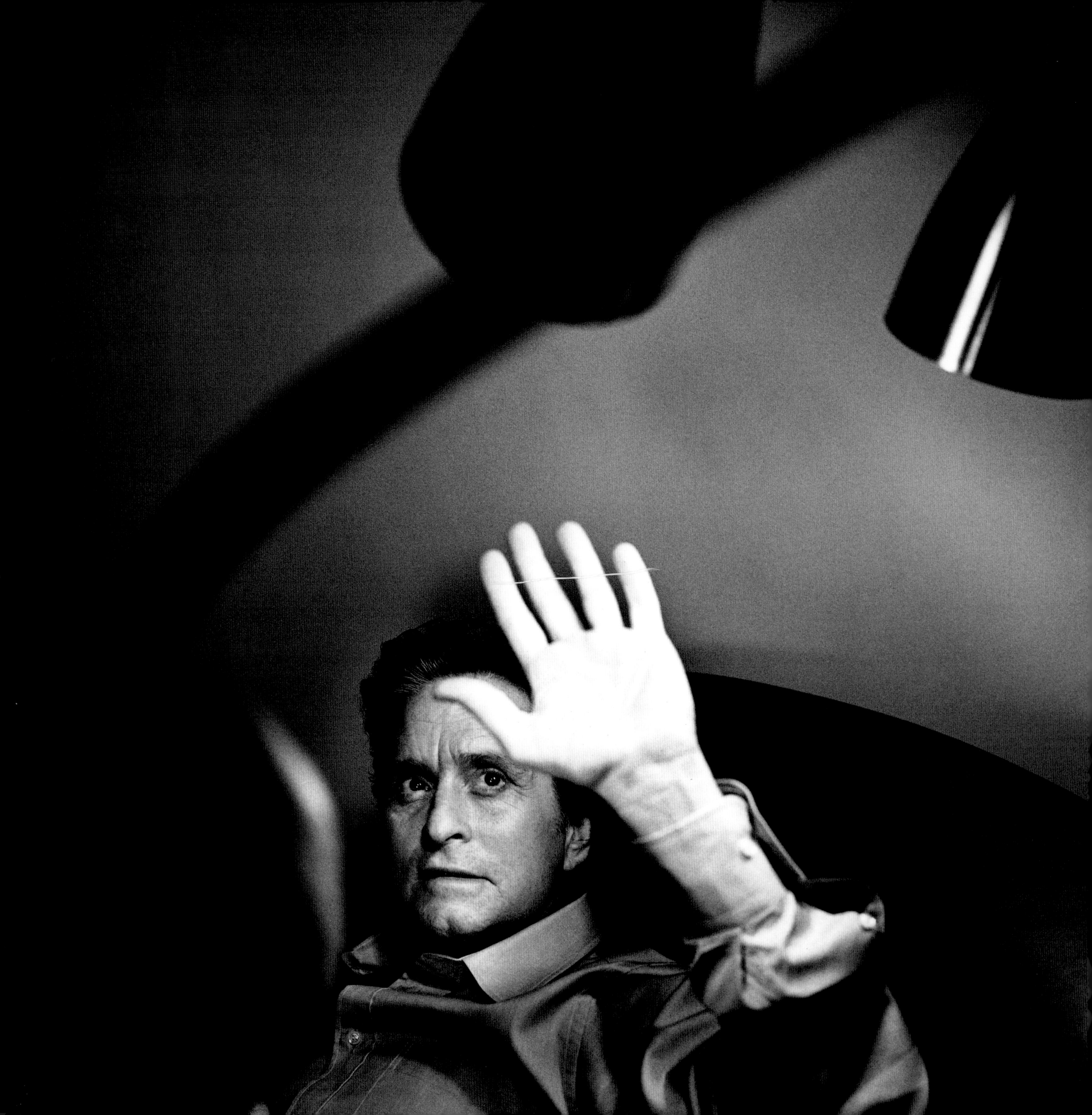

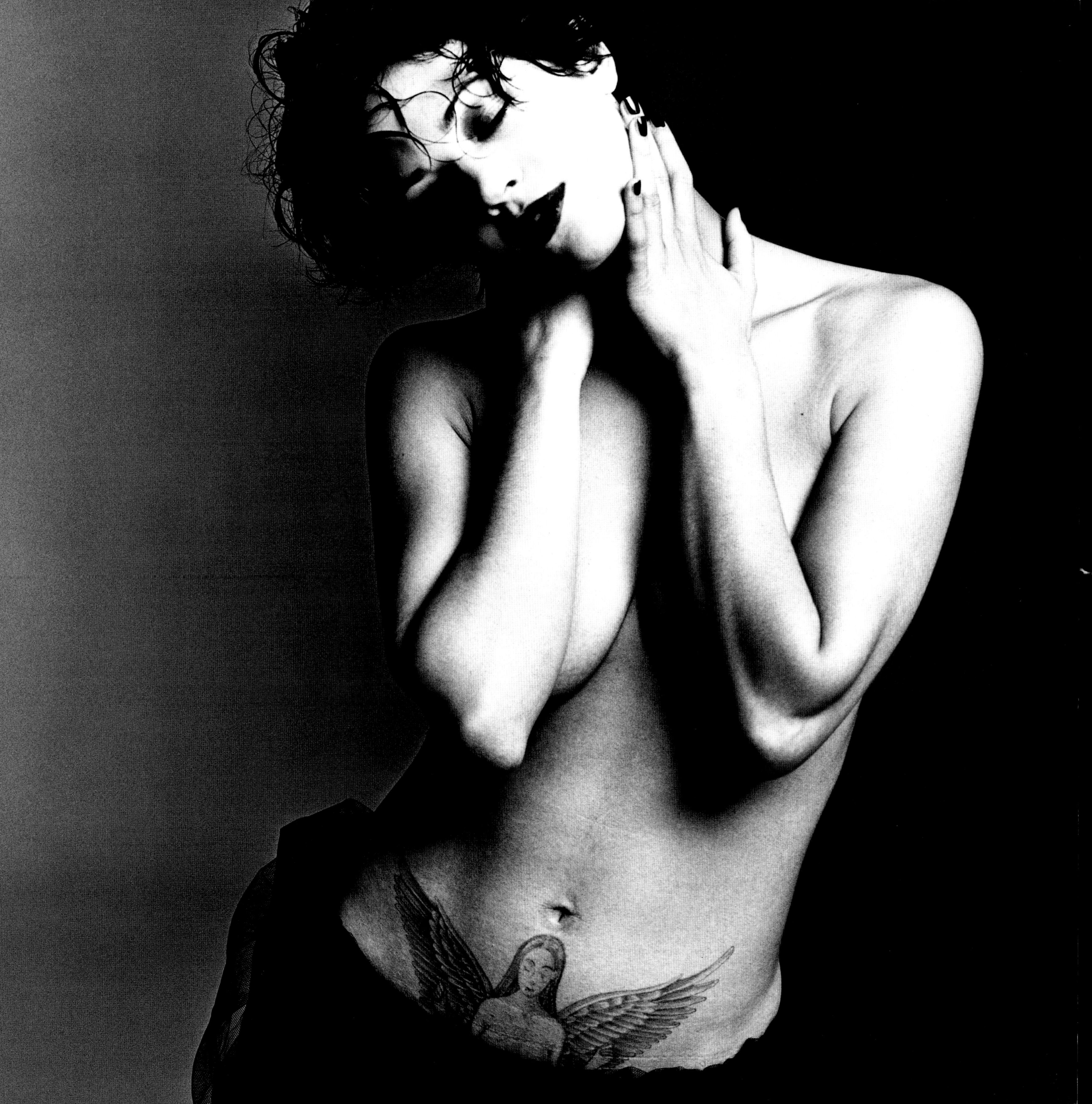

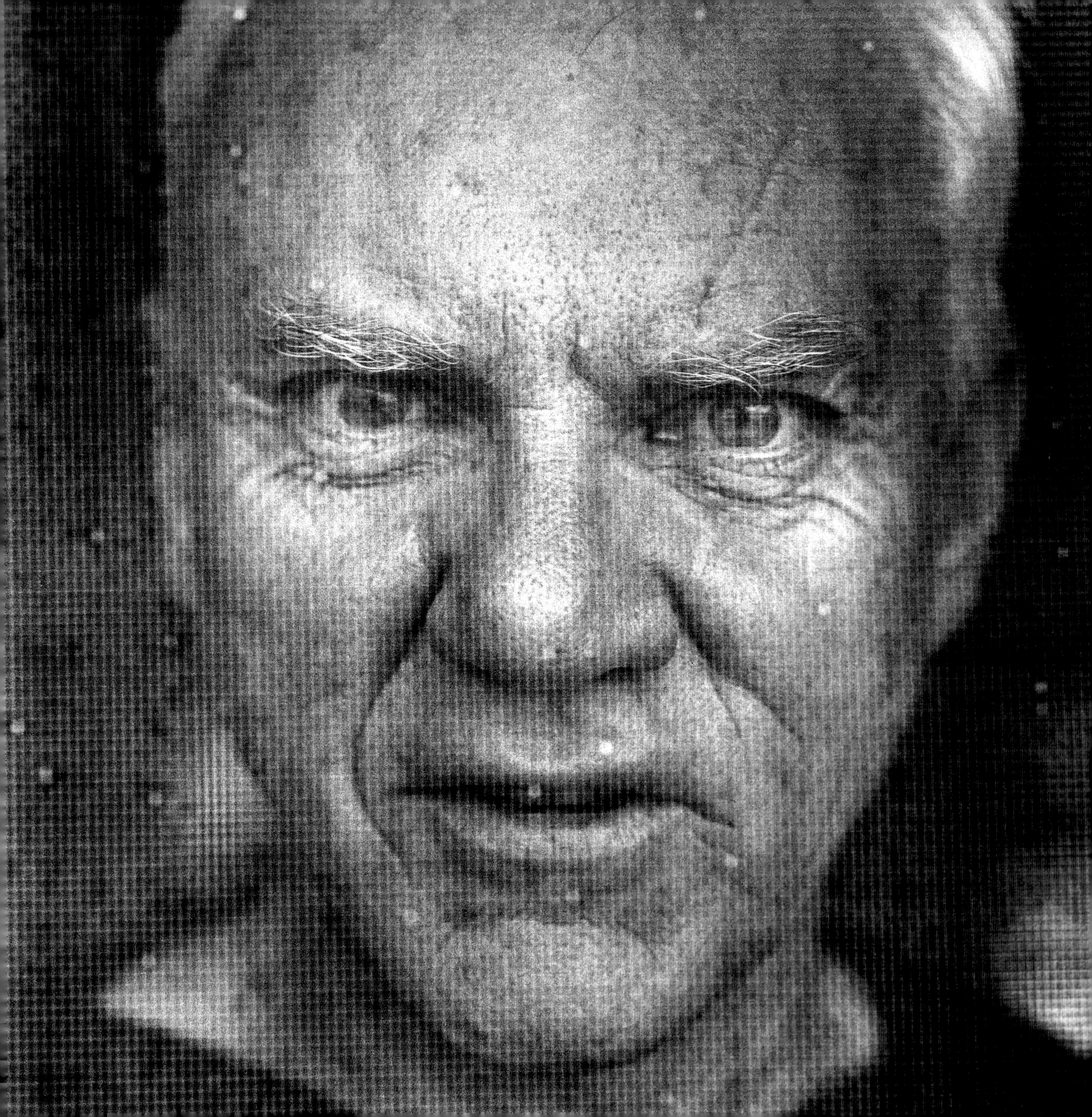

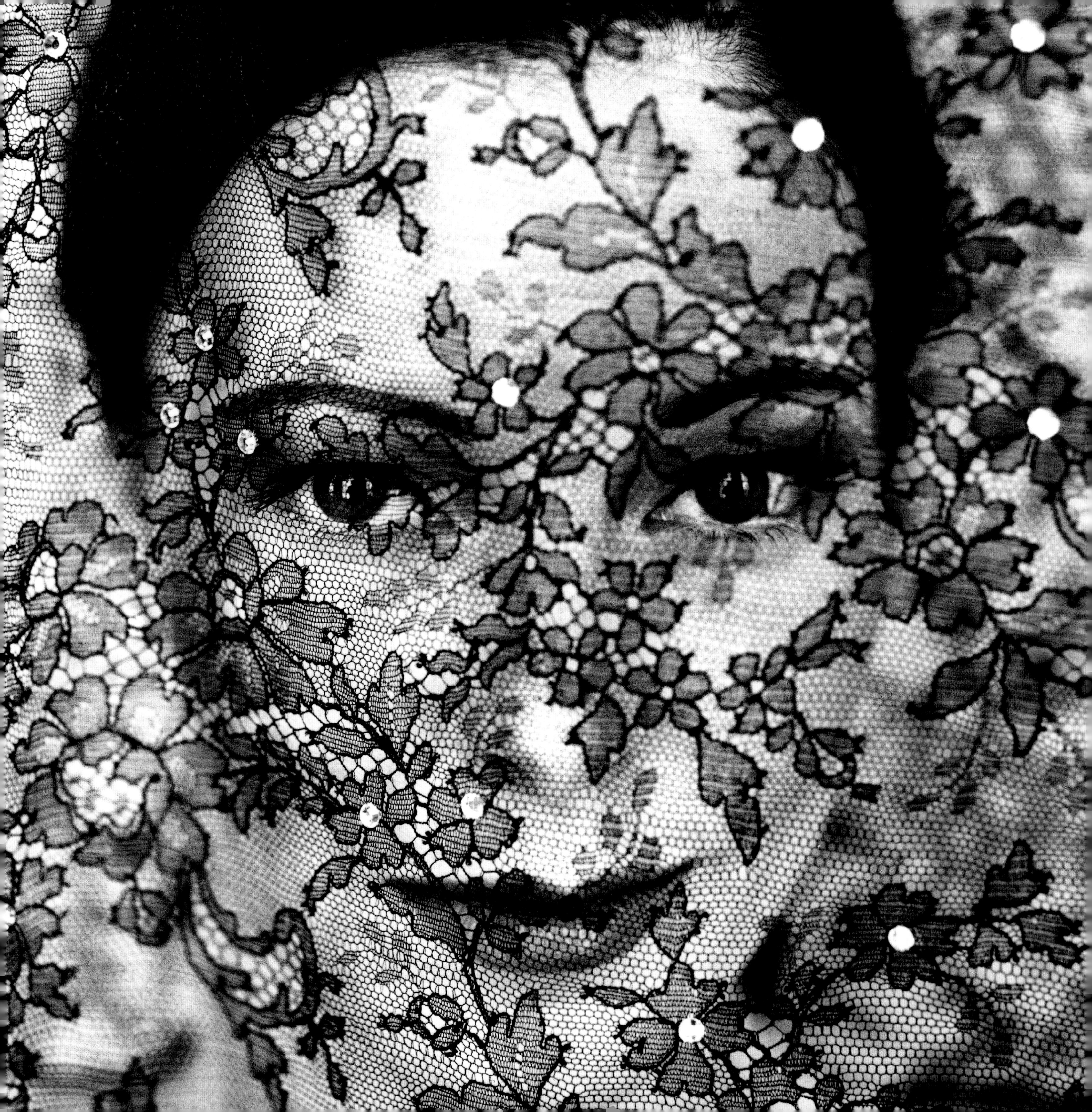

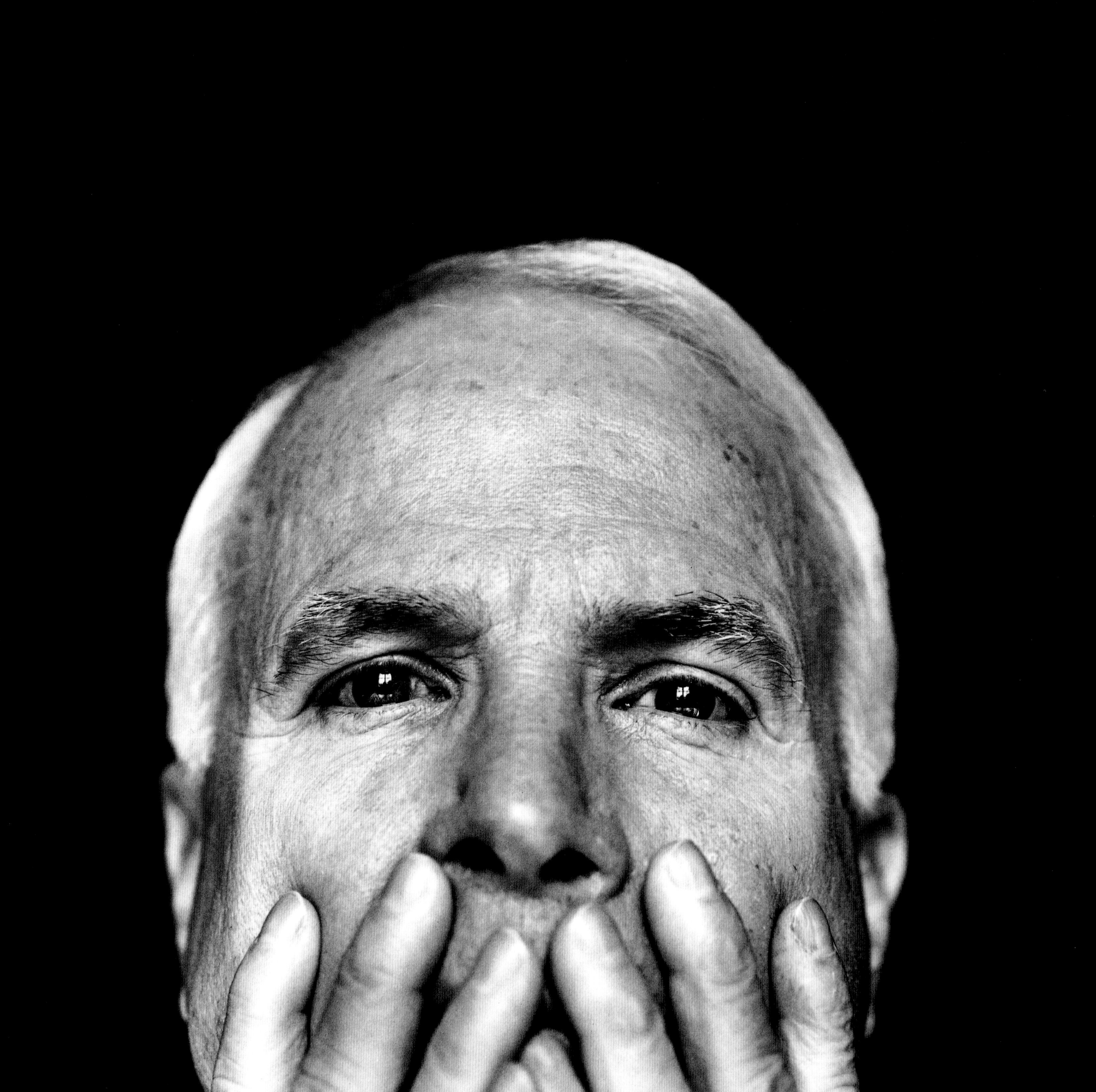

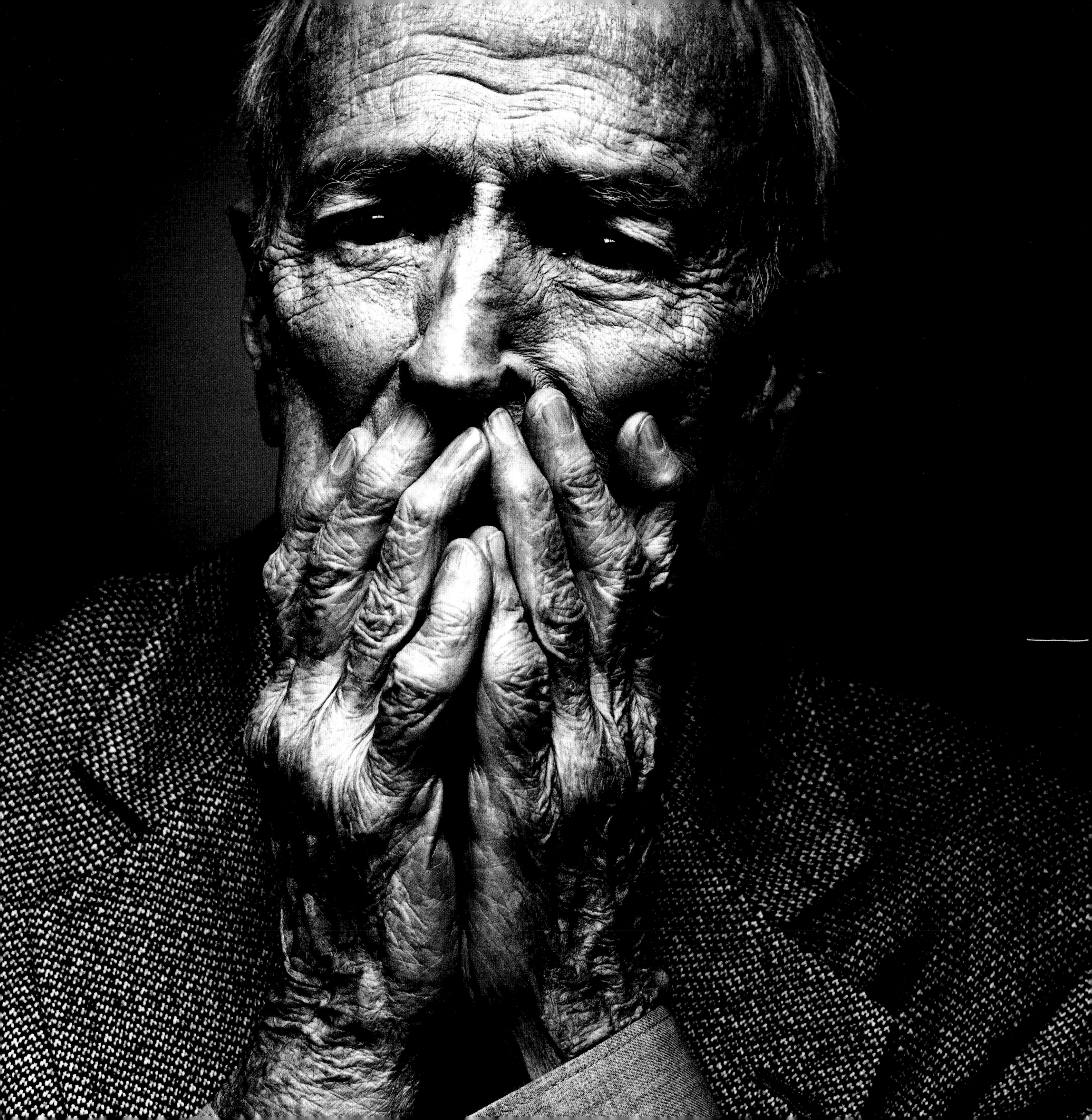

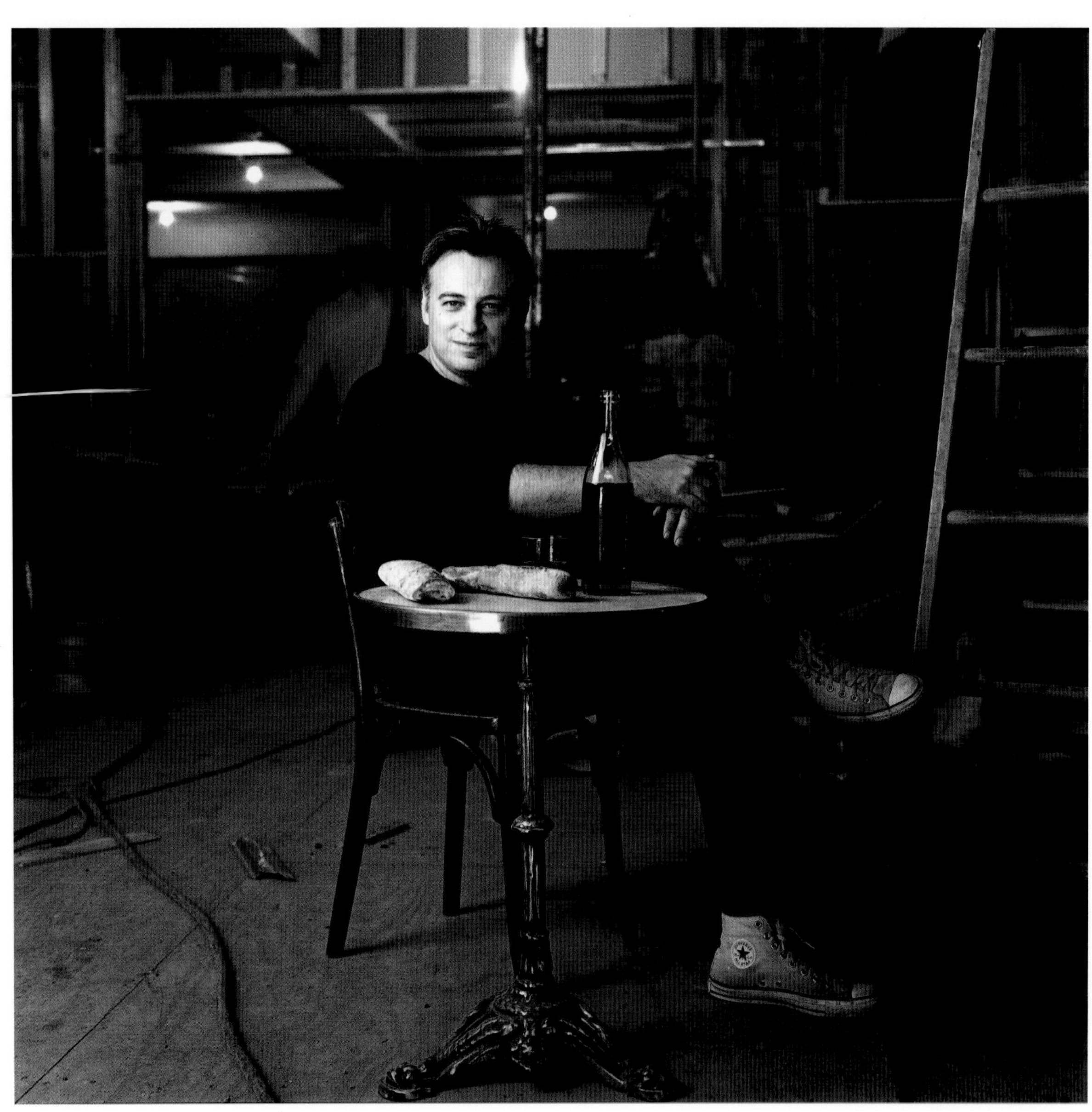

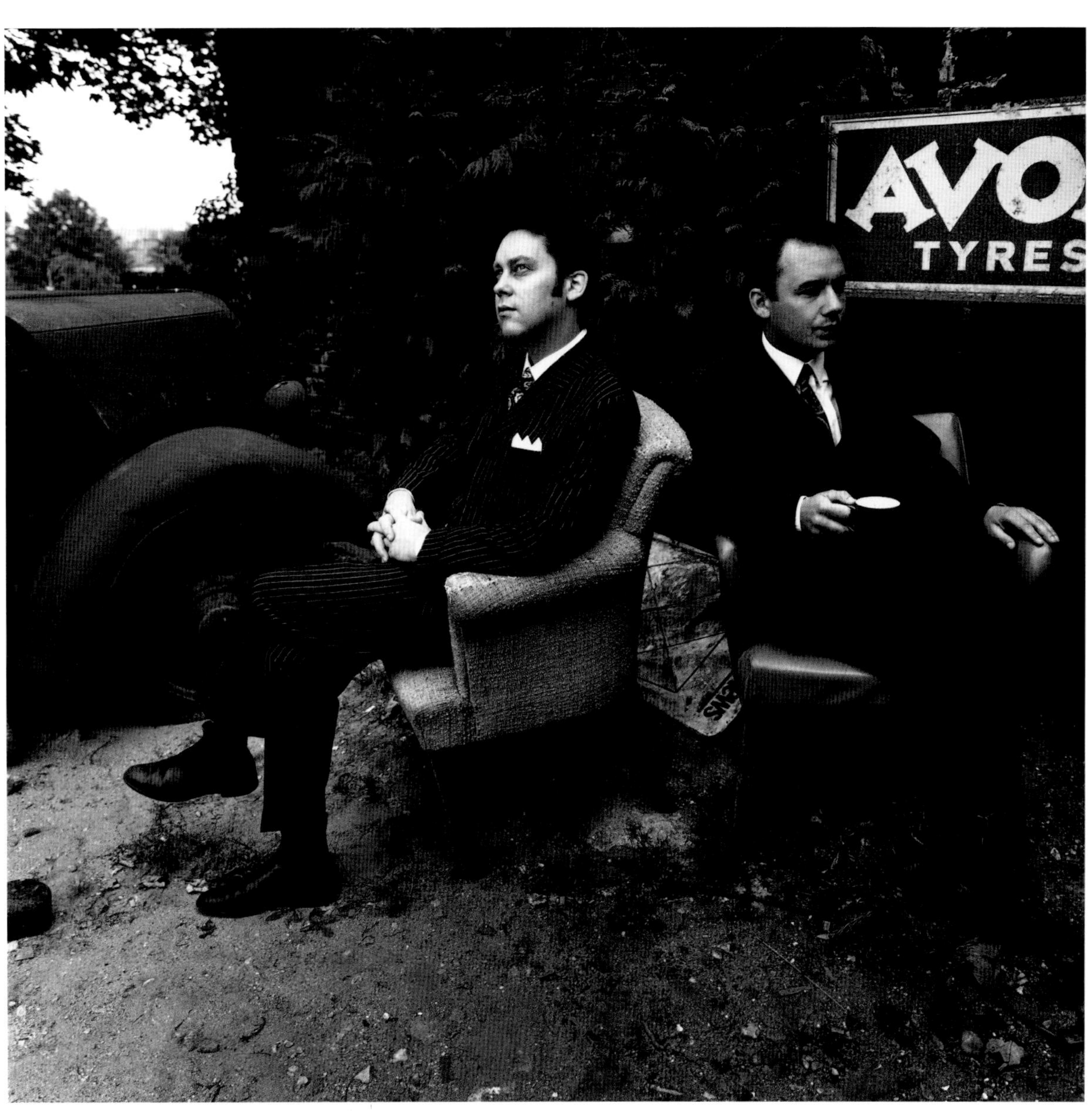

AVO
TYRES

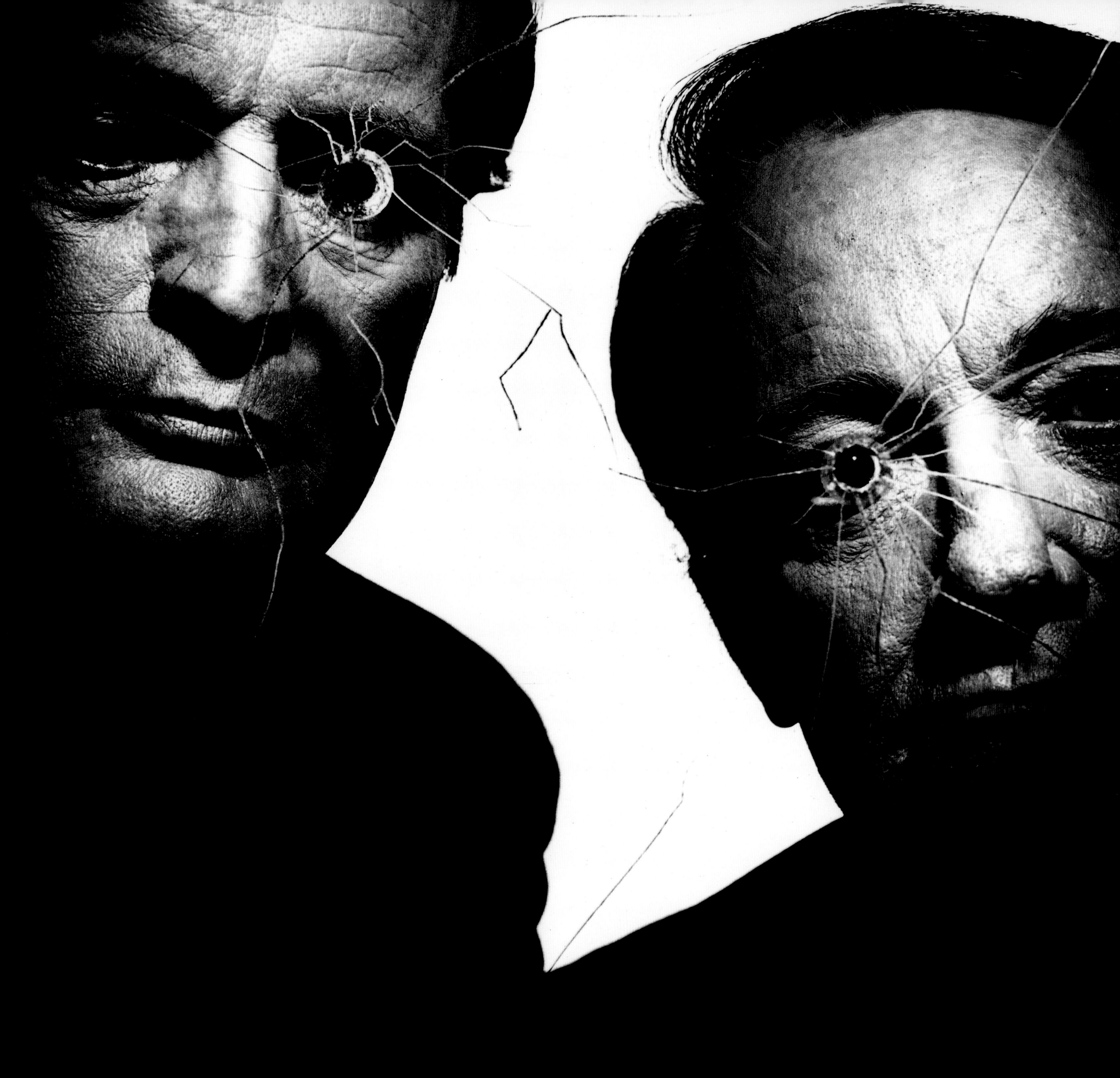

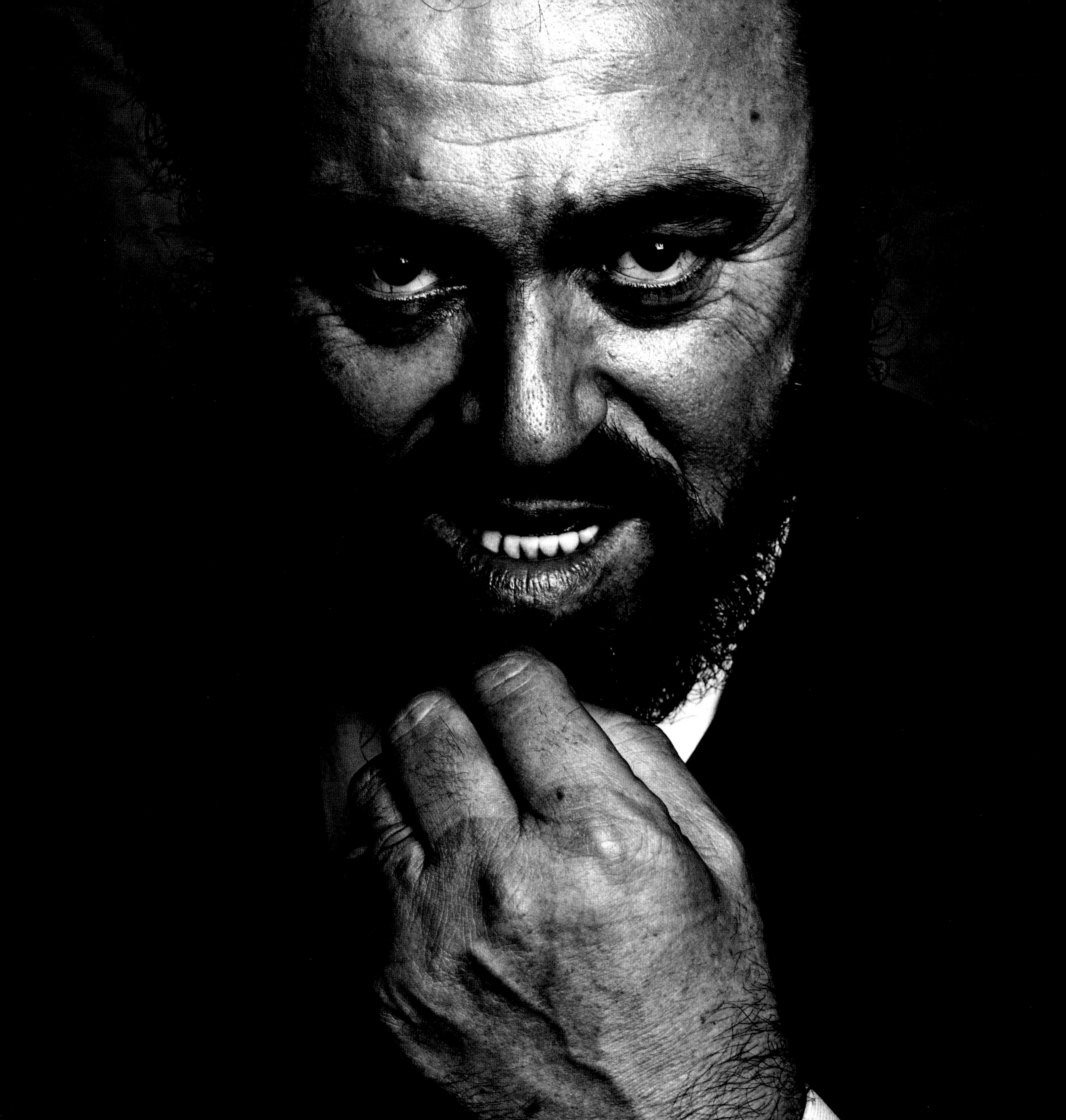

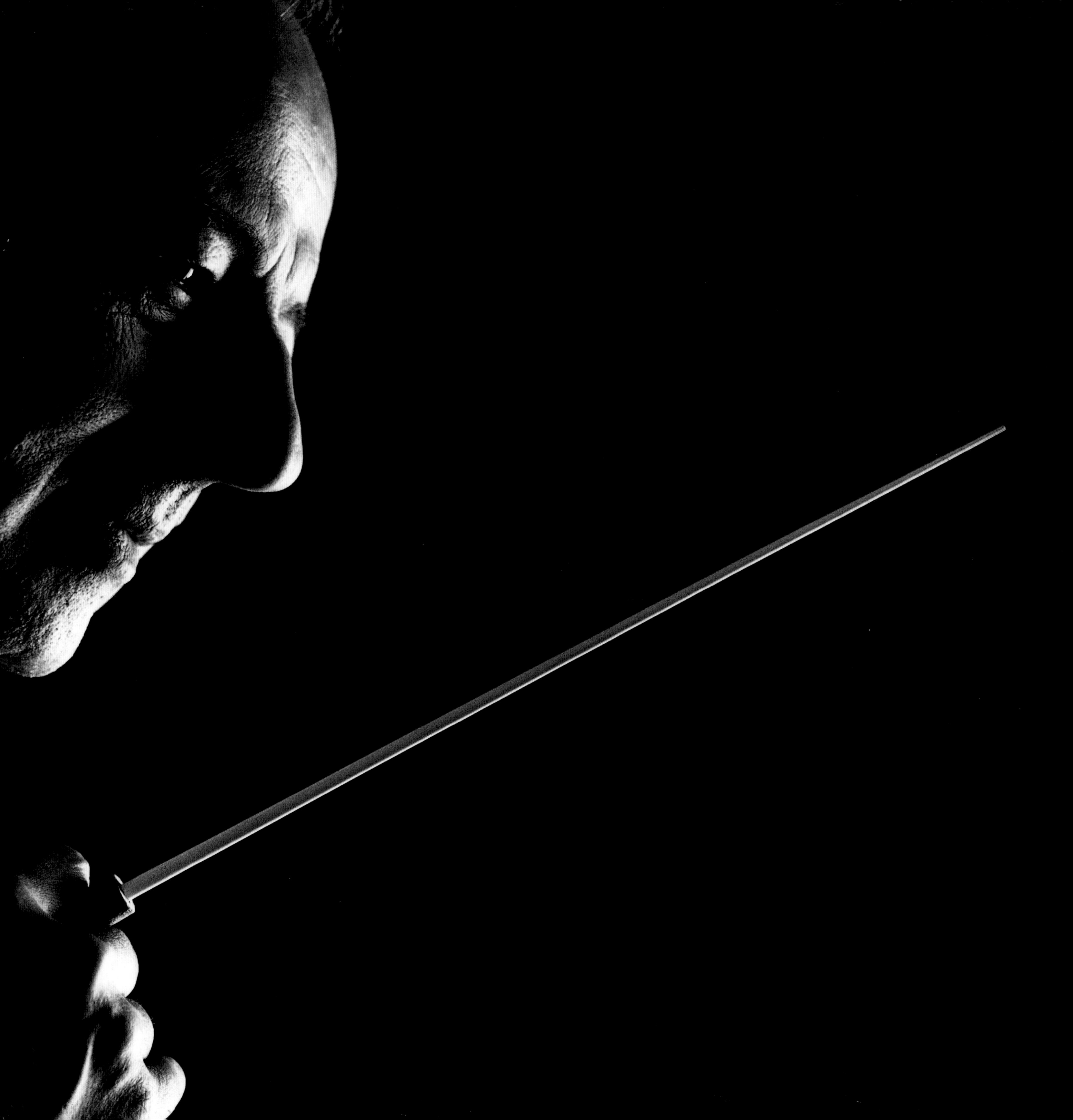

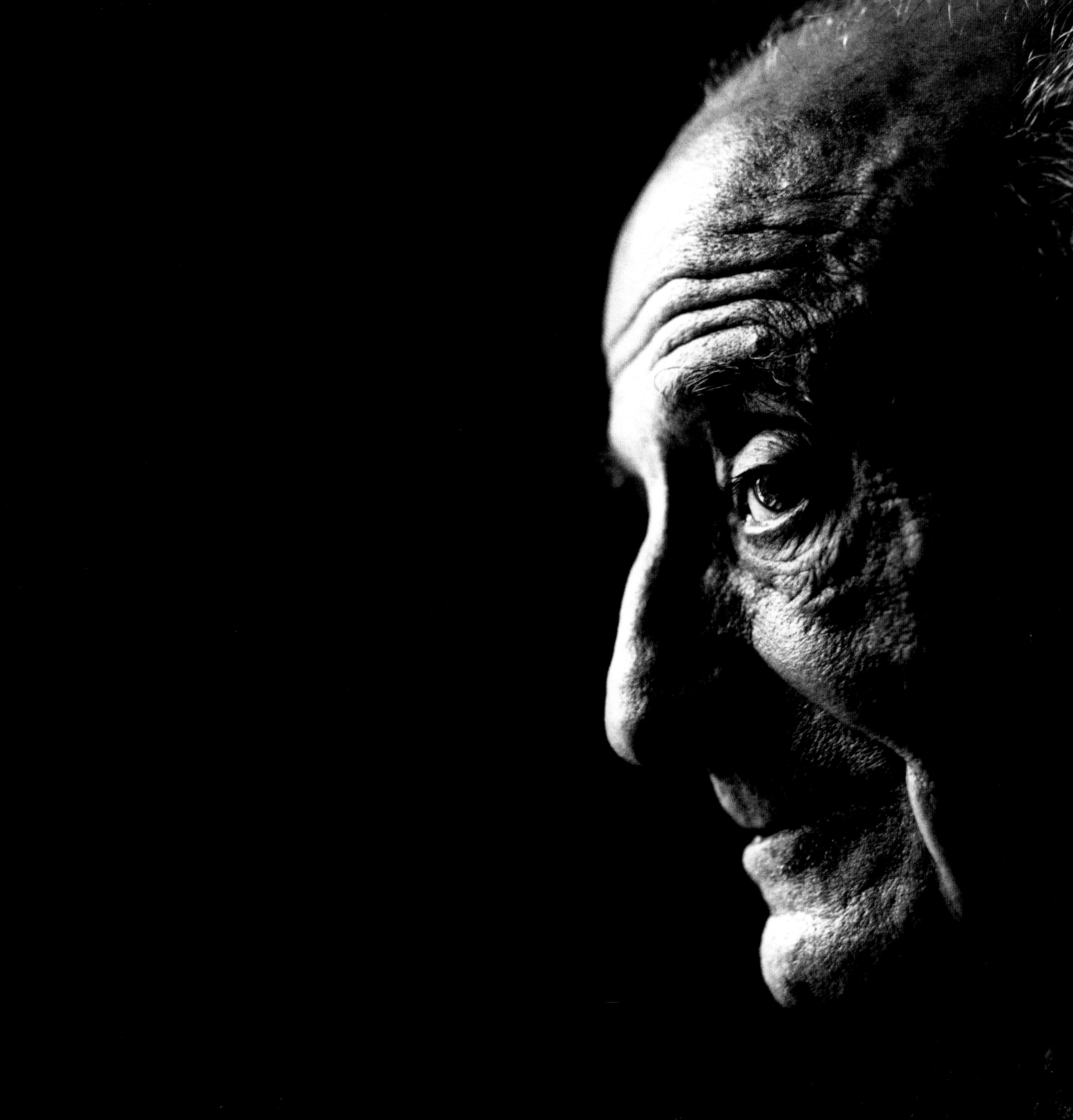

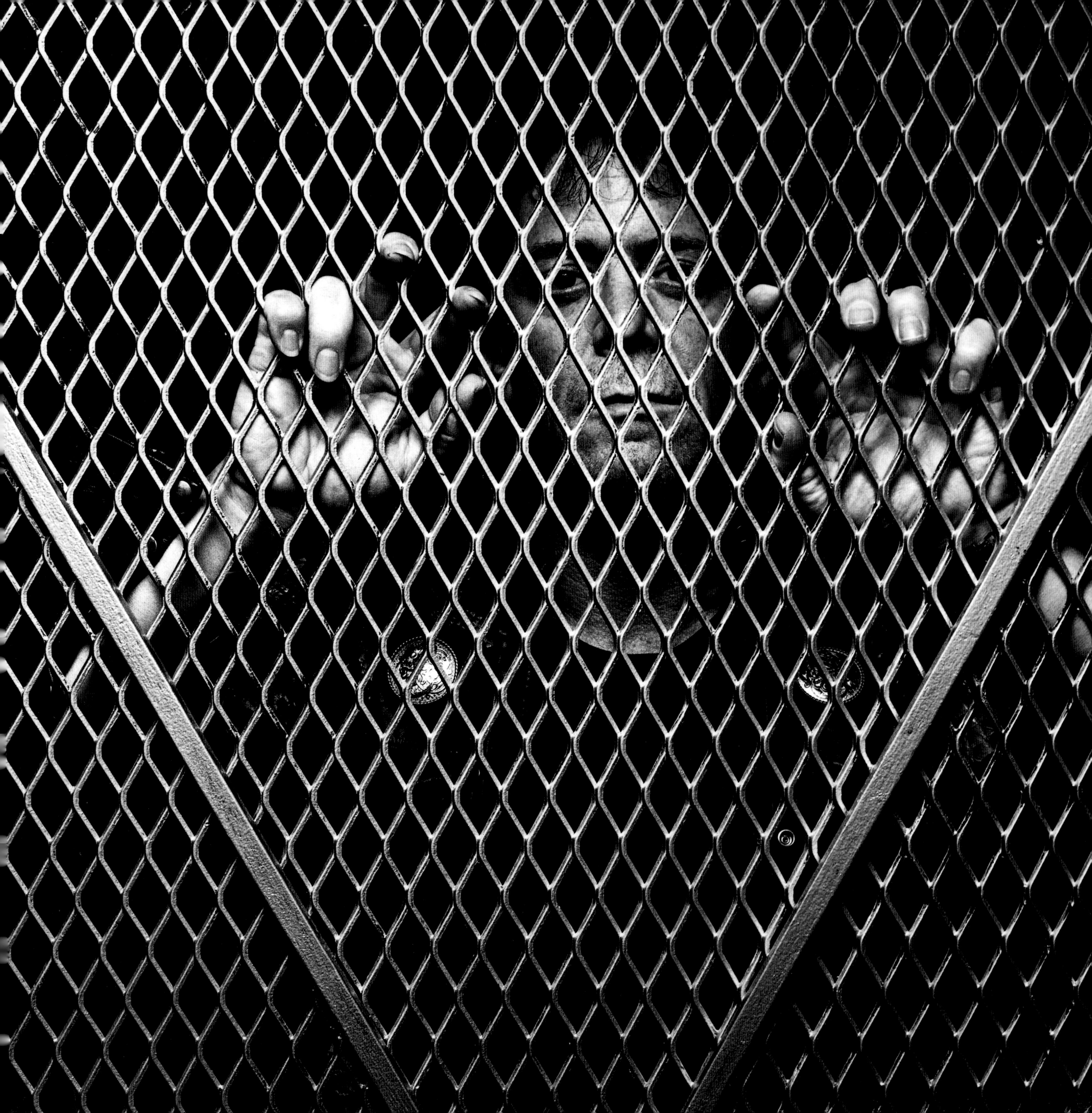

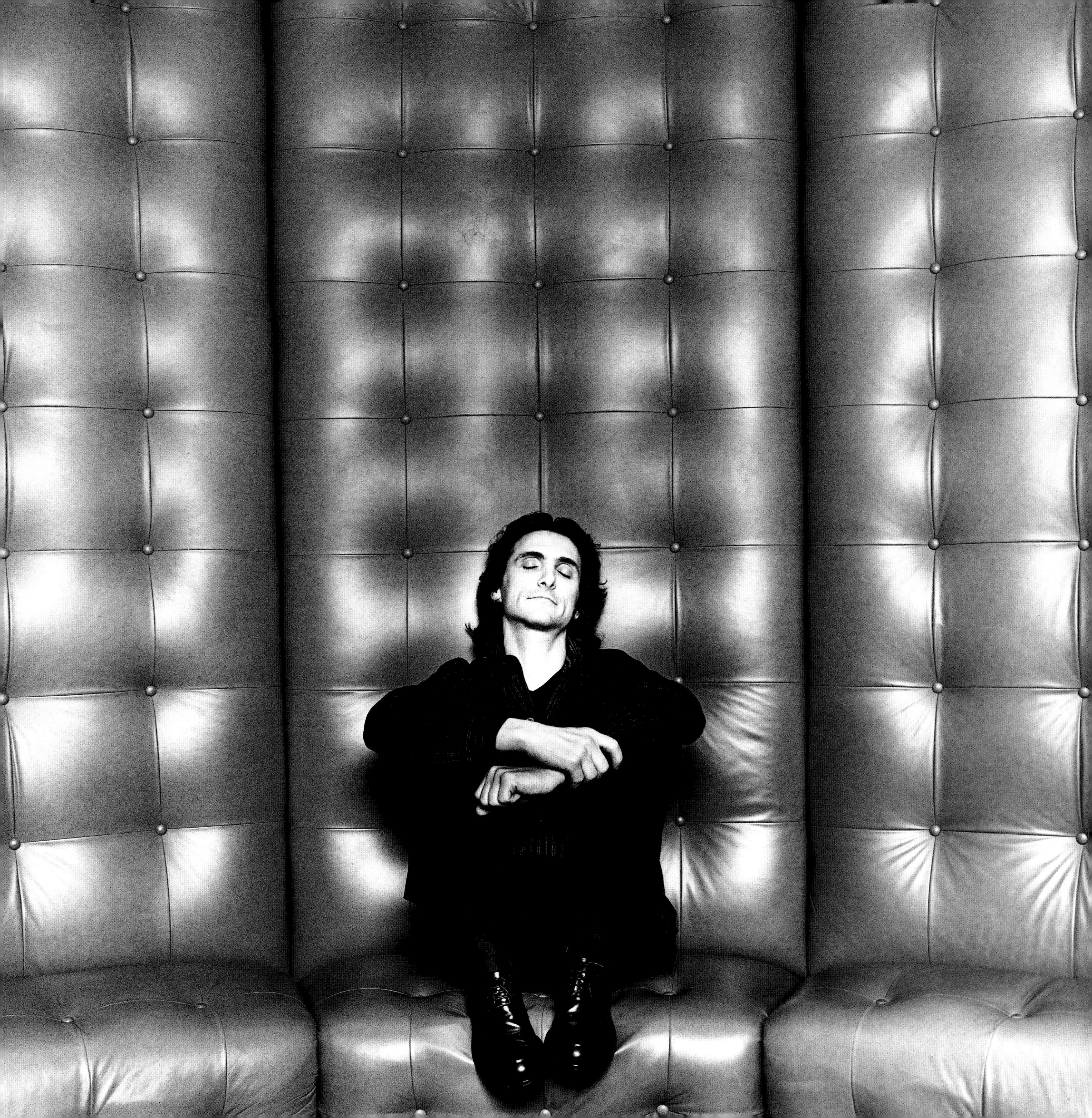

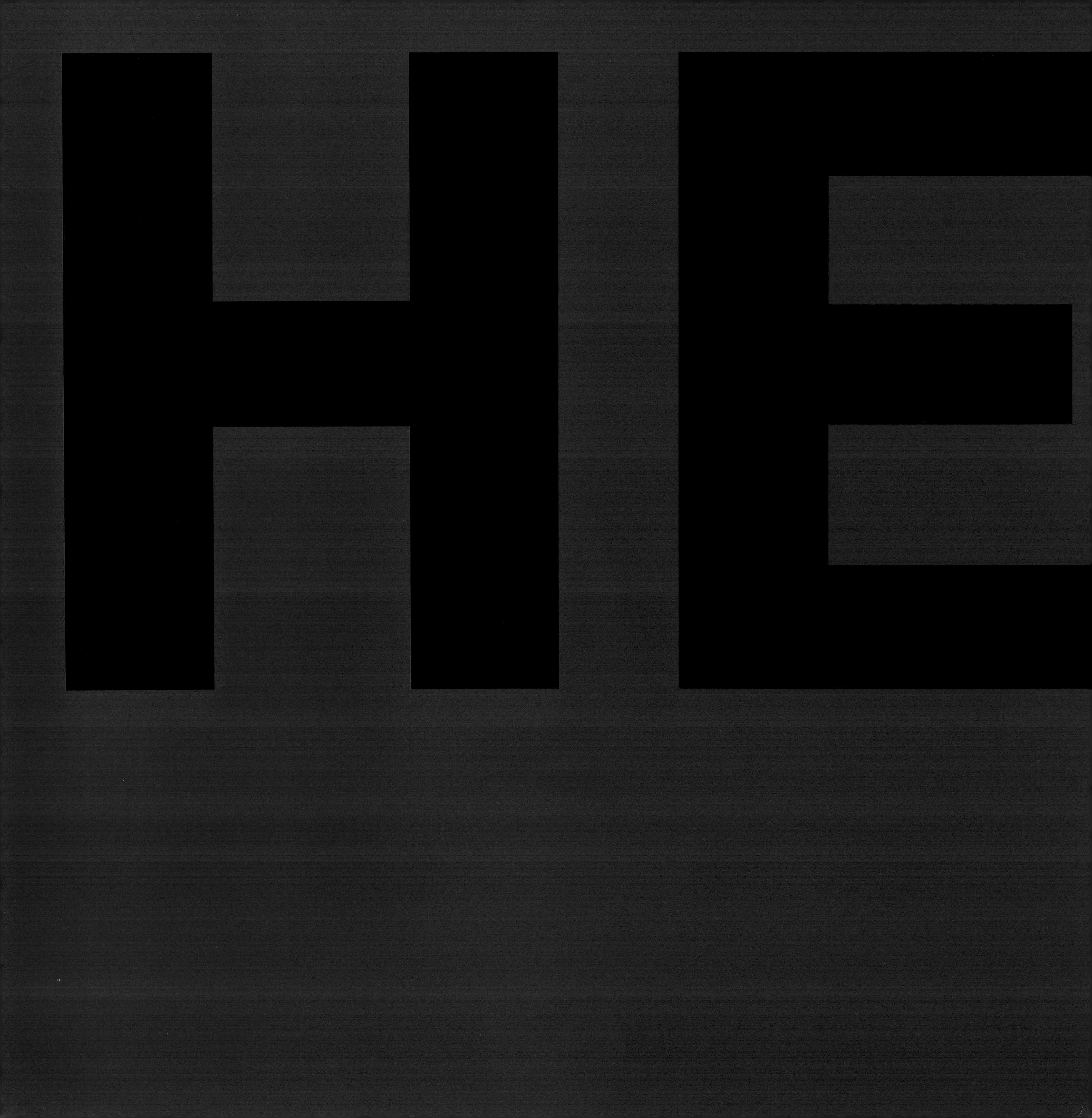

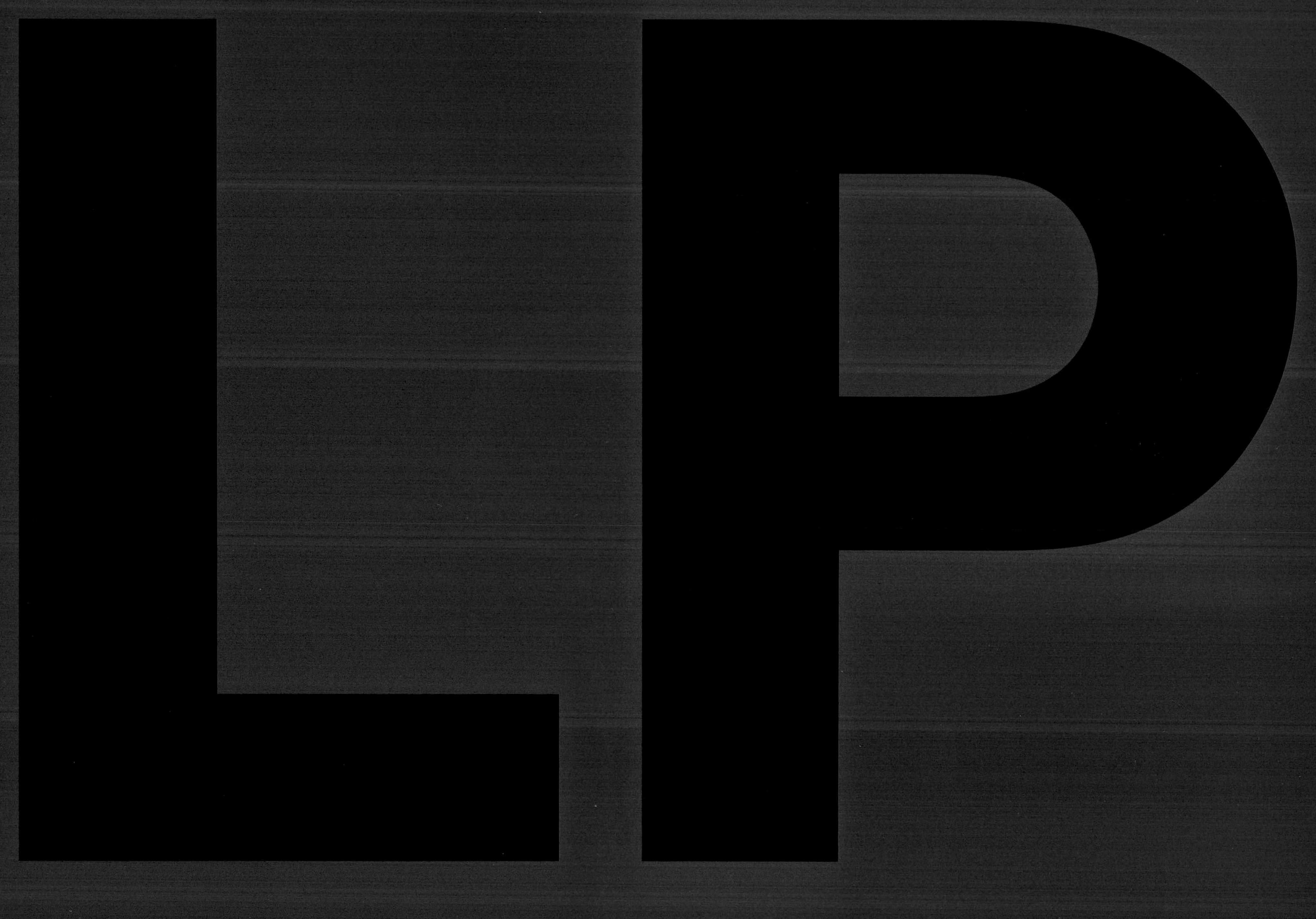

ALEXANDER MCQUEEN'S REPLY
TO MY SUGGESTION THAT
SOMETHING BE WRITTEN ACROSS
HIS FOREHEAD.

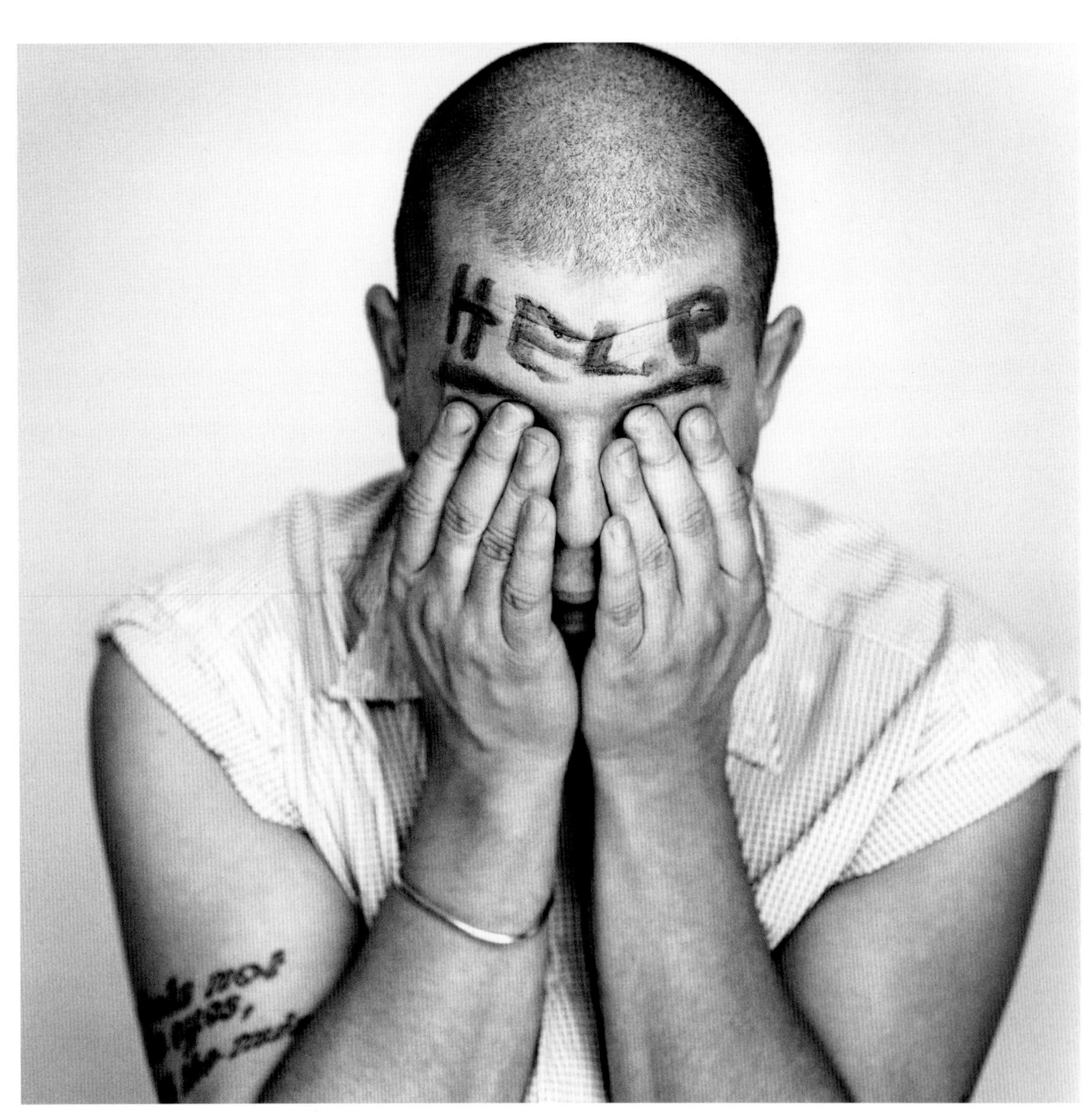

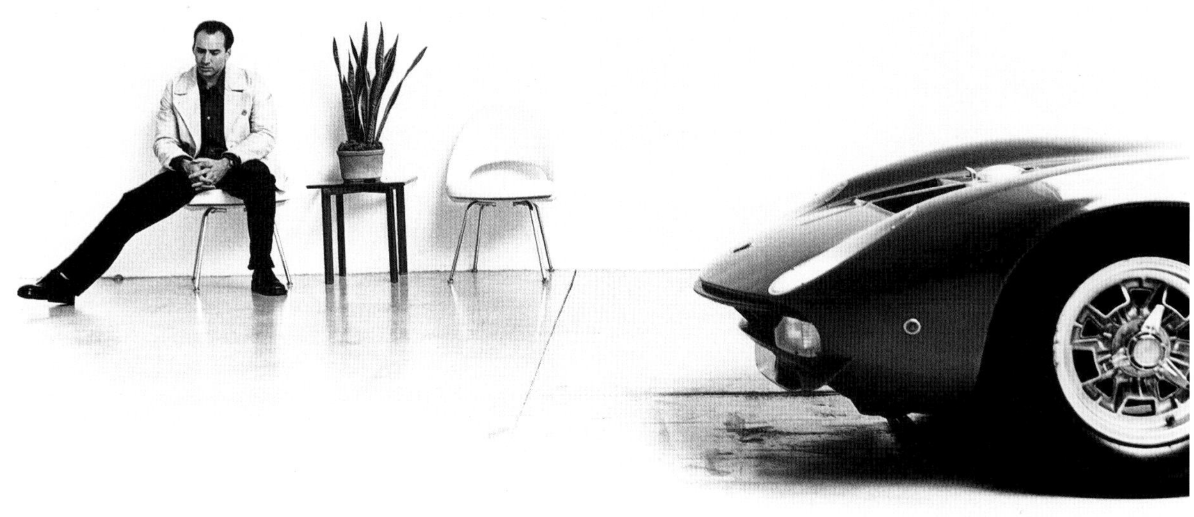

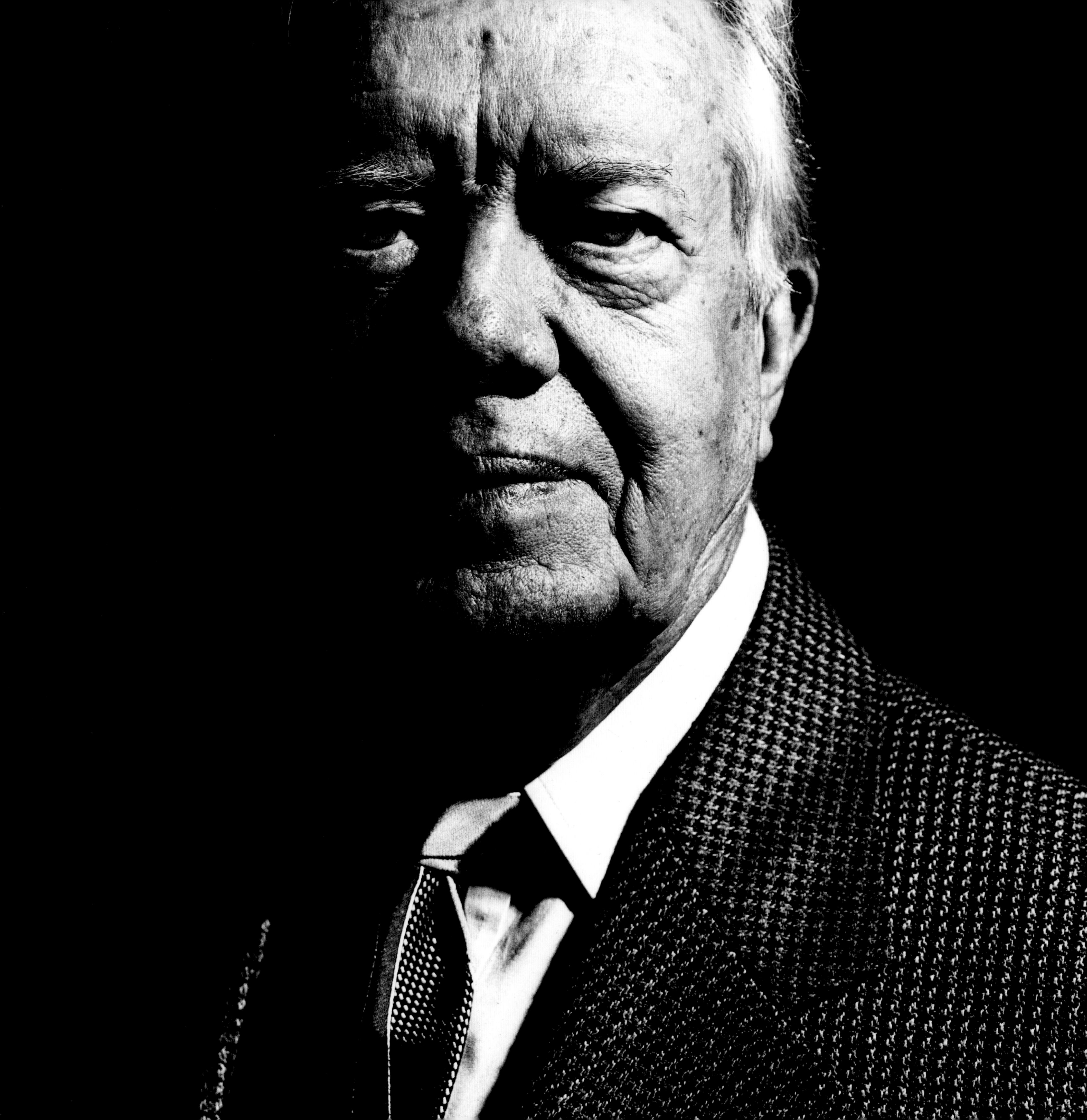

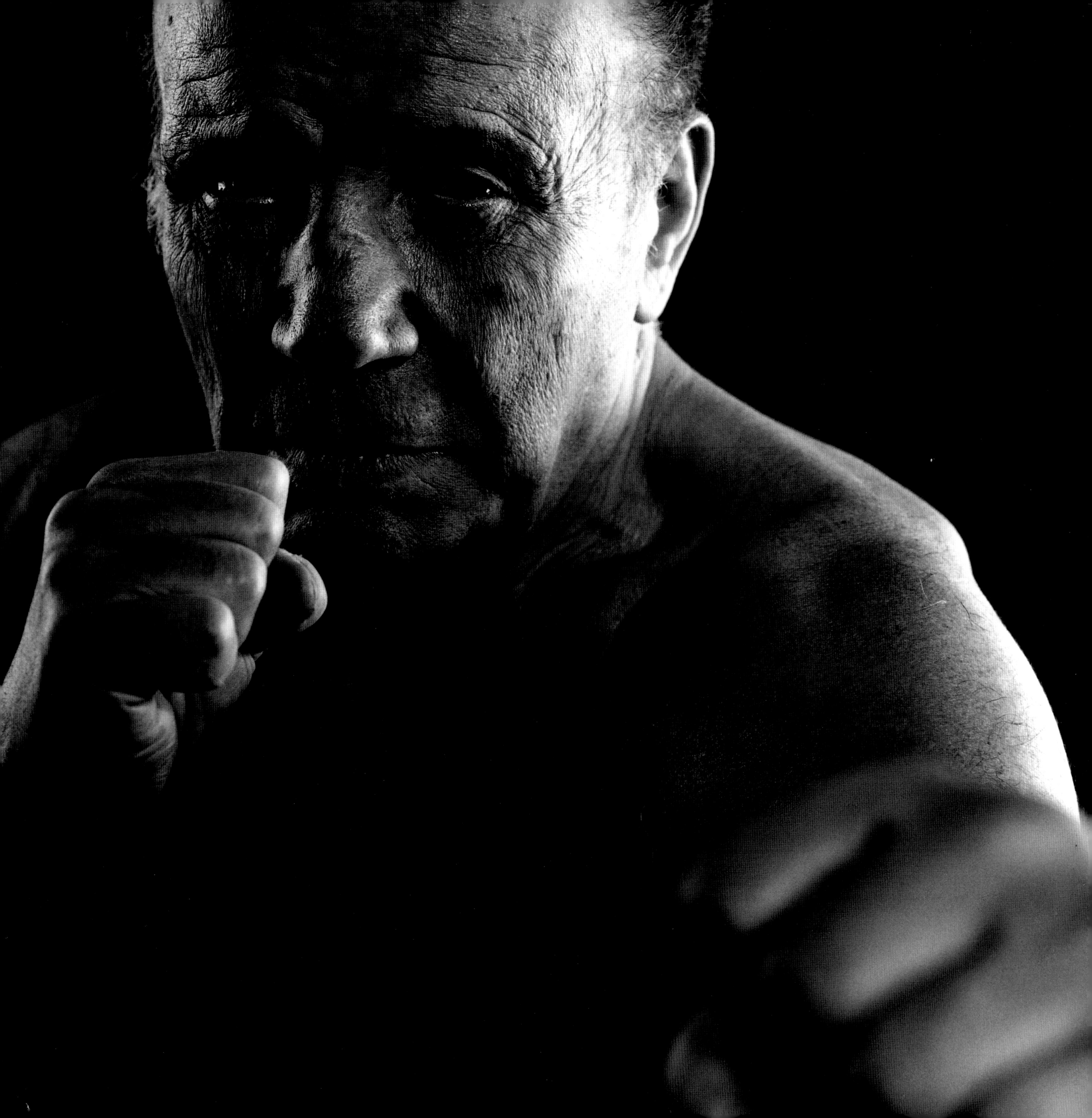

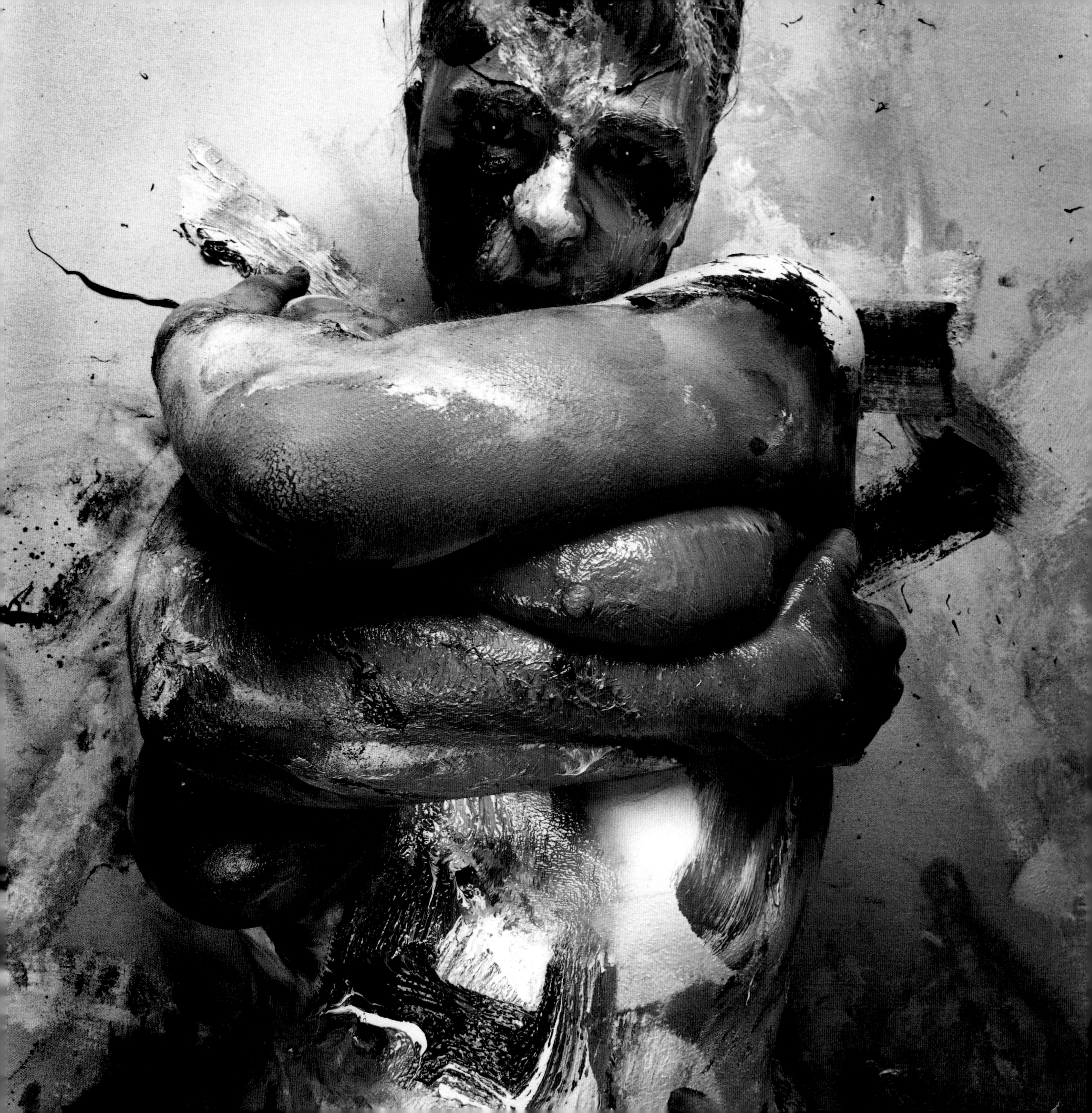

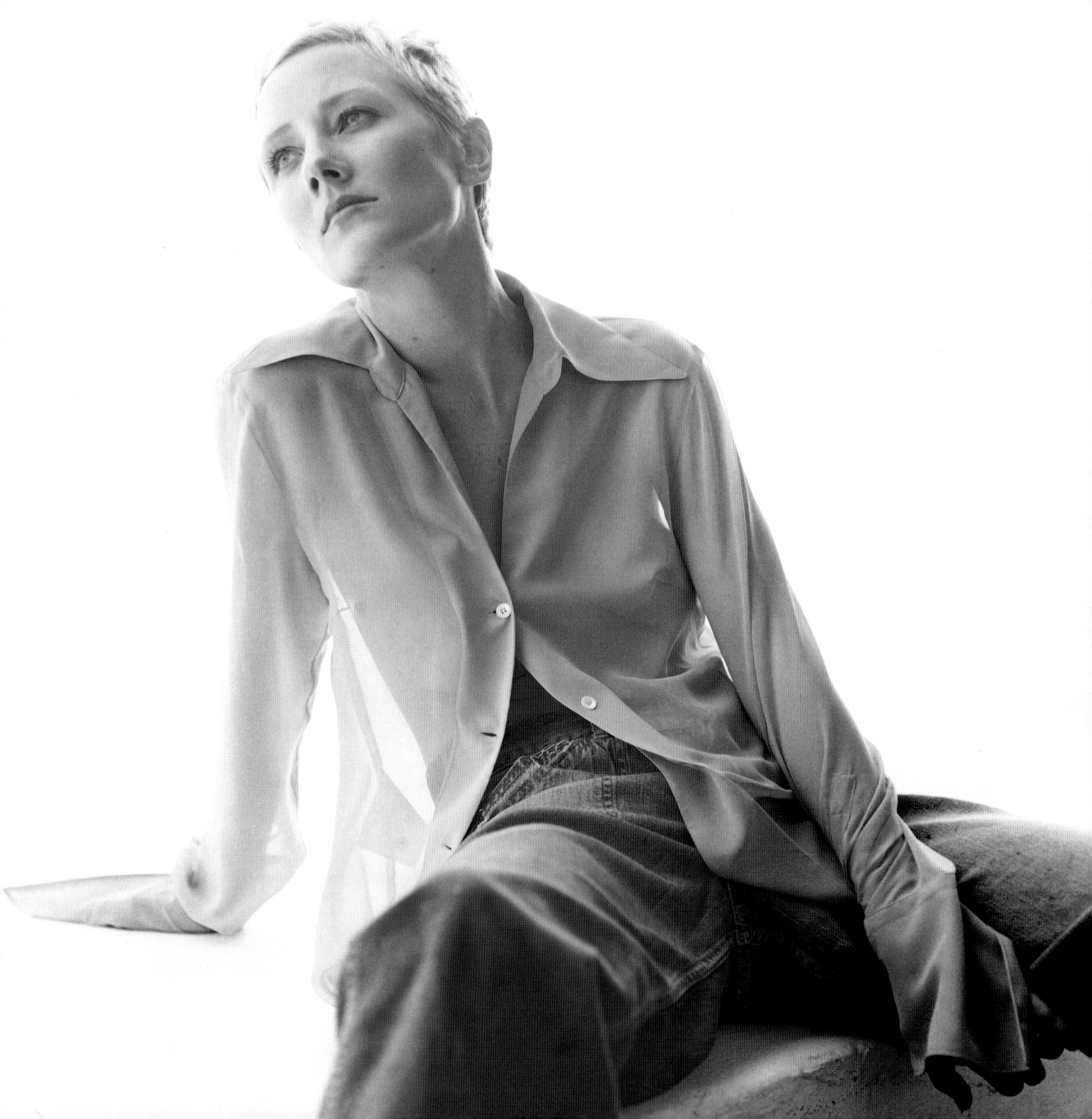

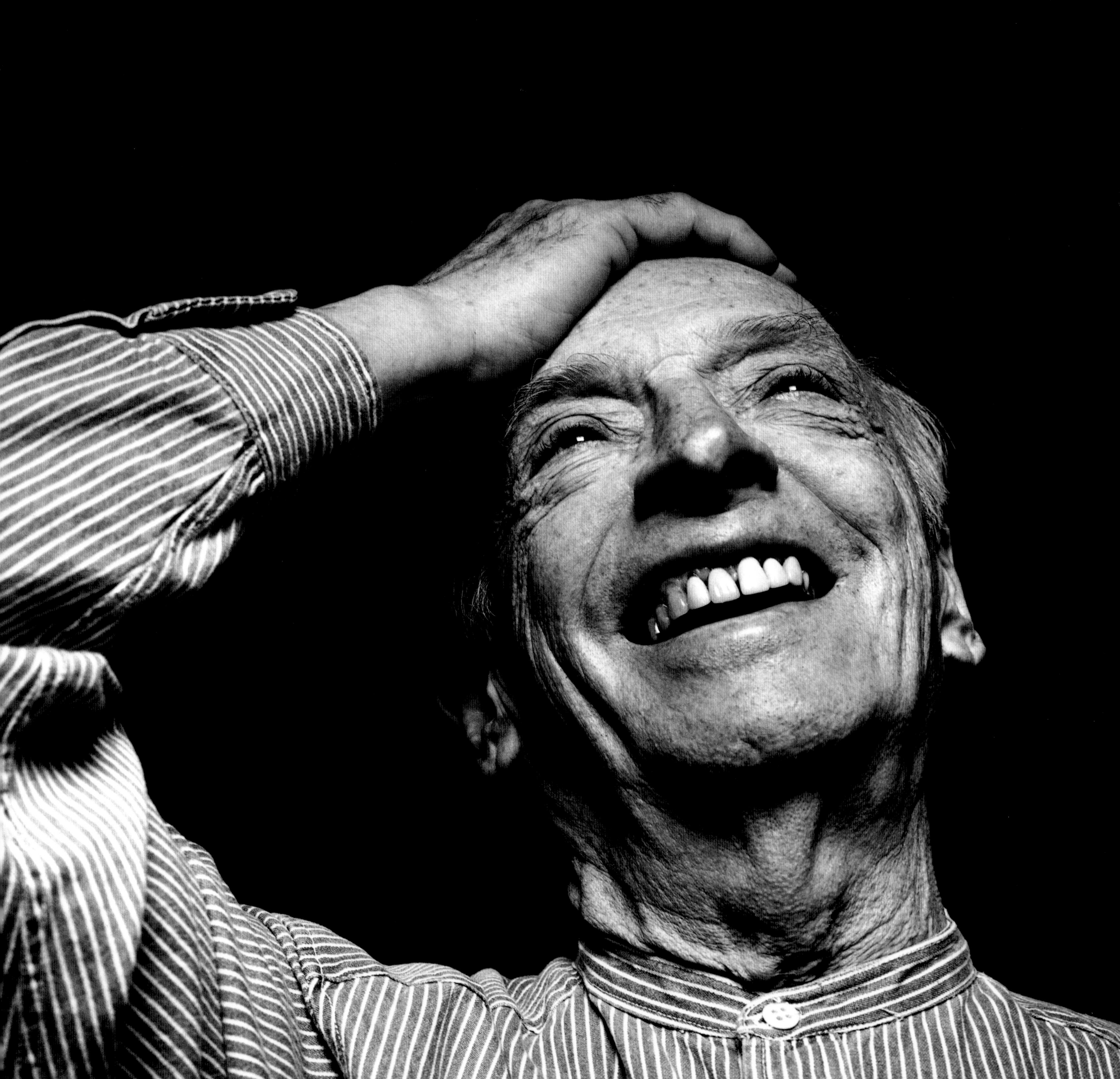

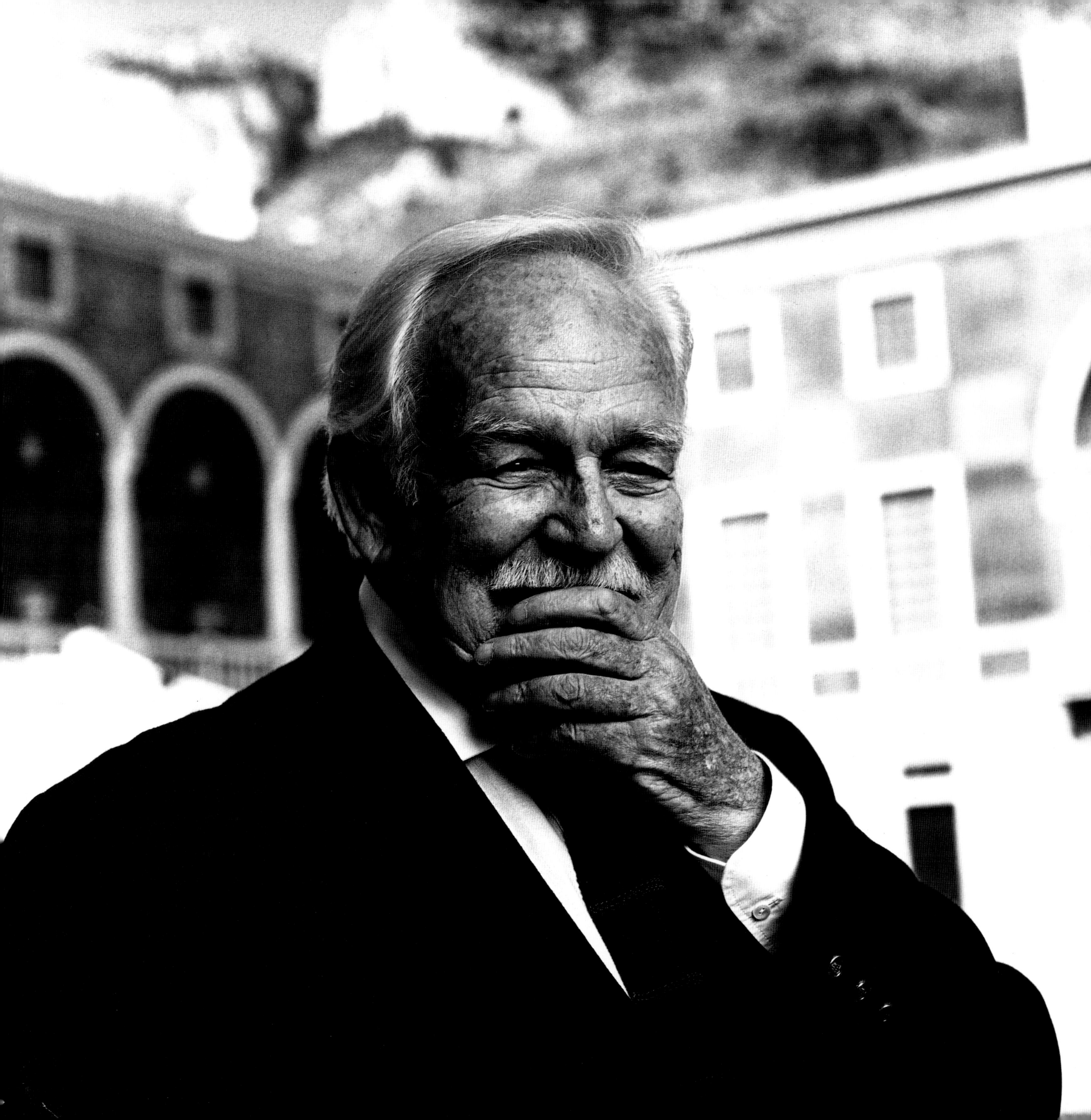

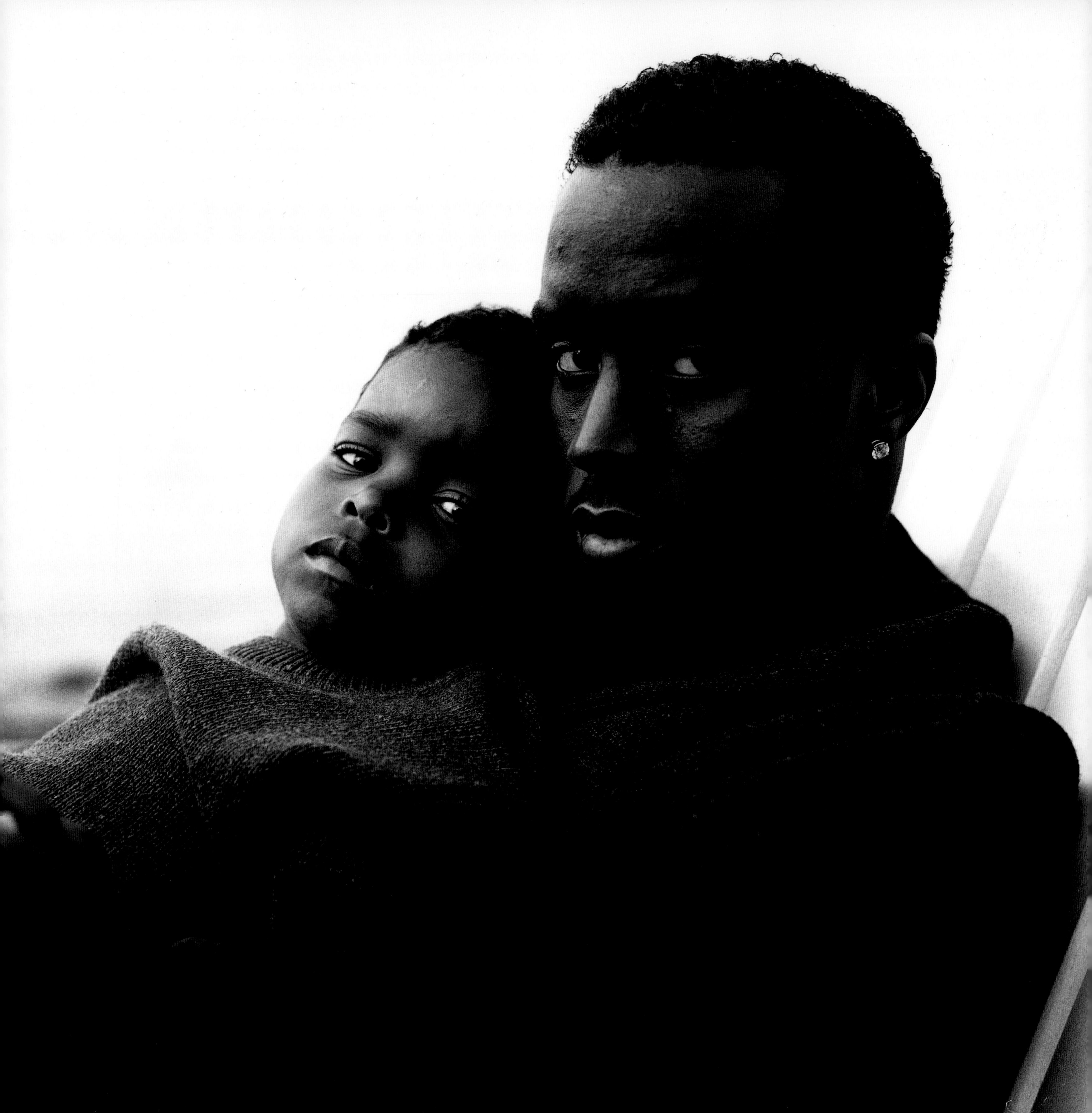

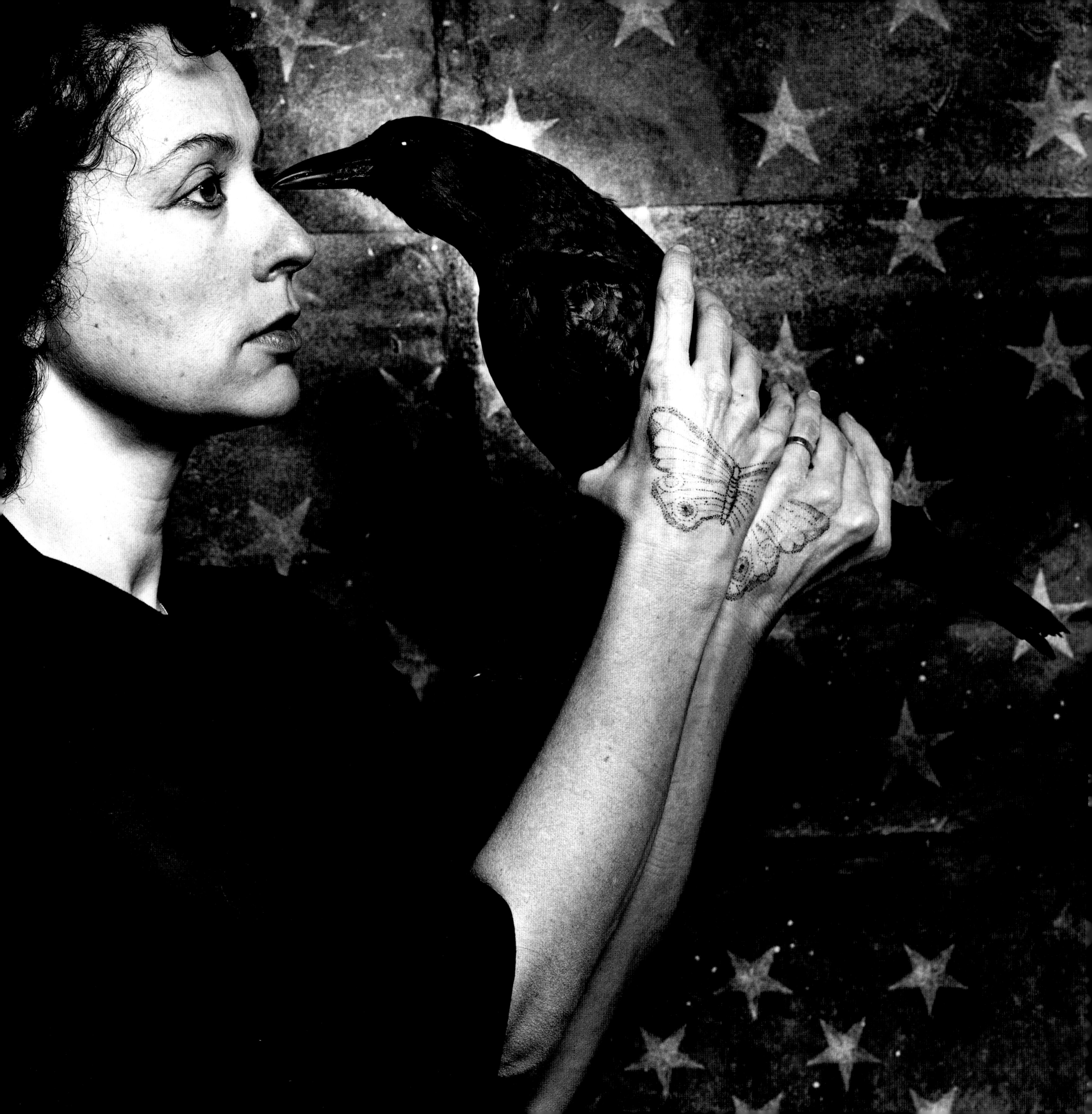

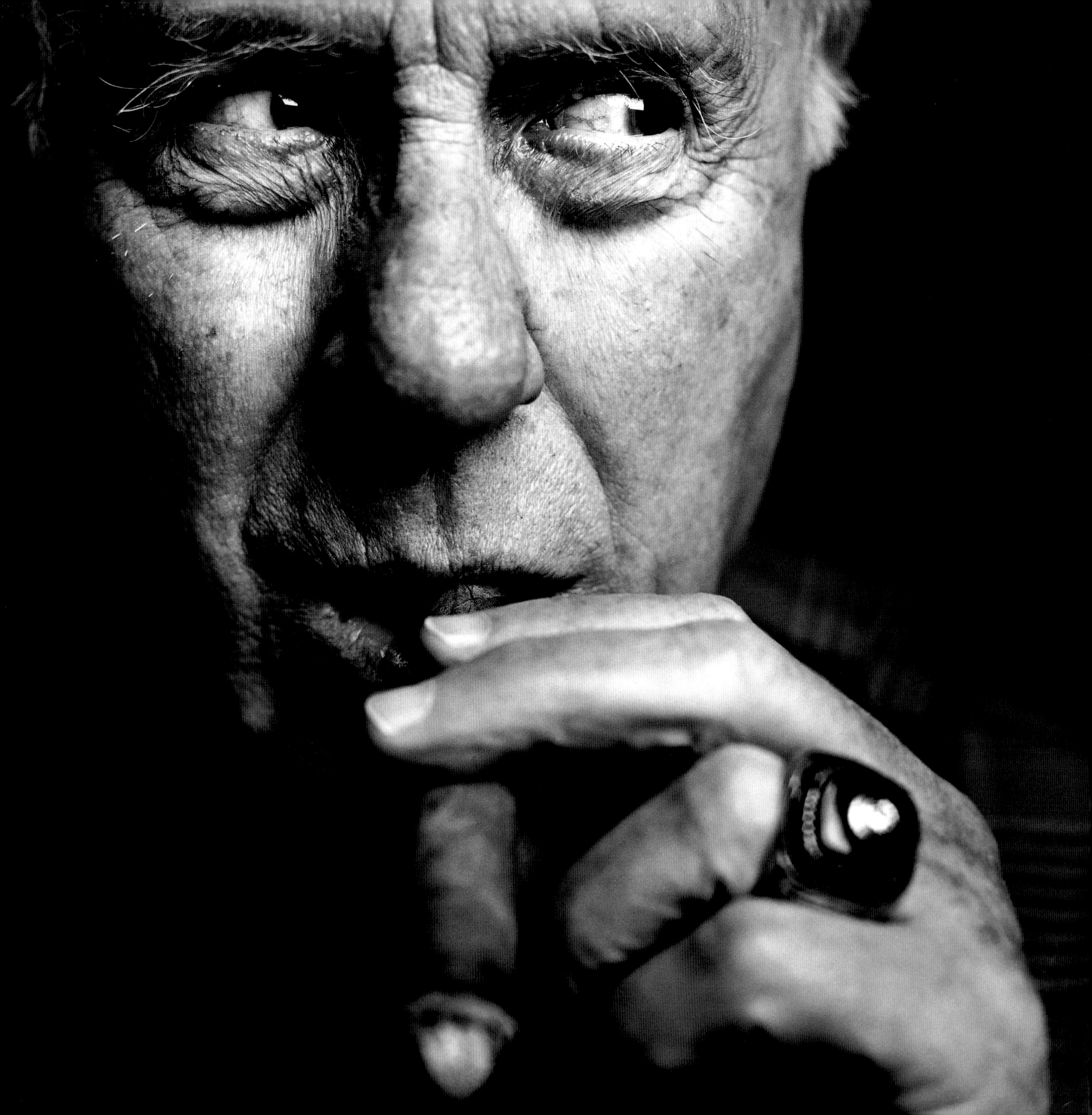

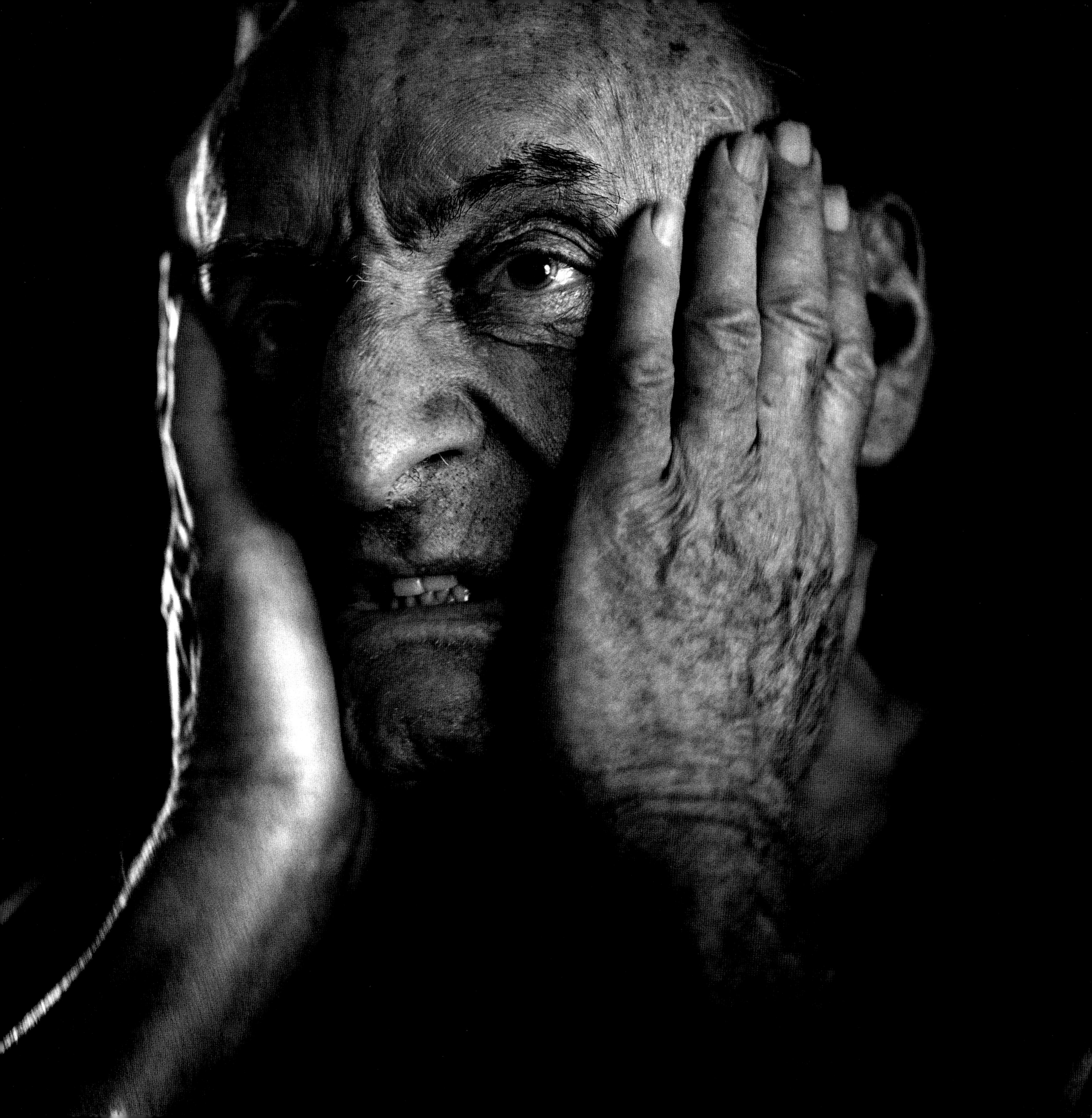

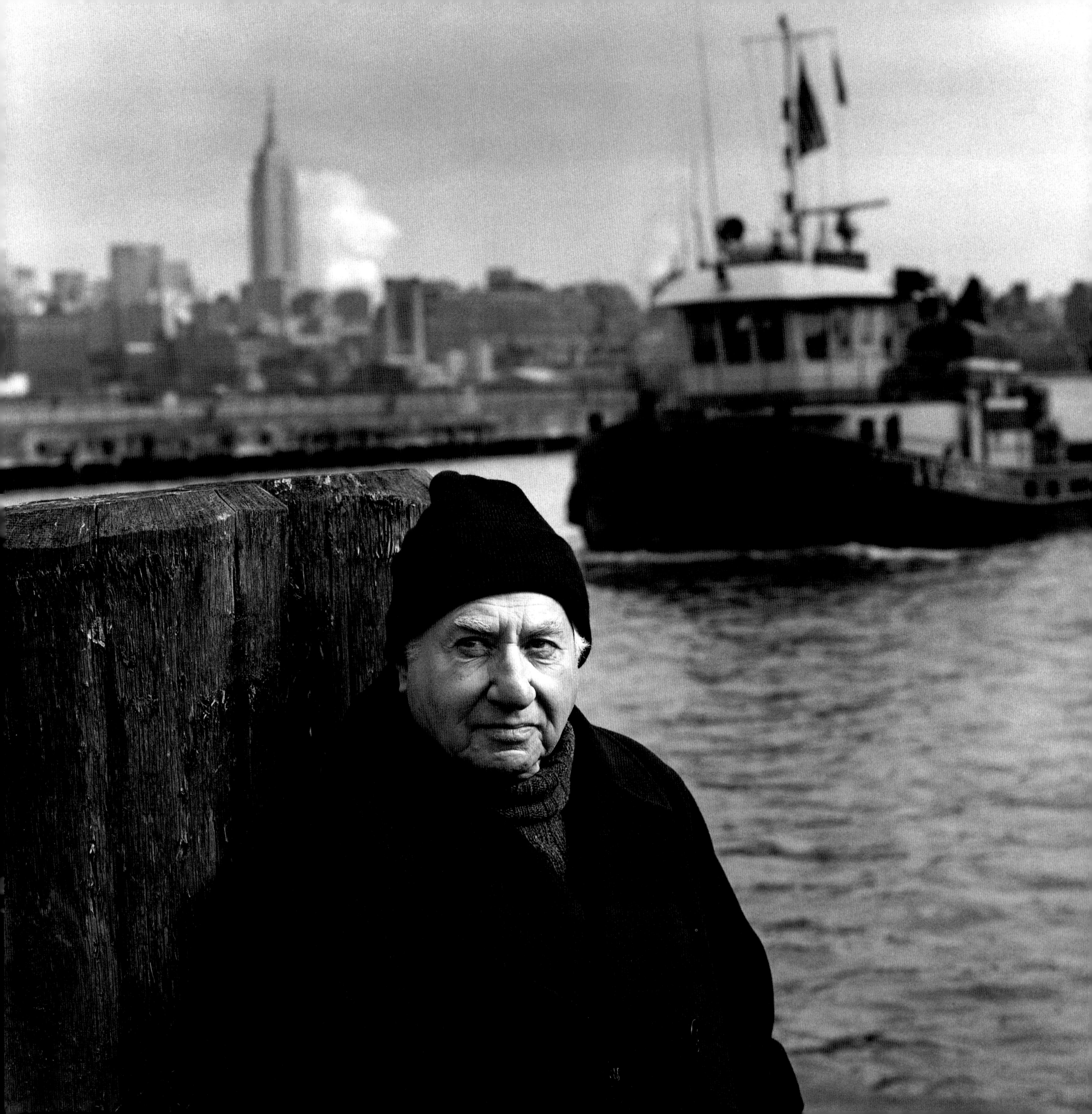

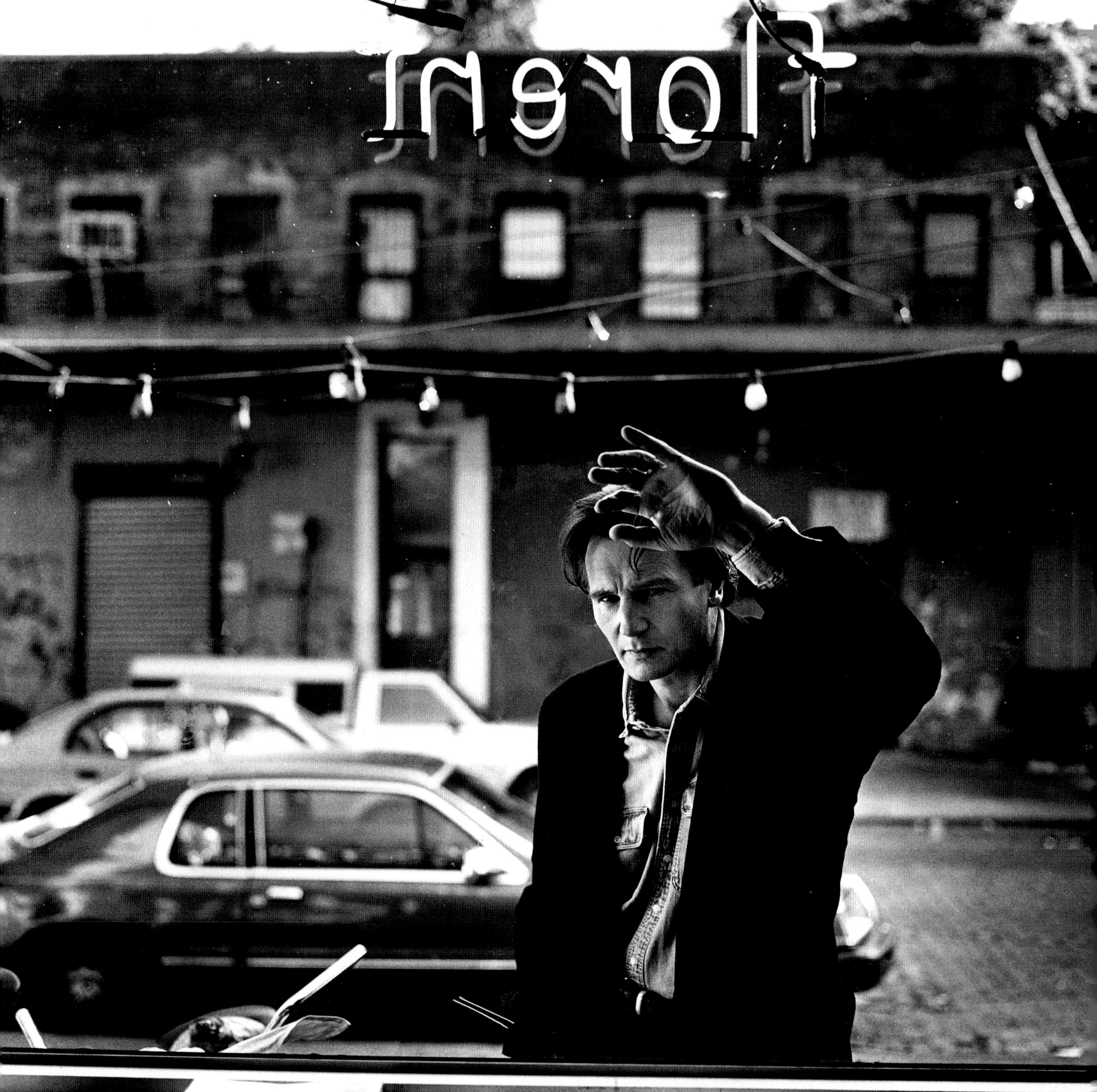
Florent

YOU'RE PA
FOR TWO
YOU'VE GO
TWO HOUR

YING ME

OURS...

T ME FOR

S!

VINNIE JONES MADE IT VERY
CLEAR HOW LONG HE WOULD STAY
FOR HIS PORTRAIT.

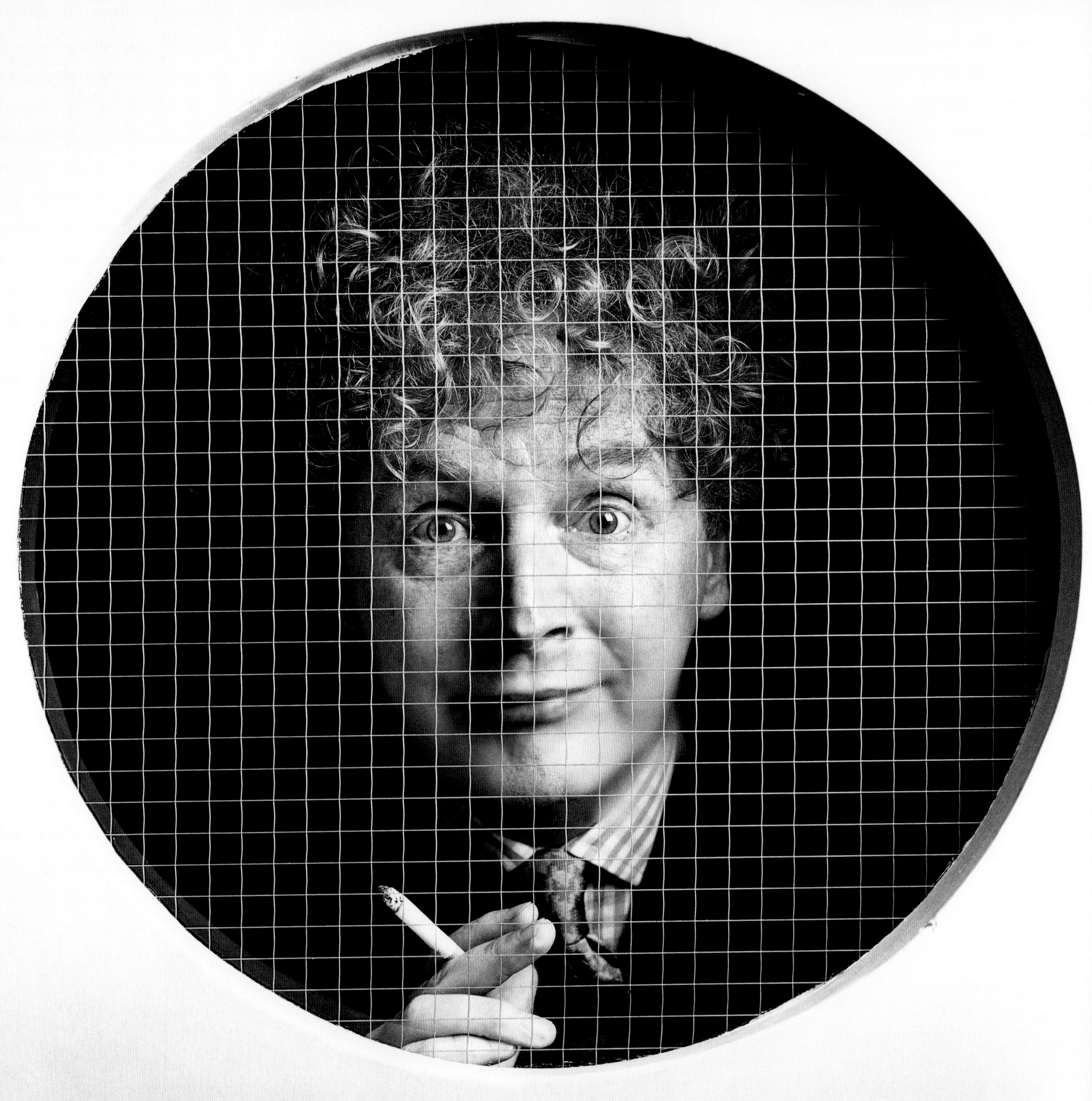

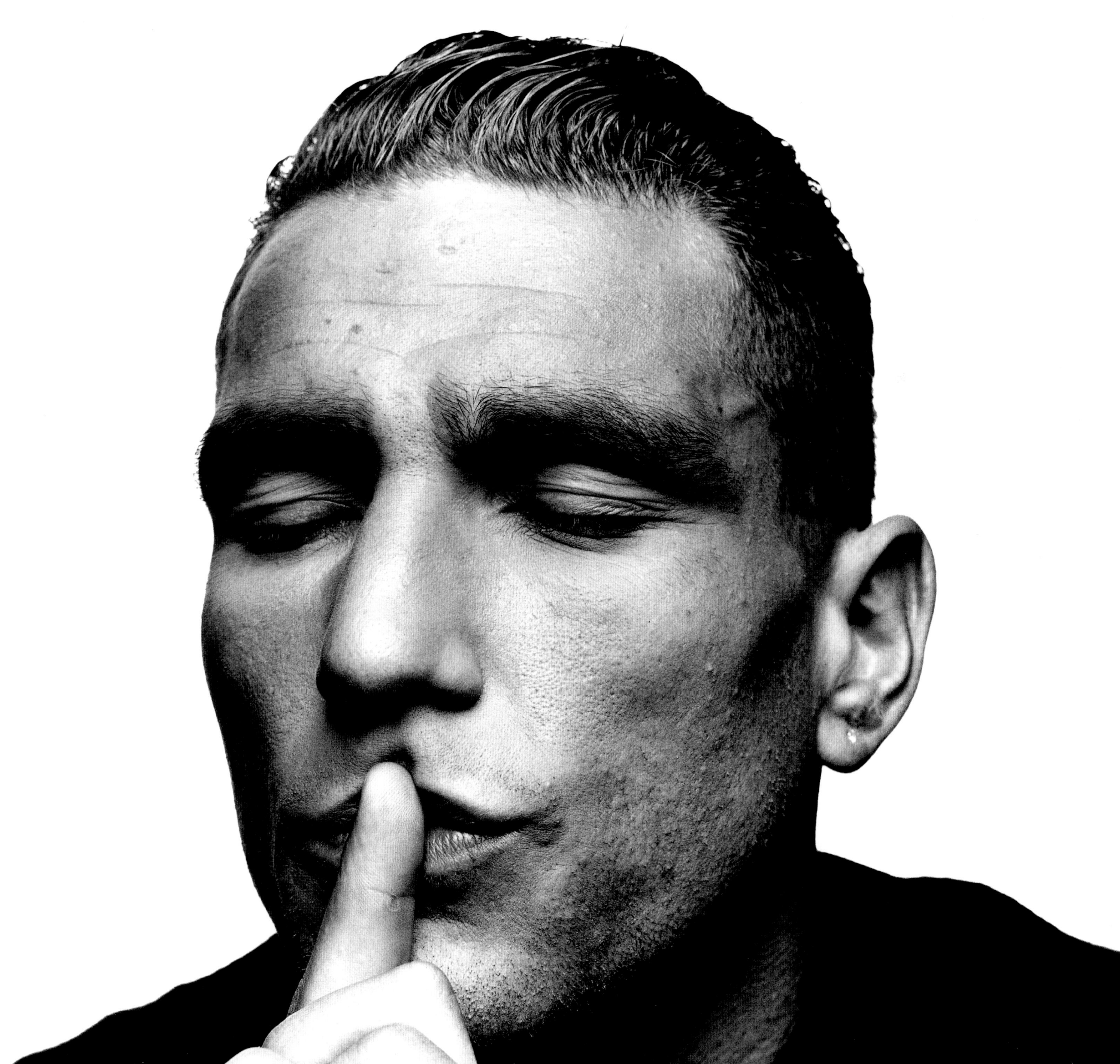

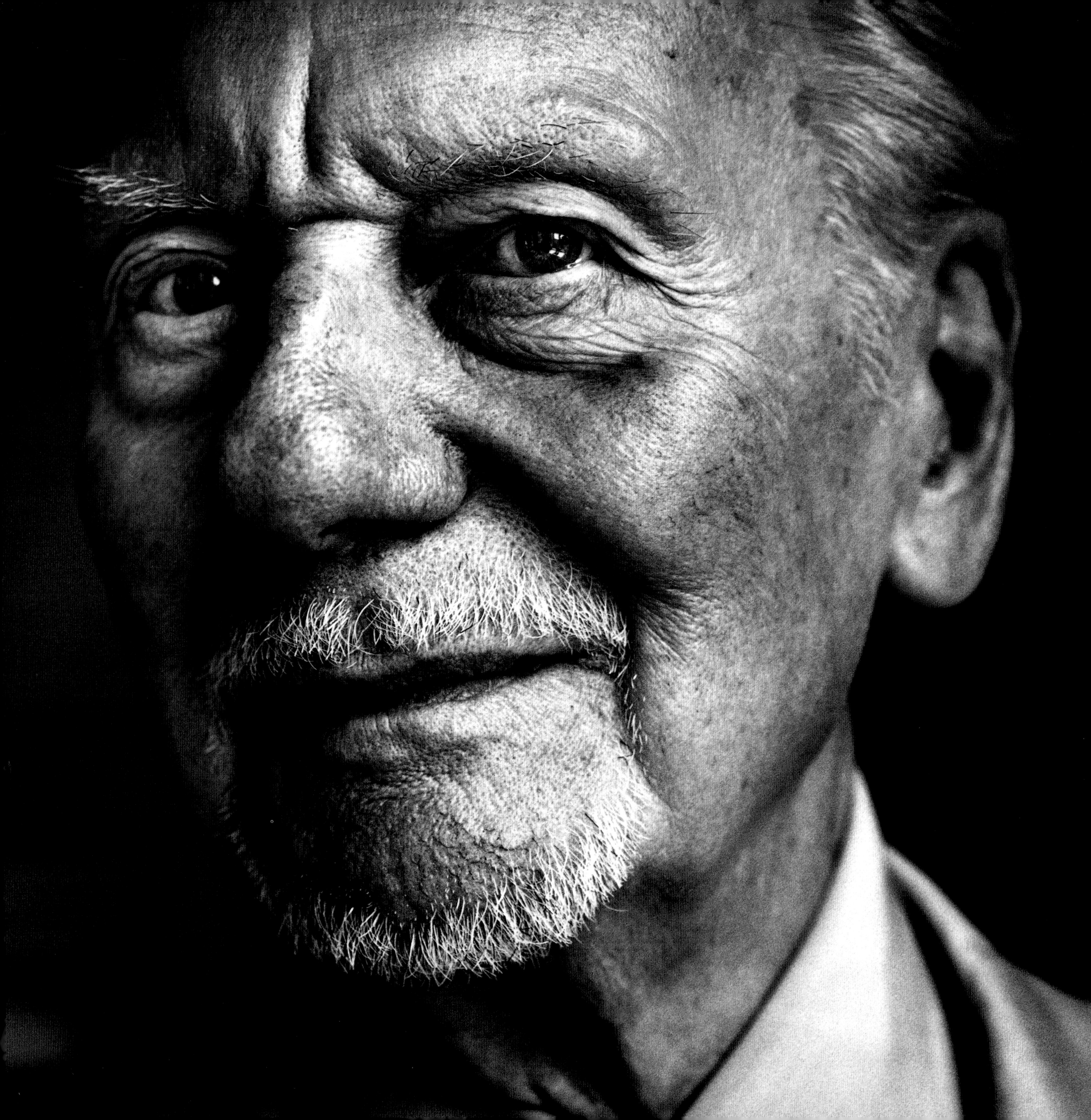

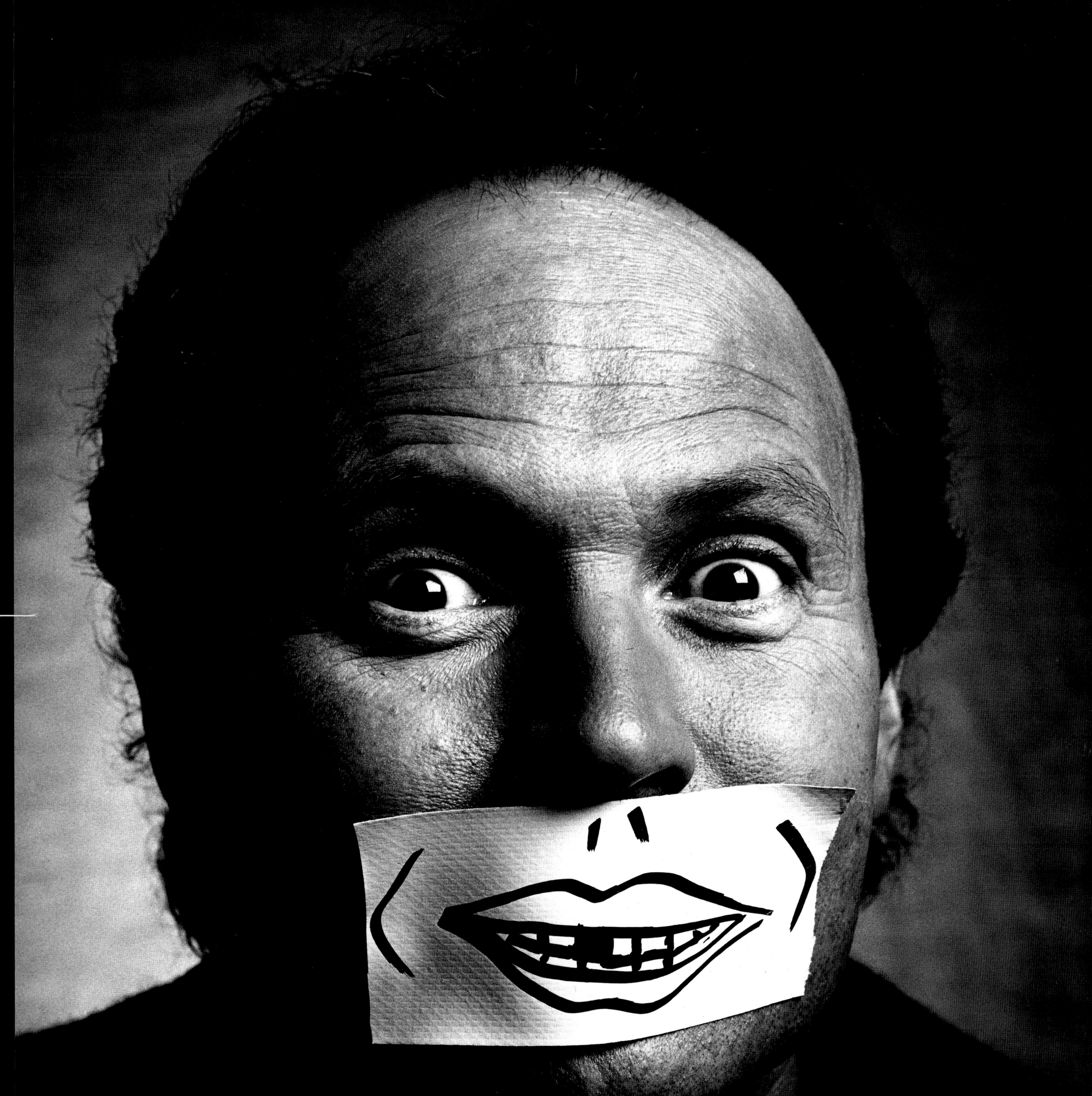

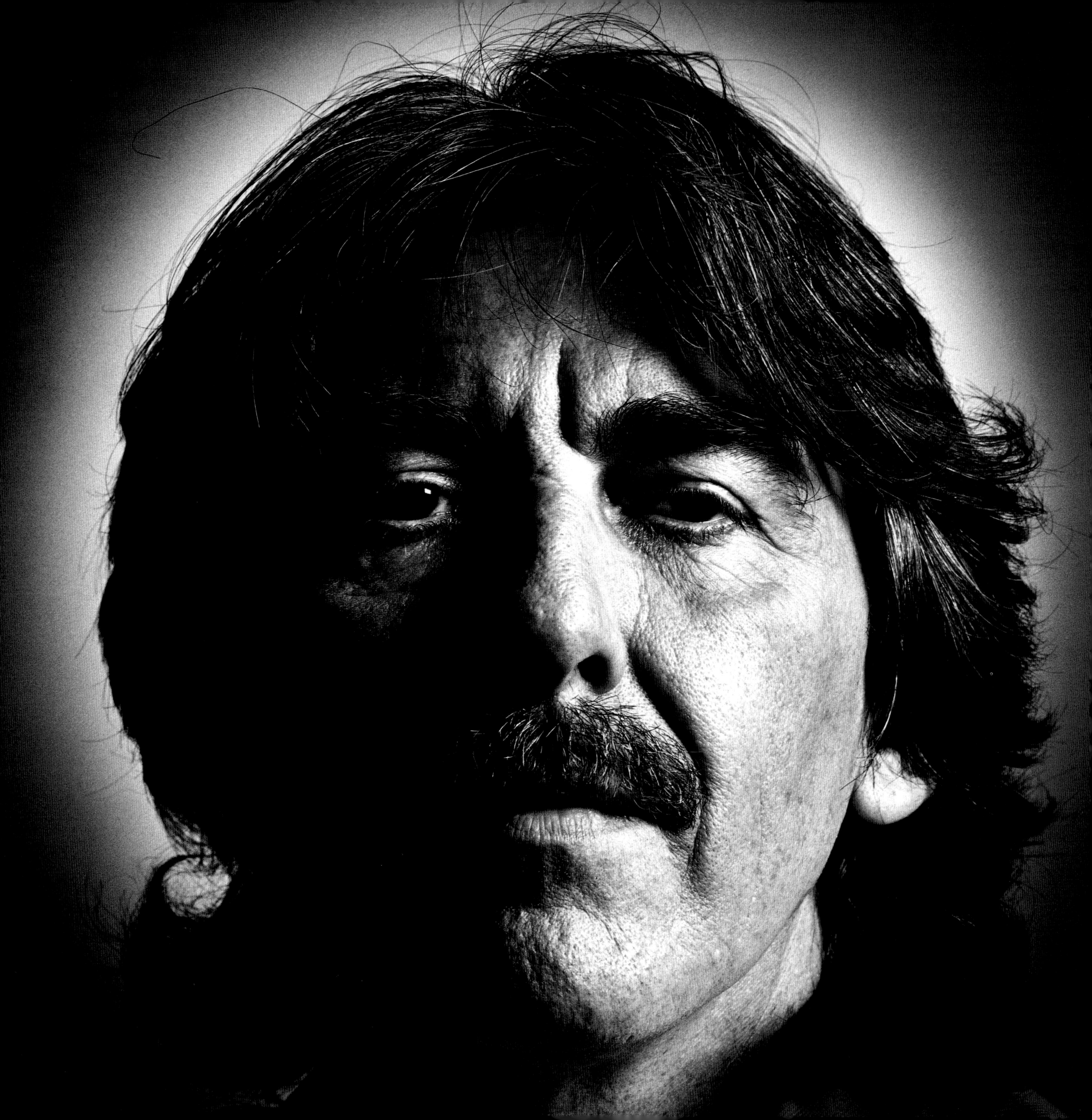

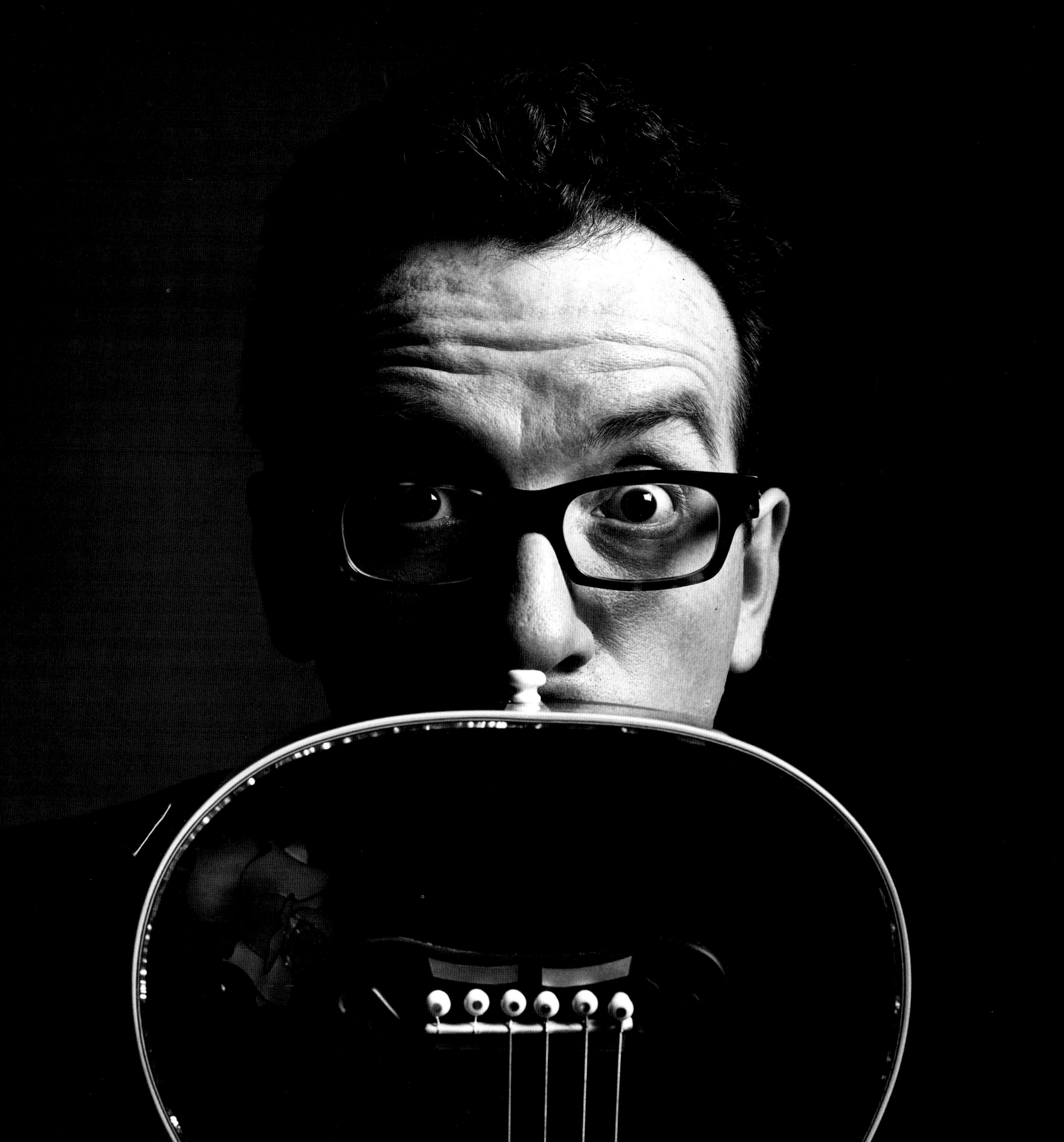

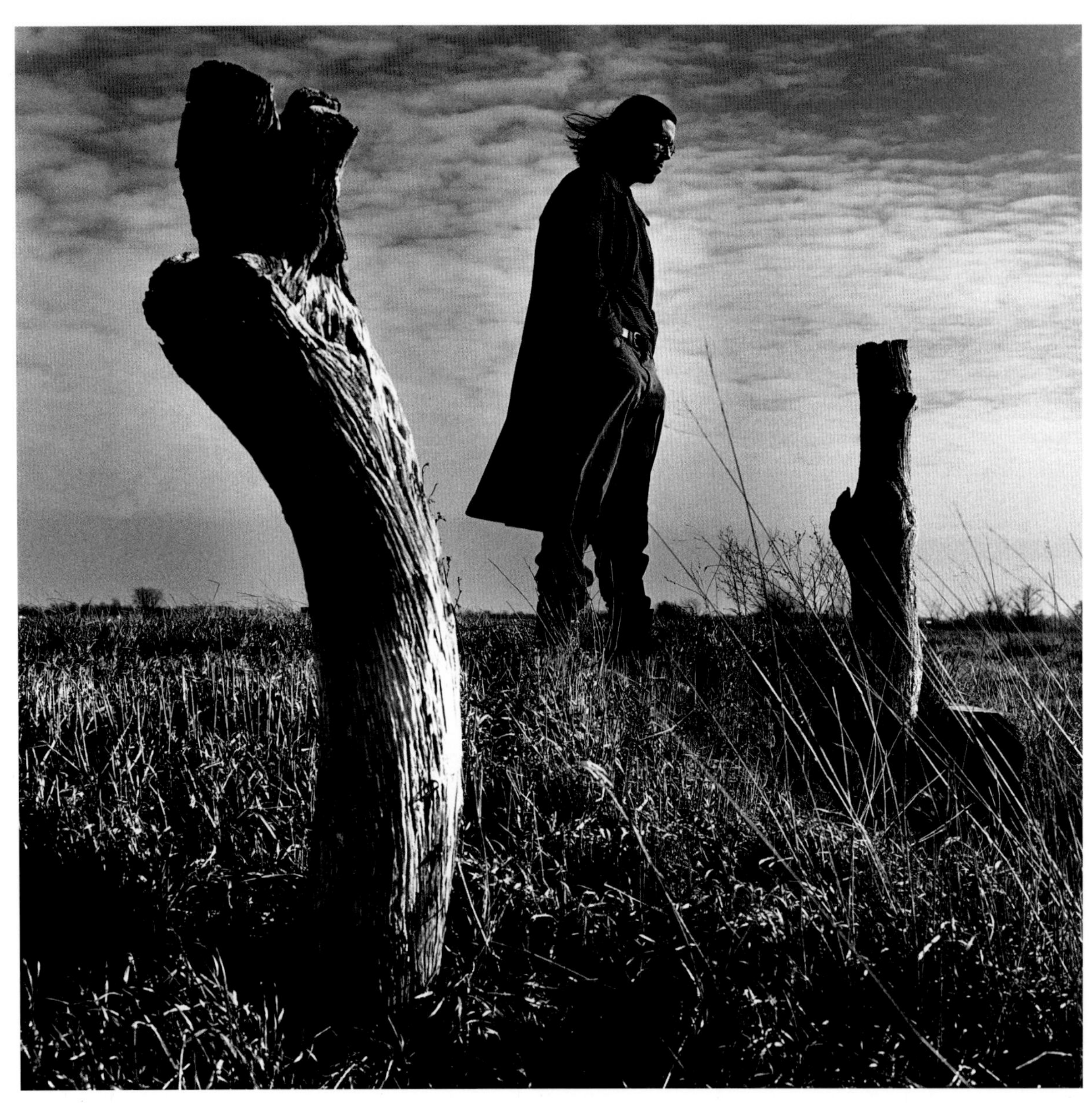

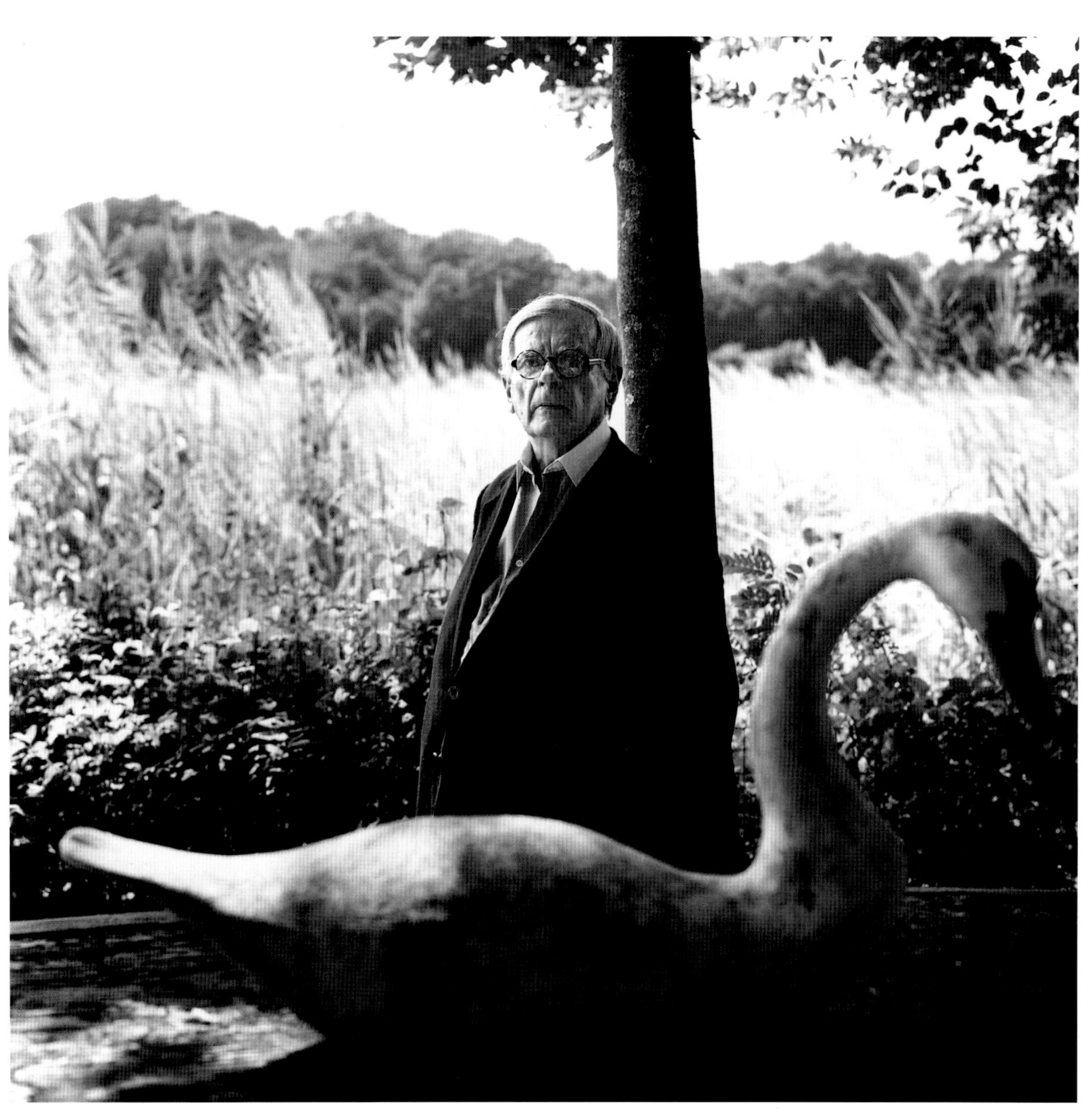

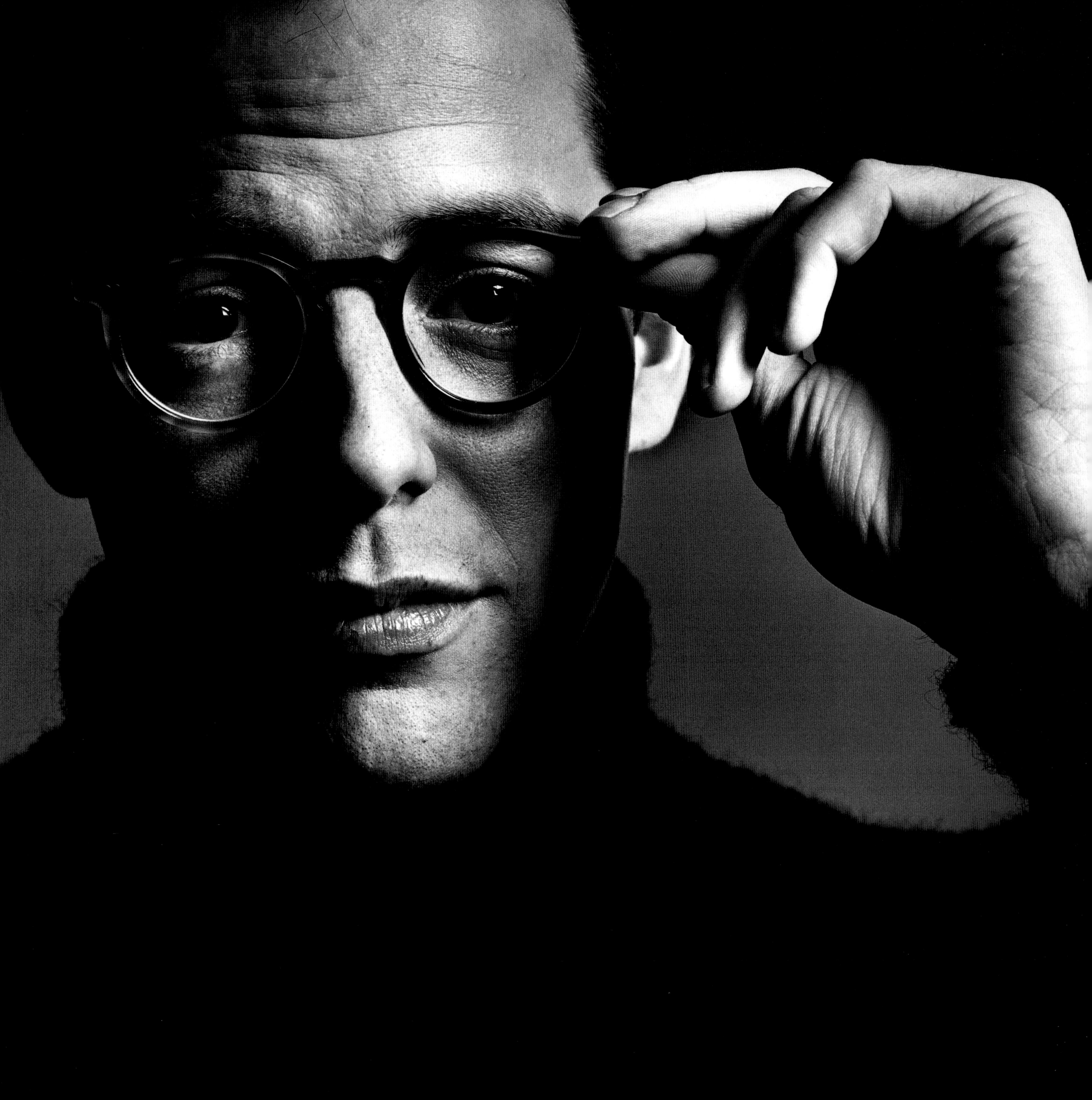

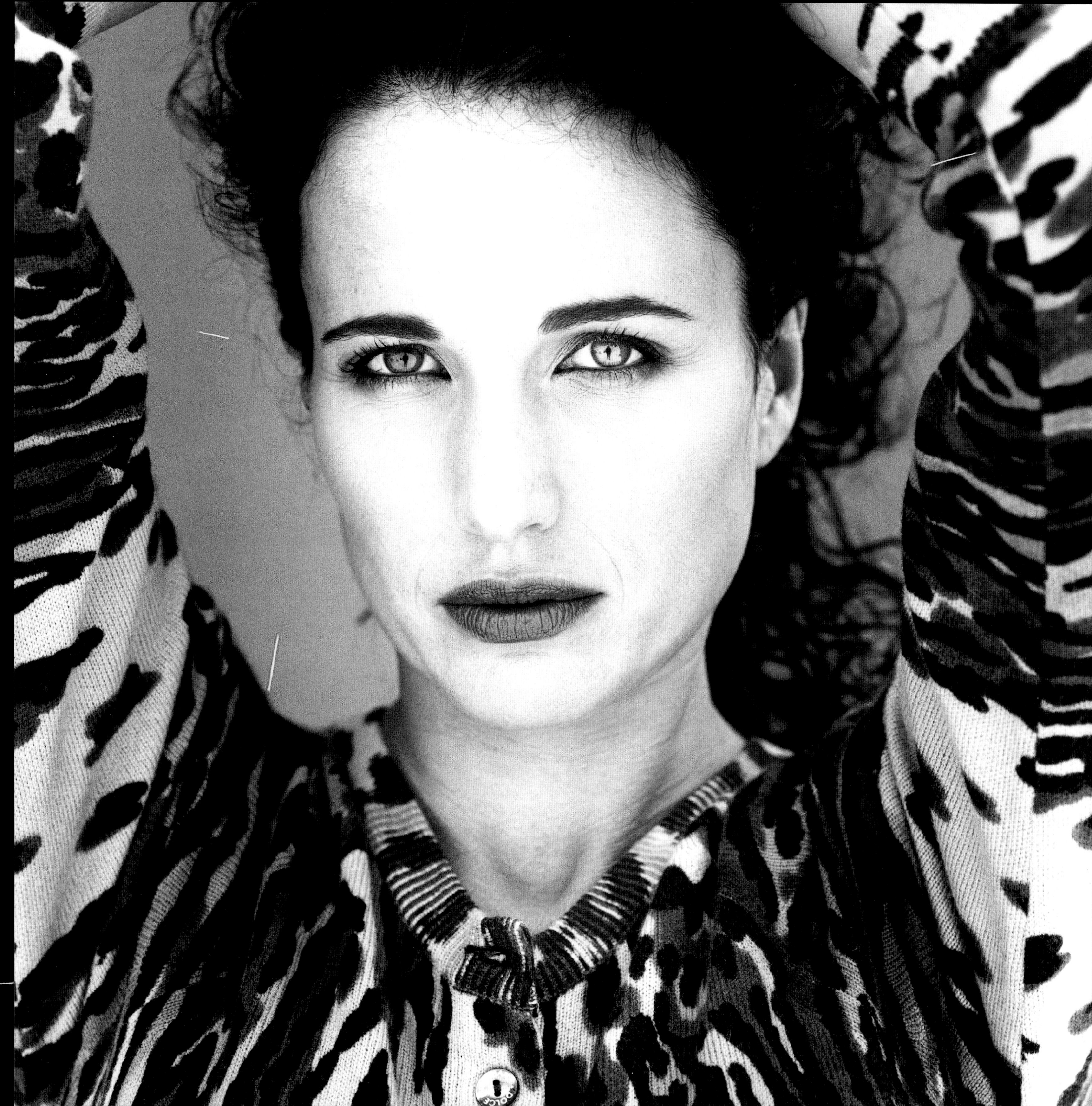

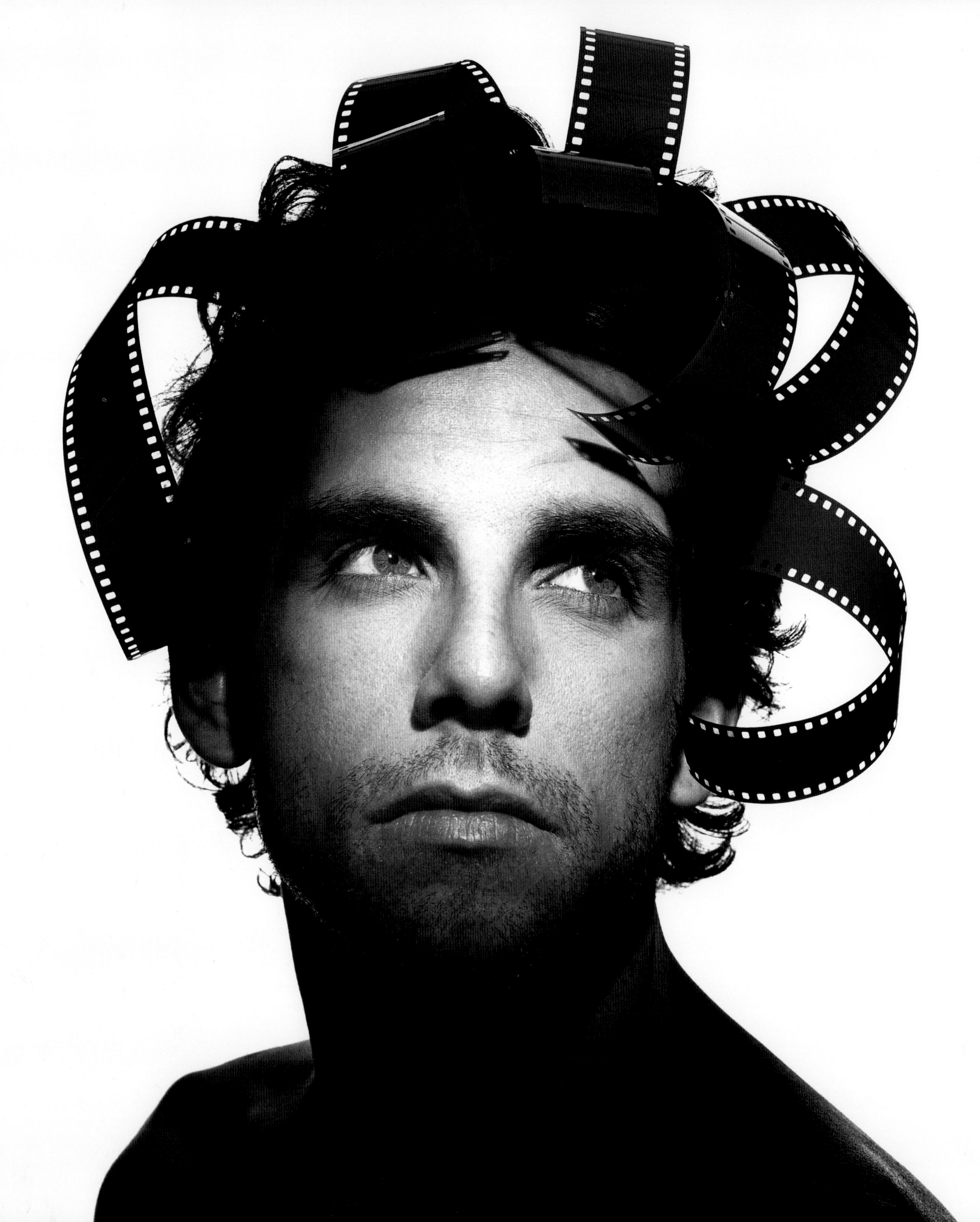

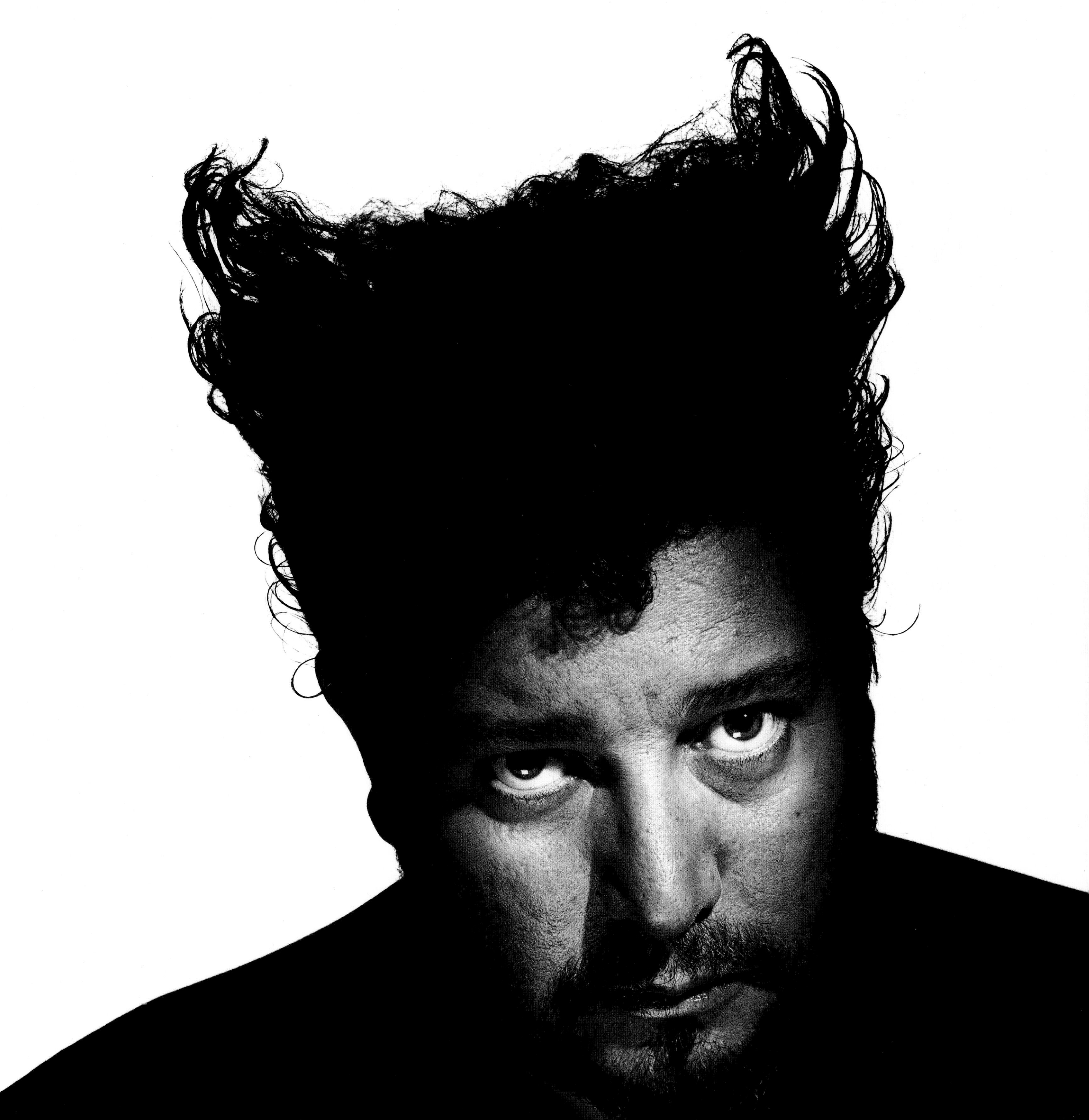

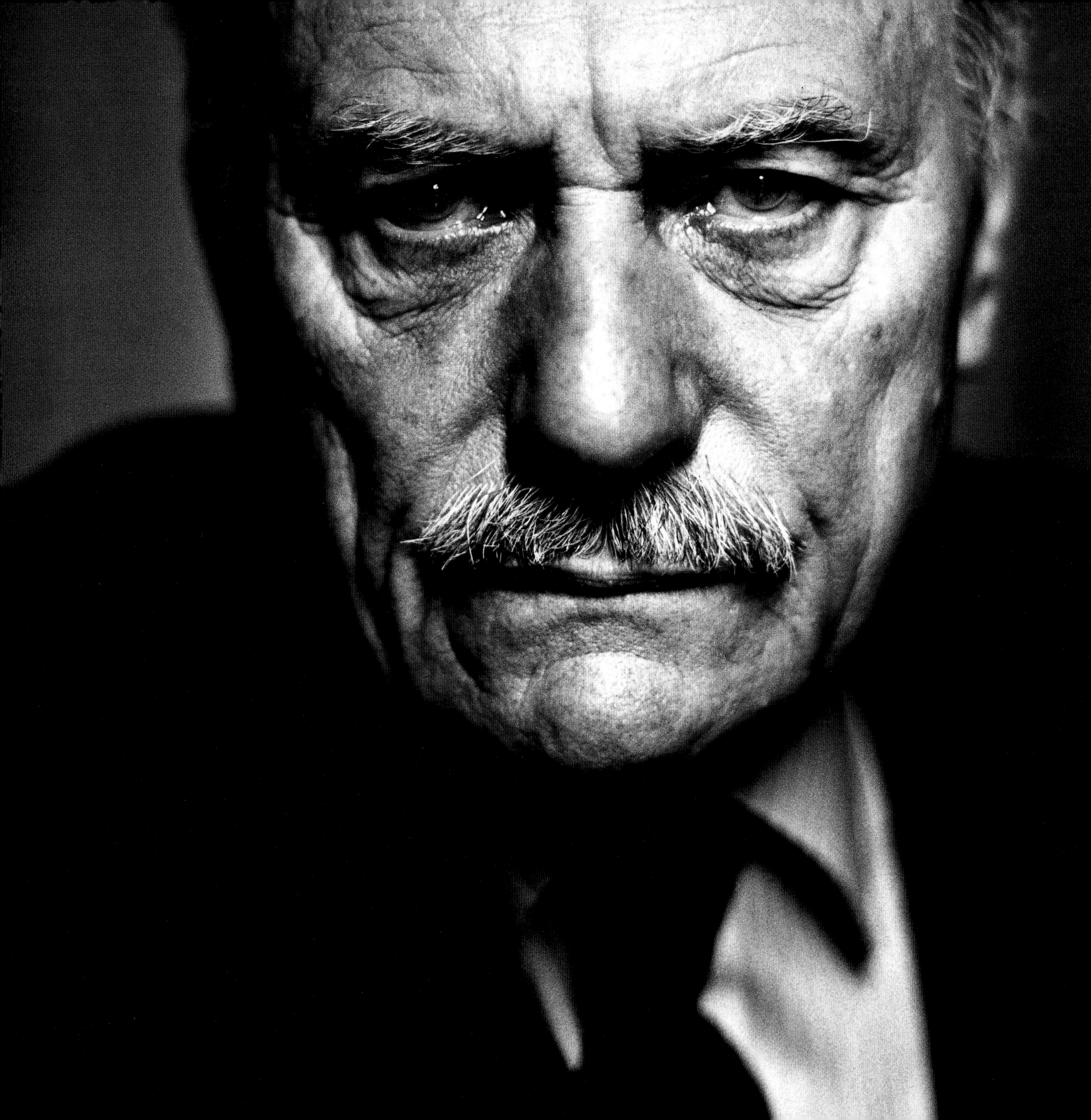

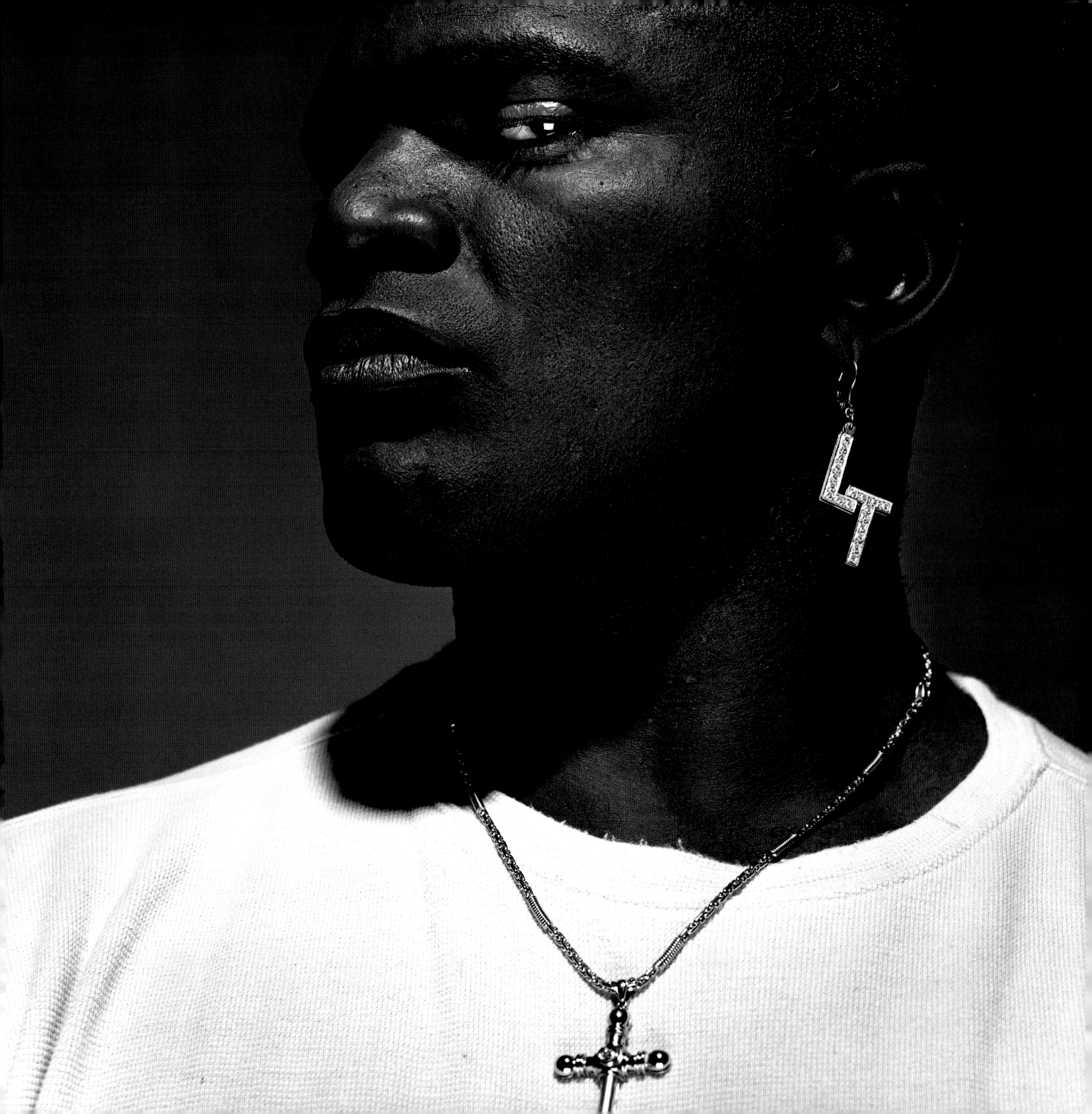

THERE AIN
NOTHING F
FUNNY TO
ABOUT HE

T
***ING
LAUGH
RE, SON.

THIS IS WHAT YOU'LL GET
WHEN YOU ASK TOMMY LEE JONES
FOR A SMILE.

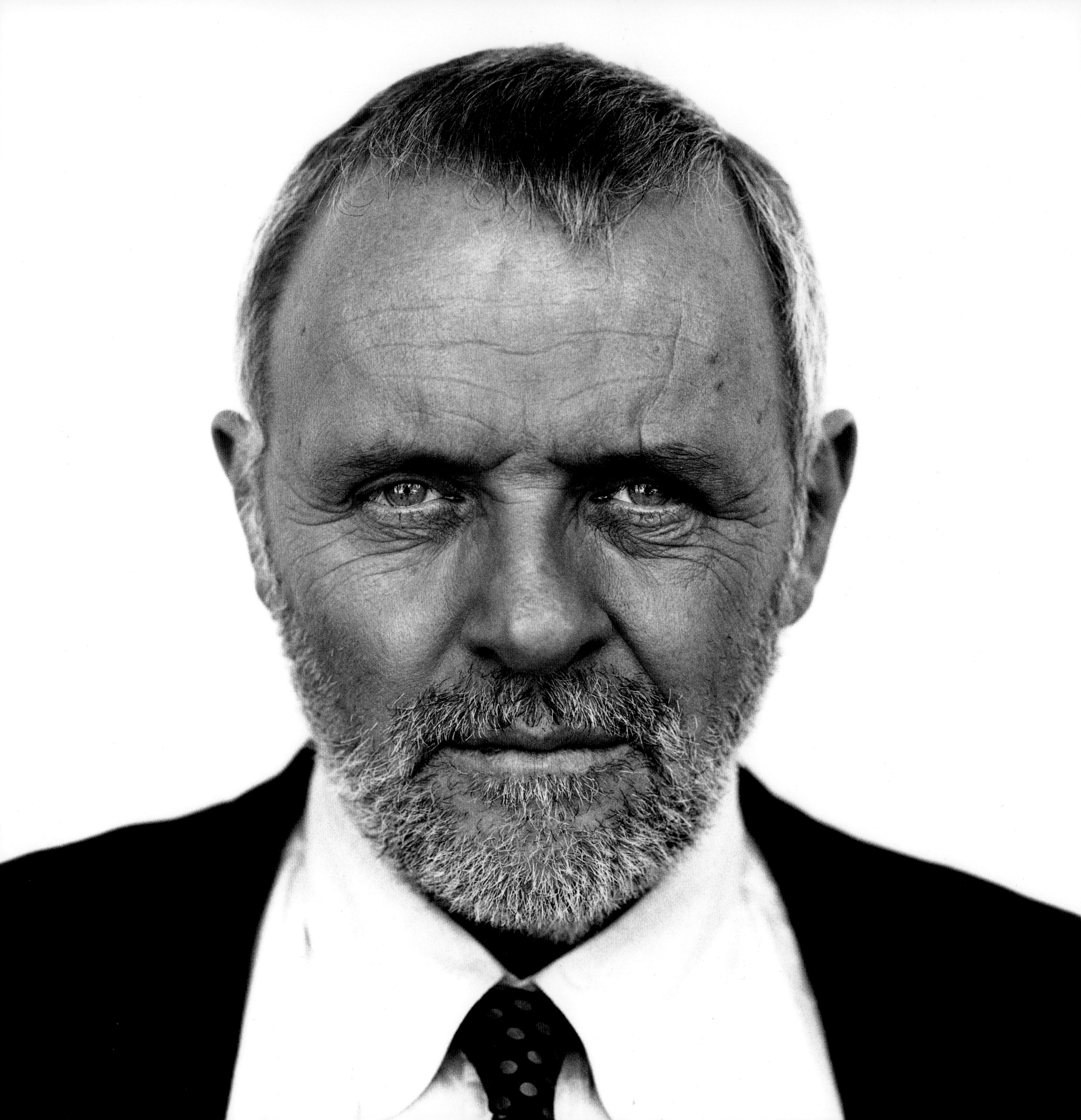

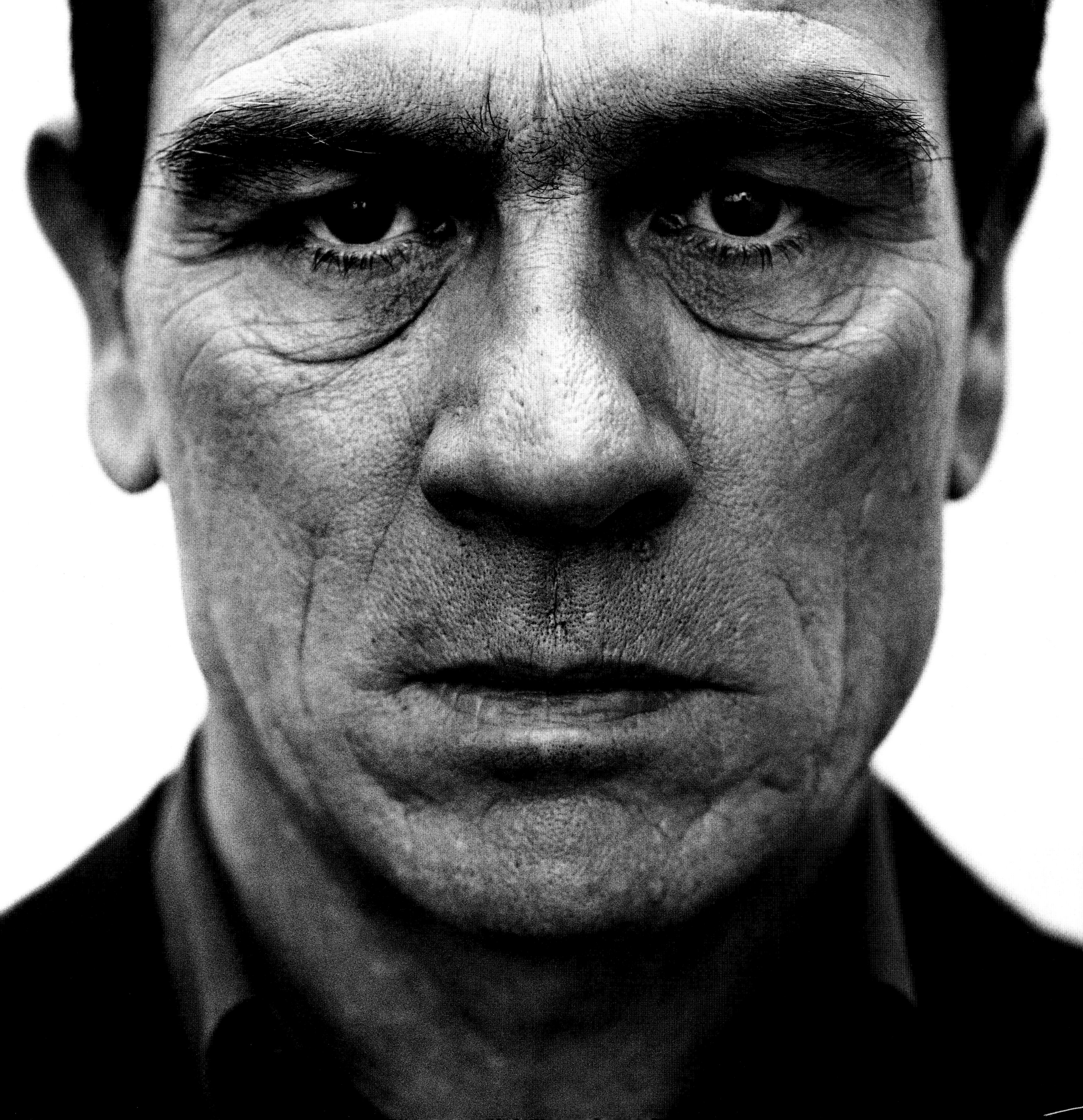

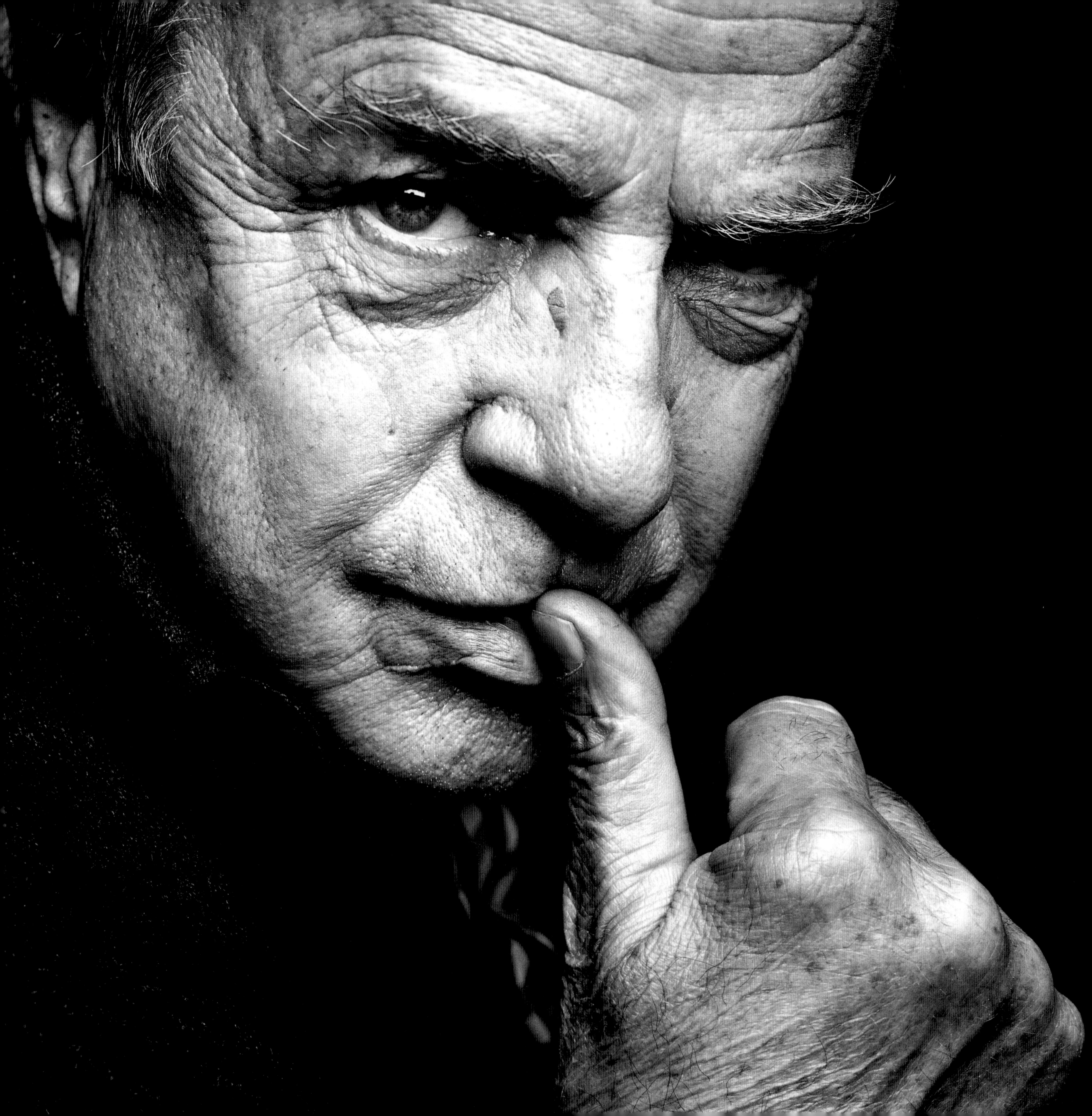

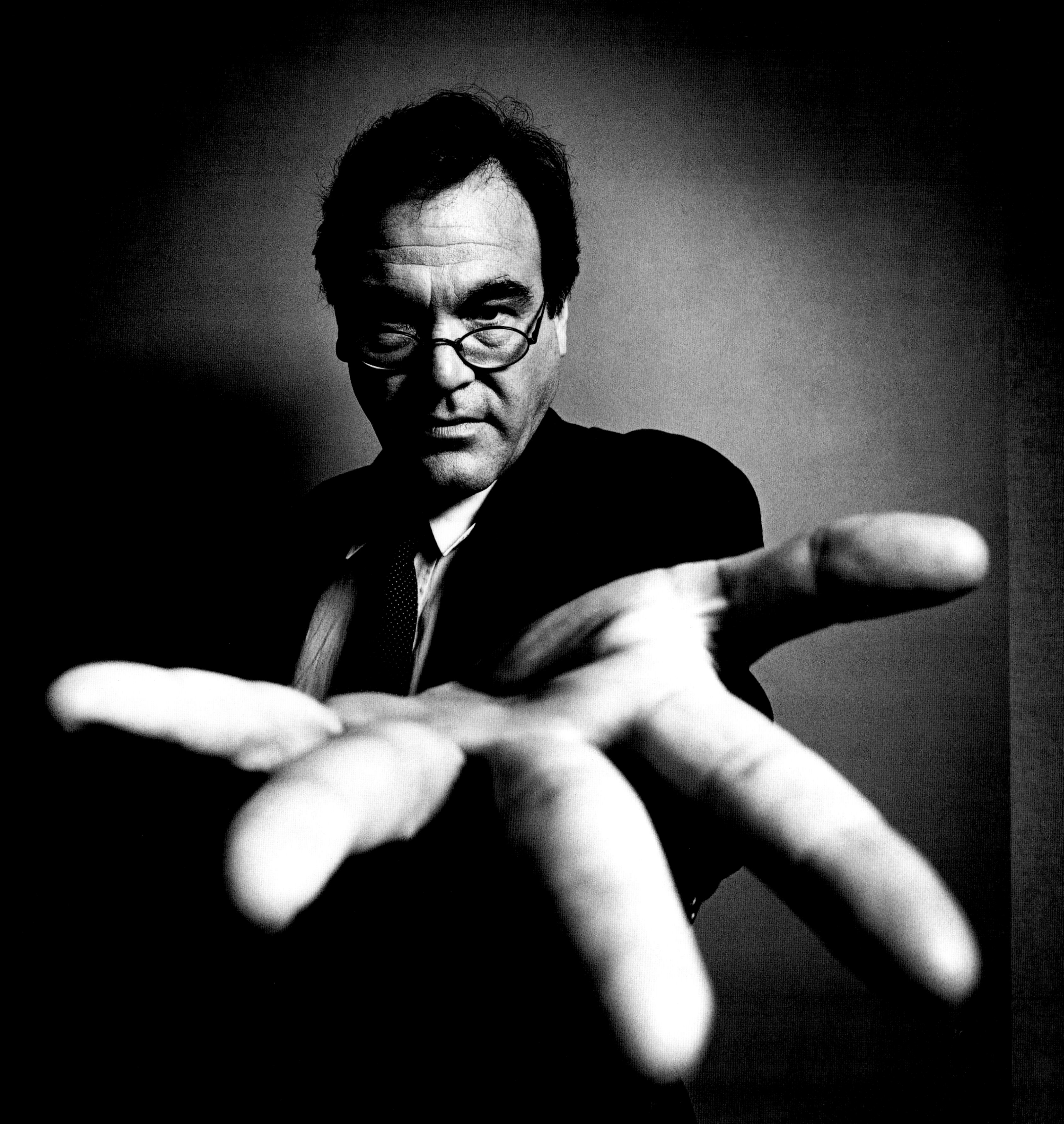

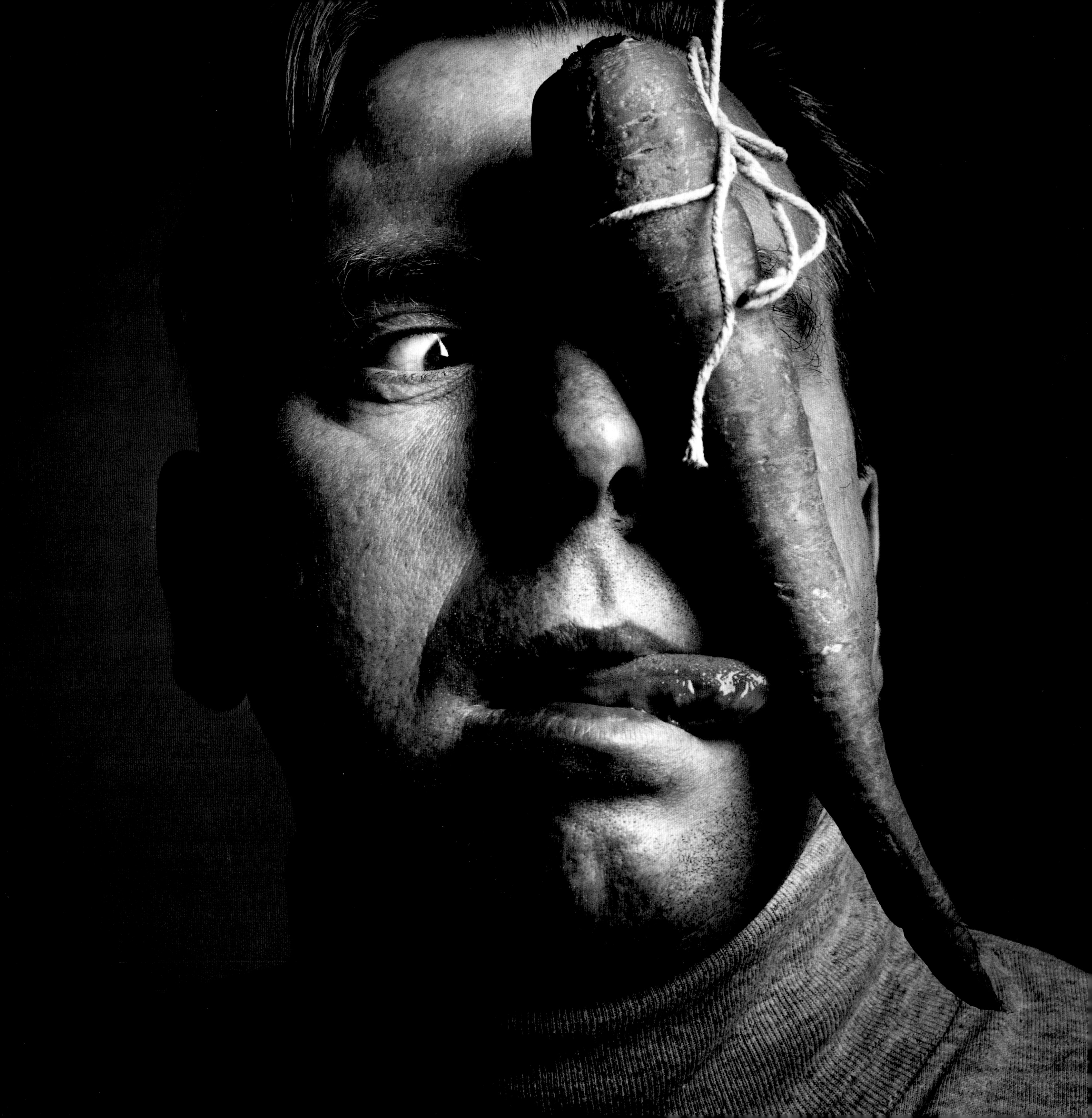

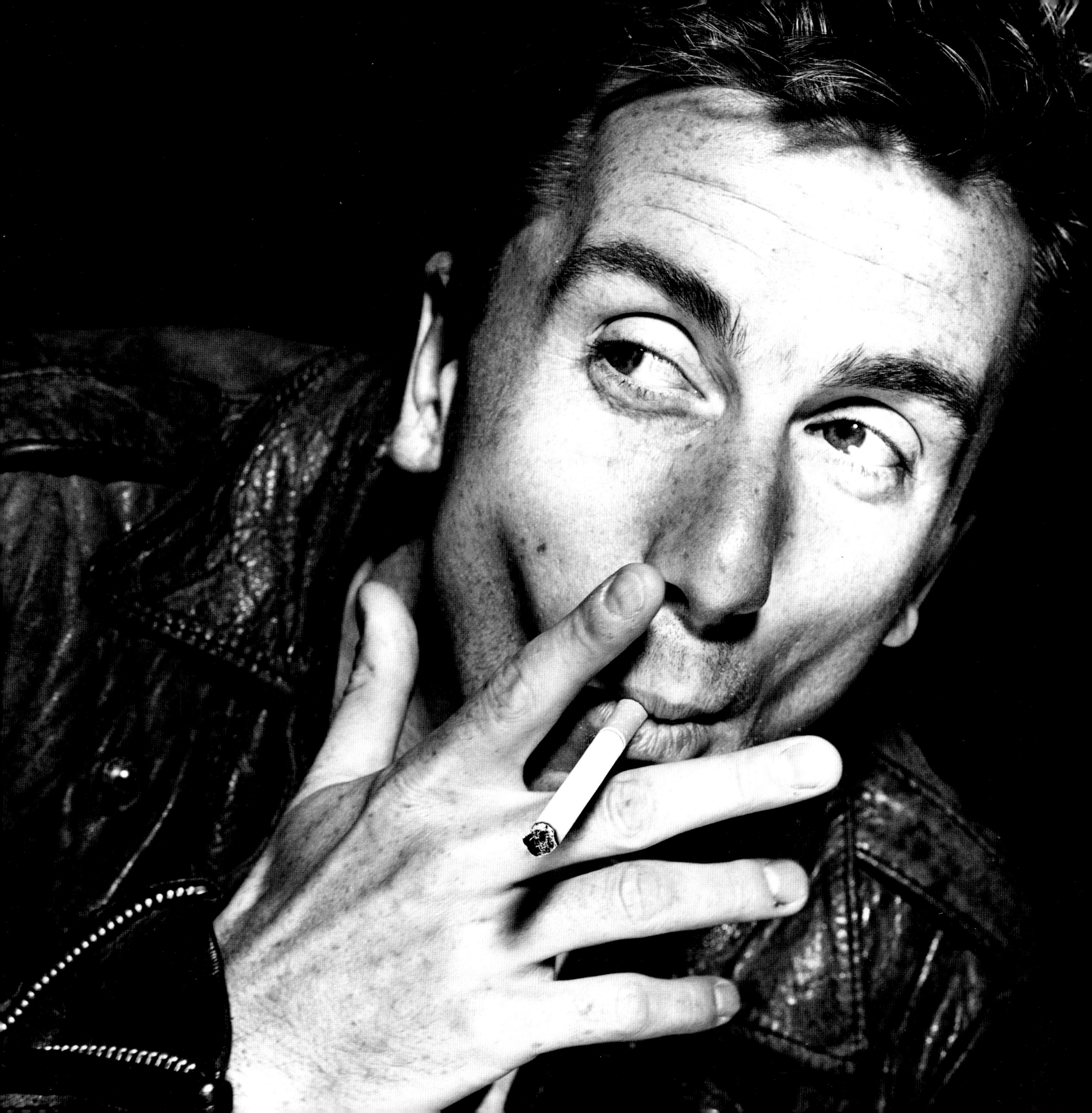

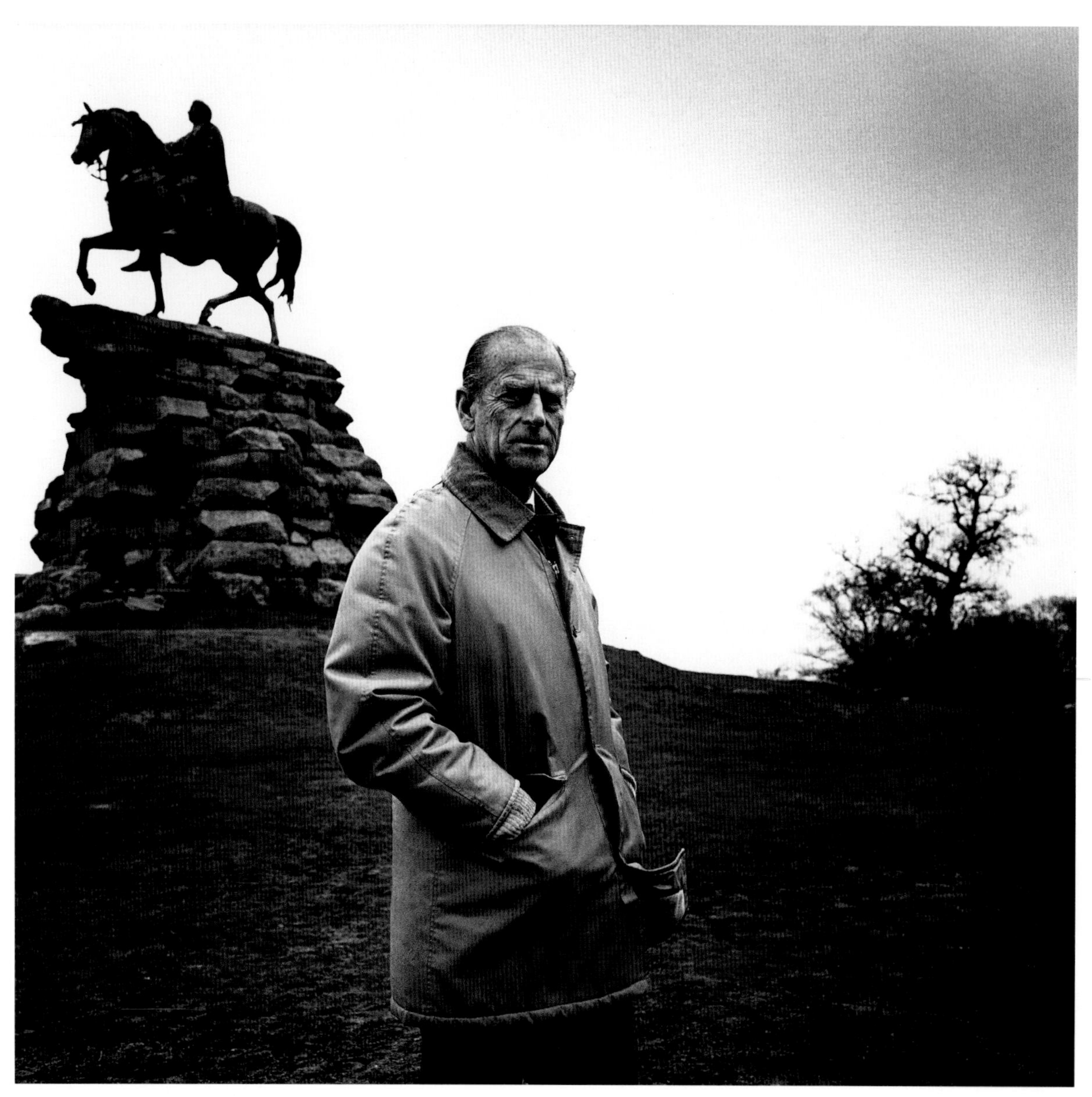

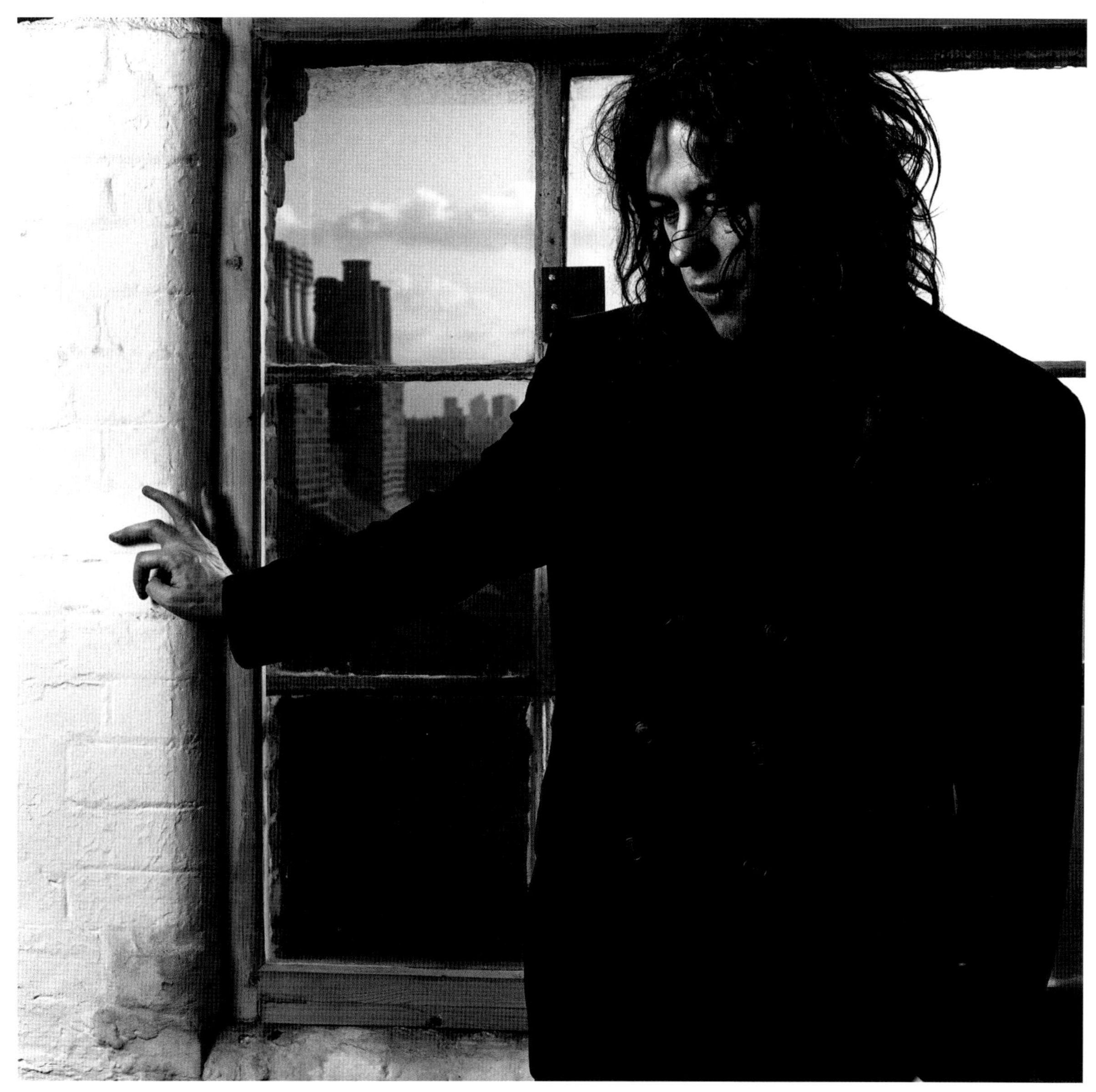

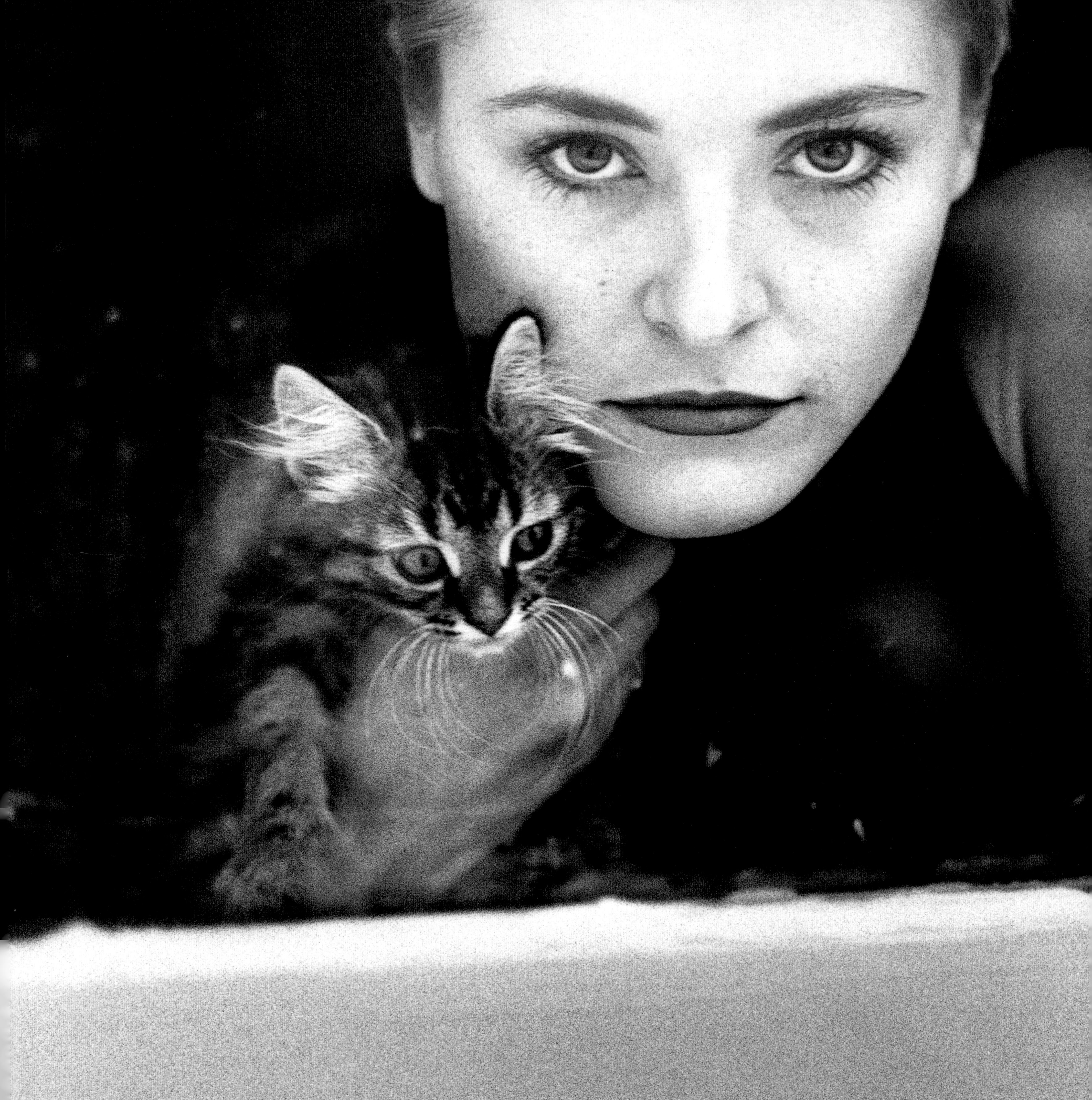

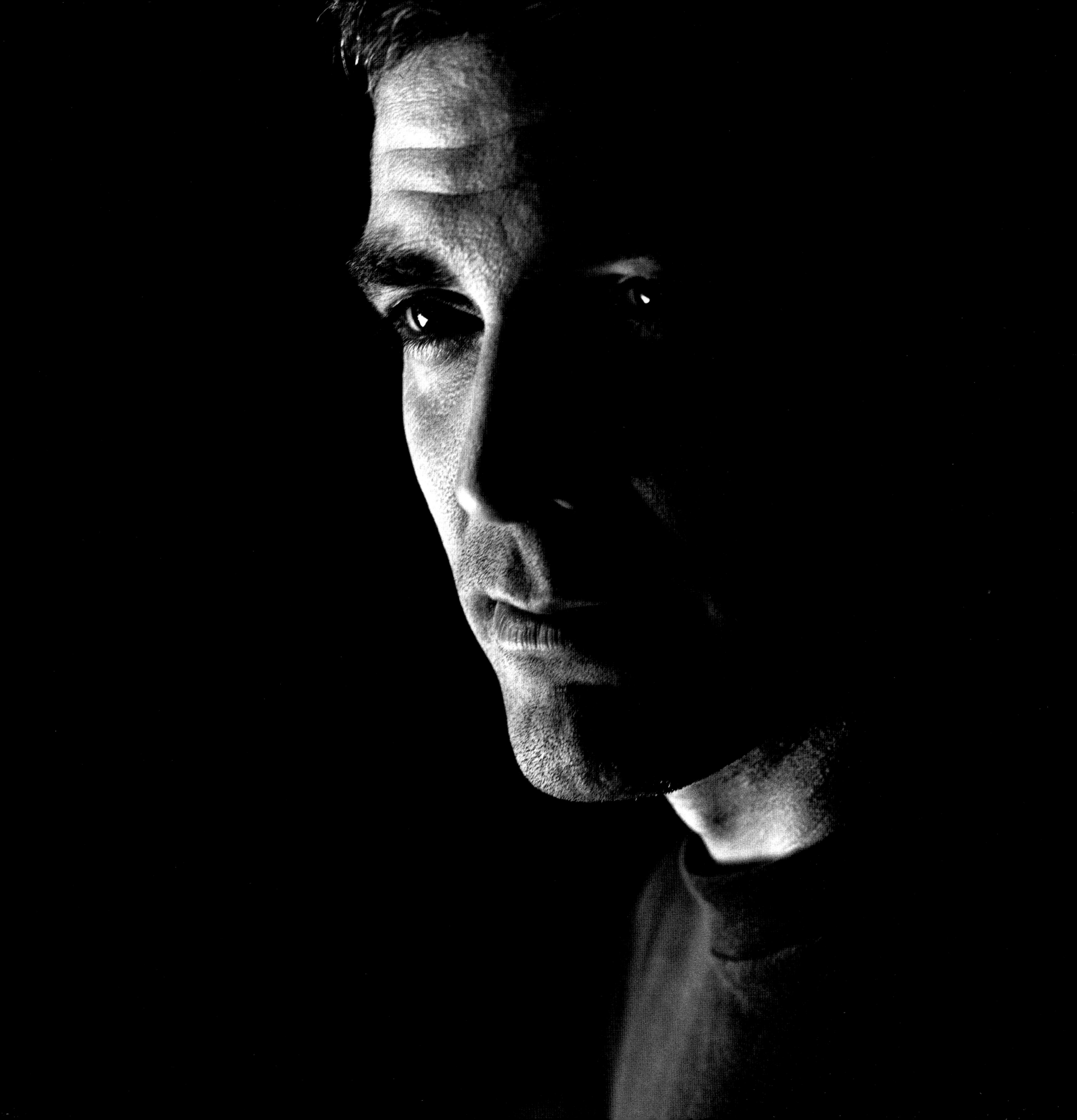

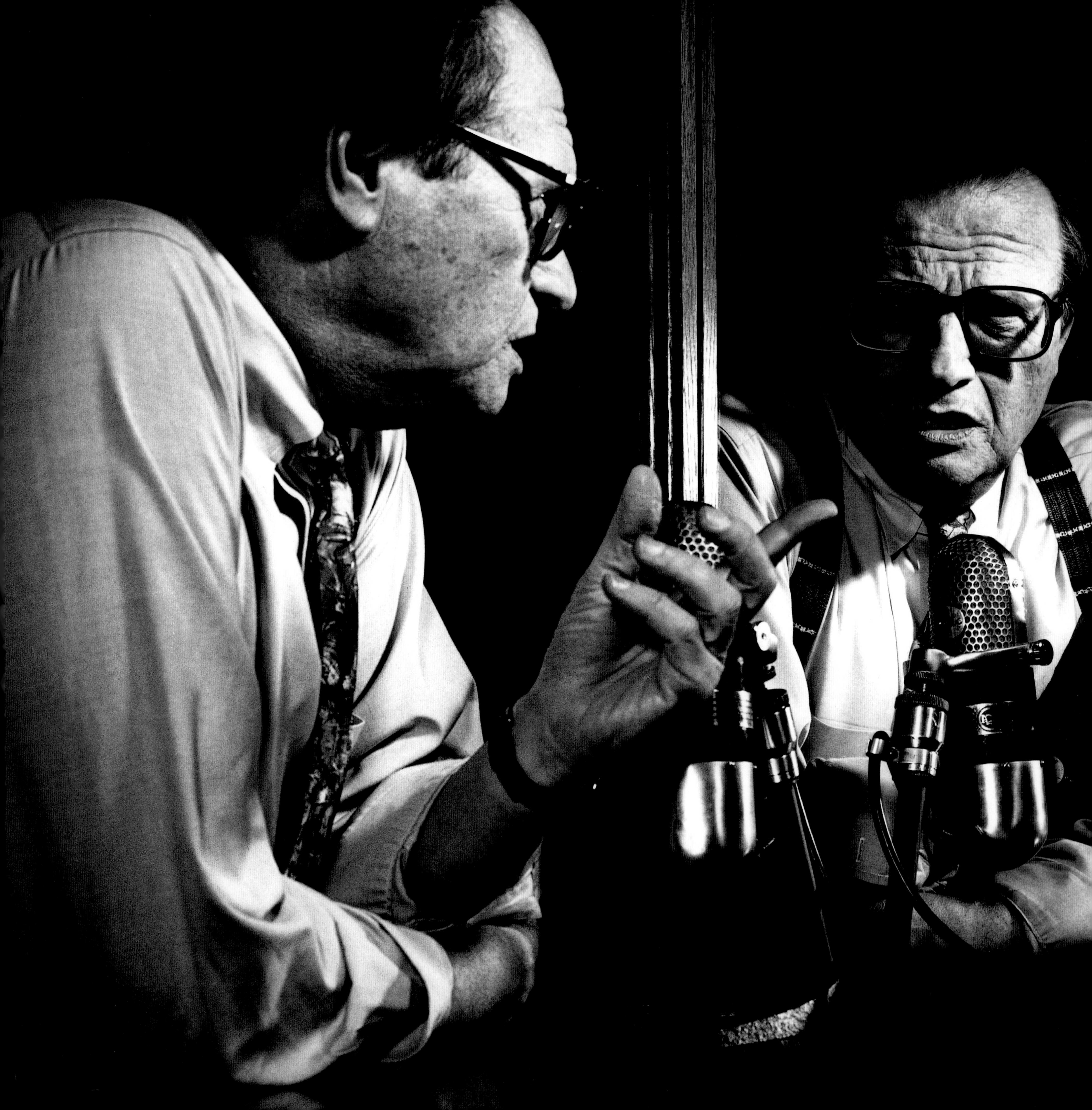

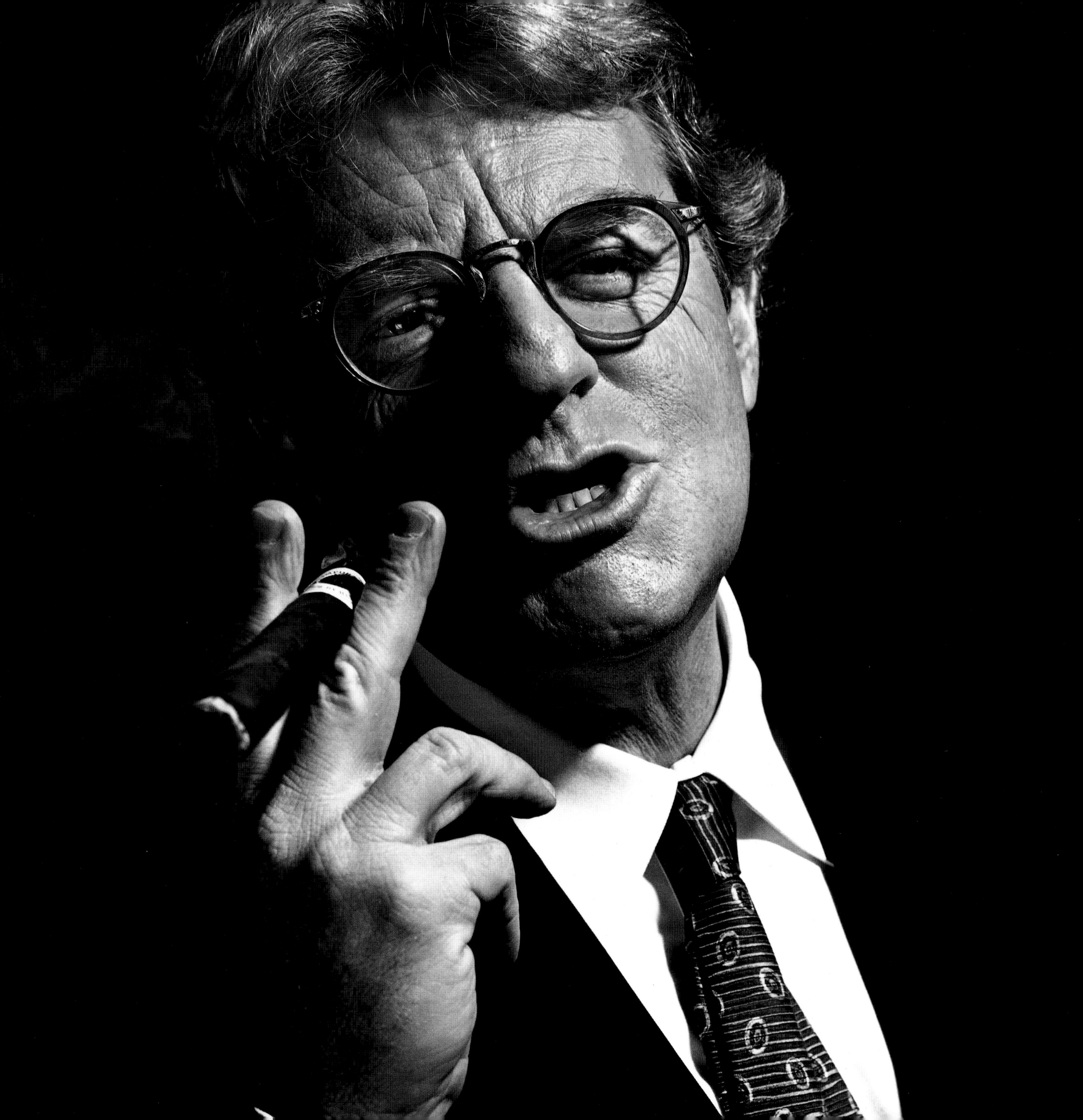

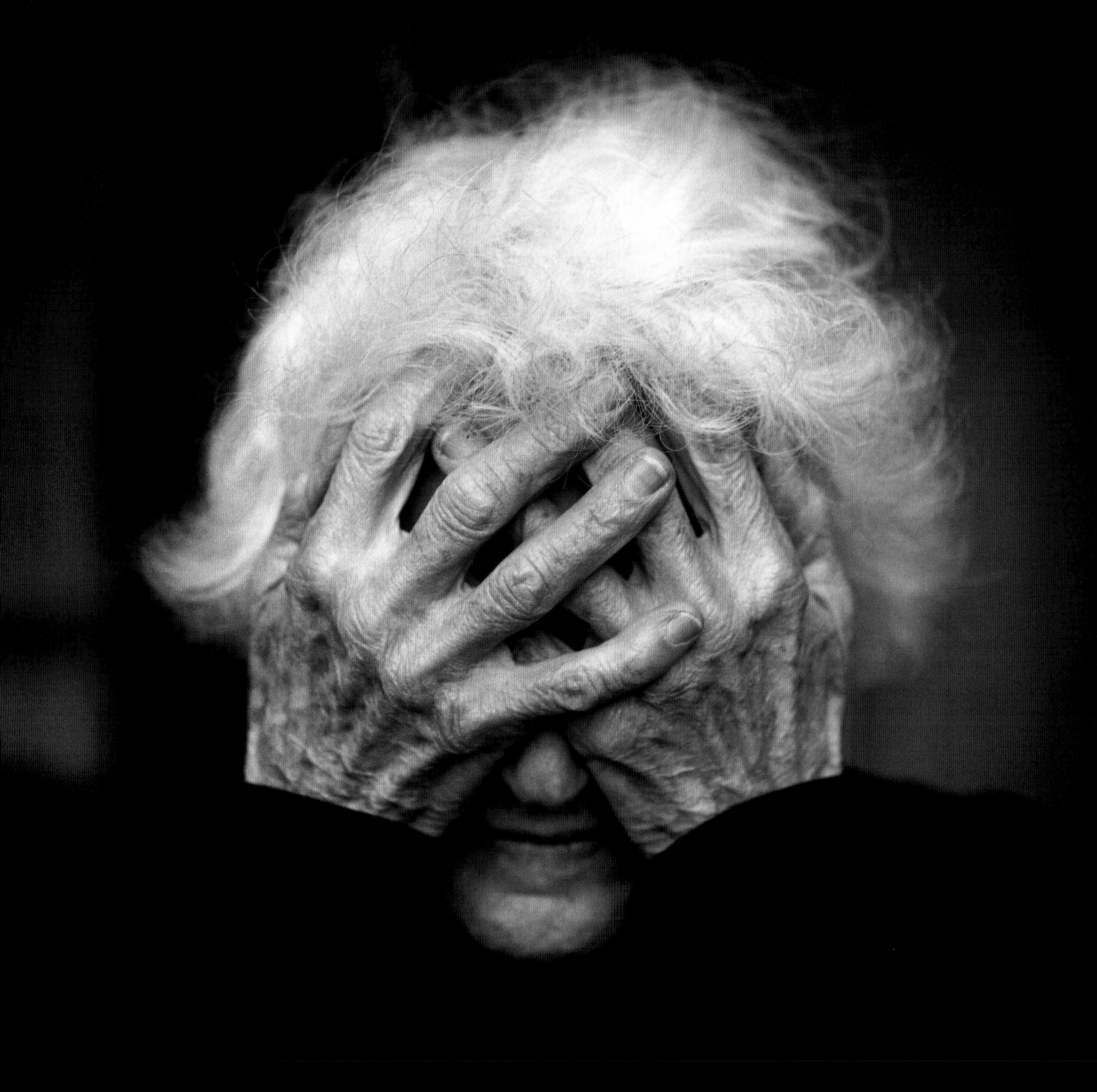

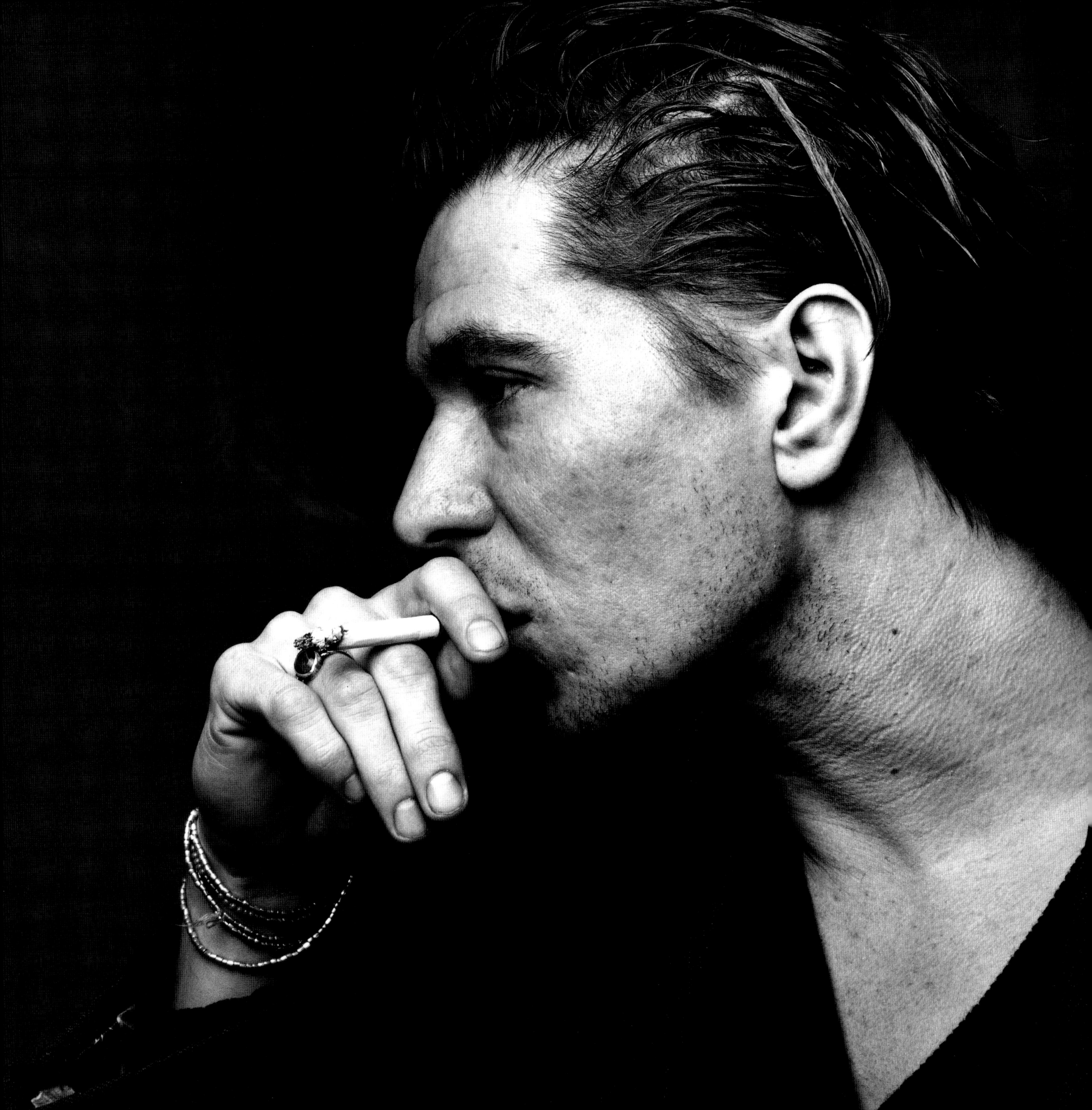

MY DEAR E
I NO LONG
JUST WHO
ME IS ANY

OY:
ER KNOW
THE REAL
MORE.

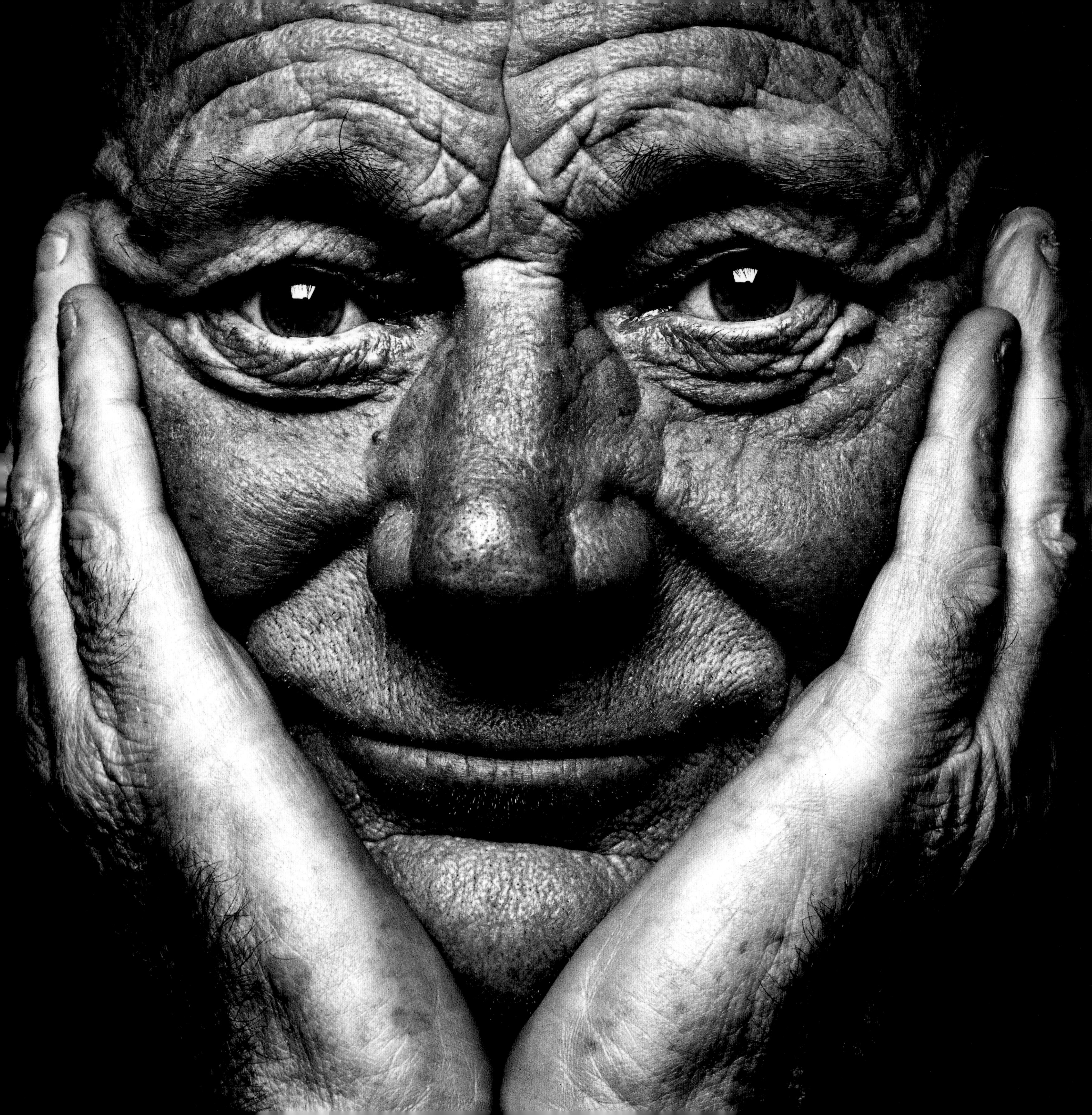

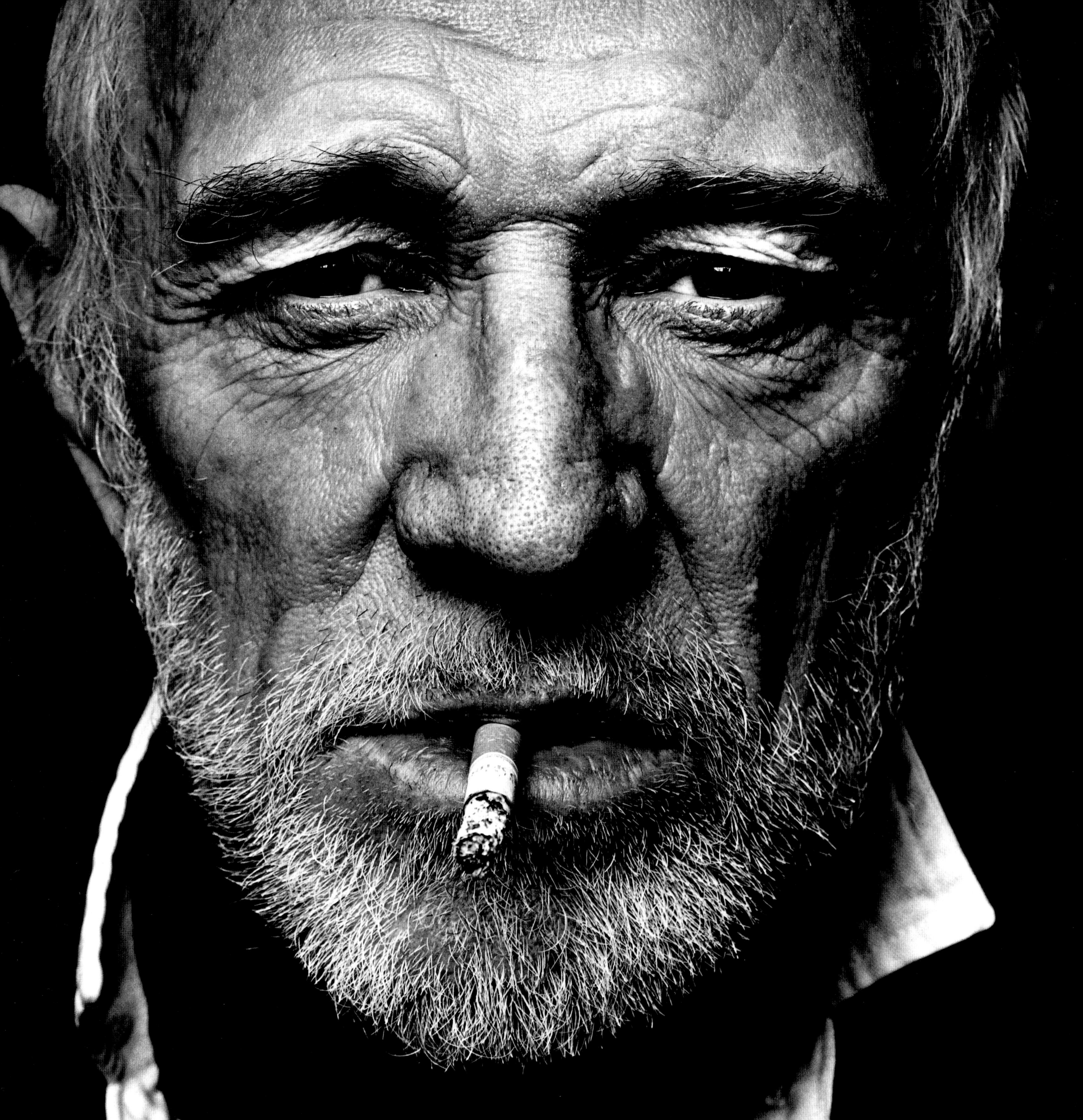

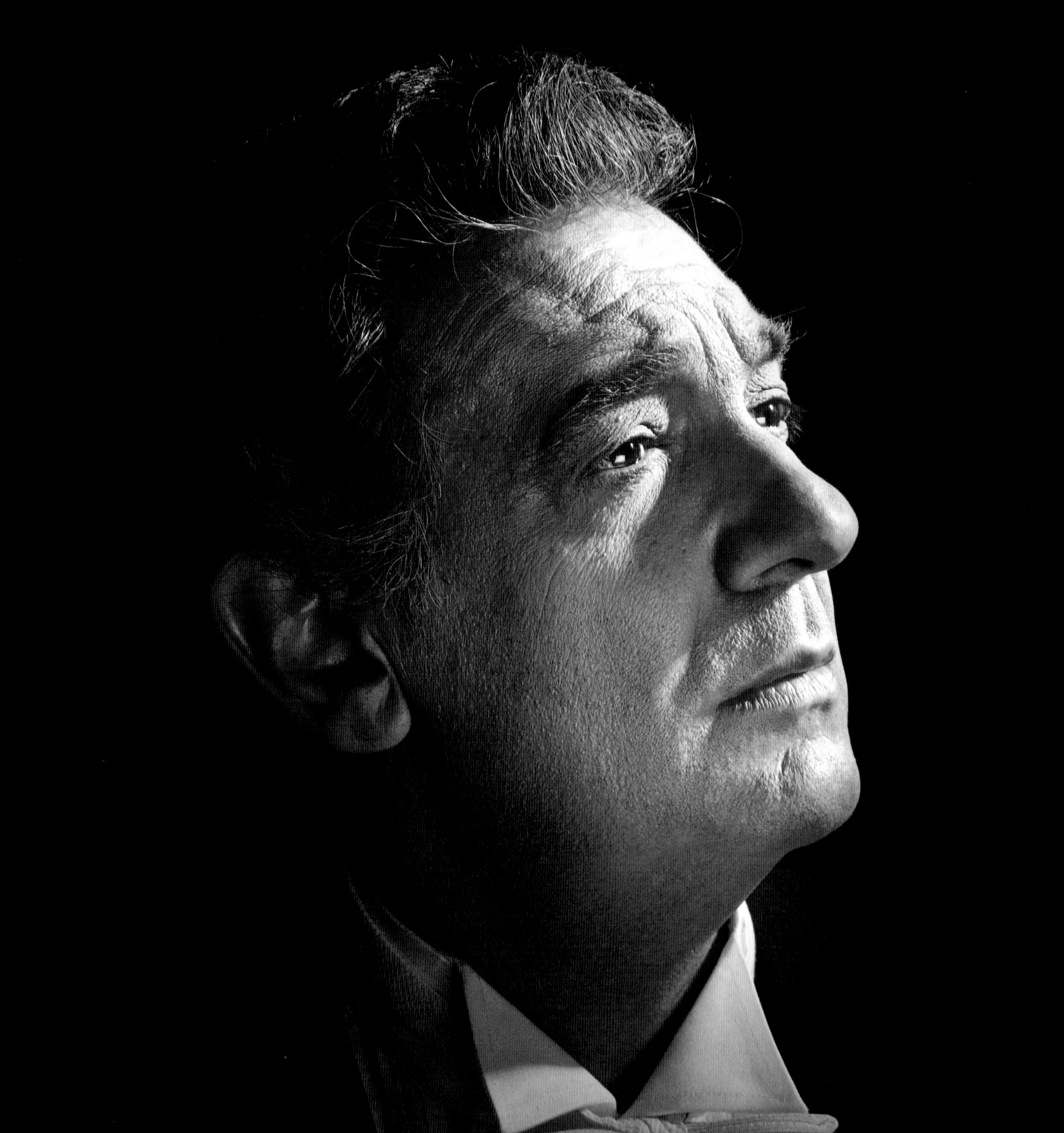

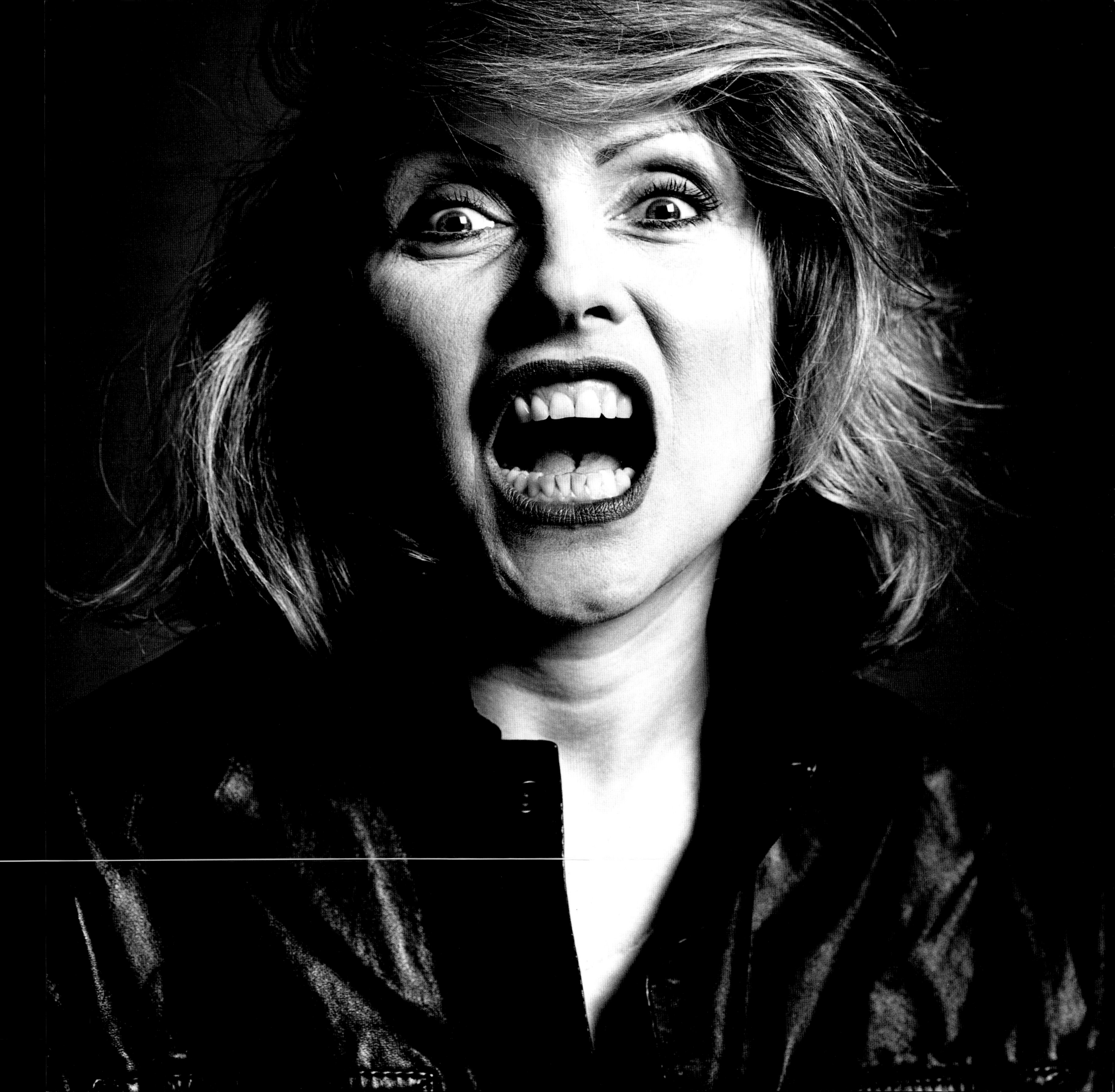

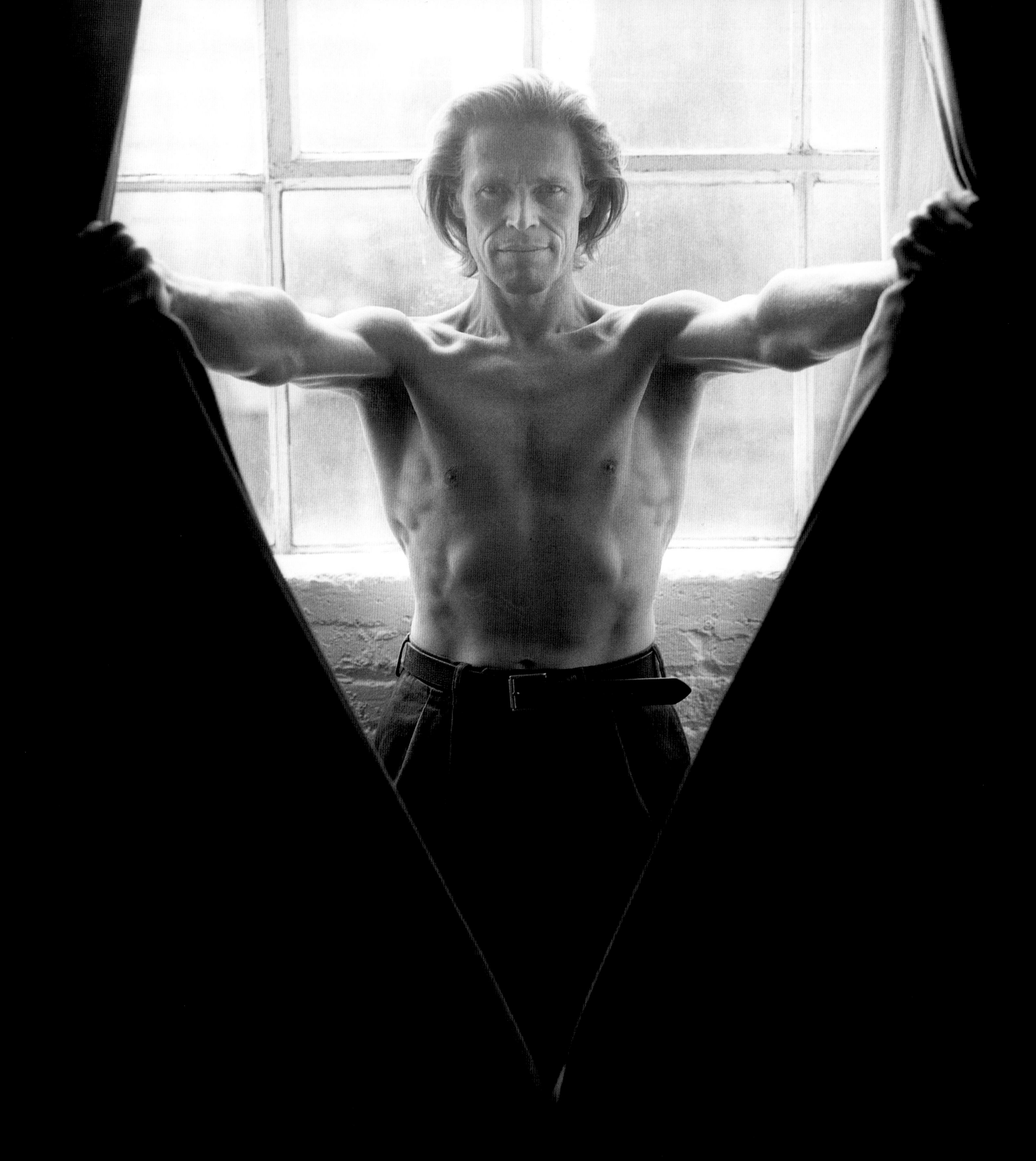

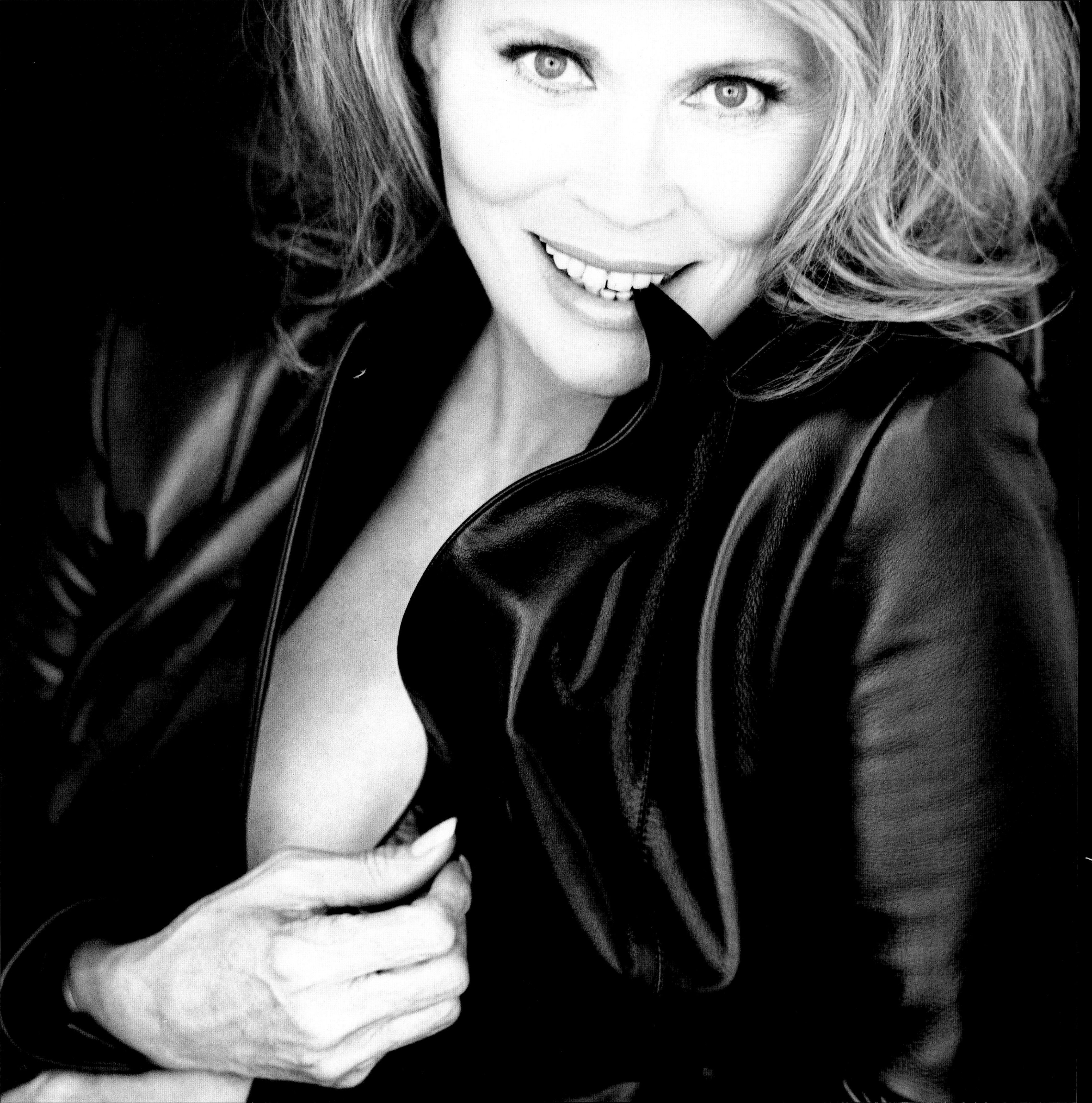

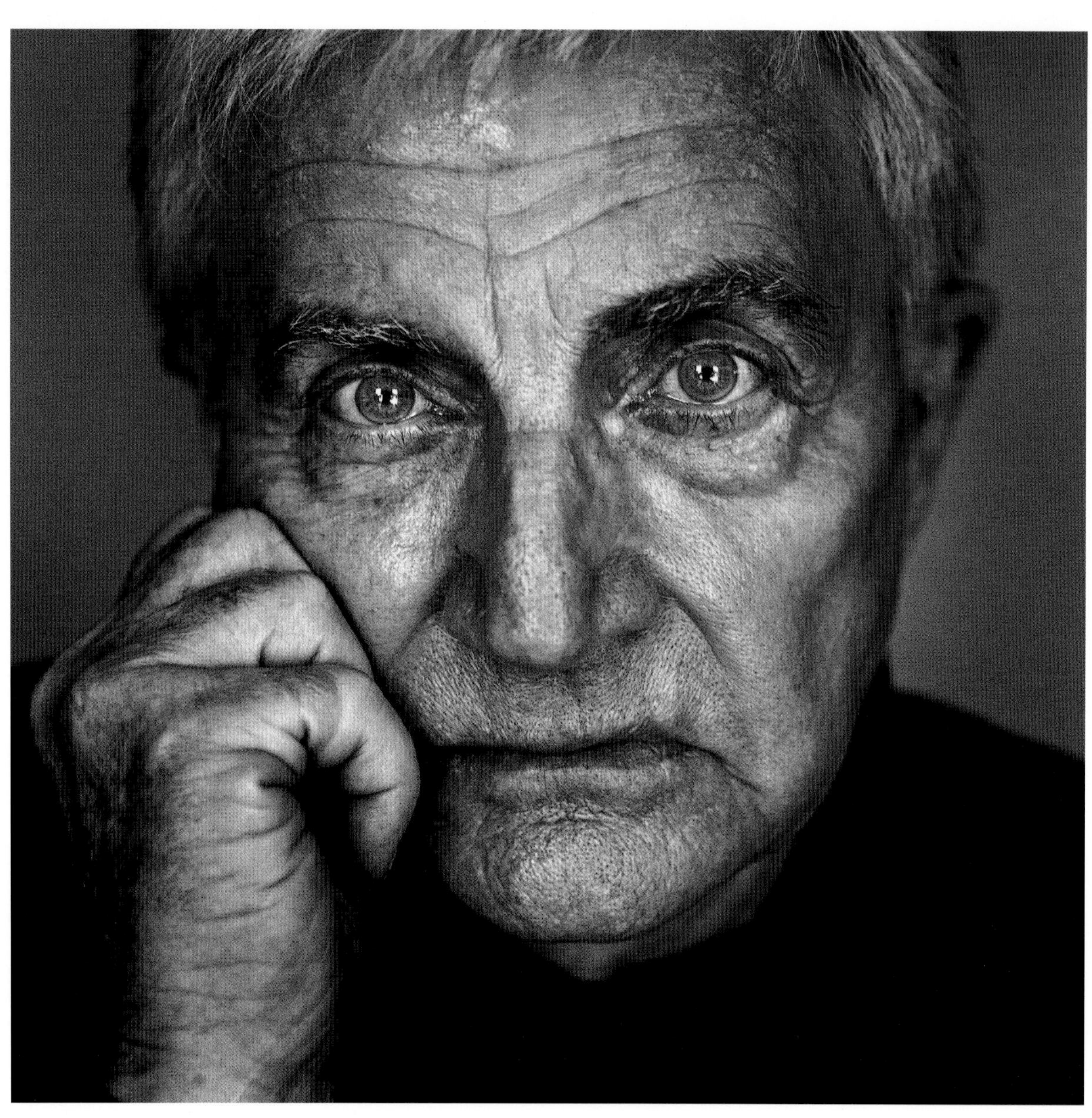

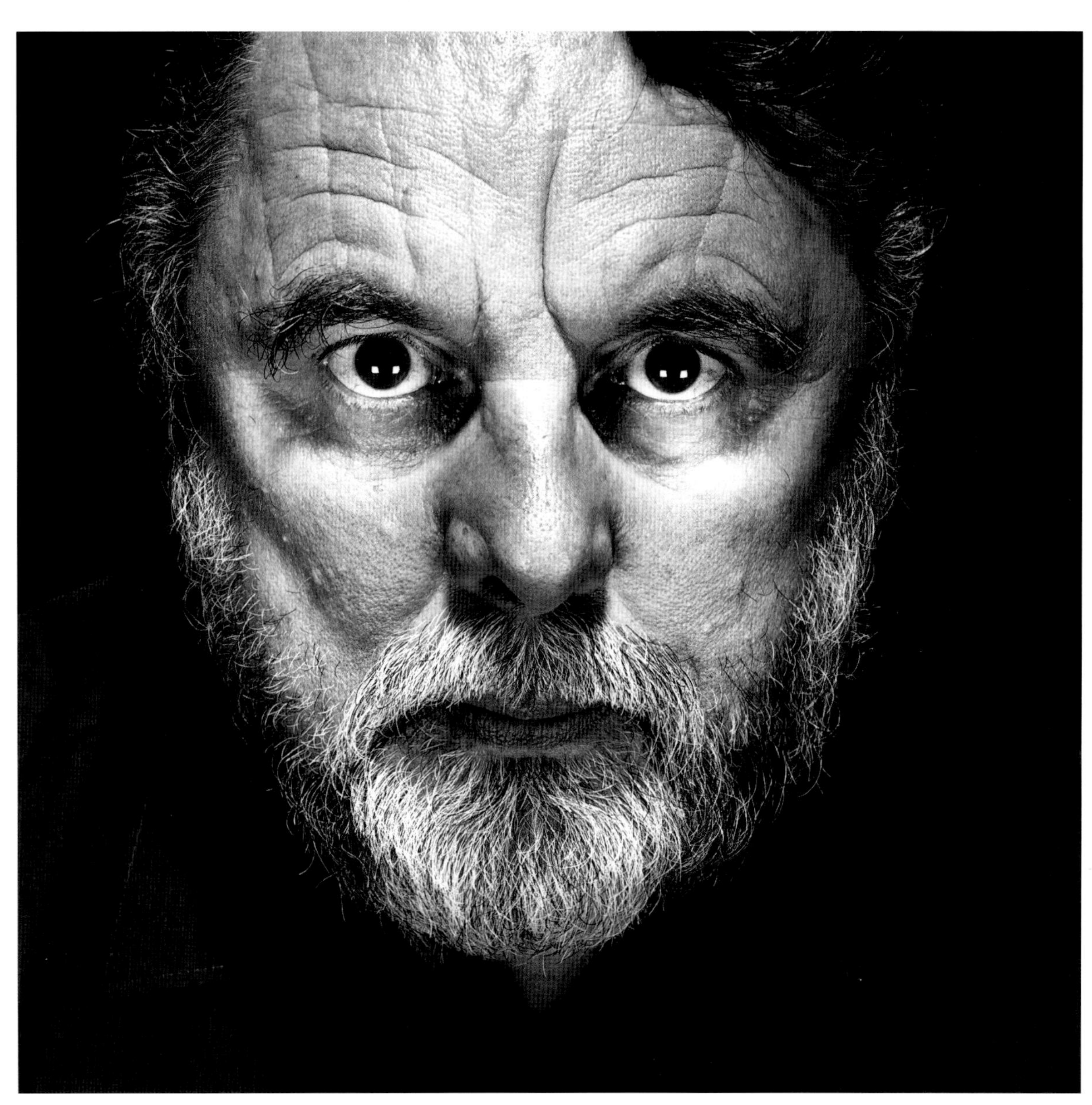

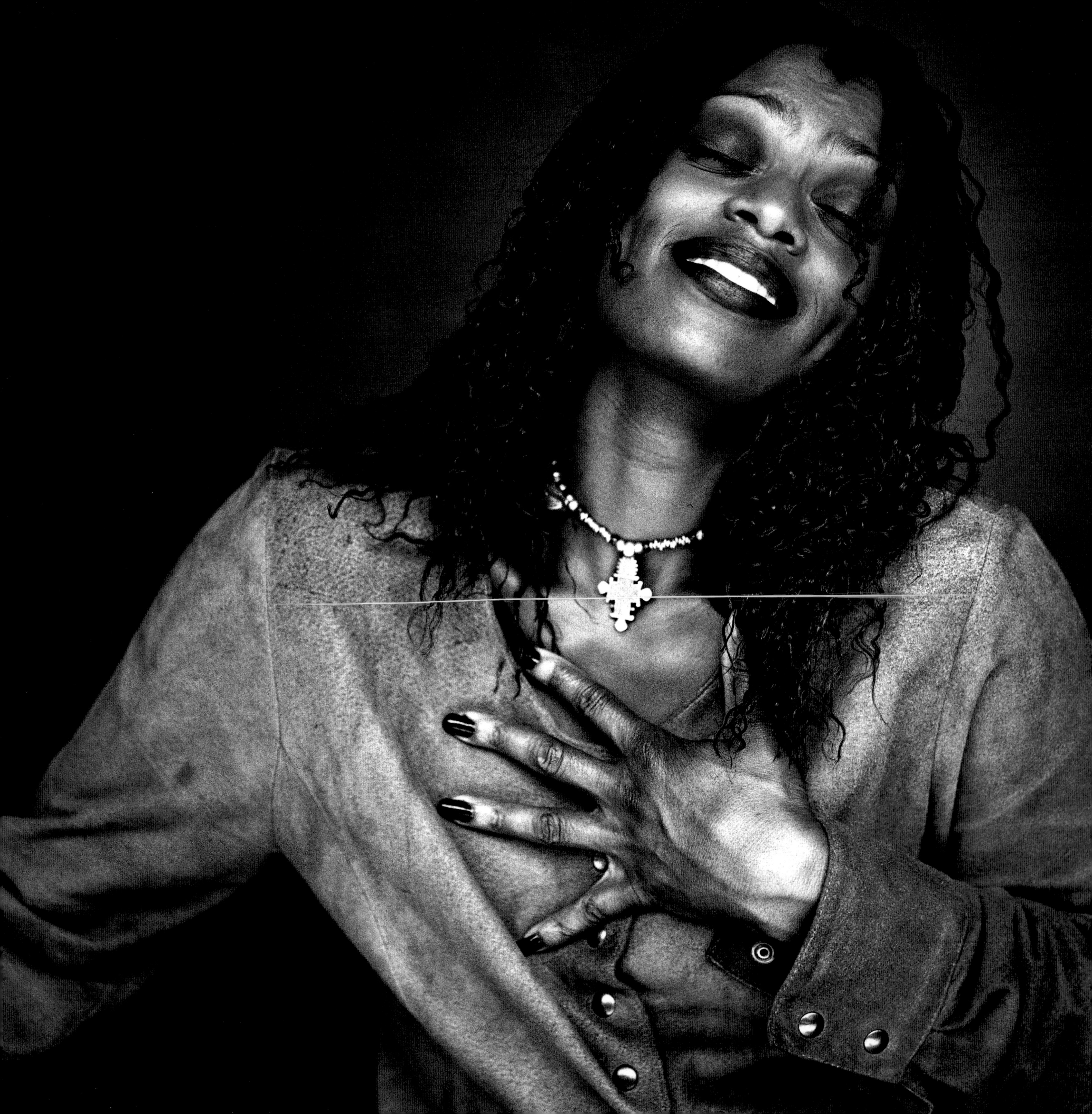

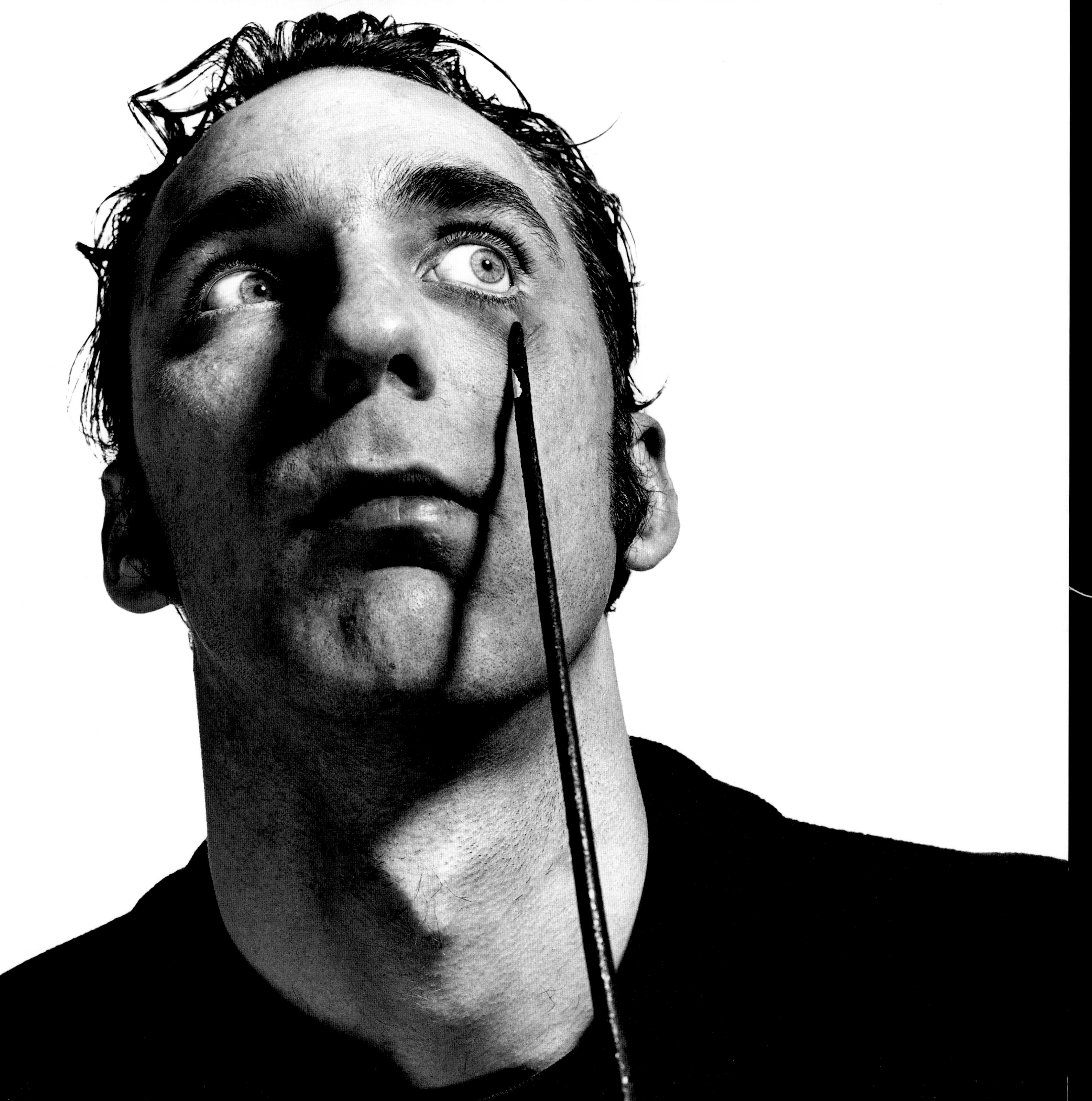

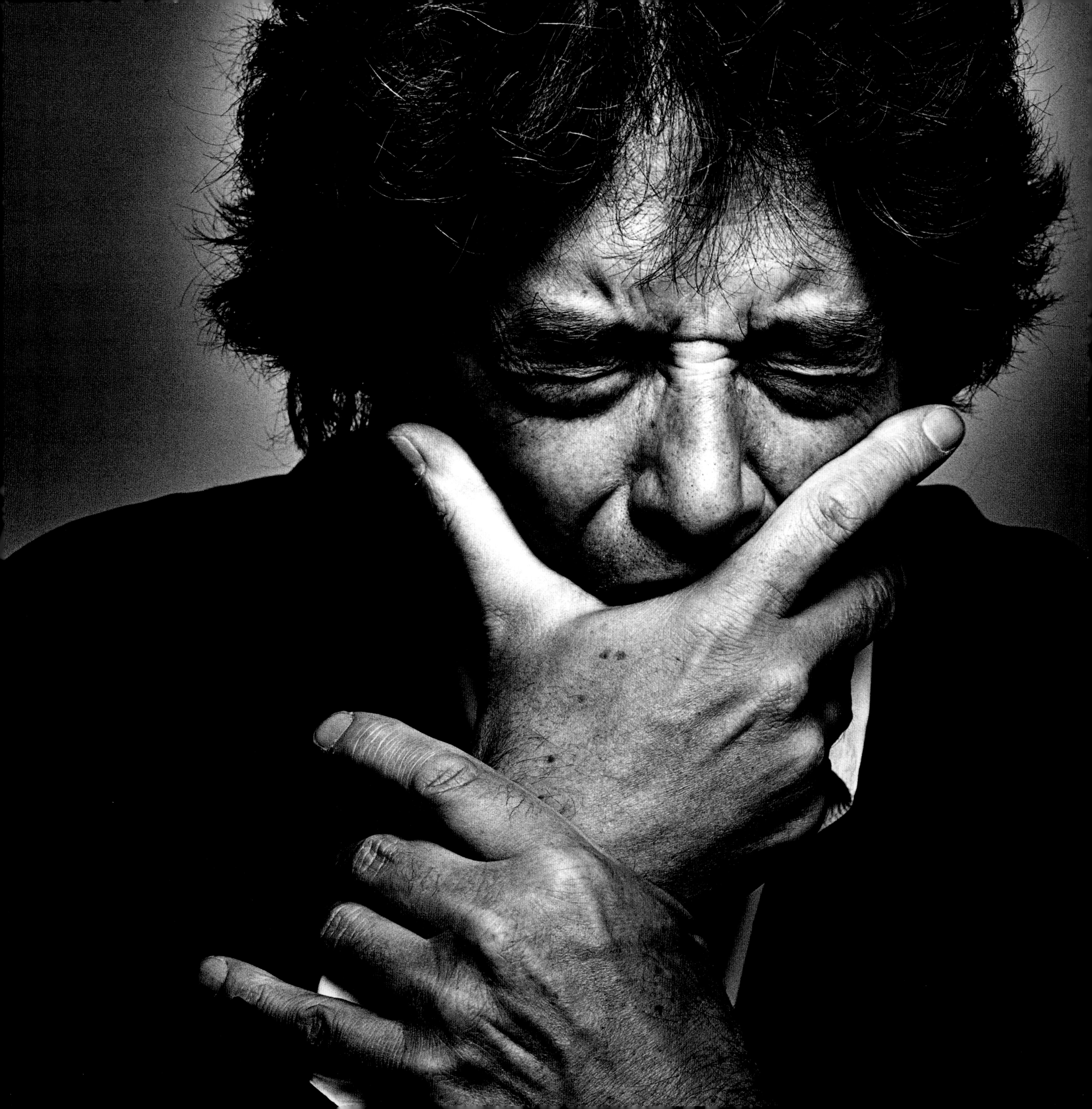

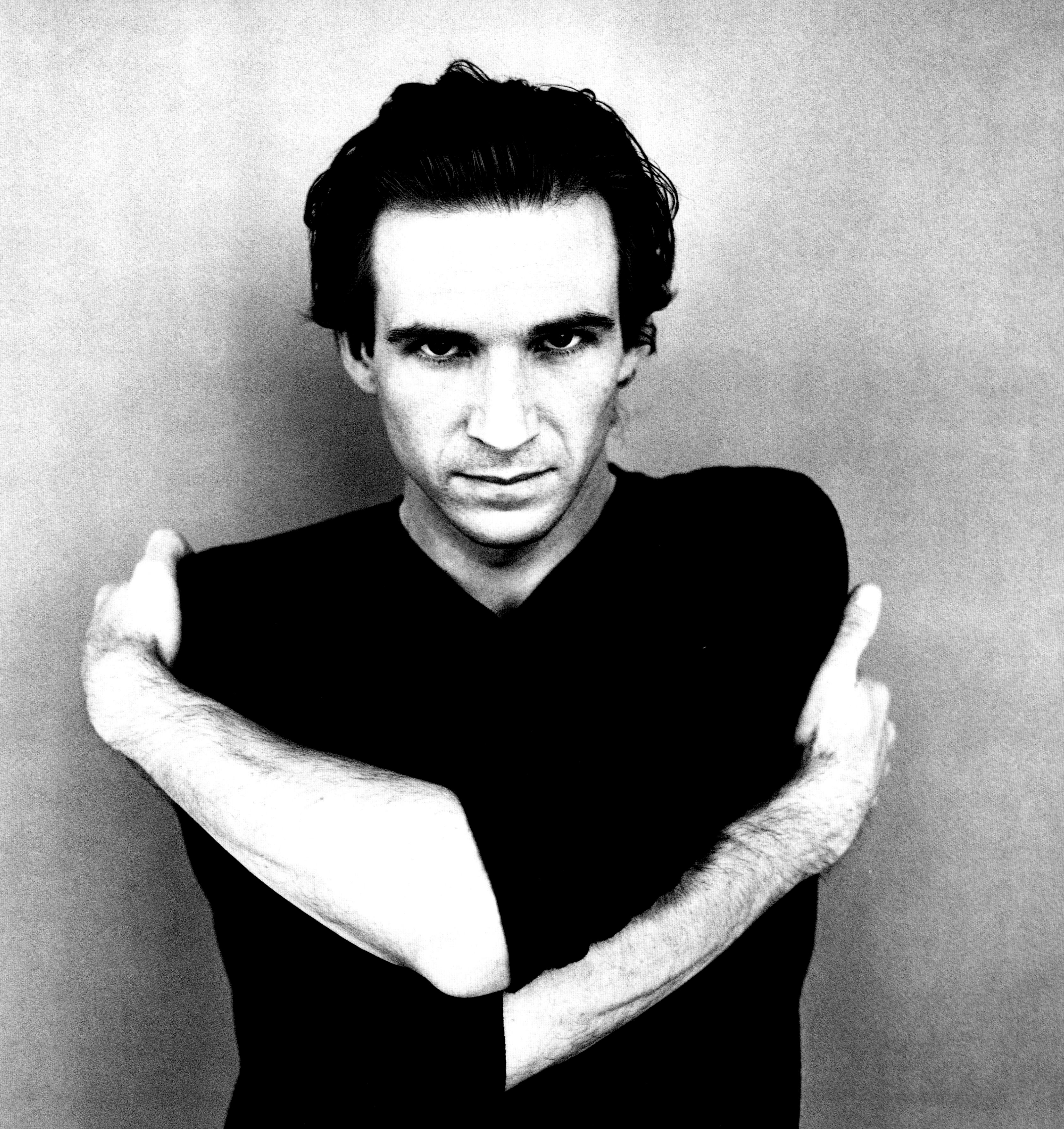

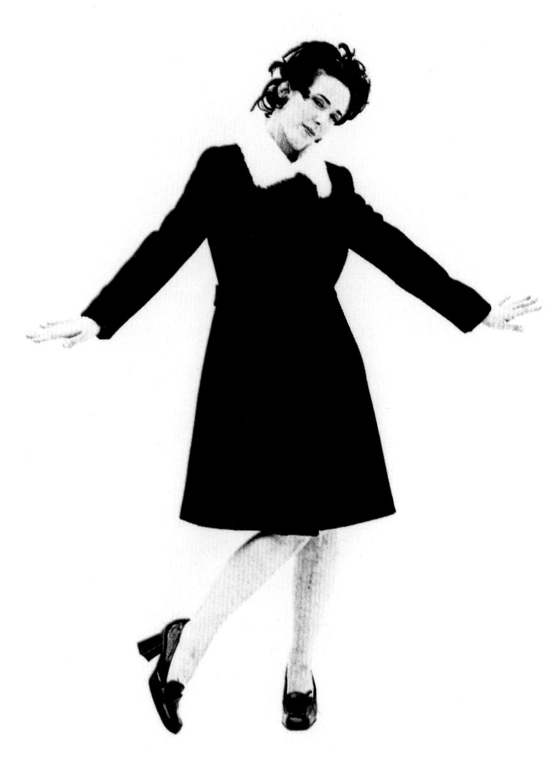

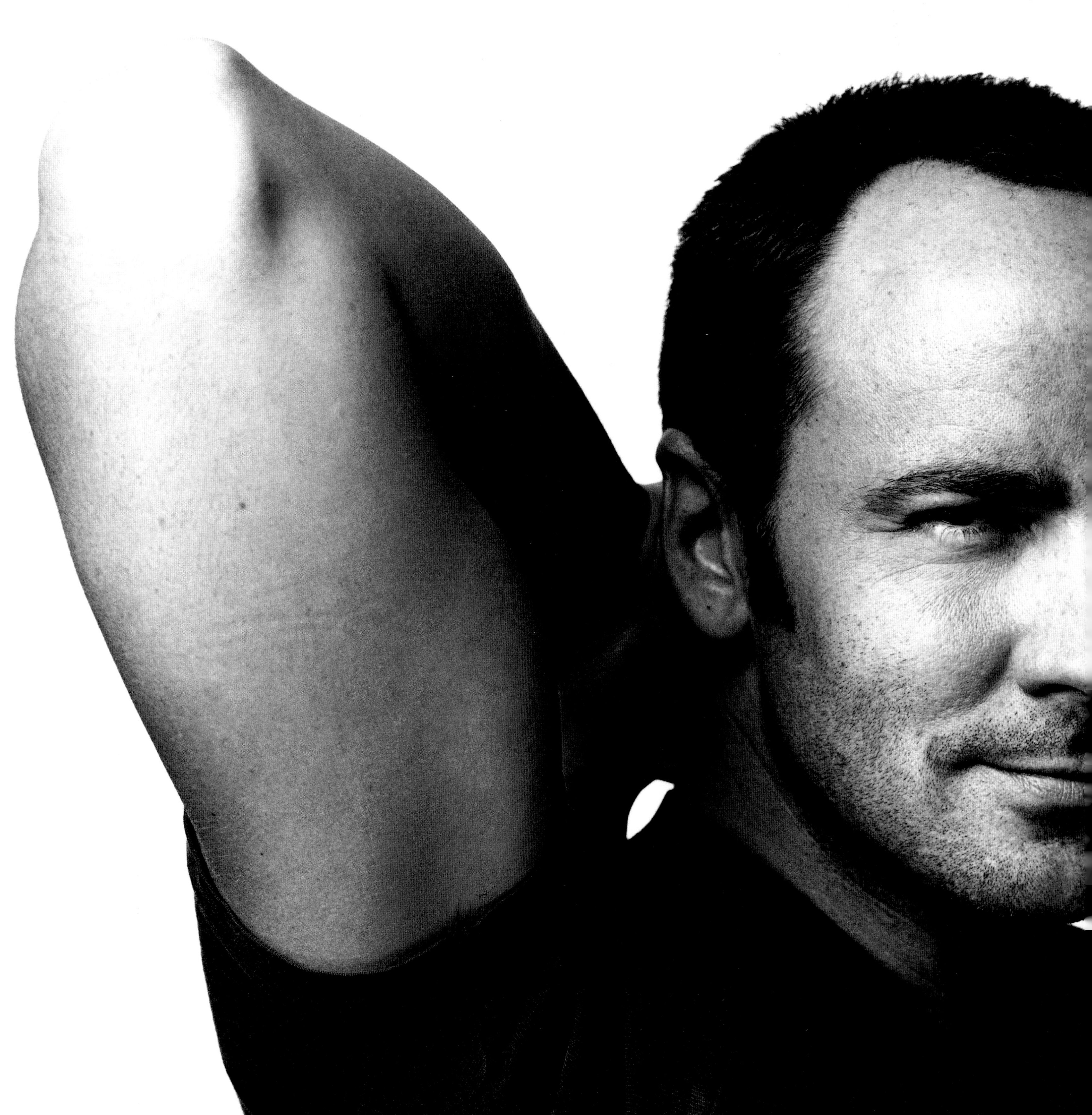

AND I'VE G
UMBRELLA
THAT MATC

OT AN

HES TOO!

RUBY DECIDING ON WHAT KIND OF
OUTFIT TO WEAR.

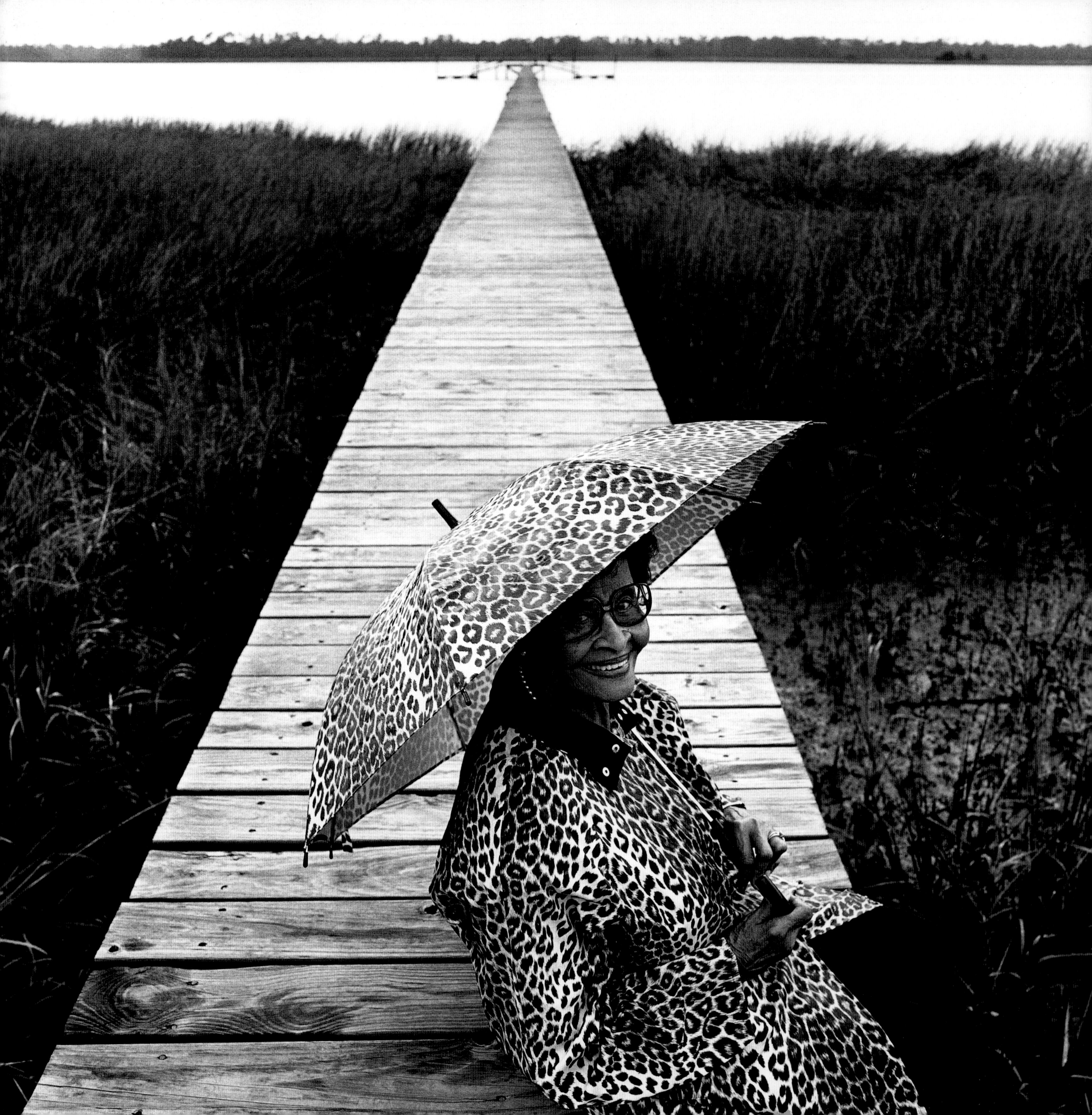

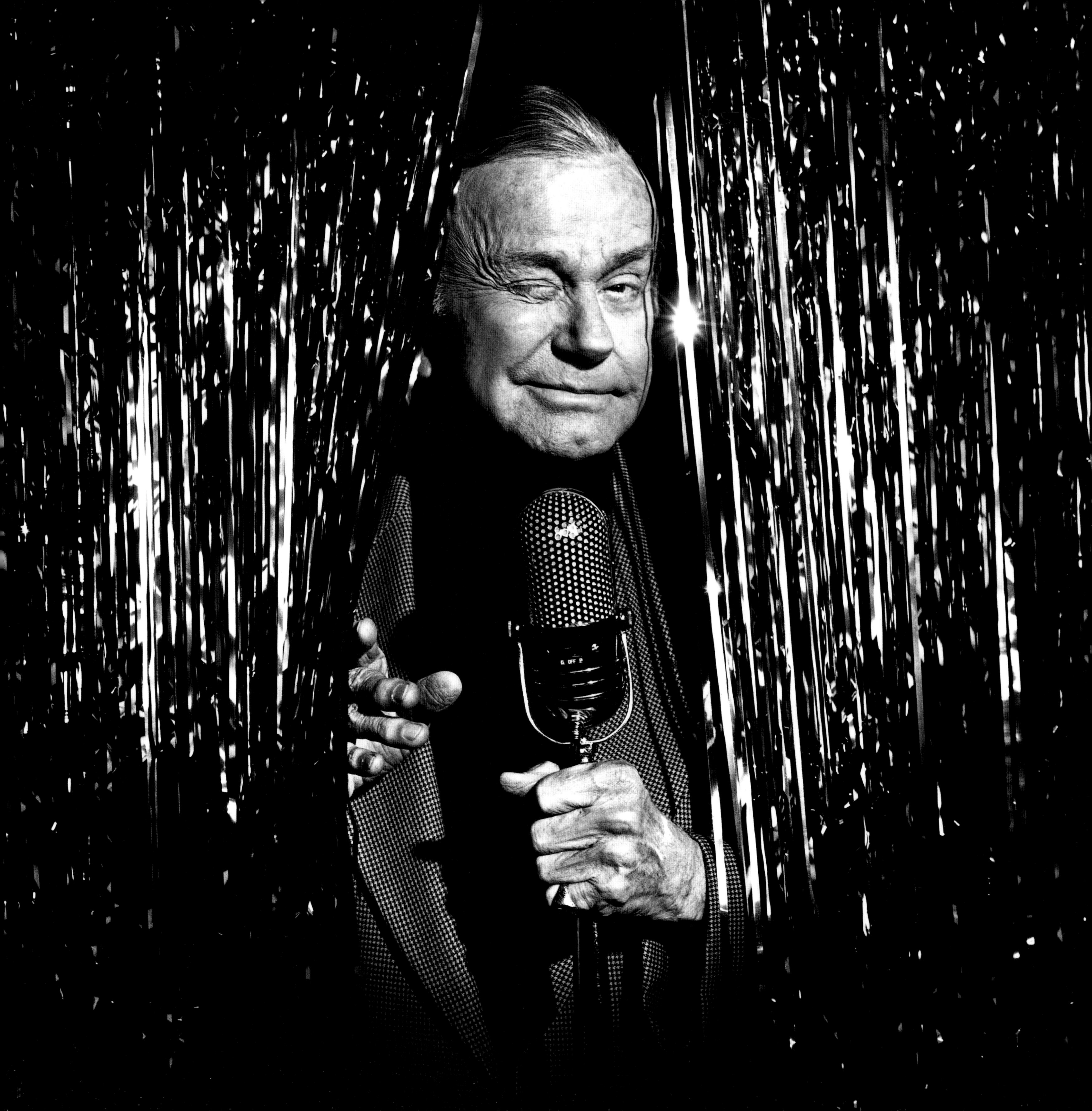

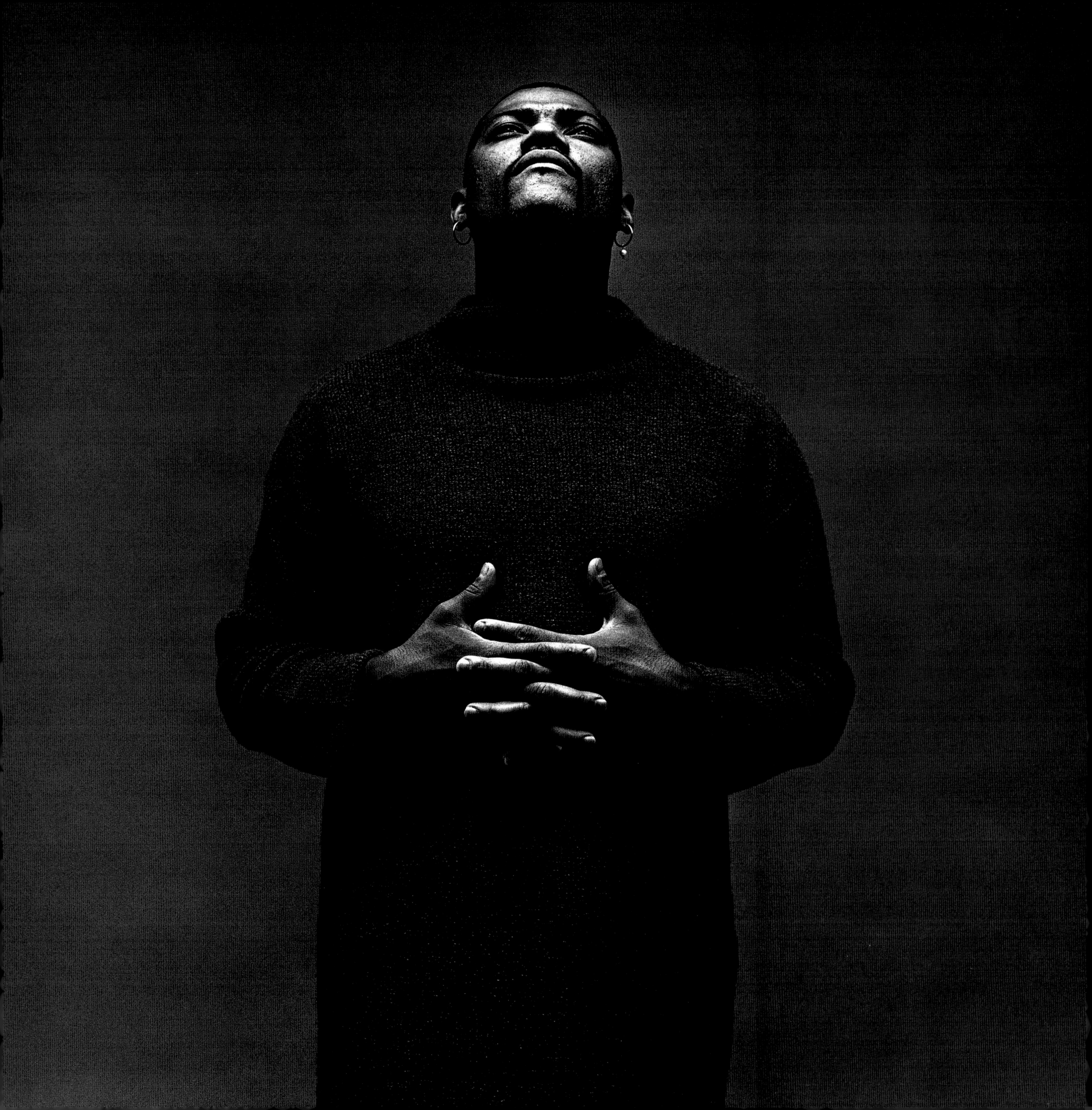

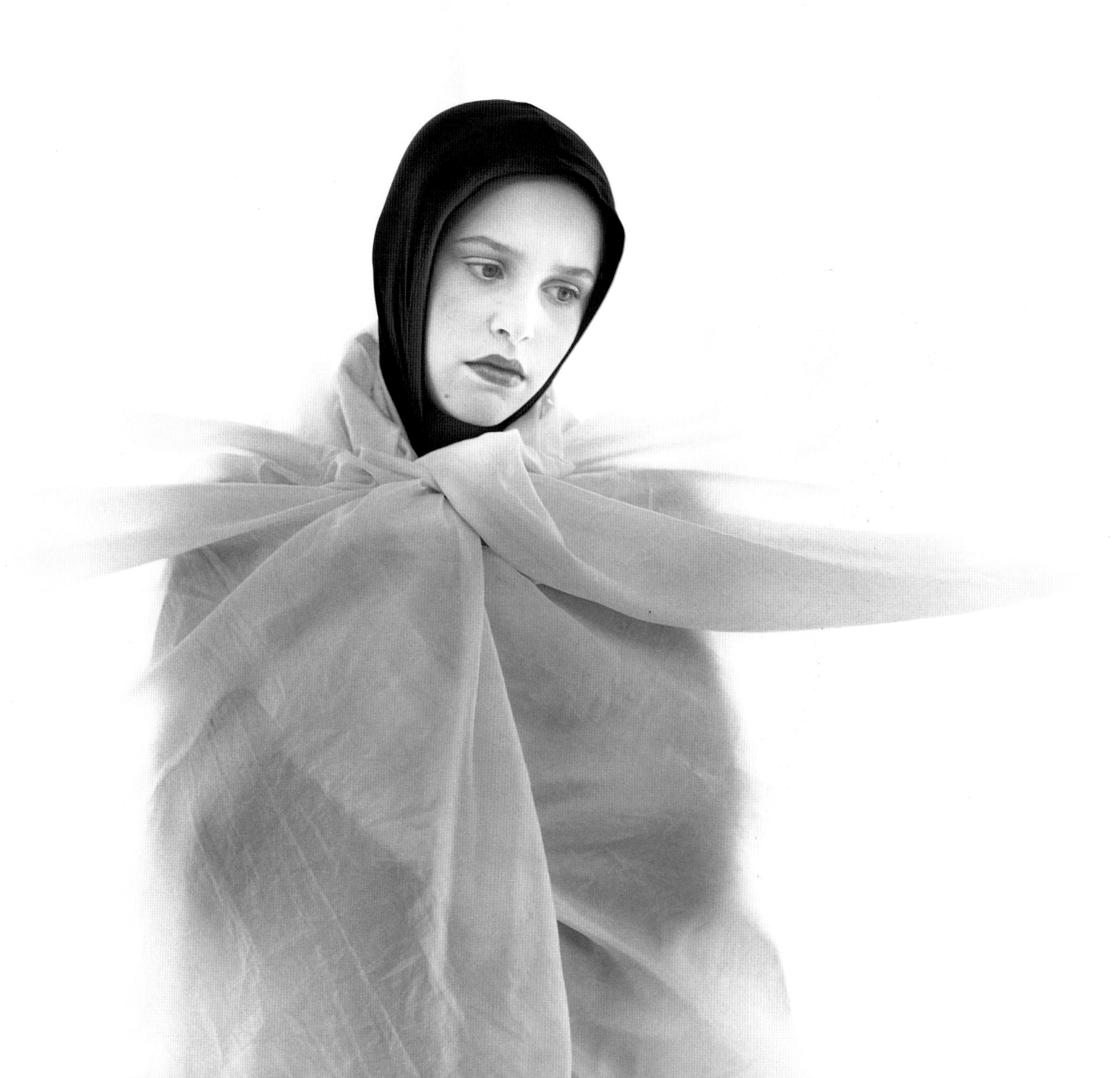

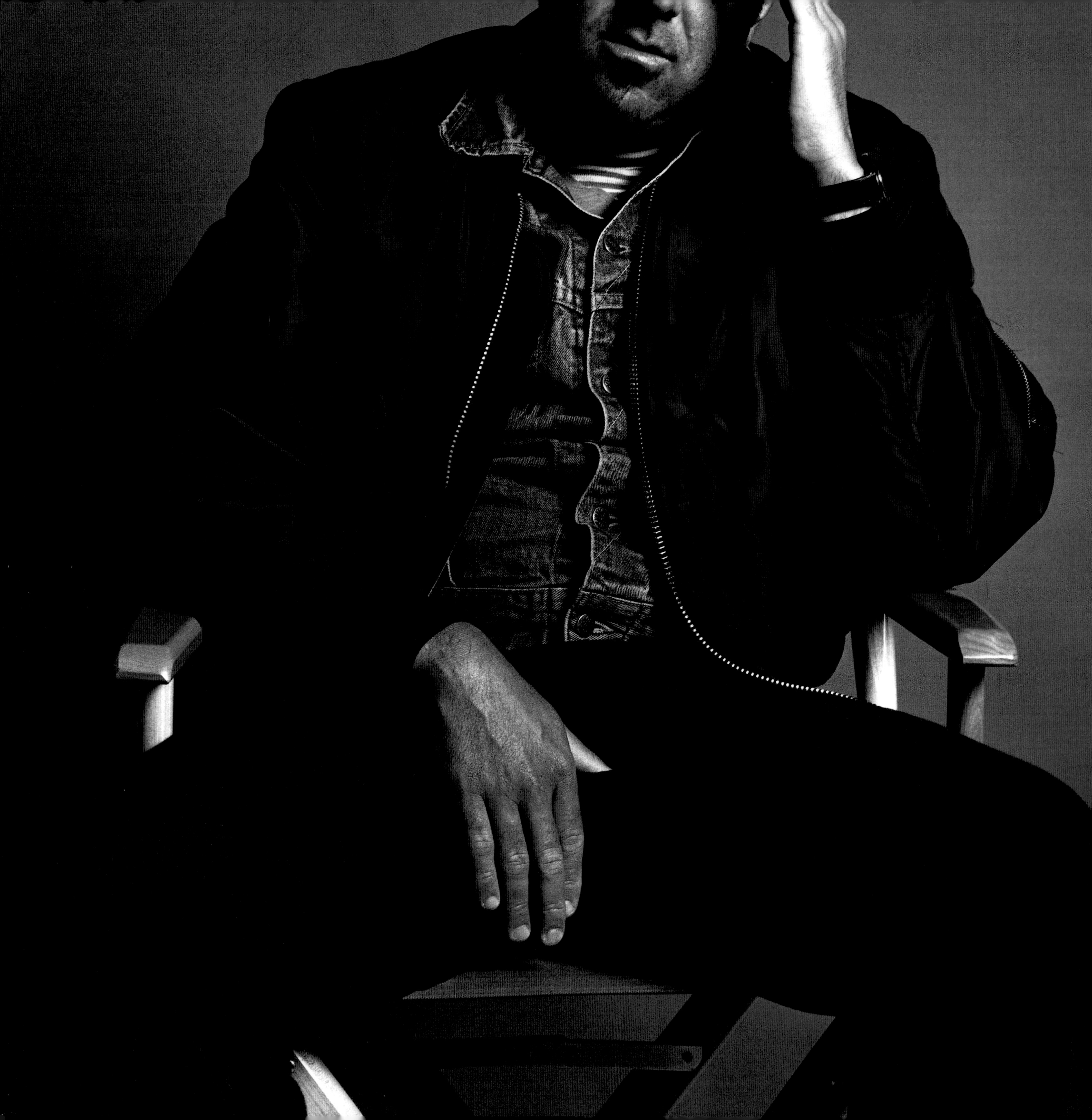

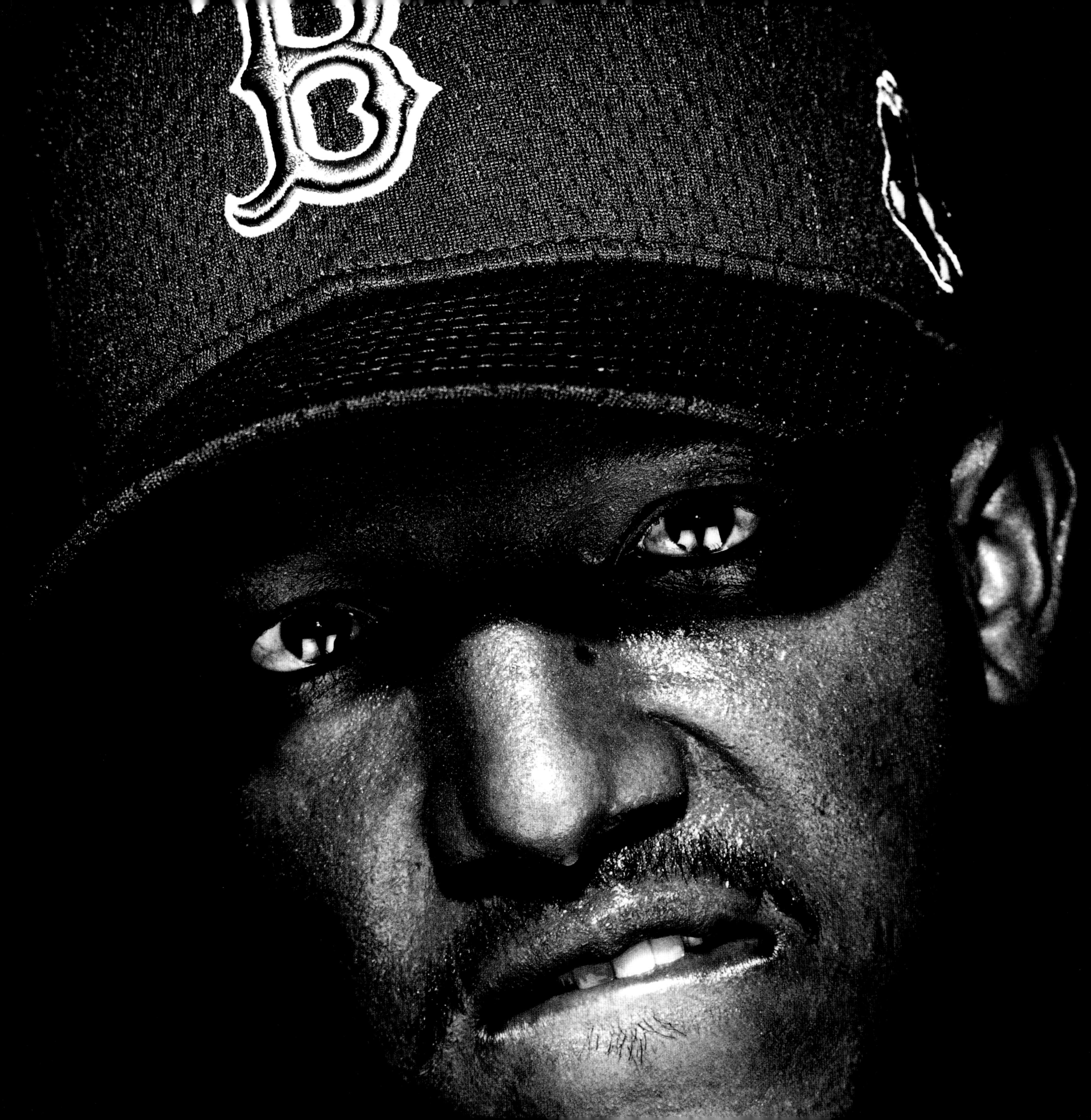

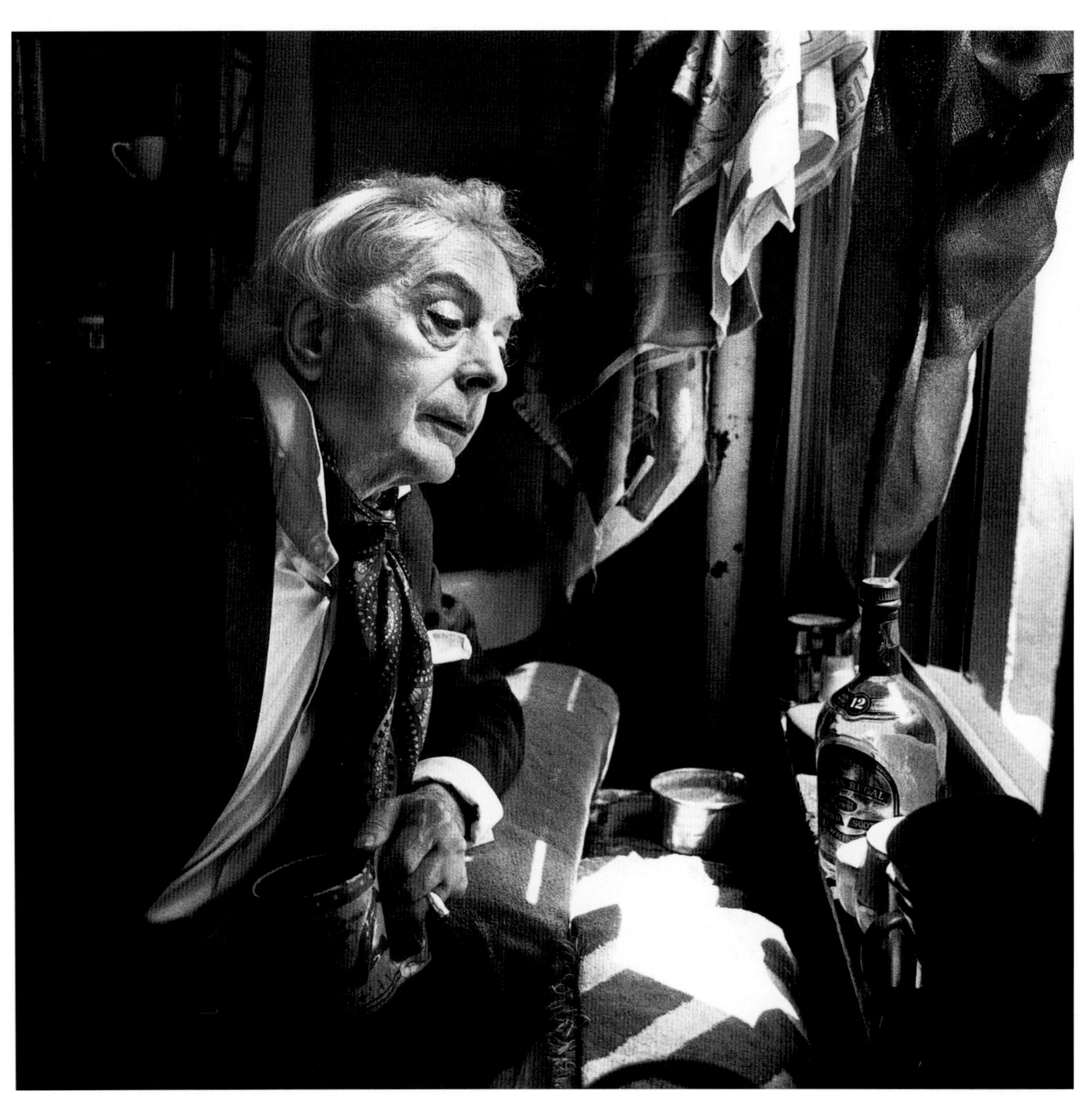

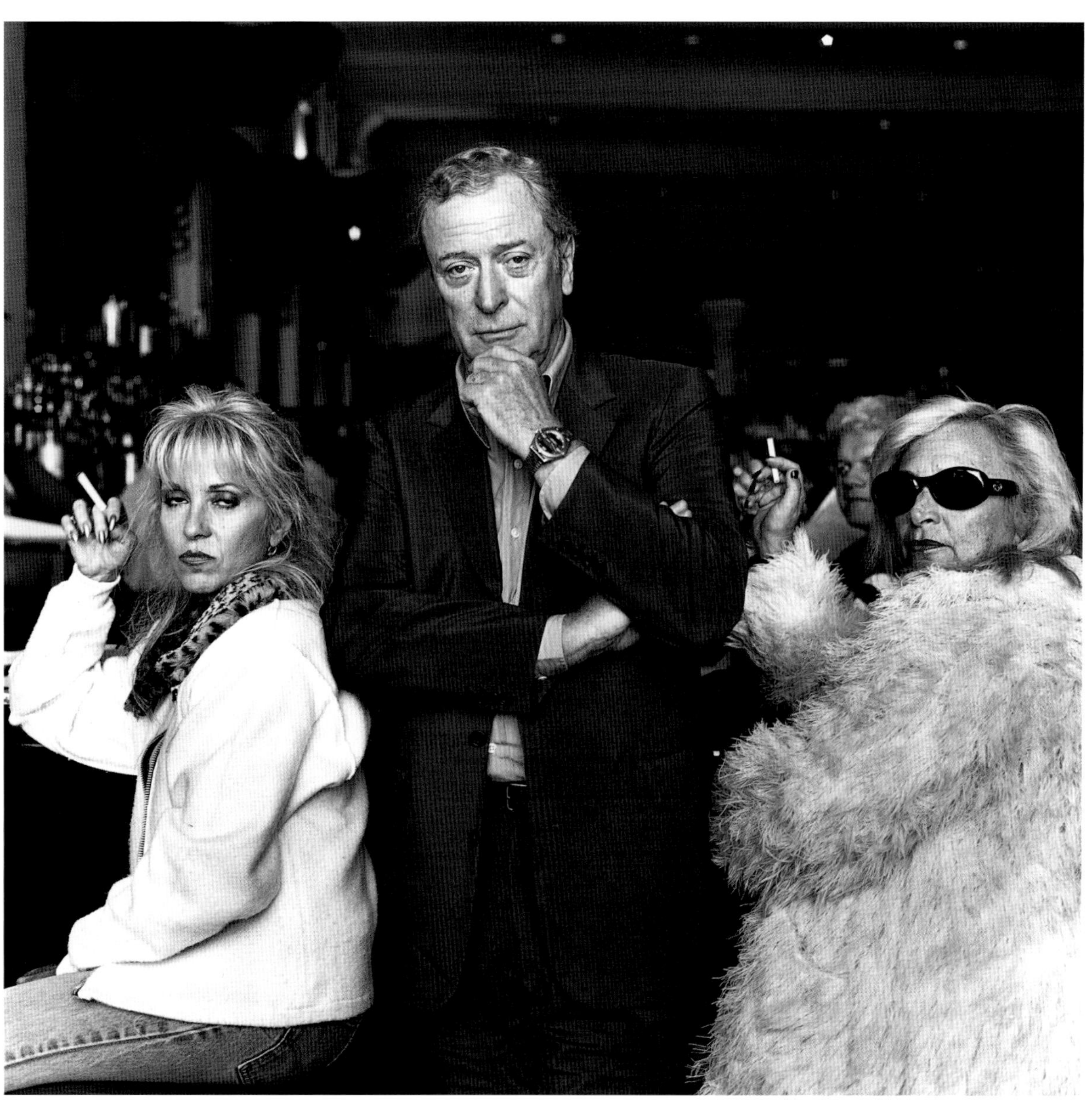

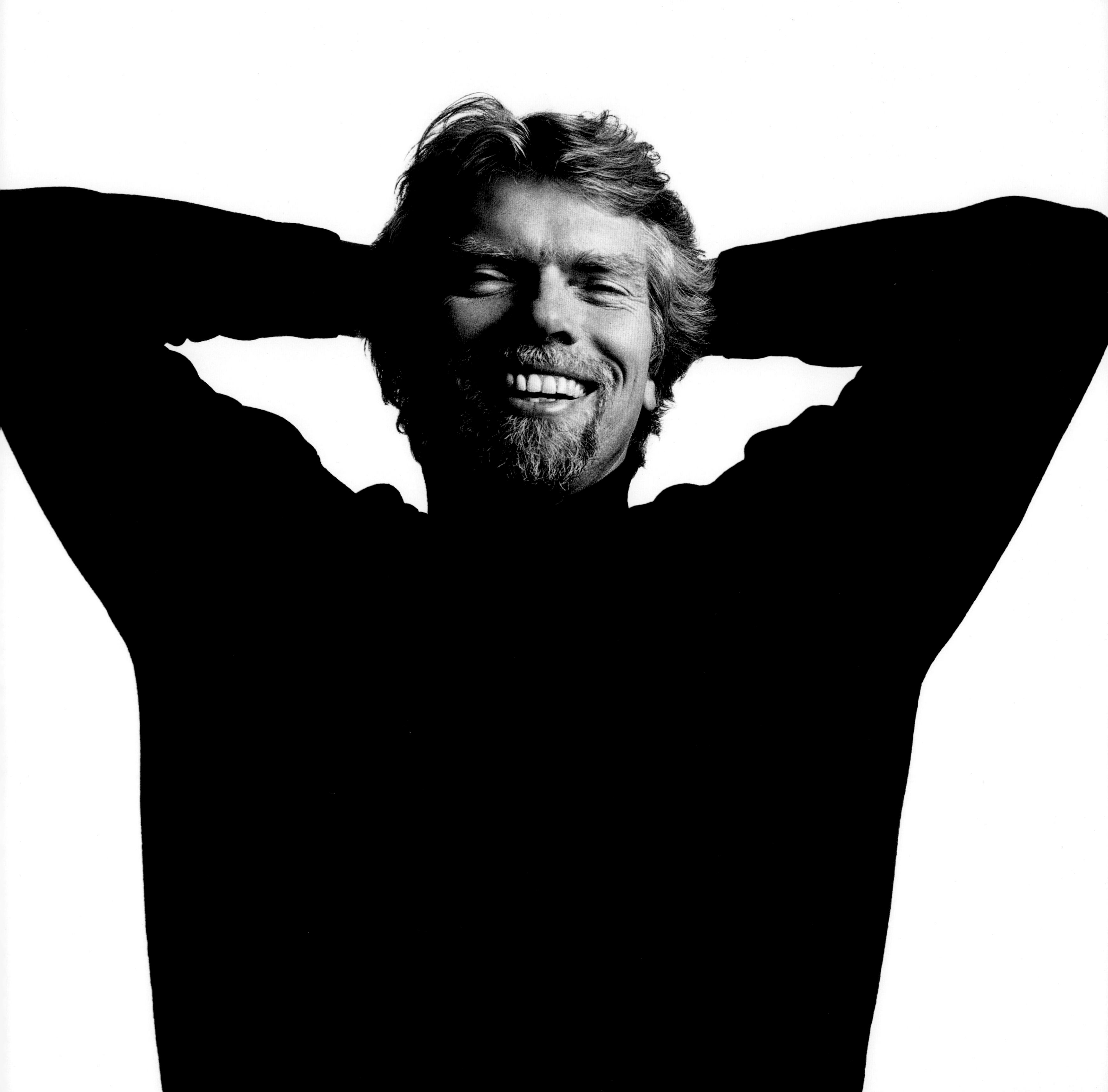

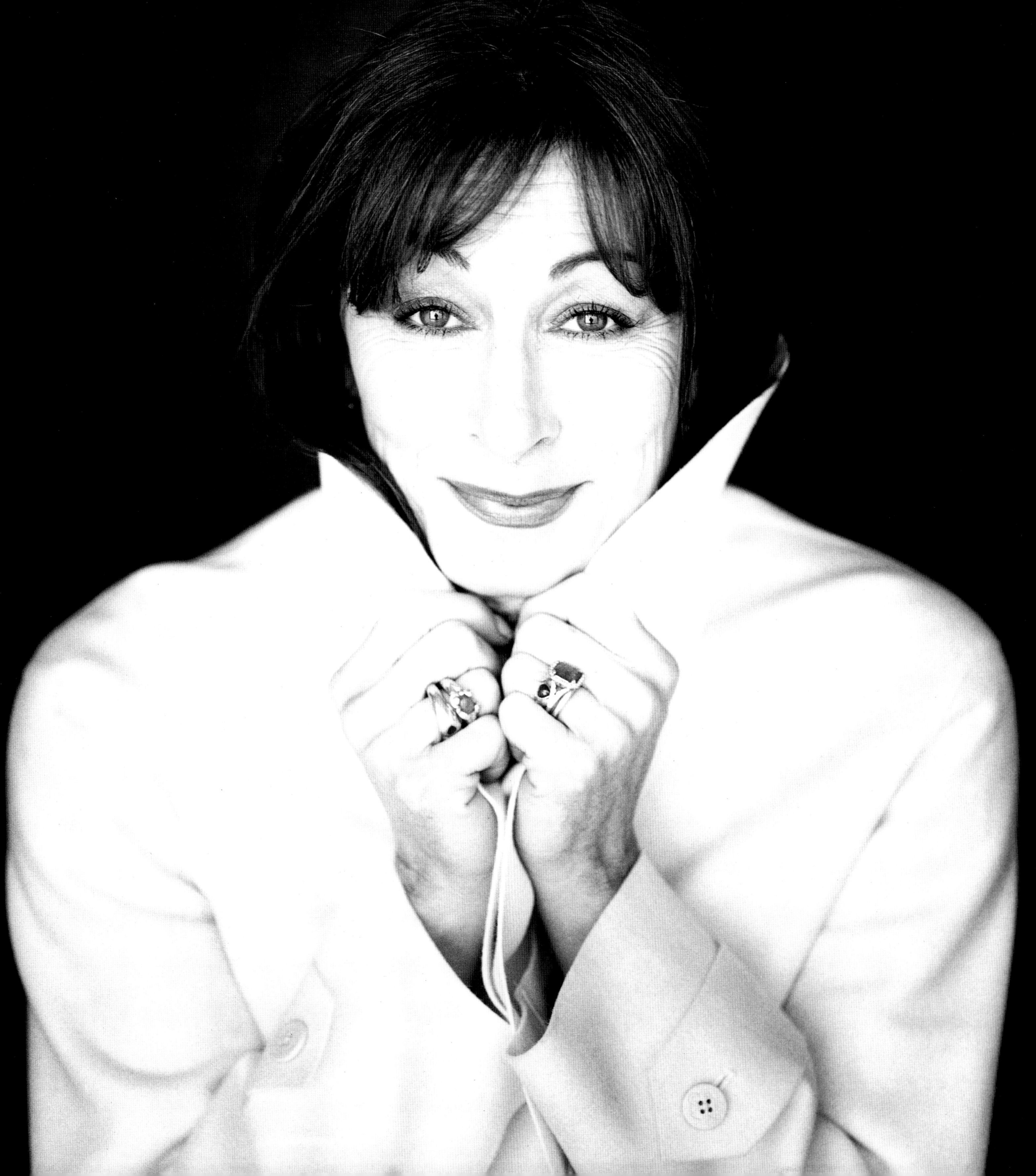

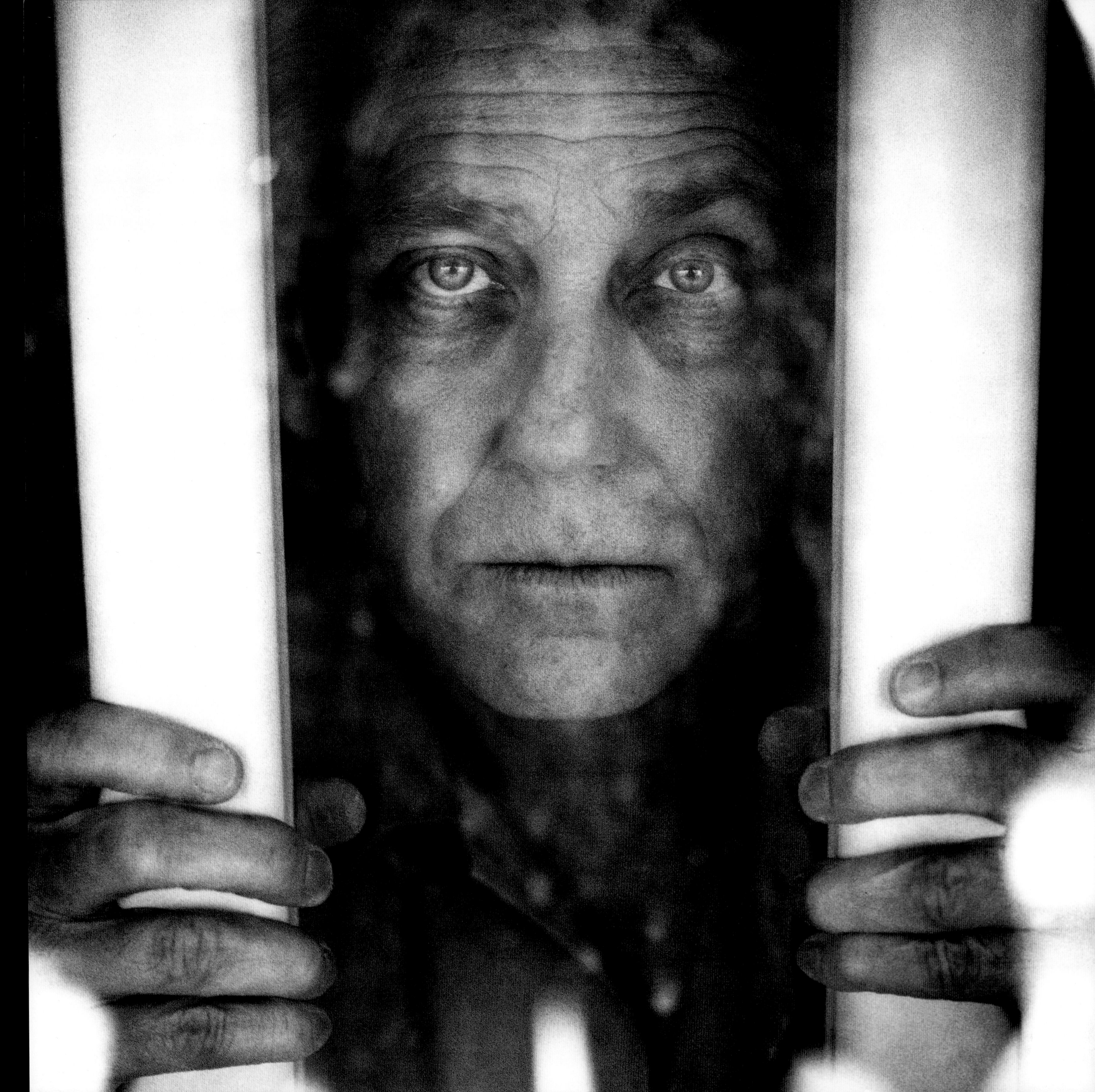

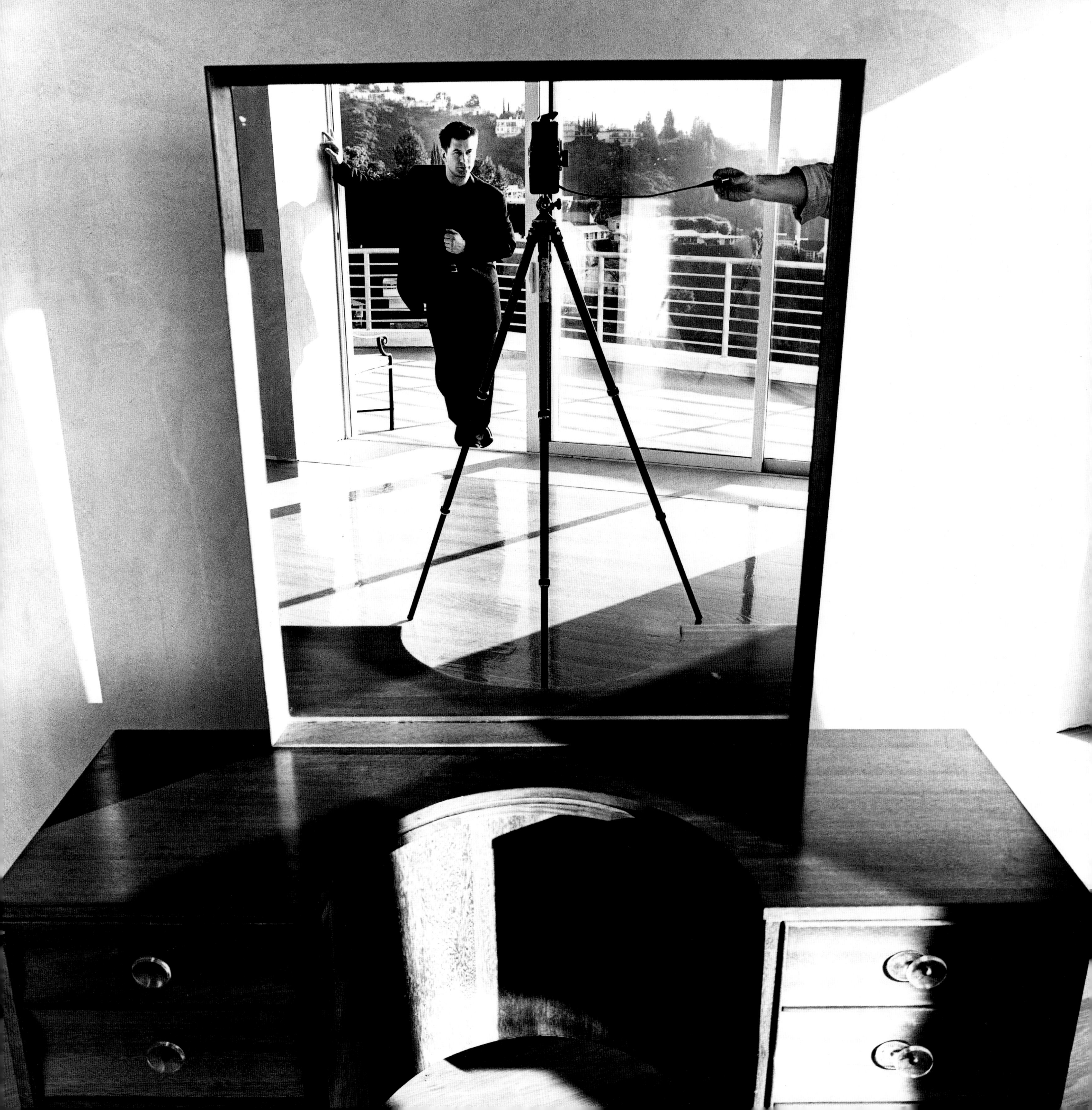

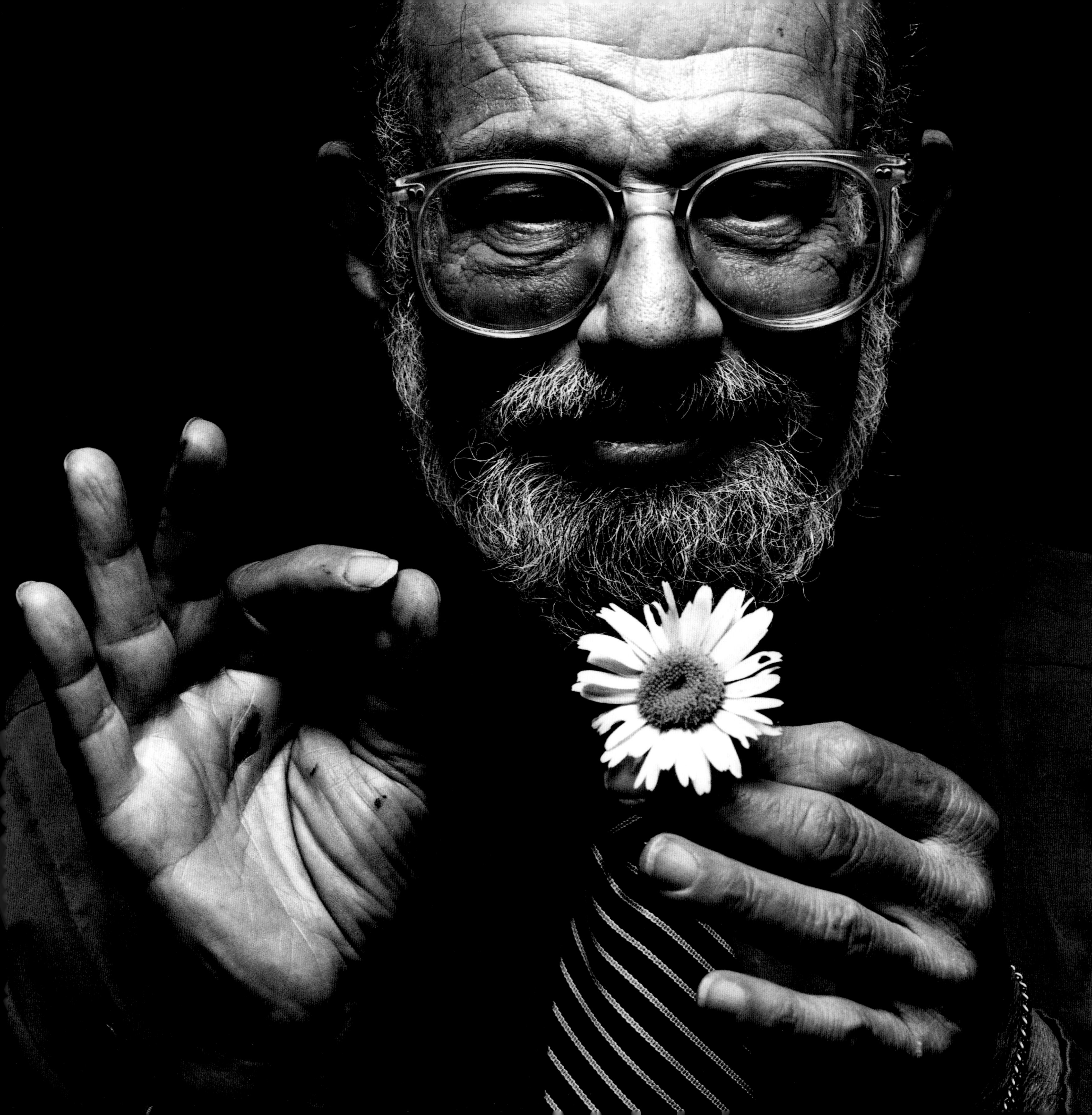

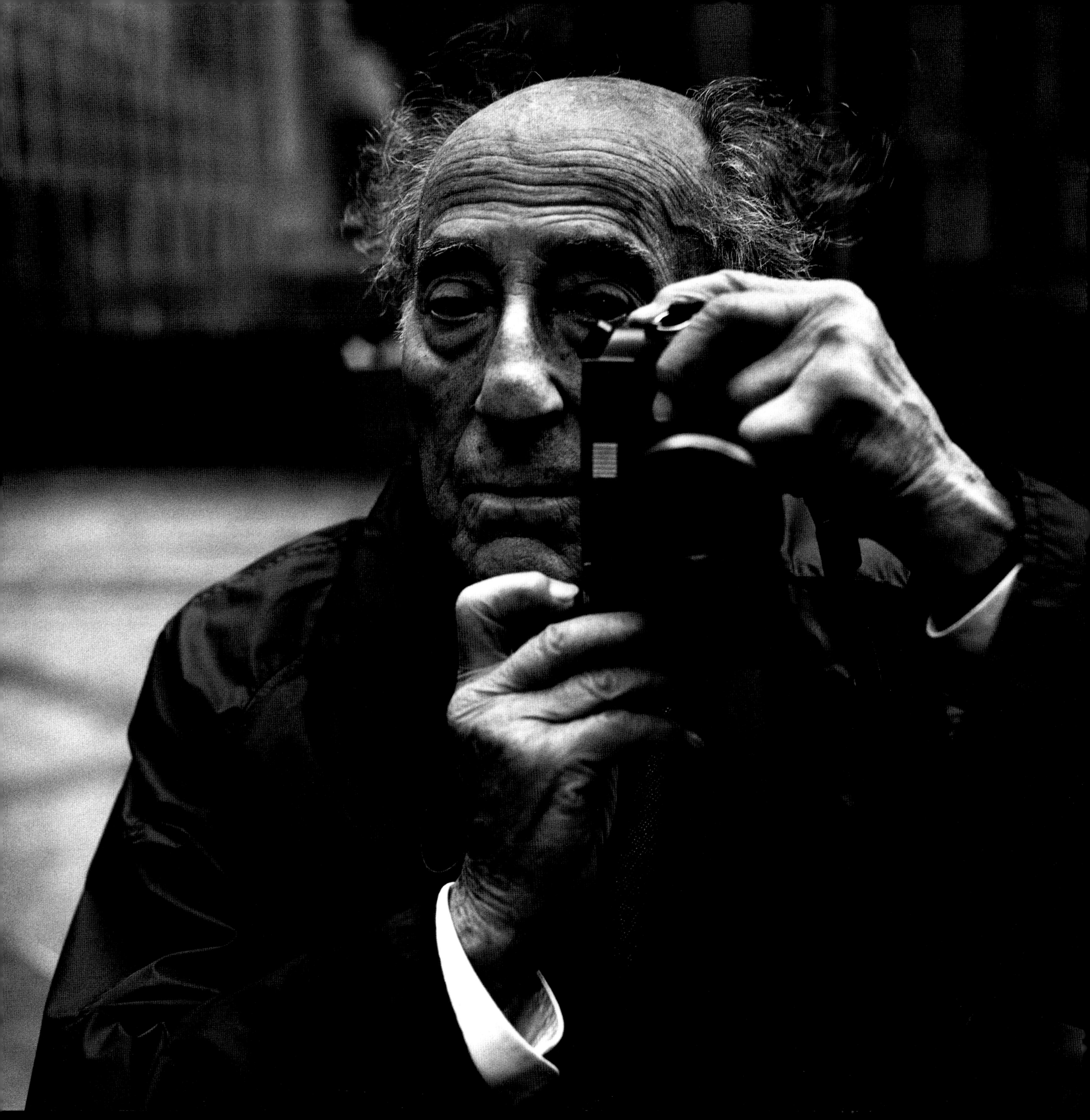

THEY'RE A
TRYING TO
ME.... LET'
LIKE THIS!

ALWAYS CENSOR DO IT

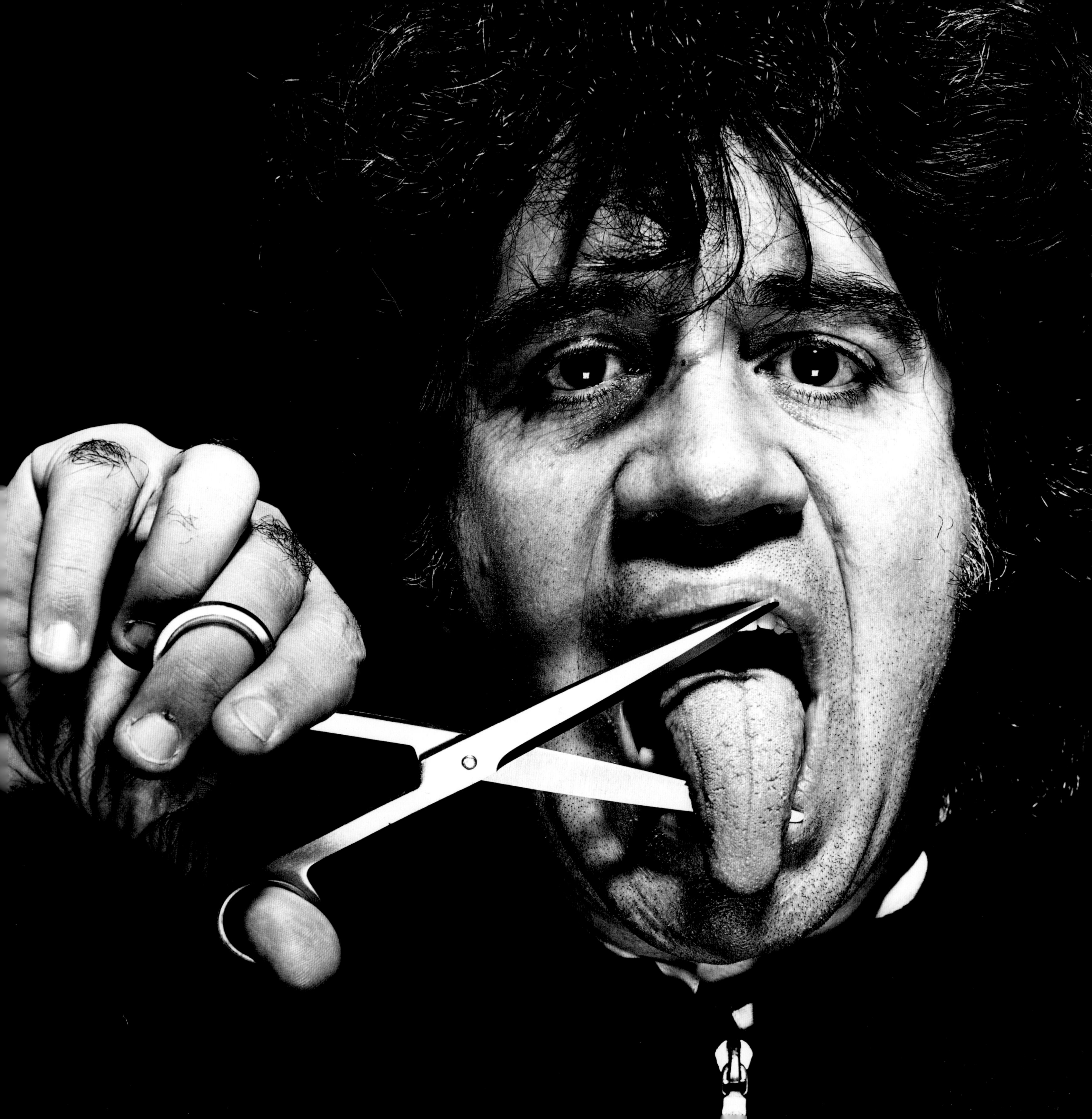

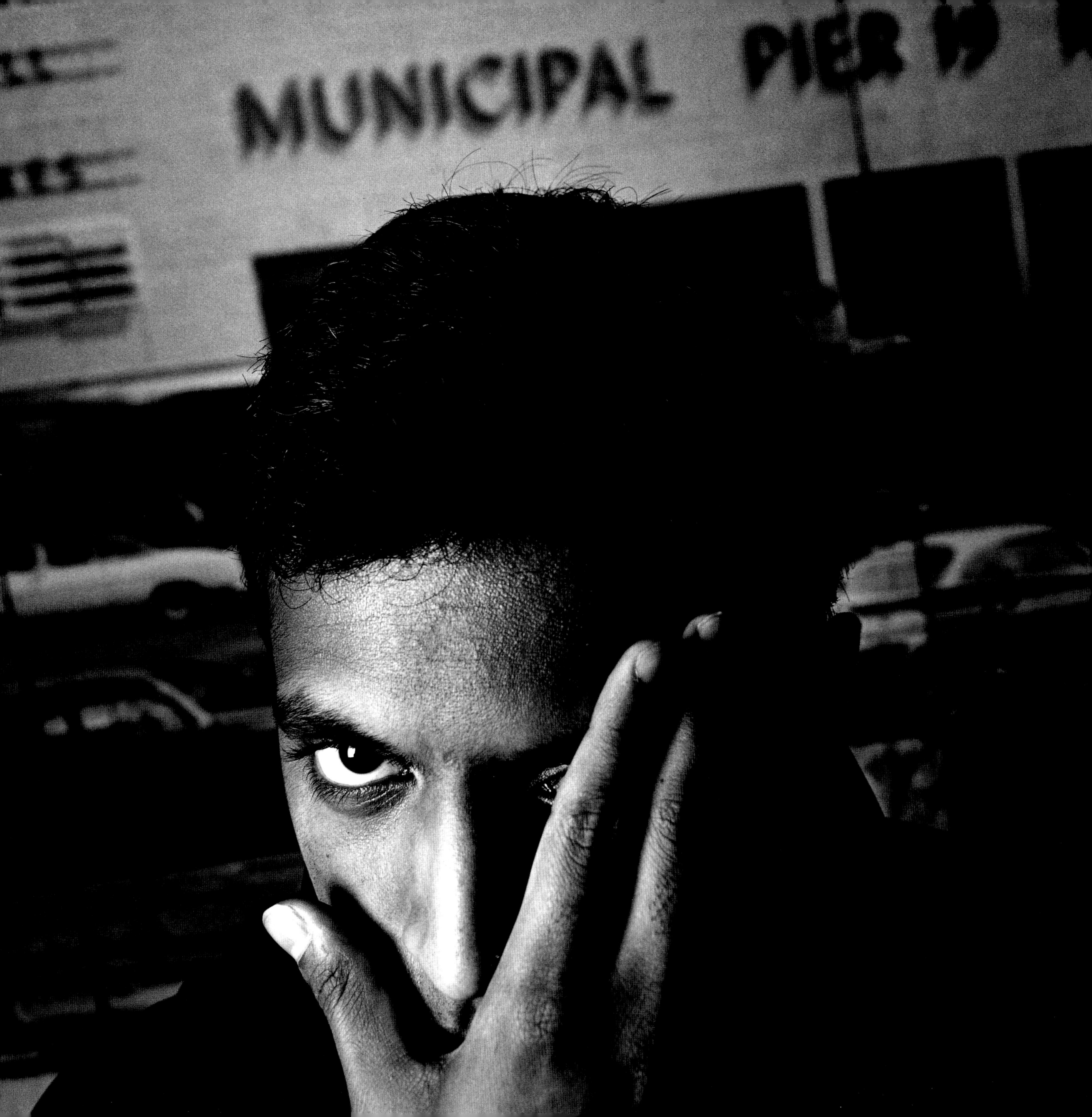

MUNICIPAL PIER 19

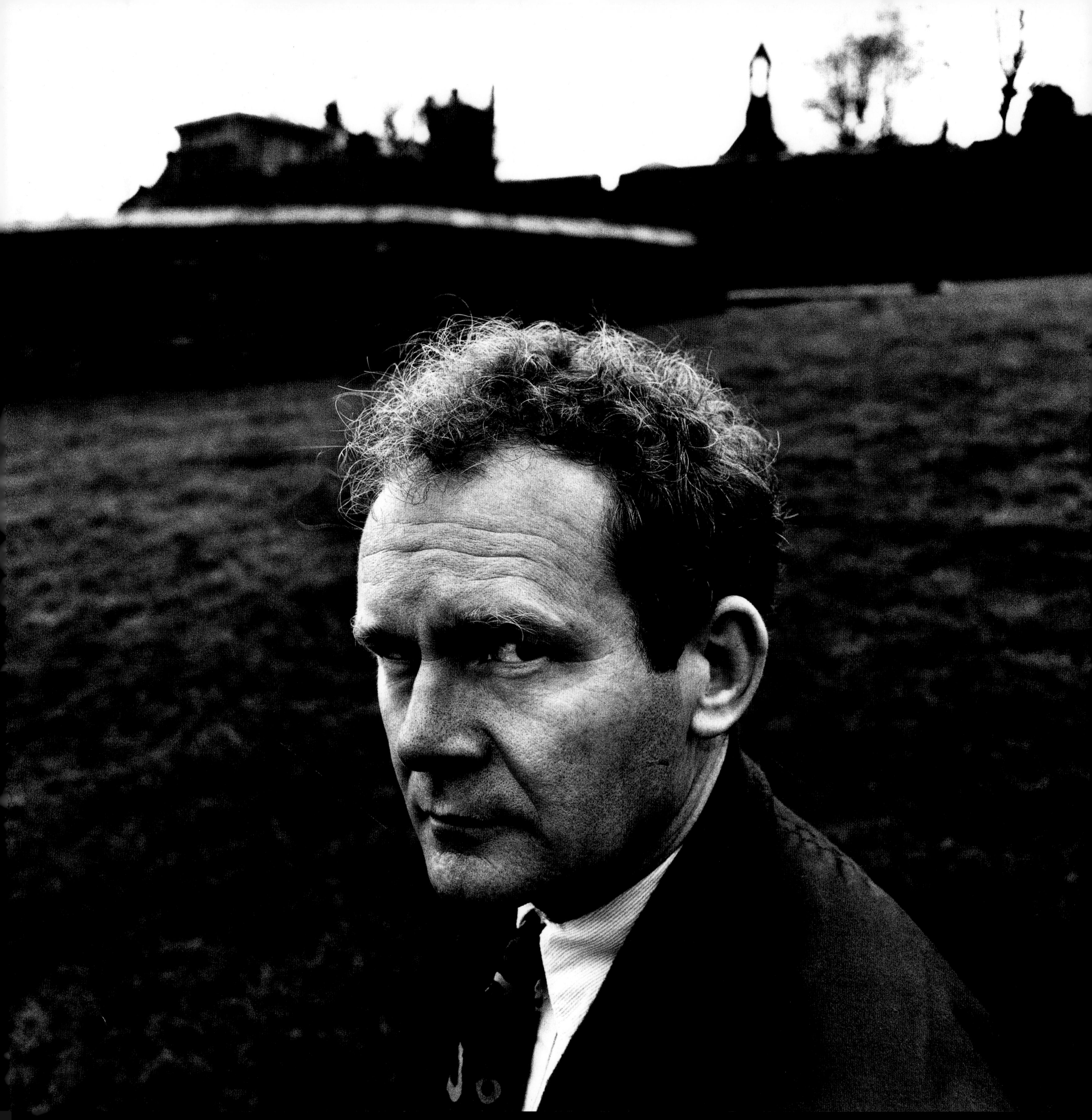

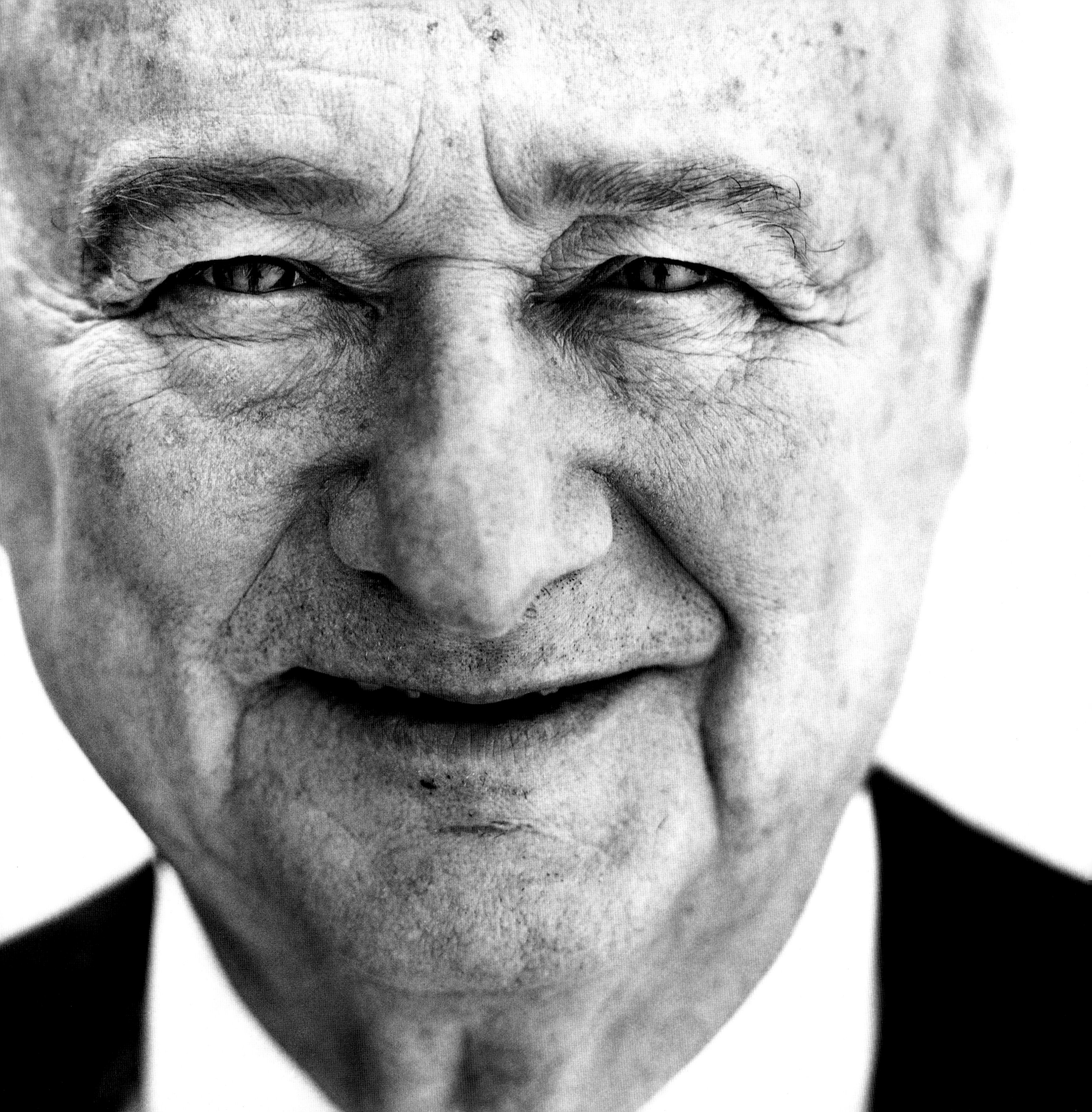

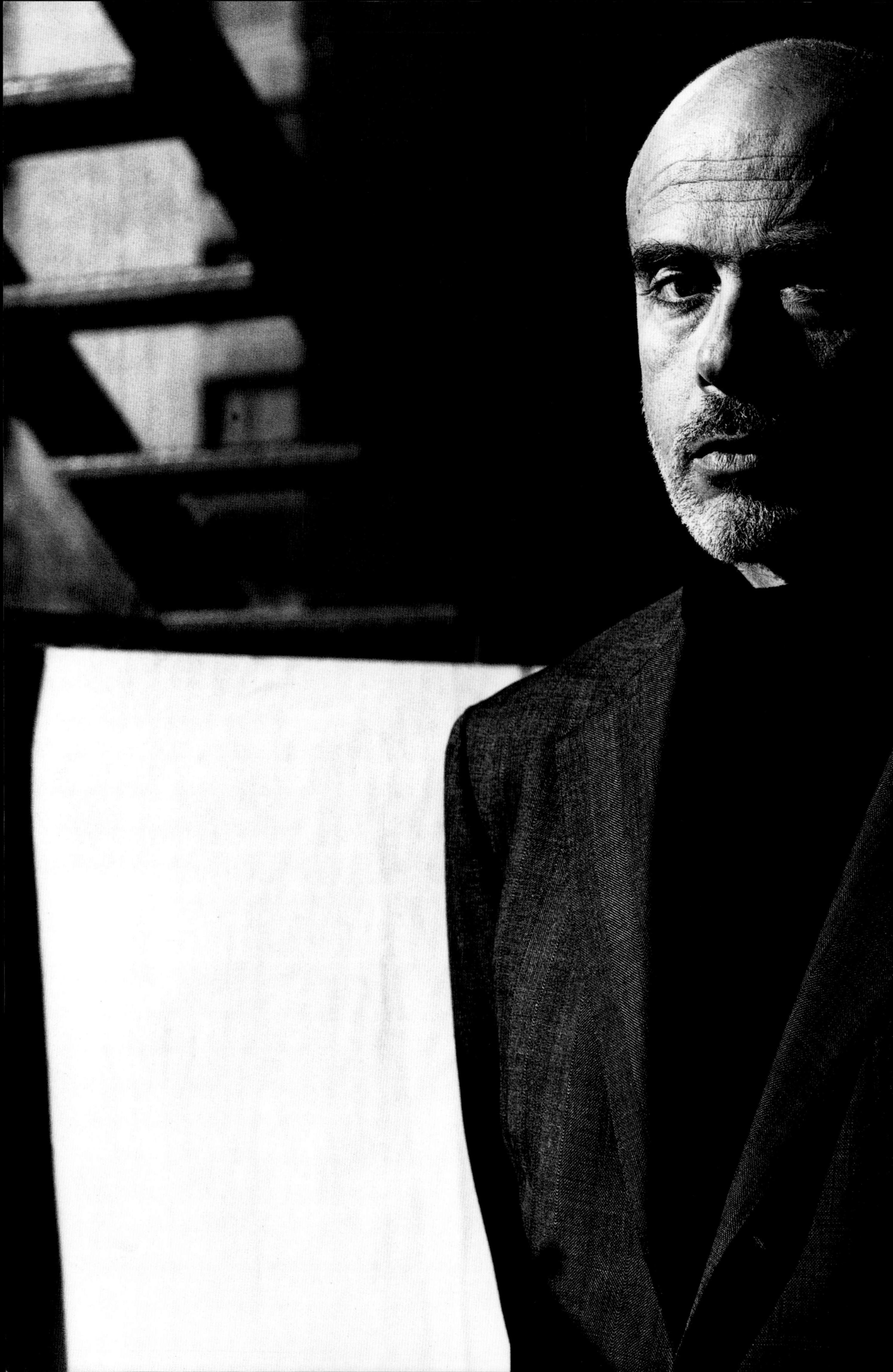

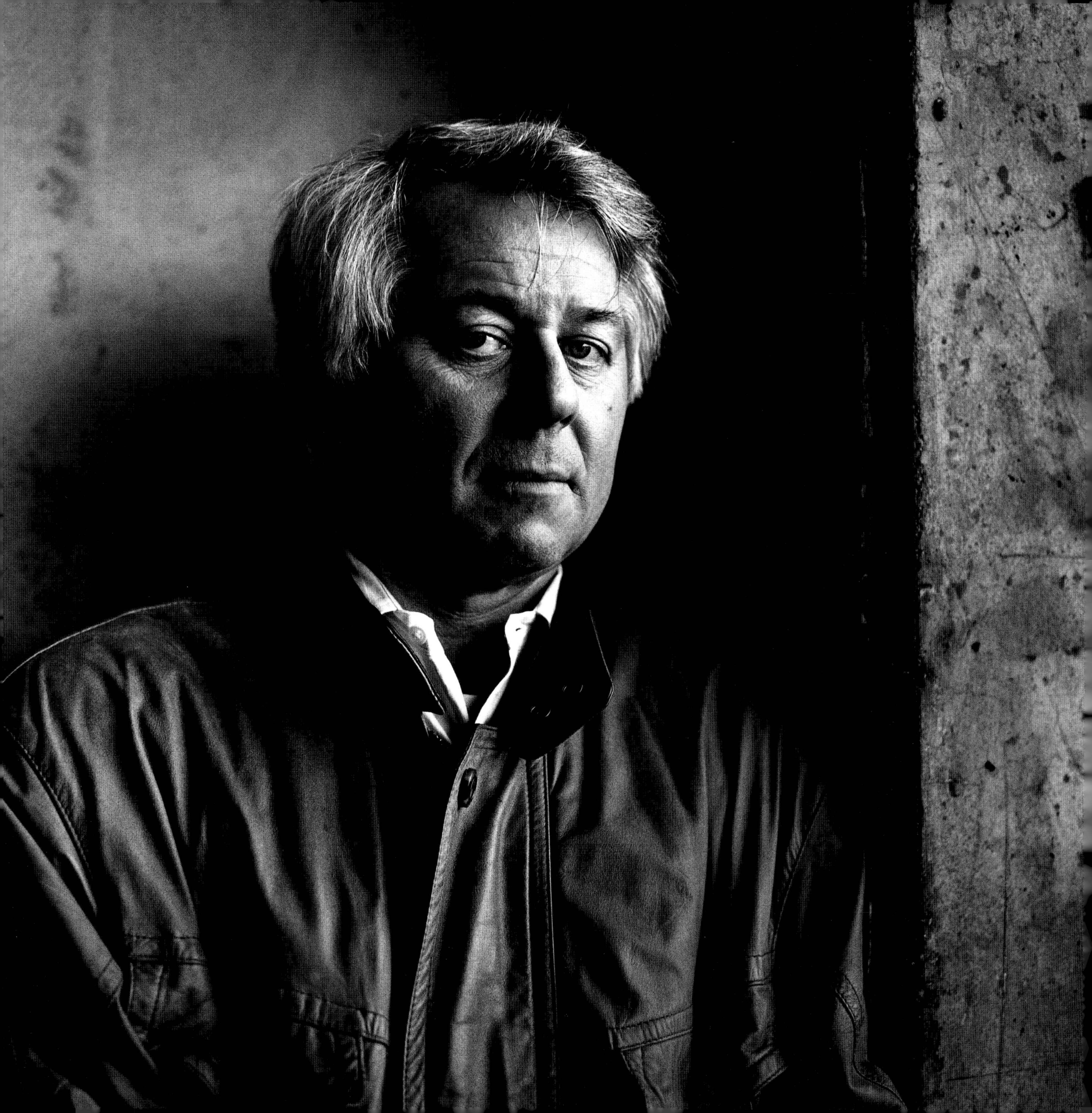

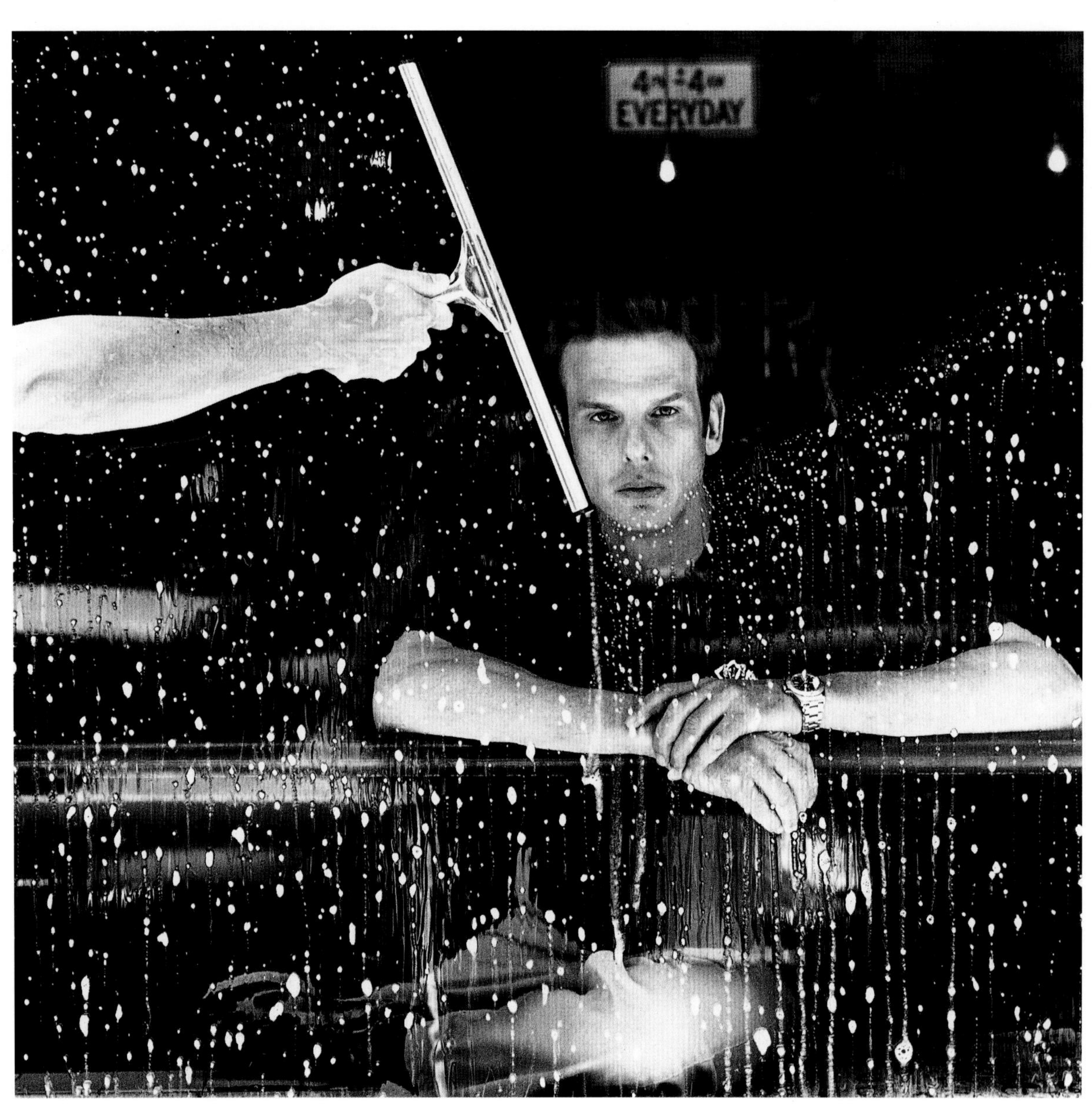

EVERYDAY

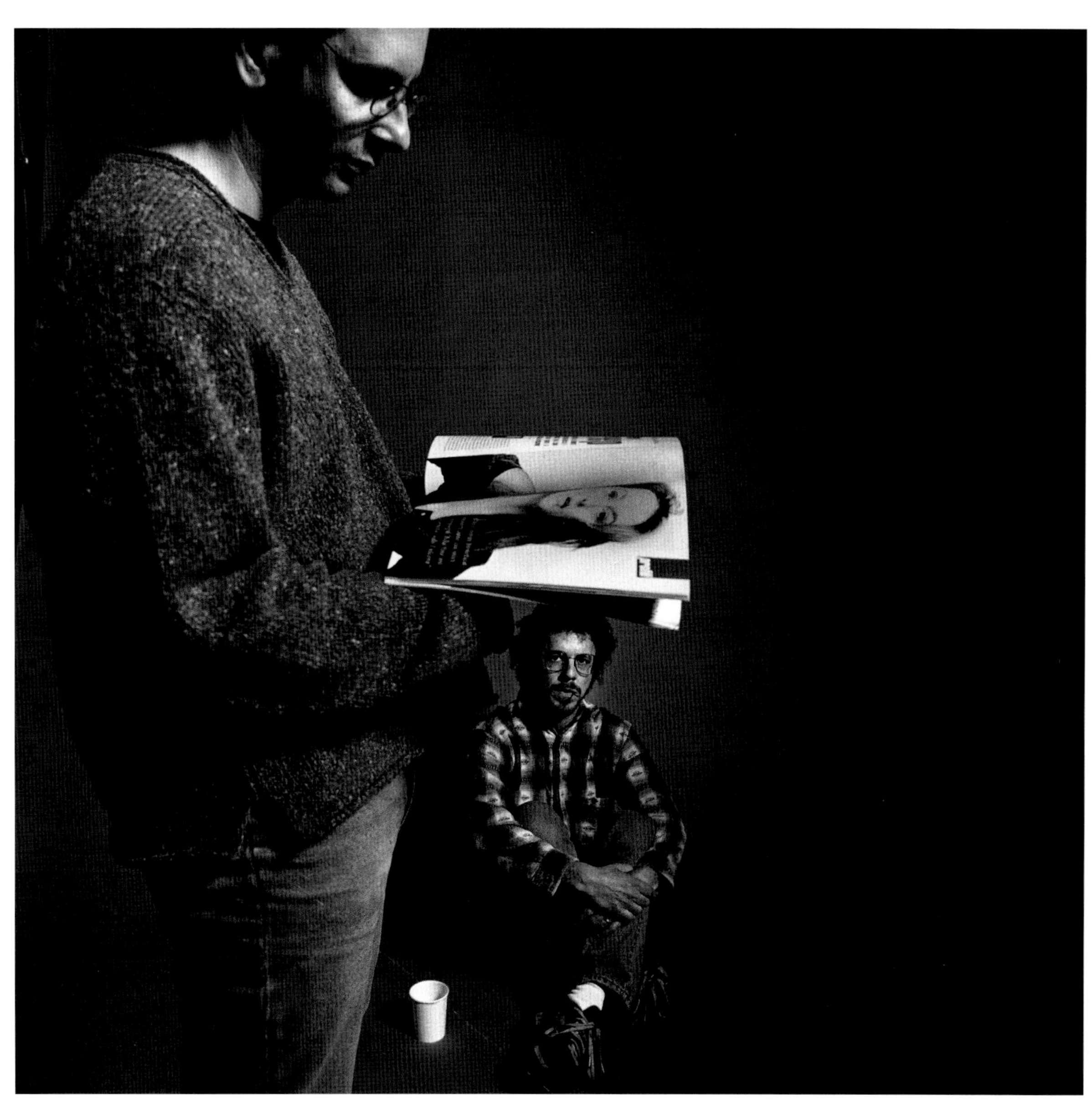

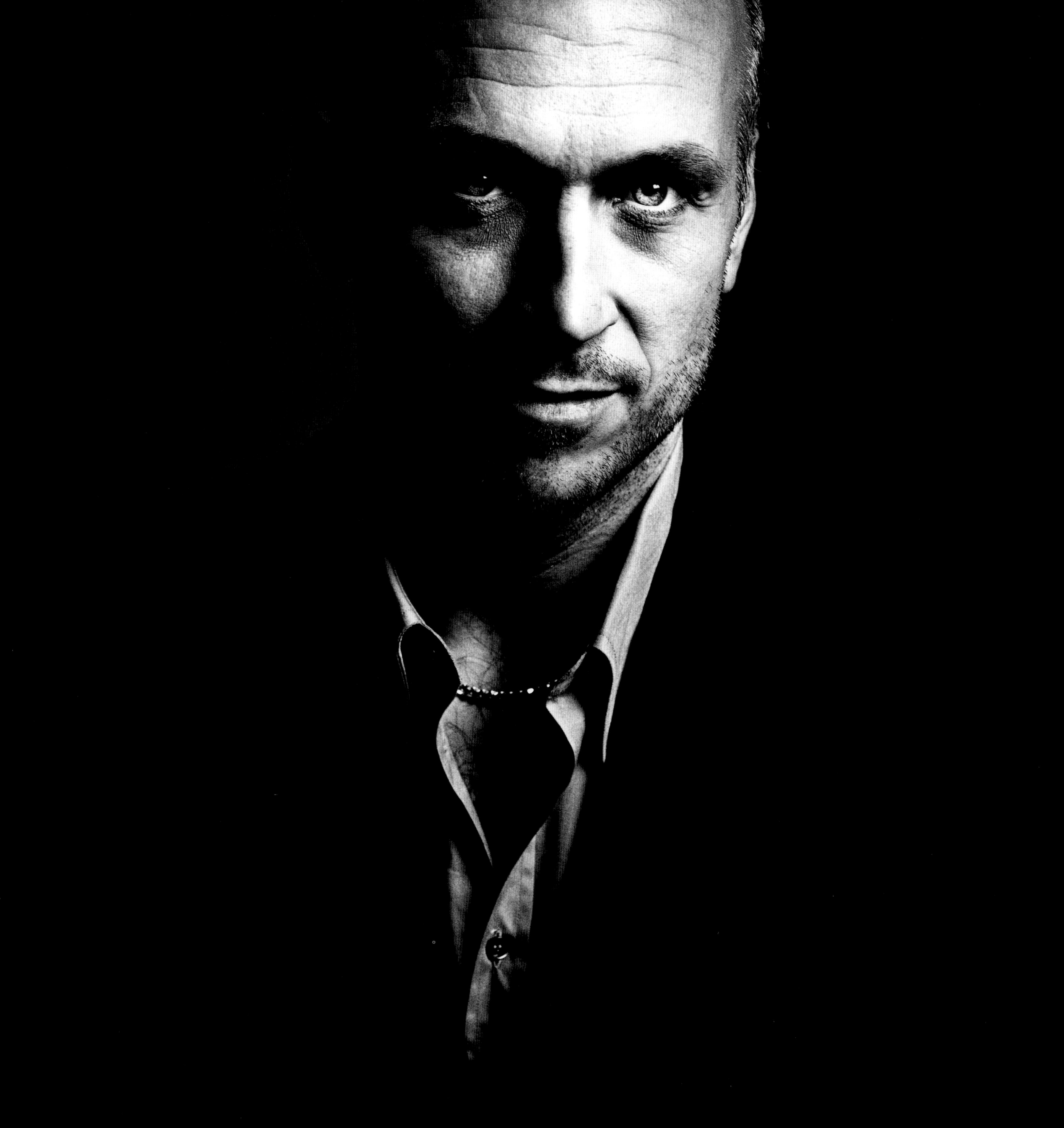

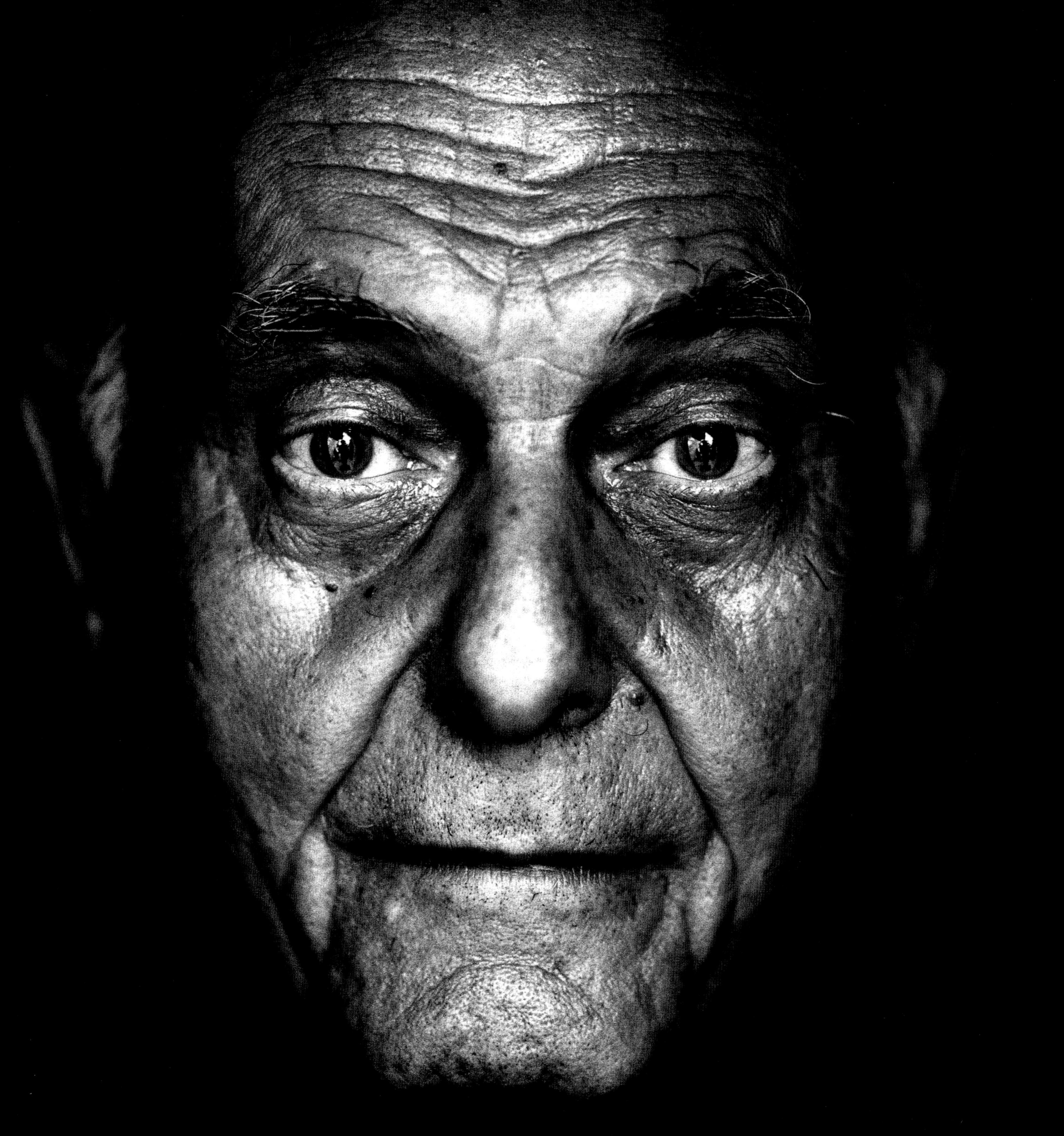

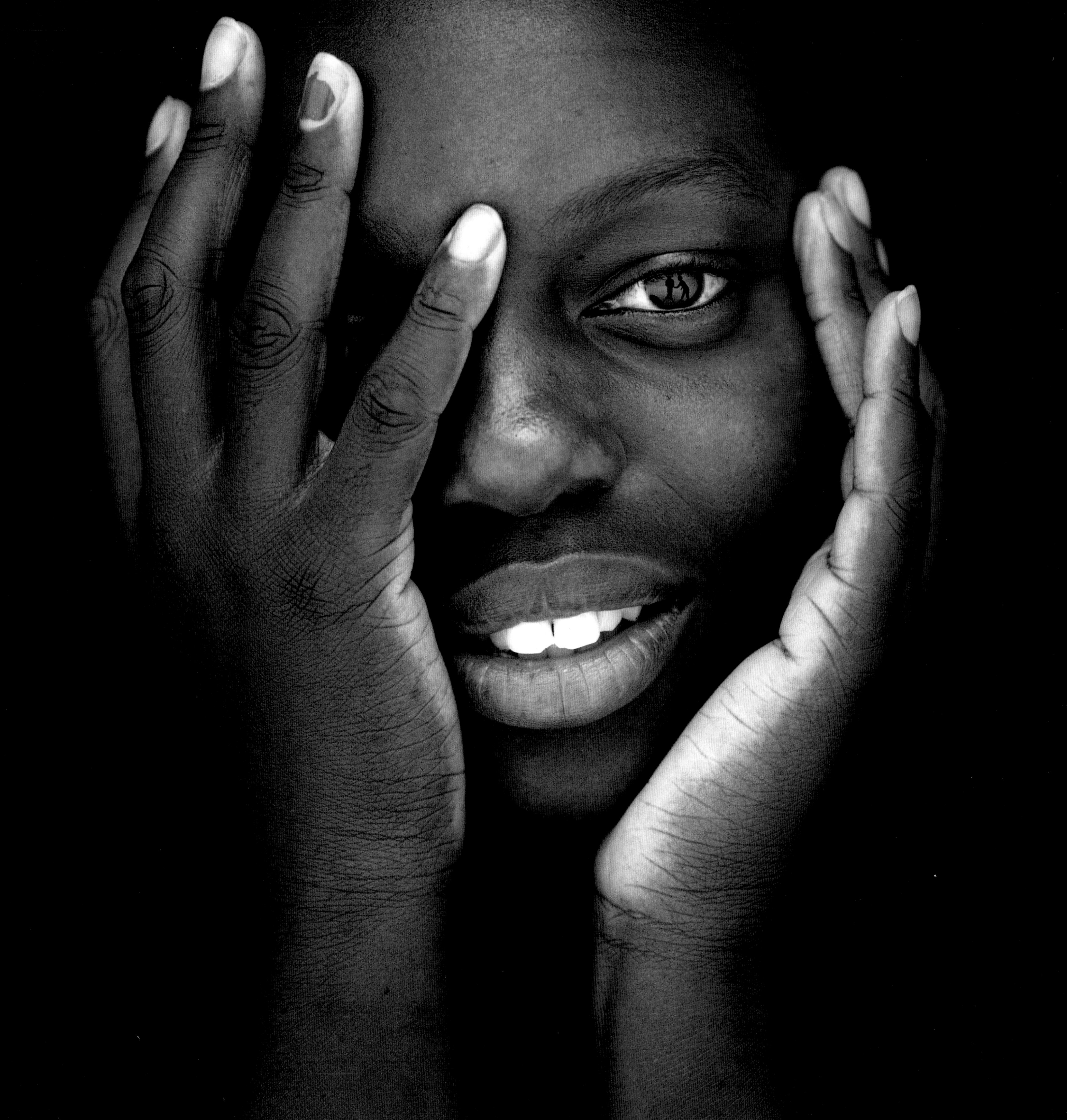

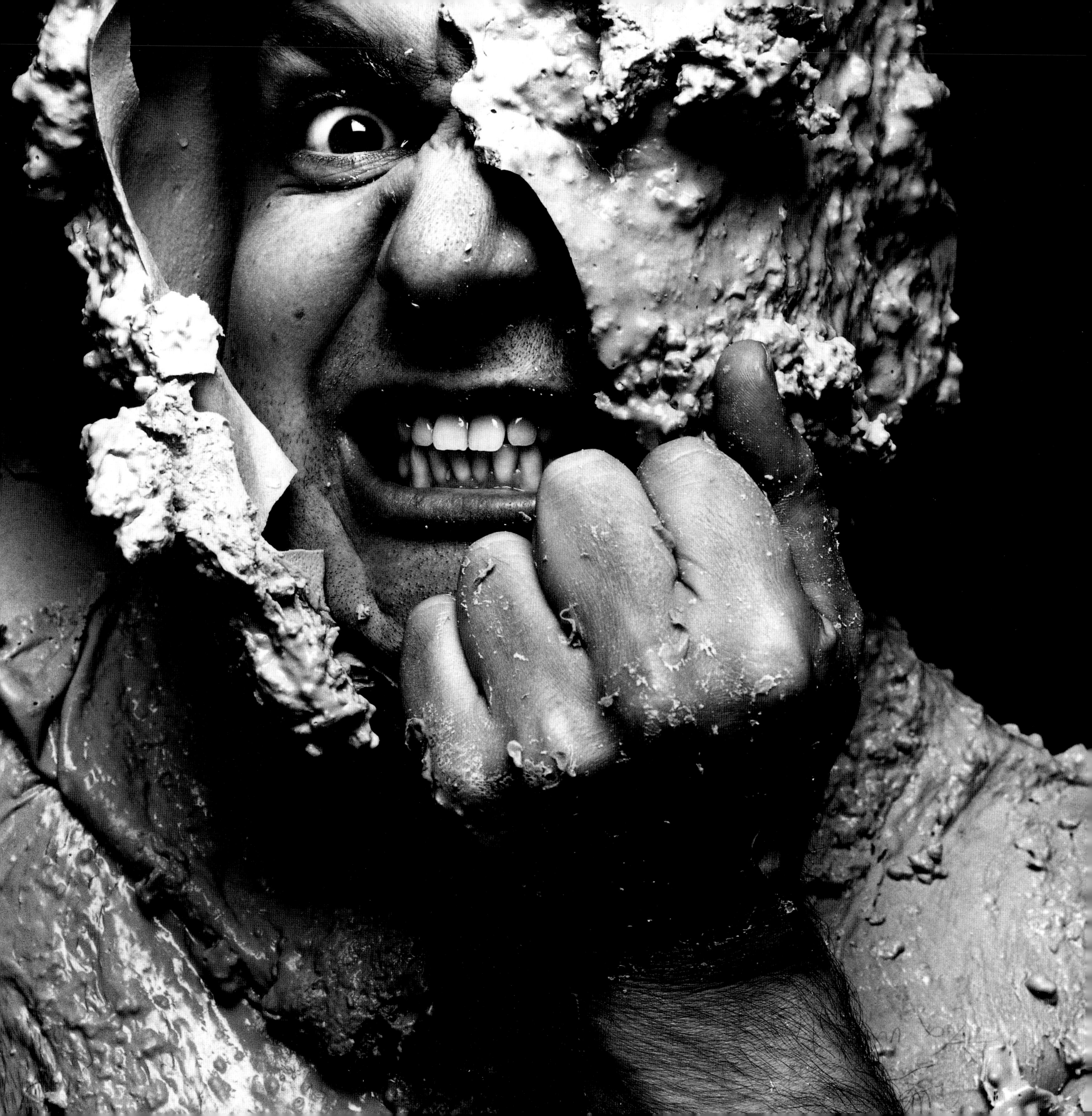

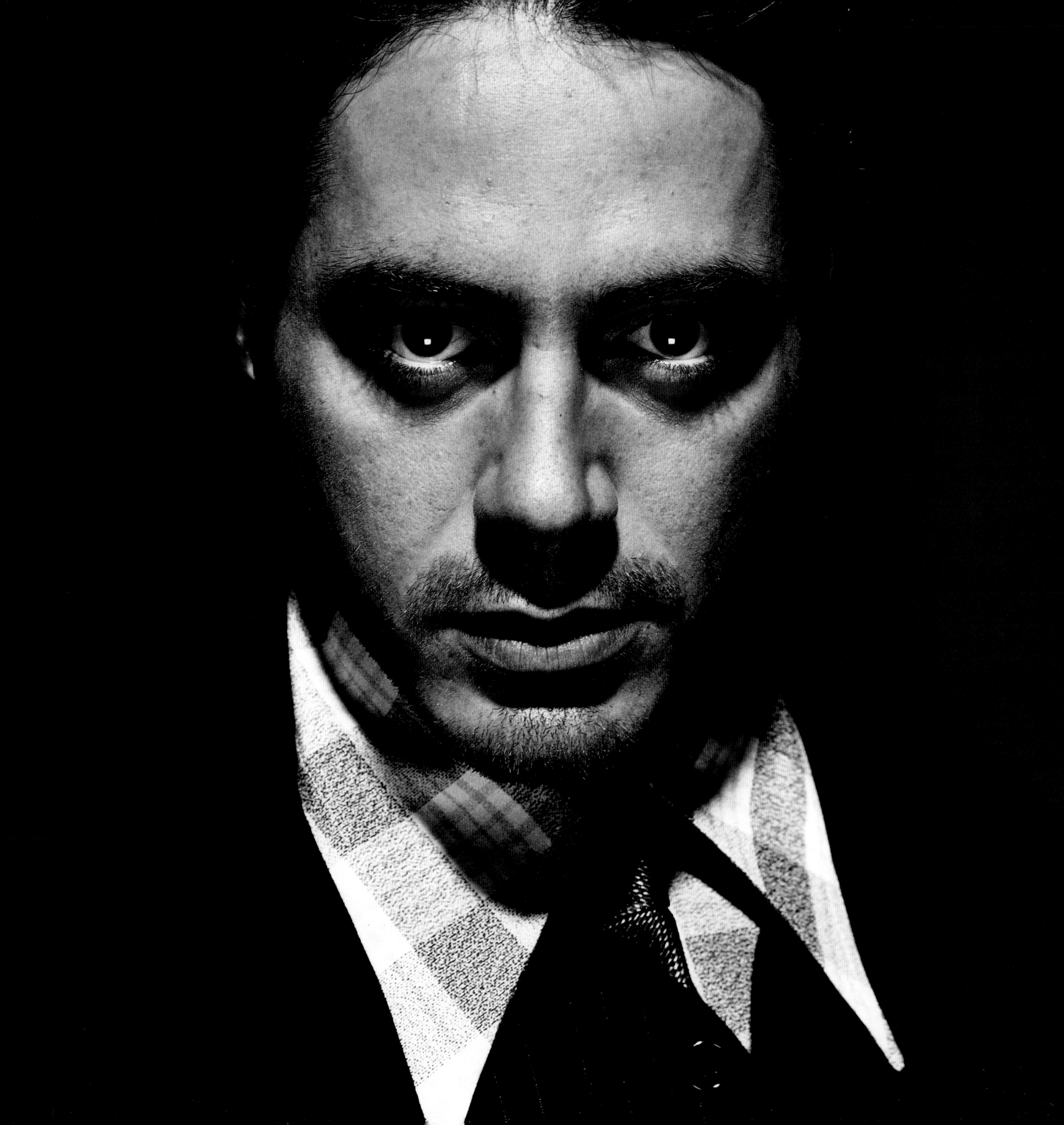

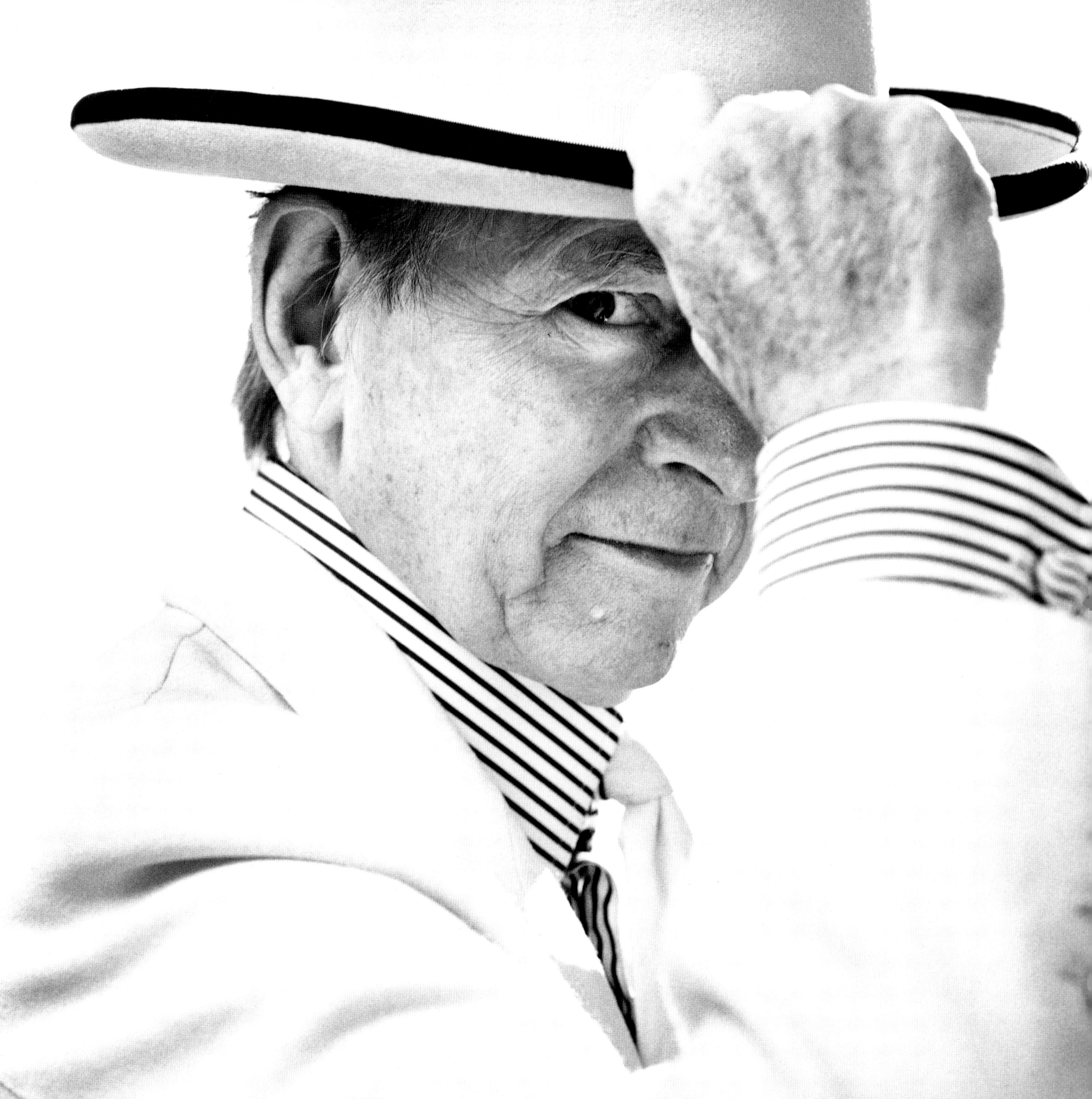

WHO IS WHO?

PHILIP JOHNSON

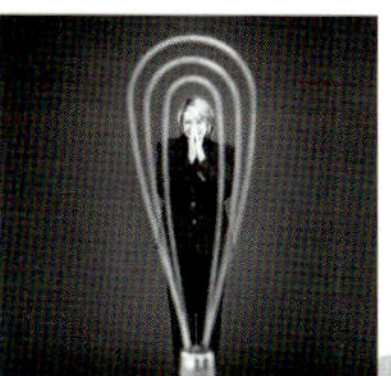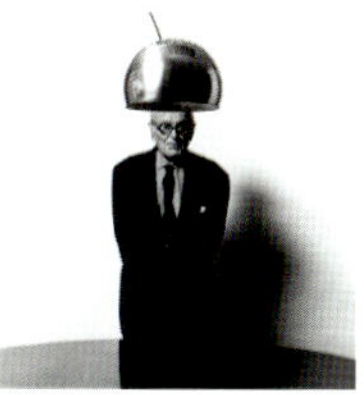

MARTHA STEWART
1998, INDUSTRIA
SUPERSTUDIO,
NEW YORK CITY

PHILIP JOHNSON
1996, THE LIPSTICK BUILDING,
NEW YORK CITY

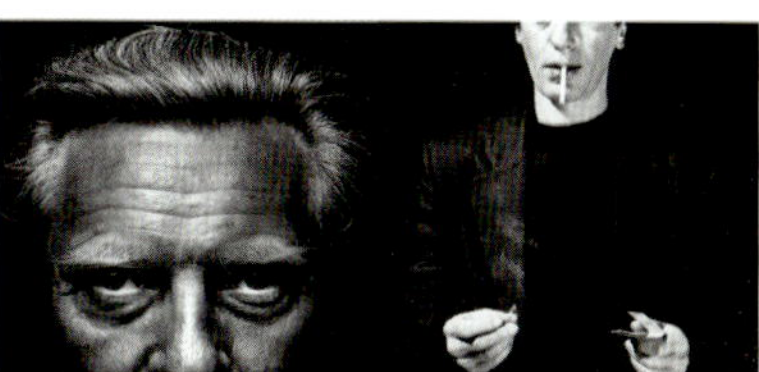

SIR MICHAEL HESELTINE
1989, SIR MICHAEL'S HOME,
LONDON

MARTIN AMIS
1995, INDUSTRIA
SUPERSTUDIO,
NEW YORK CITY

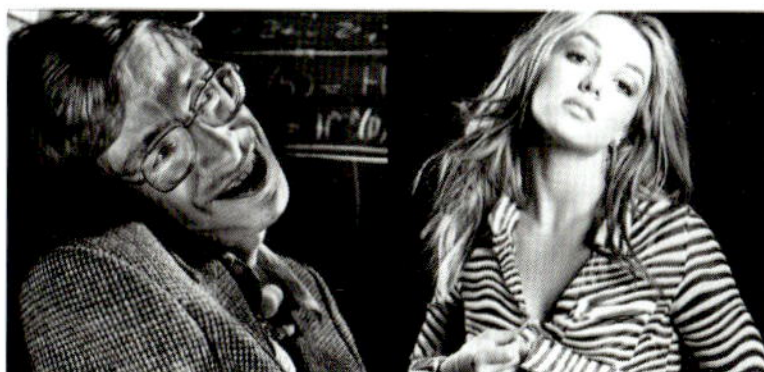

PROFESSOR
STEPHEN HAWKING
1991, CAMBRIDGE
UNIVERSITY, ENGLAND

BRITNEY SPEARS
2000, MALIBU,
CALIFORNIA

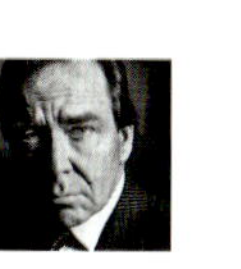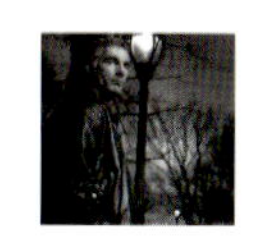

LORD SNOWDON
1992, SNOWDON'S STUDIO,
LONDON

JOHN SAYLES
1997, CENTRAL PARK,
NEW YORK CITY

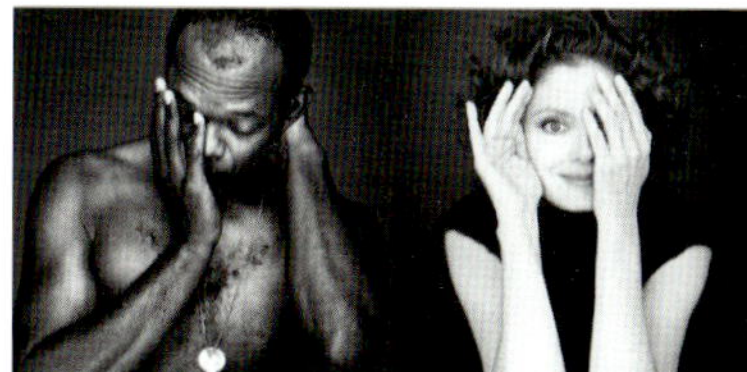

SAMUEL L JACKSON
1997, SMASHBOX STUDIOS,
LOS ANGELES

SUSAN SARANDON
1998, PIER 59 STUDIOS,
NEW YORK CITY

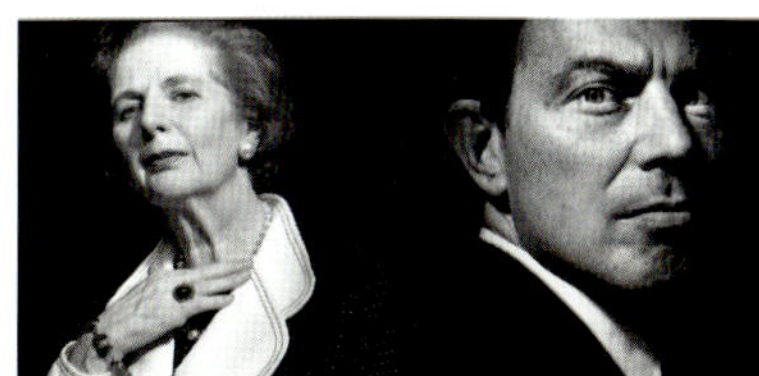

LADY MARGARET THATCHER
1993, LADY THATCHER'S
OFFICE, LONDON

TONY BLAIR
1994, THE HOUSE OF
COMMONS, LONDON

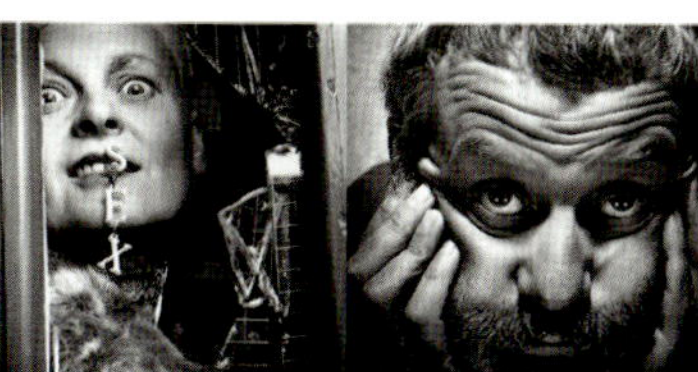

VIVIENNE WESTWOOD
1992, THE LANTERNS,
LONDON

MIKE LEIGH
1993, WEST LONDON,
ENGLAND

JOHN CUSACK

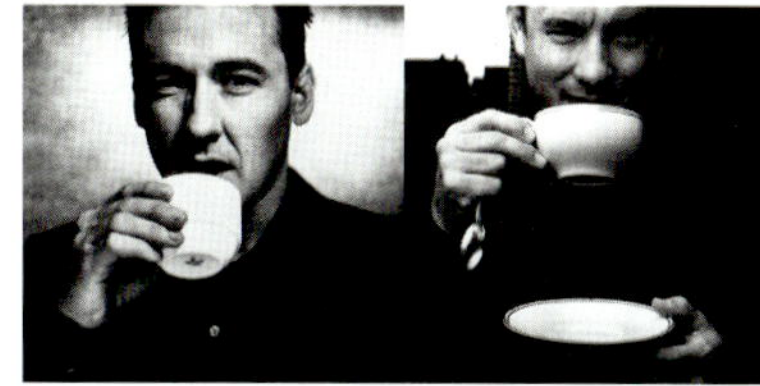

JOHN CUSACK
1997, SHERATON MIRAGE,
PORT DOUGLAS,
QUEENSLAND, AUSTRALIA

TOM HANKS
1996, HOTEL PLAZA ATHENEE,
NEW YORK CITY

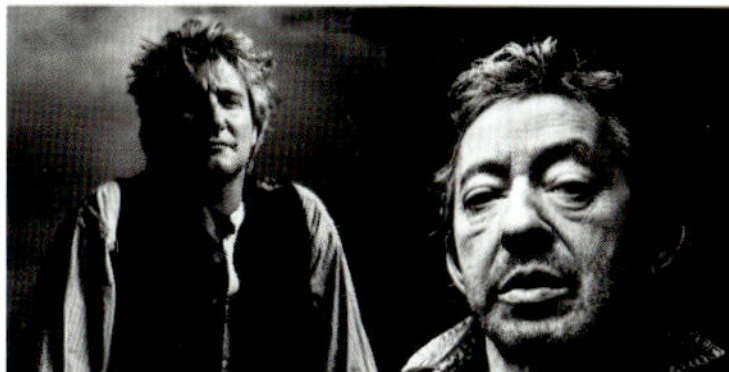

ROD STEWART
1995, ROD'S HOME,
BEVERLY HILLS,
CALIFORNIA

SERGE GAINSBOURG
1989, SERGE'S HOME,
PARIS

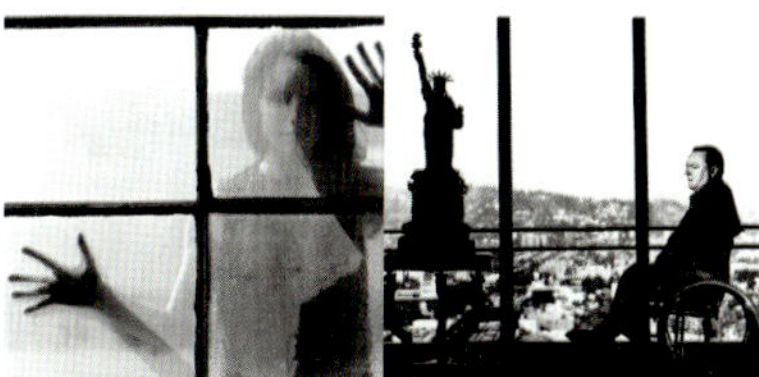

MADELEINE STOWE
1999, SMASHBOX STUDIOS,
LOS ANGELES

LARRY FLYNT
1997, LARRY'S OFFICE,
LOS ANGELES

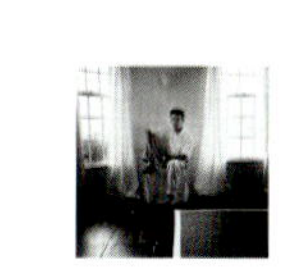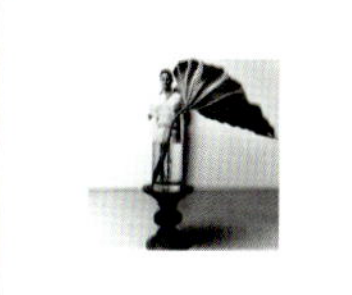

CALVIN KLEIN
1995, CALVIN'S HOME,
EAST HAMPTON,
NEW YORK

IAN SHRAGER
1999, IAN'S OFFICE,
NEW YORK CITY

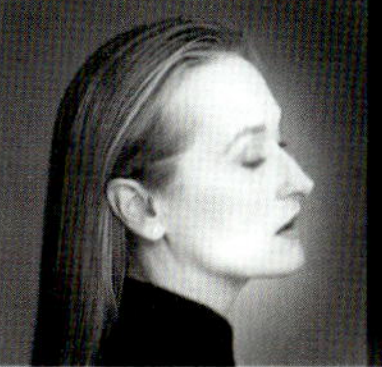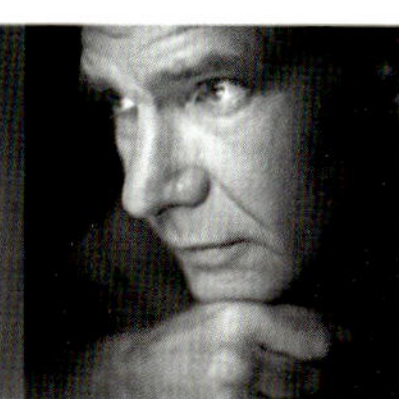

MERYL STREEP
1994, INDUSTRIA
SUPERSTUDIO,
NEW YORK CITY

HARRISON FORD
1998, INDUSTRIA
SUPERSTUDIO,
NEW YORK CITY

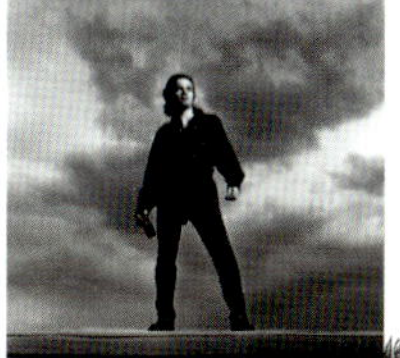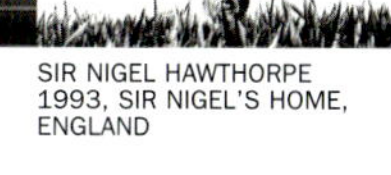

EWAN MCGREGOR
1997, INDUSTRIA
SUPERSTUDIO,
NEW YORK CITY

SIR NIGEL HAWTHORPE
1993, SIR NIGEL'S HOME,
ENGLAND

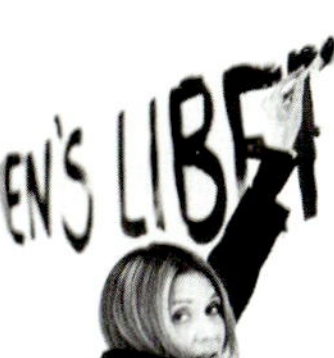

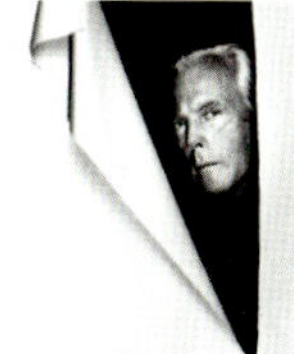

GLORIA STEINEM
1998, INDUSTRIA
SUPERSTUDIO,
NEW YORK CITY

GIORGIO ARMANI
1994, INDUSTRIA
SUPERSTUDIO,
MILAN, ITALY

PRESS OFFICER
AT THE WHITE HOUSE

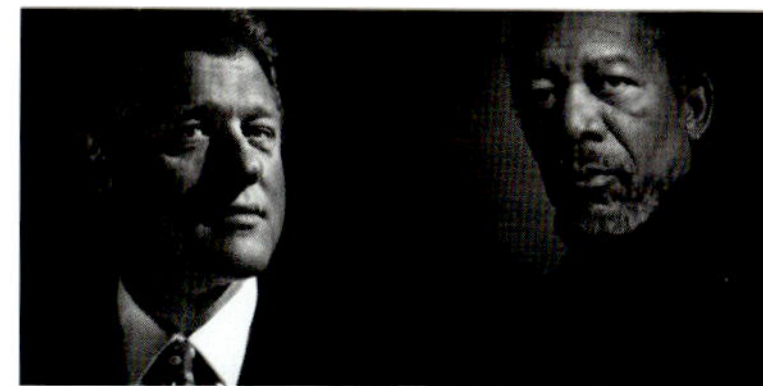

PRESIDENT BILL CLINTON
1996, THE OVAL OFFICE,
THE WHITE HOUSE,
WASHINGTON, D.C.

MORGAN FREEMAN
1997, INDUSTRIA
SUPERSTUDIO,
NEW YORK CITY

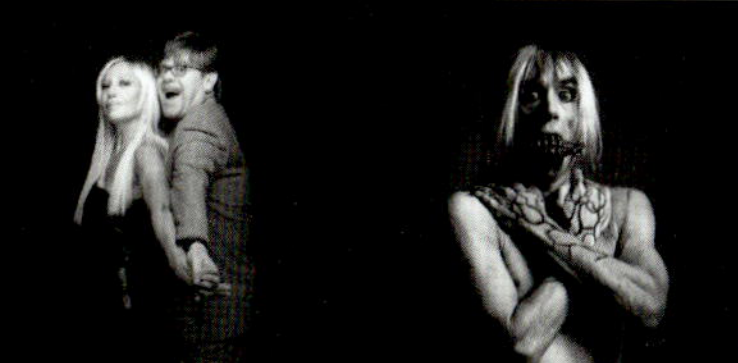

ELTON JOHN AND
DONATELLA VERSACE
1997, VERSACE MANSION,
NEW YORK CITY

IGGY POP
1996, INDUSTRIA
SUPERSTUDIO,
NEW YORK CITY

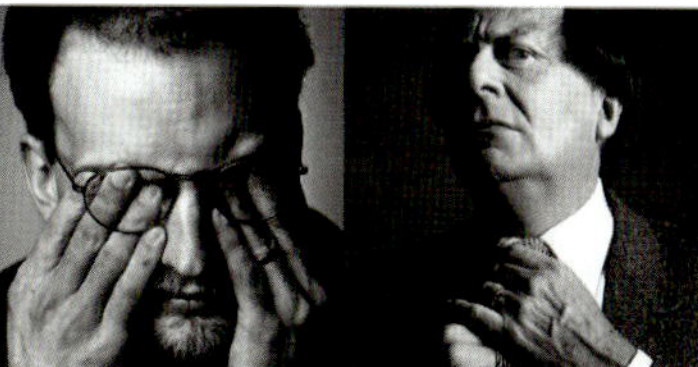

STEVEN SODERBERGH
1991, PINEWOOD STUDIOS,
LONDON

BARRY HUMPHRIES
1995, SOUTHERN LIGHT
STUDIOS, LONDON

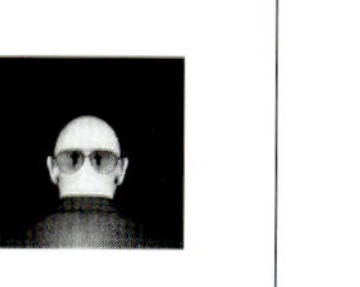

JERRY DELLA FEMINA
1998, INDUSTRIA
SUPERSTUDIO,
NEW YORK CITY

THE CAST OF *THE ICE STORM*
1997, INDUSTRIA
SUPERSTUDIO,
NEW YORK CITY

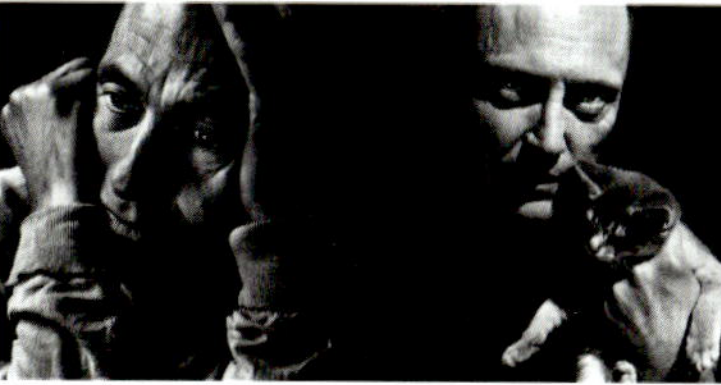

FRANK AUERBACH
1991, HOLBORN STUDIOS,
LONDON

CHRISTOPHER WALKEN
1995, CHRISTOPHER'S HOME,
NEW YORK CITY

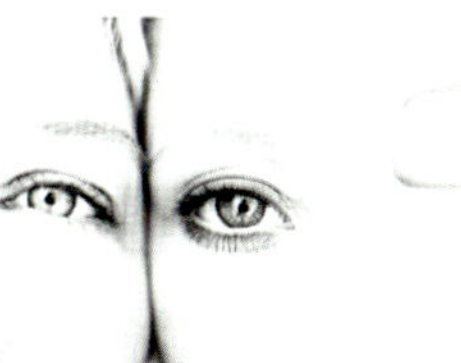

ANNE HECHE AND
ELLEN DEGENERES
1998, INDUSTRIA SUPER-
STUDIO, NEW YORK CITY

DENNIS QUAID
1999, SMASHBOX STUDIOS,
LOS ANGELES

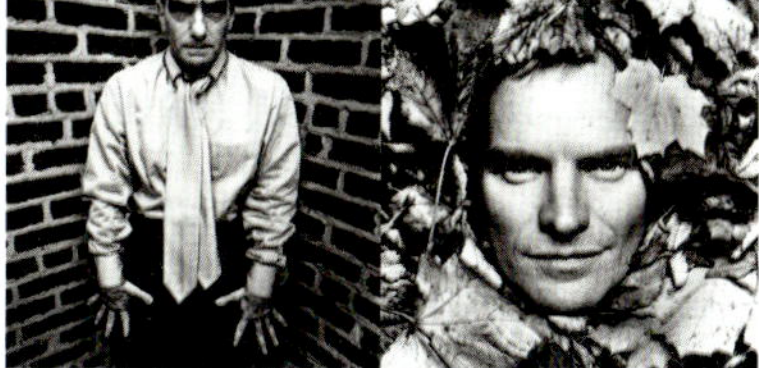

MARTIN SCORSESE
1995, NEW YORK CITY

STING
1994, STING'S HOME,
WILTSHIRE, ENGLAND

PETER GREENAWAY

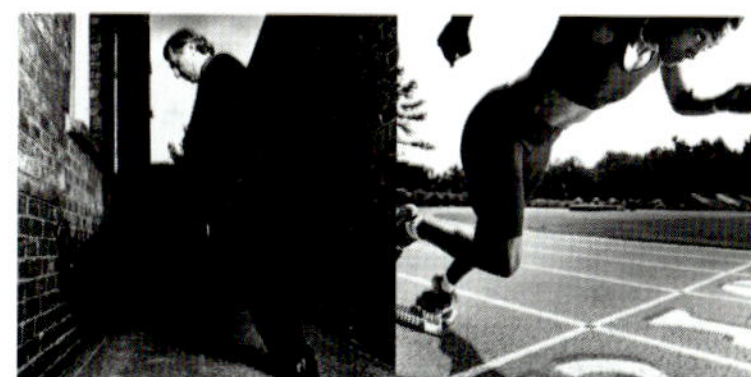

PETER GREENAWAY
1992, WEST LONDON,
ENGLAND

MARION JONES
1998, NORTH CAROLINA

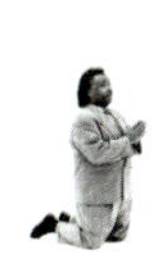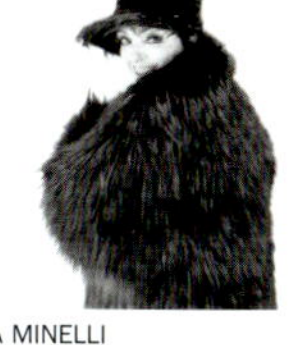

REVEREND AL SHARPTON
1998, INDUSTRIA
SUPERSTUDIO,
NEW YORK CITY

LIZA MINELLI
1998, INDUSTRIA
SUPERSTUDIO,
NEW YORK CITY

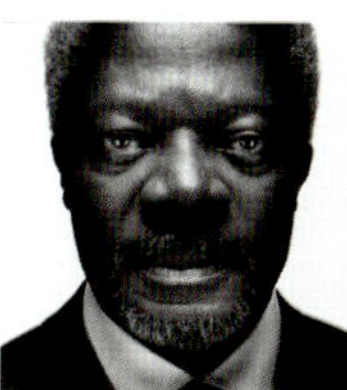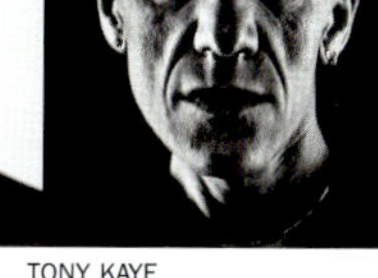

KOFI ANNAN
1998, UNITED NATIONS HQ,
NEW YORK CITY

TONY KAYE
1998, CHATEAU MARMONT,
LOS ANGELES

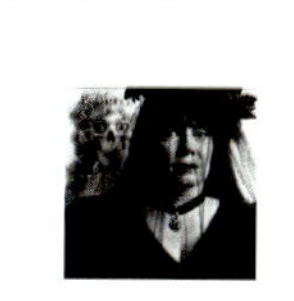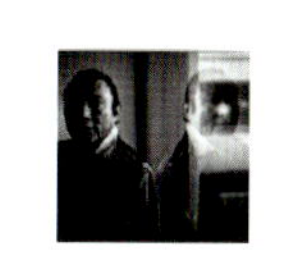

ANNE RICE
1995, ANNE'S HOME,
NEW ORLEANS,
LOUISIANA

GENERAL MANUEL NORIEGA
1995, JAIL,
FLORIDA

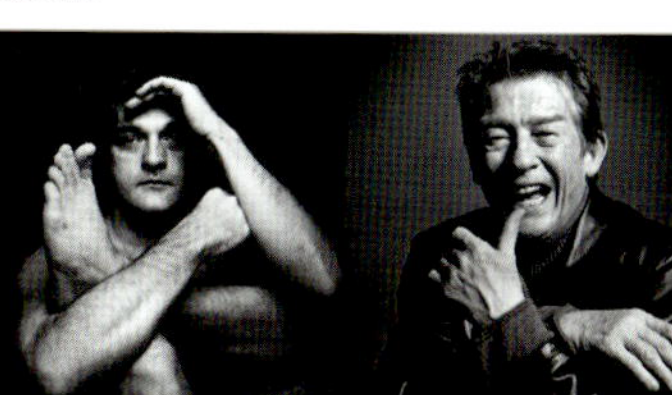

MARK MORRIS
1995, MARK'S HOME,
NEW YORK CITY

JOHN HURT
1999, SMASHBOX STUDIOS,
LOS ANGELES

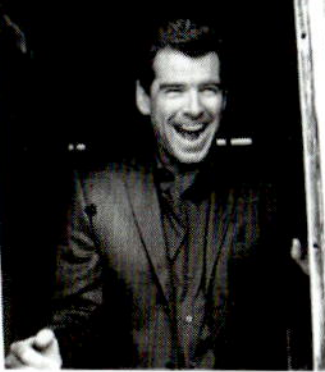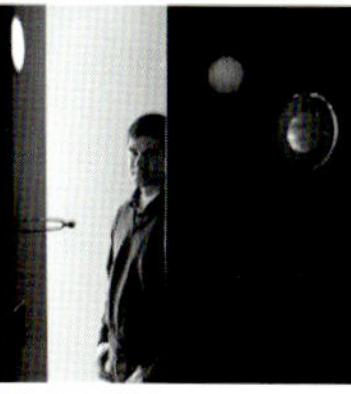

PIERCE BROSNAN
1999, CHALK FARM STUDIOS,
LONDON

GUS VAN SANT
1997, THE ROYALTON HOTEL,
NEW YORK CITY

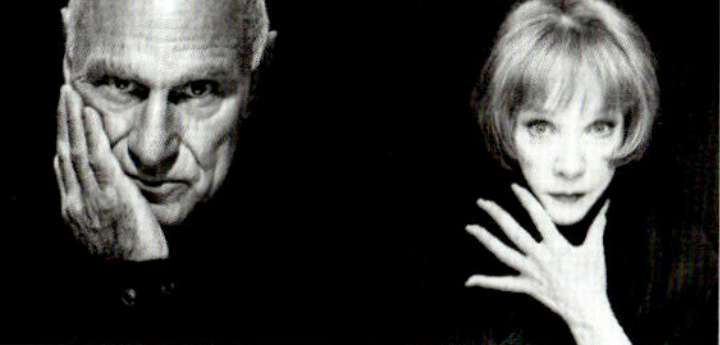

RICHARD SERRA
1998, RICHARD'S STUDIO,
NEW YORK CITY

SHIRLEY MACLAINE
1993, SMASHBOX STUDIOS,
LOS ANGELES

ASIA ARGENTO

ALEXANDER MCQUEEN

VINNIE JONES

TOMMY LEE JONES

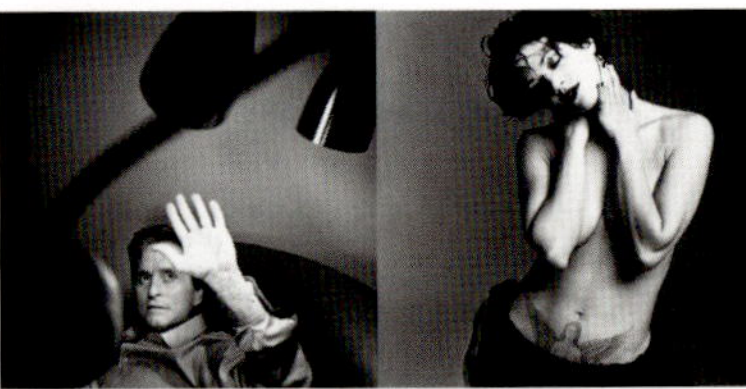

MICHAEL DOUGLAS
2000, 5TH AND SUNSET
STUDIOS, LOS ANGELES

ASIA ARGENTO
1997, ROME, ITALY

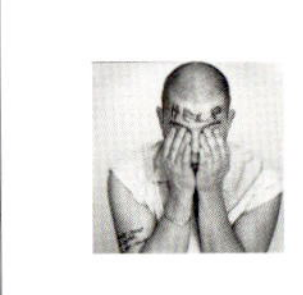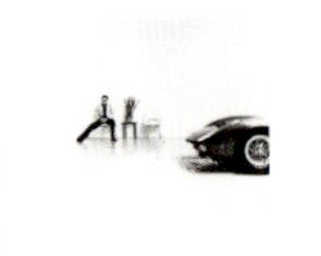

ALEXANDER MCQUEEN
1999, INDUSTRIA
SUPERSTUDIO,
NEW YORK CITY

NICOLAS CAGE
1997, SMASHBOX STUDIOS,
LOS ANGELES

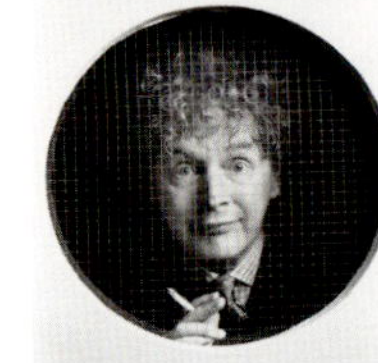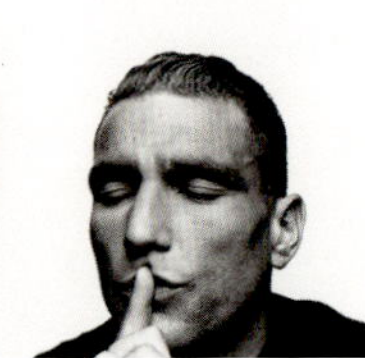

MALCOLM MCLAREN
1991, KENSINGTON PLACE,
LONDON

VINNIE JONES
1991, THE WORX STUDIOS,
LONDON

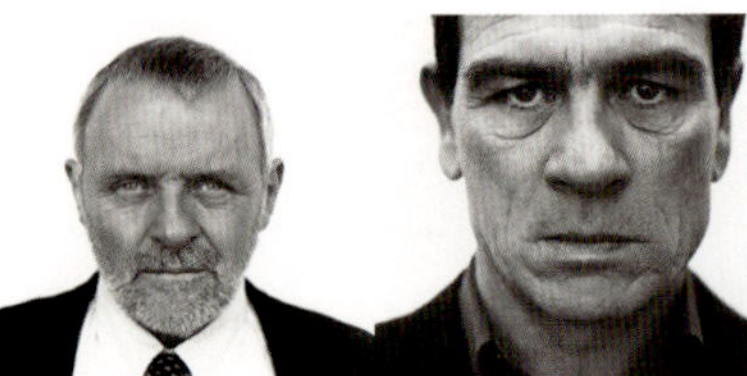

SIR ANTHONY HOPKINS
1993, PHOTO PRODUCTIONS,
NEW YORK CITY

TOMMY LEE JONES
1997, SMASHBOX STUDIOS,
LOS ANGELES

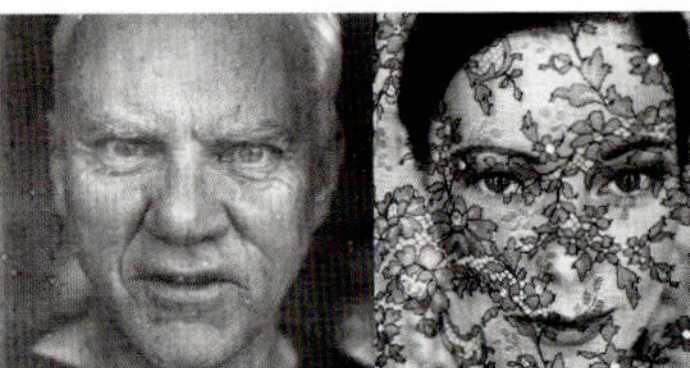

MALCOLM MCDOWELL
2000, MALCOLM'S HOME,
OJAI, CALIFORNIA

RUTHIE HENSHALL
1999, THE SPACE STUDIO,
NEW YORK CITY

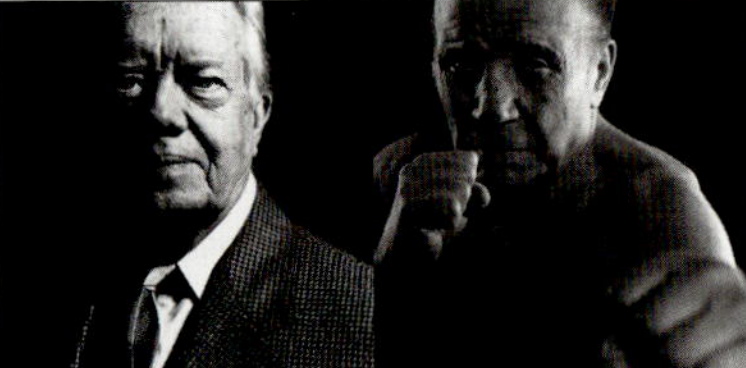

PRESIDENT JIMMY CARTER
1998, THE CARTER CENTER,
ATLANTA, GEORGIA

JAKE LAMOTTA
1999, INDUSTRIA
SUPERSTUDIO,
NEW YORK CITY

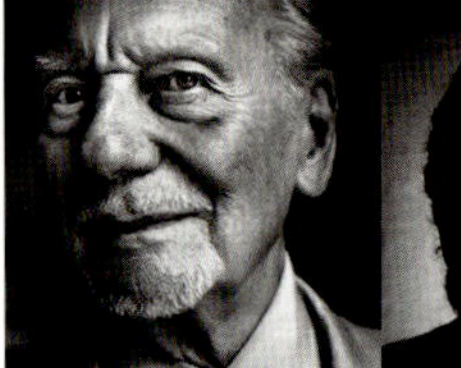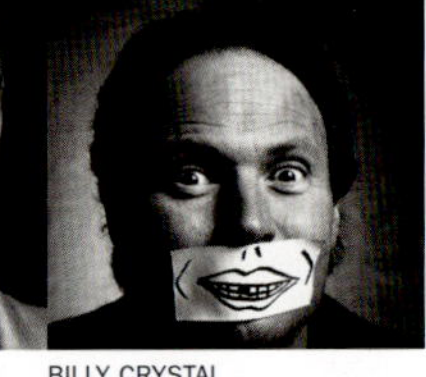

SIR JOHN GIELGUD
1991, SIR JOHN'S HOME,
ENGLAND

BILLY CRYSTAL
1993, THE BERKLEY SQUARE
HOTEL, LONDON

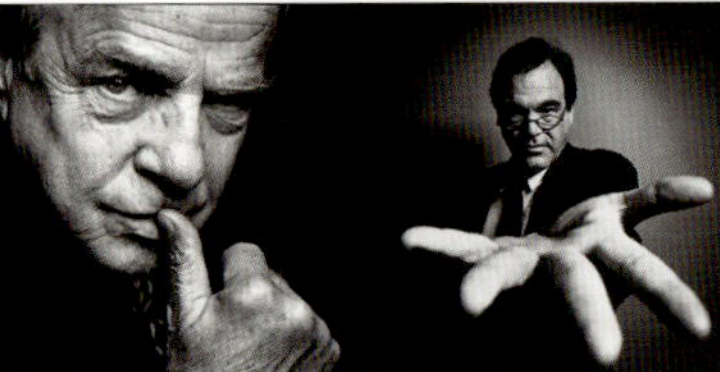

FRANCO ZEFFIRELLI
1998, THE LINCOLN CENTER,
NEW YORK CITY

OLIVER STONE
1995, THE MUSEUM OF
MODERN ART, NEW YORK CITY

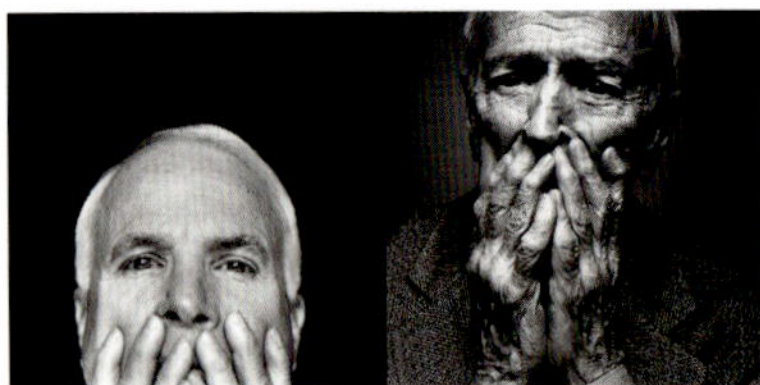

SENATOR JOHN MCCAIN
2000, THE RUSSELL
BUILDING, WASHINGTON, D.C.

WILLIAM MAXWELL
1997, WILLIAM'S HOME,
NEW YORK CITY

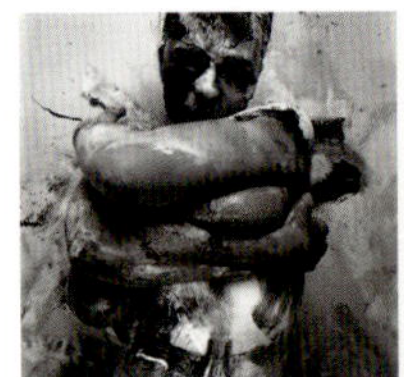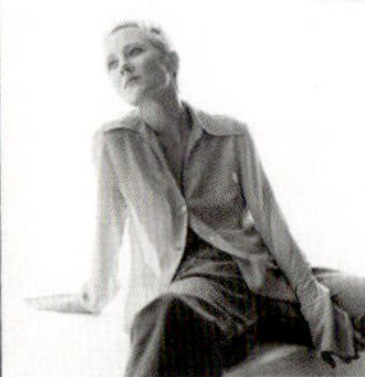

JENNY SAVILLE
1995, JENNY'S STUDIO,
LONDON

ANNE HECHE
1998, INDUSTRIA
SUPERSTUDIO,
NEW YORK CITY

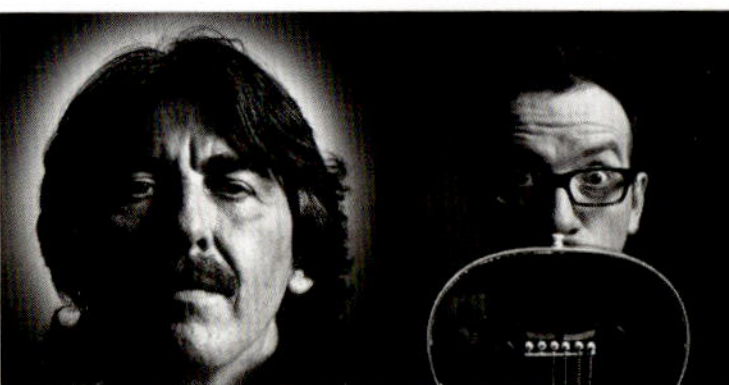

GEORGE HARRISON
1993, KENSINGTON PLACE,
LONDON

ELVIS COSTELLO
1994, SOUTHERN LIGHT
STUDIOS, LONDON

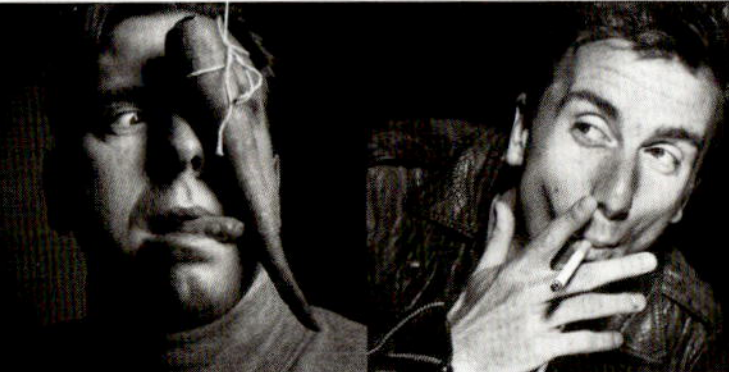

TIMOTHY SPALL
1993, NATIONAL THEATER,
LONDON

TIM ROTH
1993, WEST LONDON,
ENGLAND

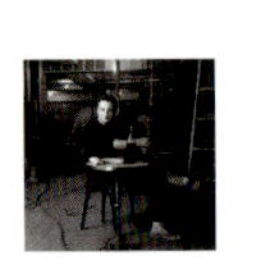

KEITH MCNALLY
1999, THE UNFINISHED
PASTIS, NEW YORK CITY

VIC REEVES AND
BOB MORTIMER
1990, CLAPHAM,
LONDON

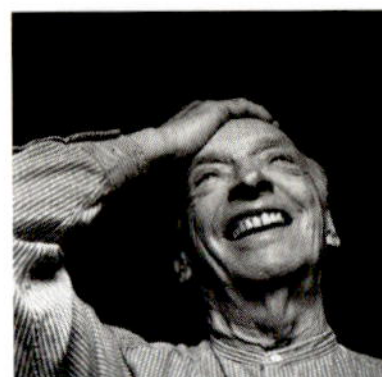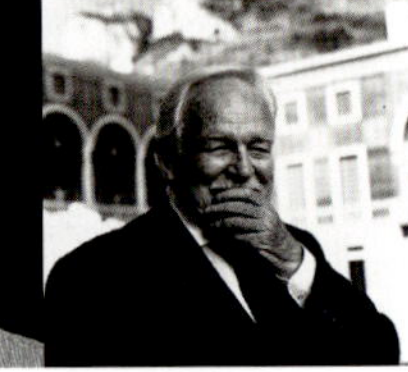

SAUL BELLOW
1995, SAUL'S APARTMENT,
BOSTON

PRINCE RAINIER OF MONACO
1997, THE PALACE,
MONTE CARLO

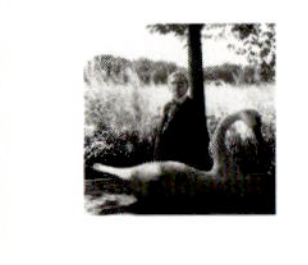

DAVID FOSTER WALLACE
1995, A FIELD OUTSIDE
BLOOMINGTON, ILLINOIS

DOMINICK DUNNE
1999, DOMINICK'S HOME,
UPSTATE NEW YORK

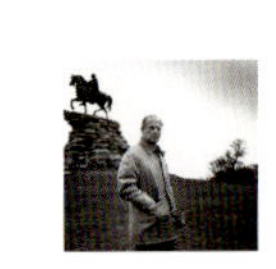

THE DUKE OF EDINBURGH
1991, WINDSOR CASTLE,
ENGLAND

BOB GELDOF
1994, CAMDEN, LONDON

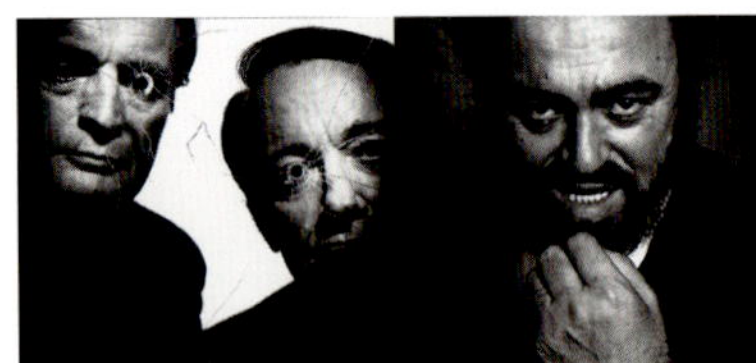

THE MAN FROM U.N.C.L.E.
1995, STUDIO ONE,
NEW YORK CITY

LUCIANO PAVAROTTI
1990, THE SAVOY HOTEL,
LONDON

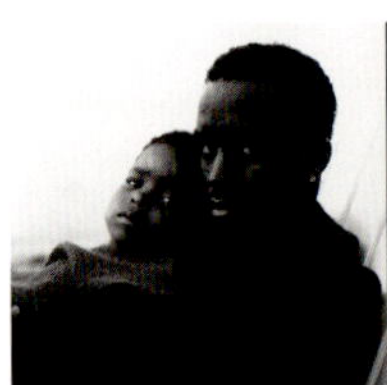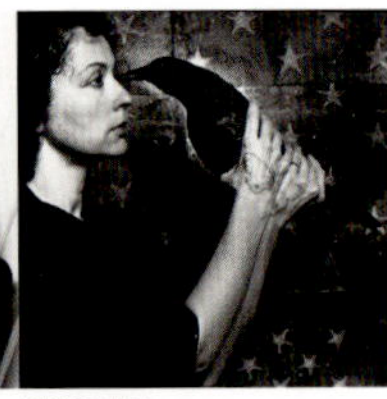

SEAN 'PUFFY' COMBS AND
SON JUSTIN
1998, PUFFY'S HOME,
EAST HAMPTON, NEW YORK

KIKI SMITH
1995, KIKI'S STUDIO,
NEW YORK CITY

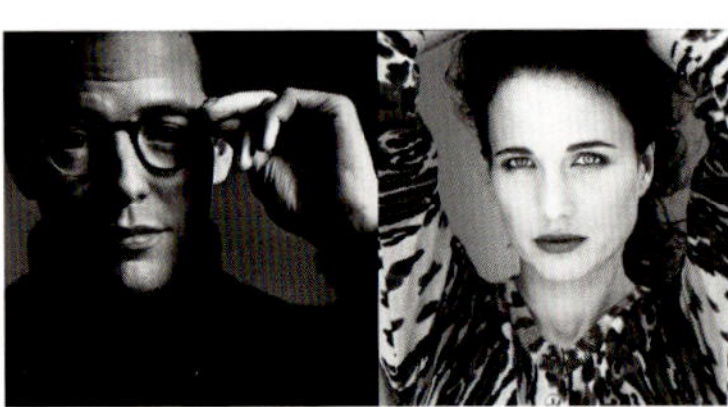

MATTHEW BRODERICK
1995, INDUSTRIA
SUPERSTUDIO,
NEW YORK CITY

ANDIE MACDOWELL
1997, INDUSTRIA
SUPERSTUDIO,
NEW YORK CITY

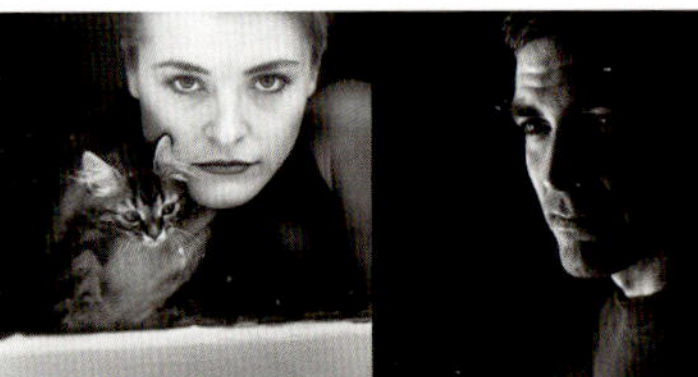

AMANDA DONOHOE
1997, CAMDEN,
LONDON

GEORGE CLOONEY
1997, HOLLYWOOD,
CALIFORNIA

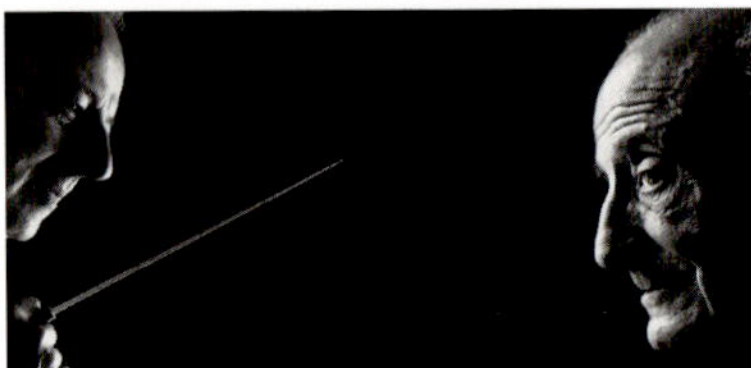

ANDRE PREVIN
1998, INDUSTRIA
SUPERSTUDIO,
NEW YORK CITY

FRED ZINNEMANN
1991, FRED'S OFFICE,
LONDON

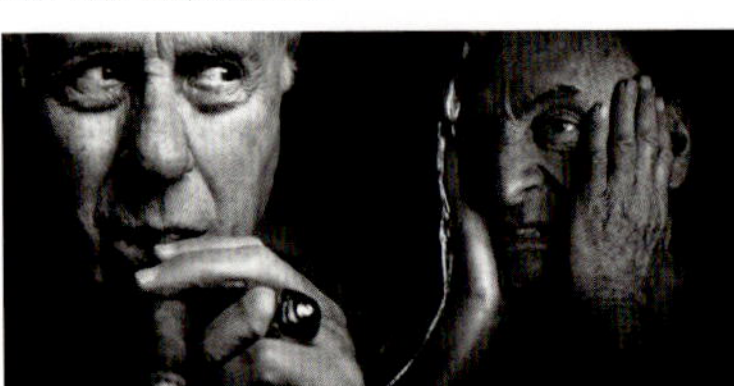

RED AUERBACH
1999, RED'S OFFICE,
WASHINGTON, D.C.

LARRY RIVERS
1999, LARRY'S STUDIO,
NEW YORK CITY

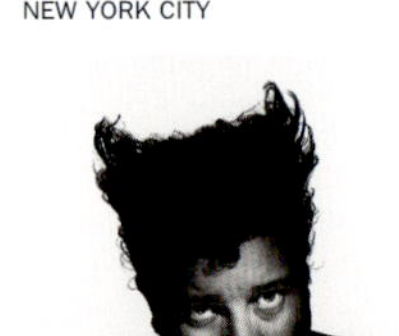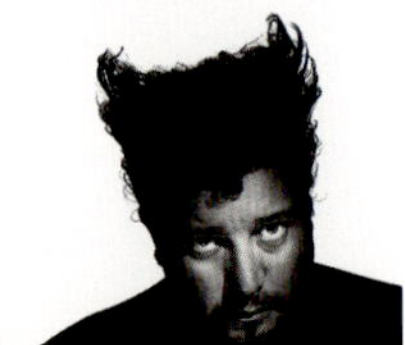

BEN STILLER
1994, LOS ANGELES

PHILIPPE STARCK
1995, INDUSTRIA
SUPERSTUDIO,
NEW YORK CITY

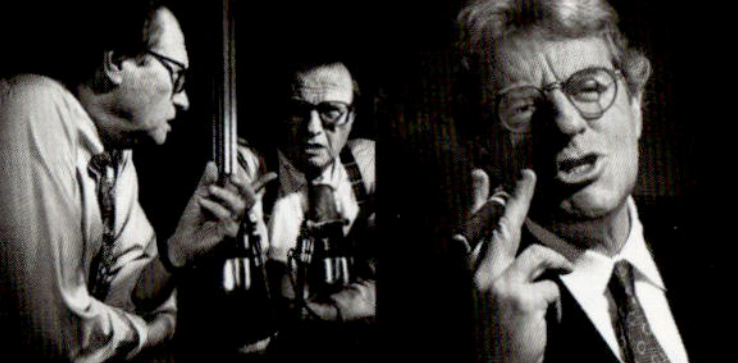

LARRY KING
1995, CNN,
WASHINGTON, D.C.

JERRY SPRINGER
1999, NBC STUDIOS,
CHICAGO, ILLINOIS

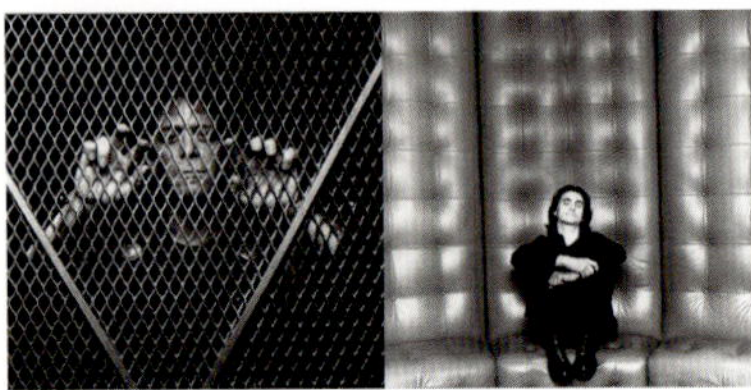

LOU REED
1996, SUN STUDIOS,
NEW YORK CITY

LAWRENCE BENDER
1997, THE ROYALTON HOTEL,
NEW YORK CITY

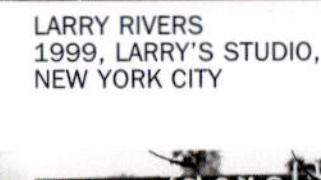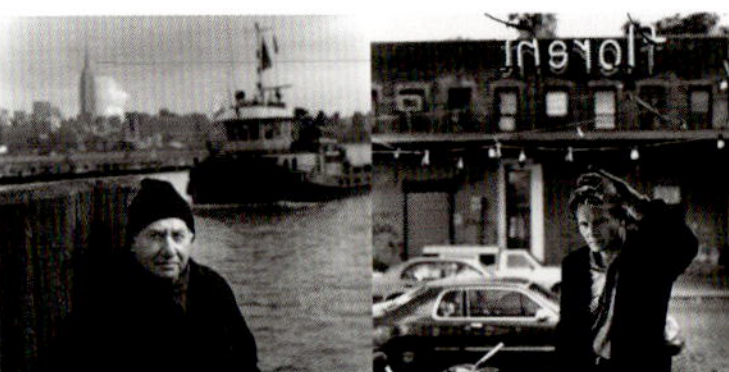

BUDD SCHULBERG
1997, HOBOKEN FERRY
TERMINAL, NEW JERSEY

LIAM NEESON
1996, FLORENT,
NEW YORK CITY

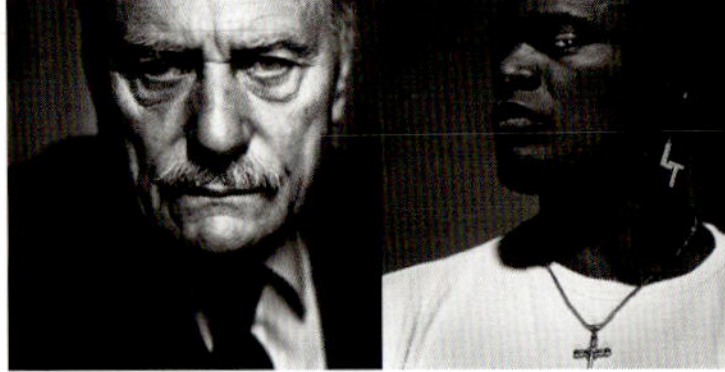

ENOCH POWELL
1989, BELGRAVIA, LONDON

LAWRENCE TAYLOR
1998, NEW JERSEY

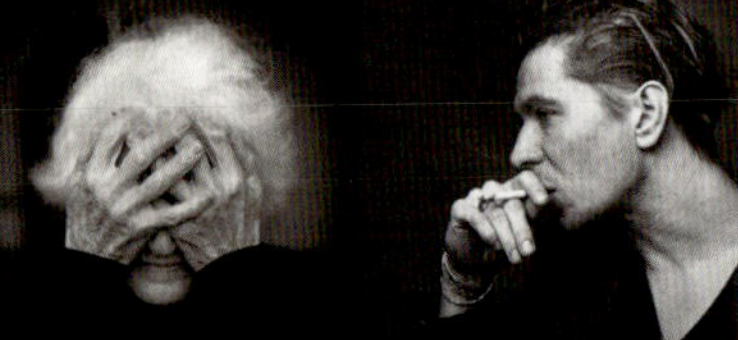

LAURA HUXLEY
1994, HOLLYWOOD,
CALIFORNIA

GARY OLDMAN
1990, SOHO,
LONDON

MY DEAR BOY:
I NO LONGER KNOW
JUST WHO THE REAL
ME IS ANYMORE.

DENHOLM ELLIOTT

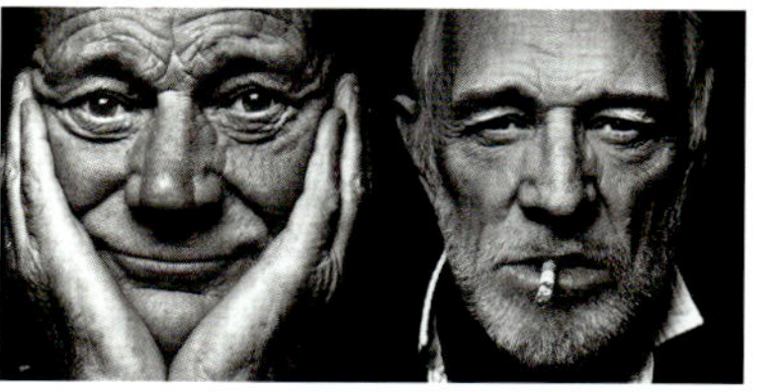

DENHOLM ELLIOTT
1998, CLAPHAM,
LONDON

RICHARD HARRIS
1990, THE SAVOY HOTEL,
LONDON

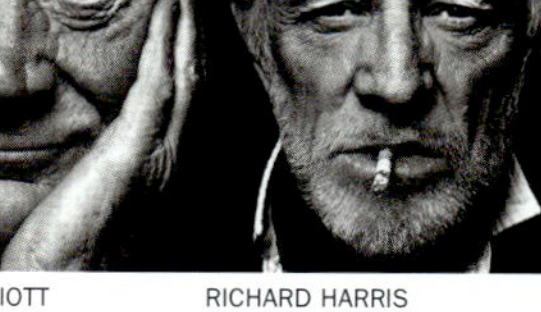

PLACIDO DOMINGO
1996, LINCOLN CENTER,
NEW YORK CITY

DEBRA HARRY
1996, CHELSEA,
NEW YORK CITY

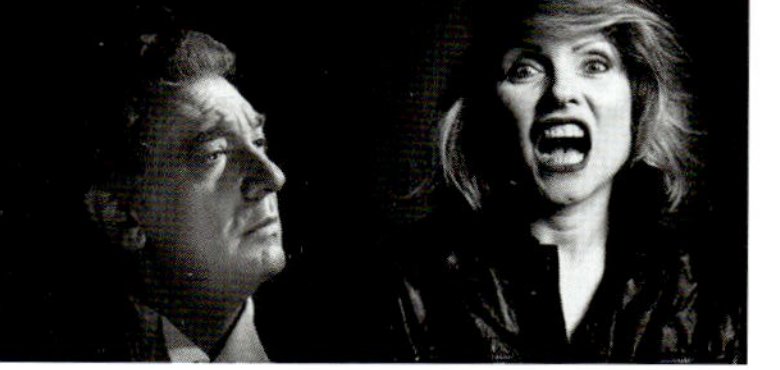

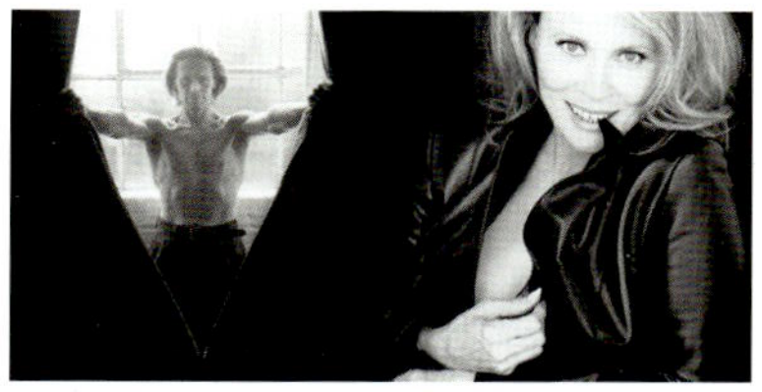

WILLEM DAFOE
1997, INDUSTRIA
SUPERSTUDIO,
NEW YORK CITY

FAYE DUNAWAY
1999, SMASHBOX STUDIOS,
LOS ANGELES

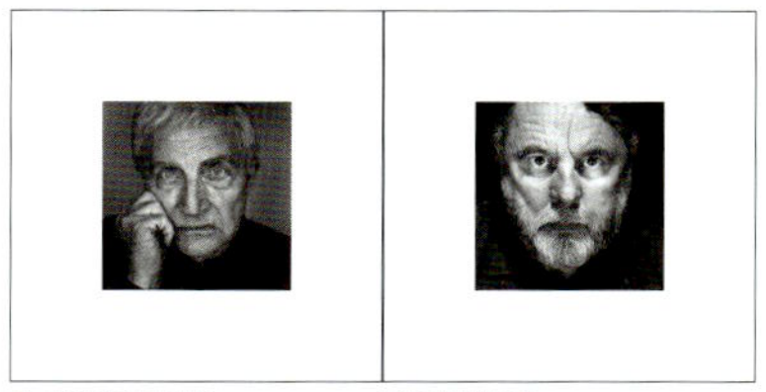

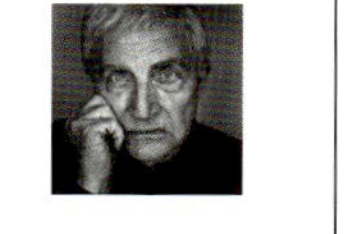

BLAKE EDWARDS
1995, SAG HARBOR,
NEW YORK

TERRY WAITE
1993, SUFFOLK,
ENGLAND

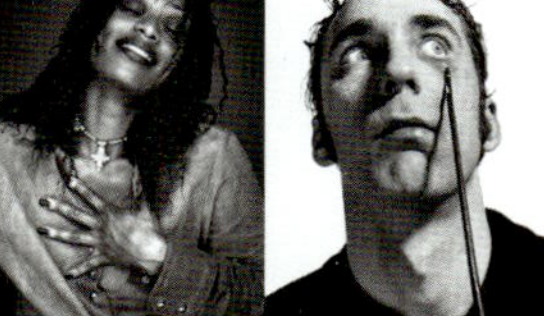

DES'REE
1995, INDUSTRIA
SUPERSTUDIO,
NEW YORK CITY

WILL SELF
1993, WILL'S HOME,
LONDON

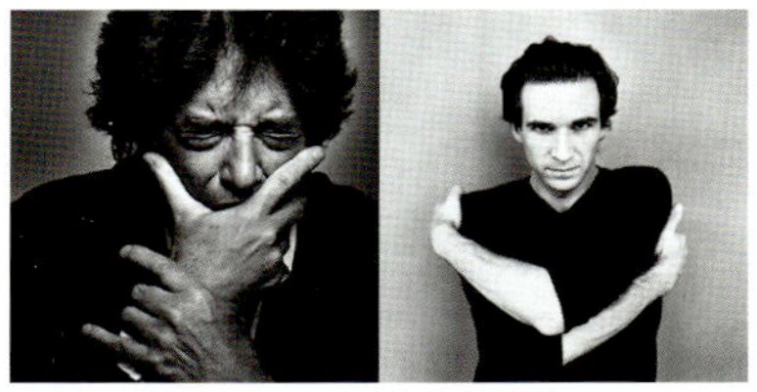

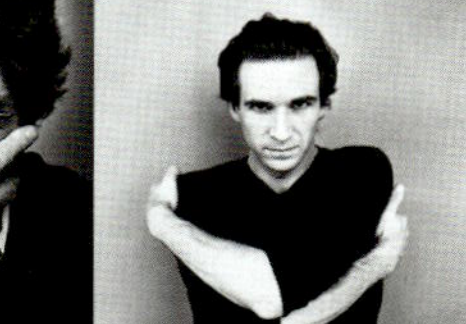

TOM STOPPARD
1991, CHELSEA,
LONDON

RALPH FIENNES
1996, SOUTHERN LIGHT
STUDIOS, LONDON

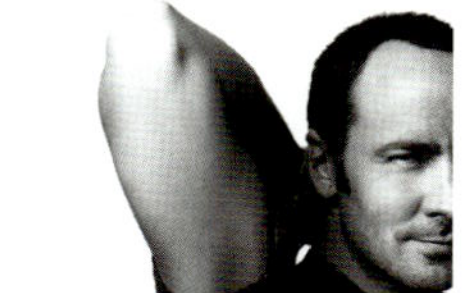
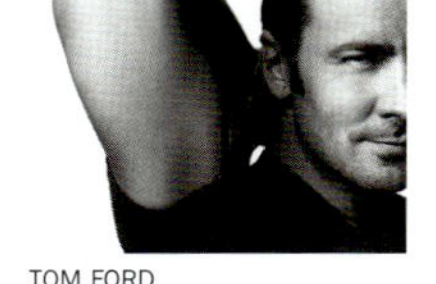
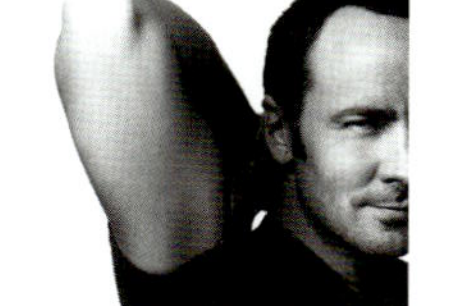

KATE SPADE
1996, INDUSTRIA
SUPERSTUDIO,
NEW YORK CITY

TOM FORD
2000, THE WORX STUDIO,
LONDON

AND I'VE
GOT AN UMBRELLA
THAT MATCHES
TOO!

RUBY

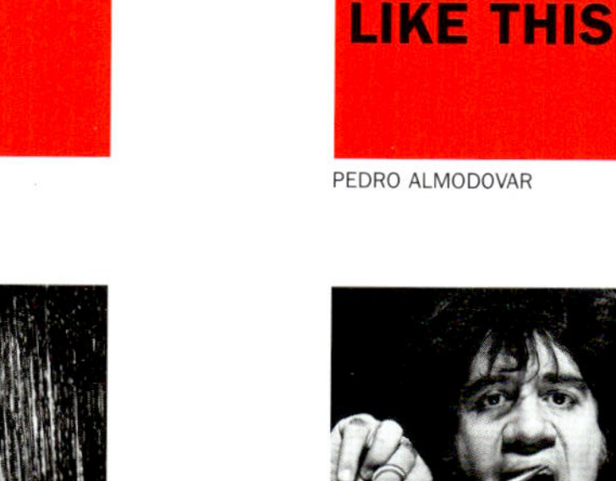

RUBY
1995, CHARLESTON,
SOUTH CAROLINA

JACK BENNY
1997, STAMFORD,
CONNECTICUT

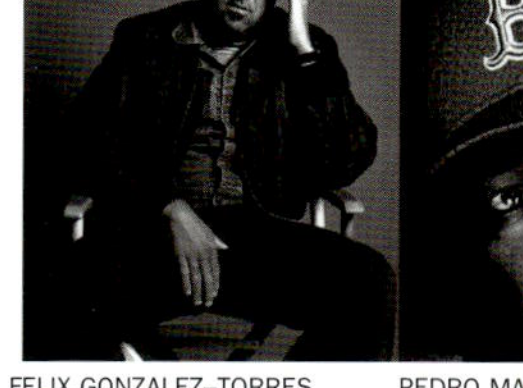

LAURENCE FISHBURNE
1995, INDUSTRIA
SUPERSTUDIO,
NEW YORK CITY

CARA DE LIZIA
1998, SMASHBOX STUDIOS,
LOS ANGELES

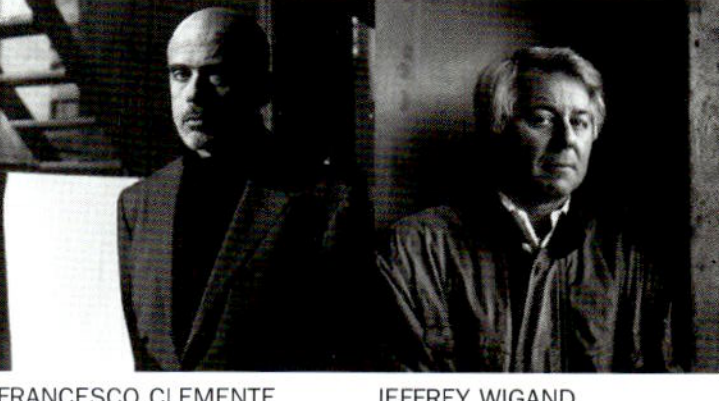

FELIX GONZALEZ–TORRES
1995, BUHL STUDIOS,
NEW YORK CITY

PEDRO MARTINEZ
2000, SANTO DOMINGO,
DOMINICAN REPUBLIC

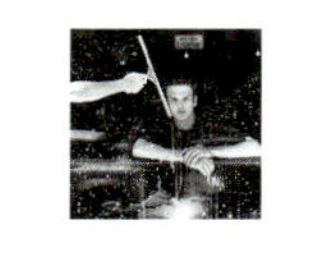
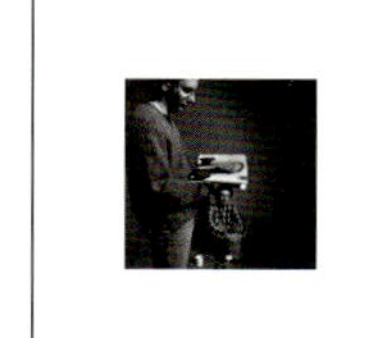

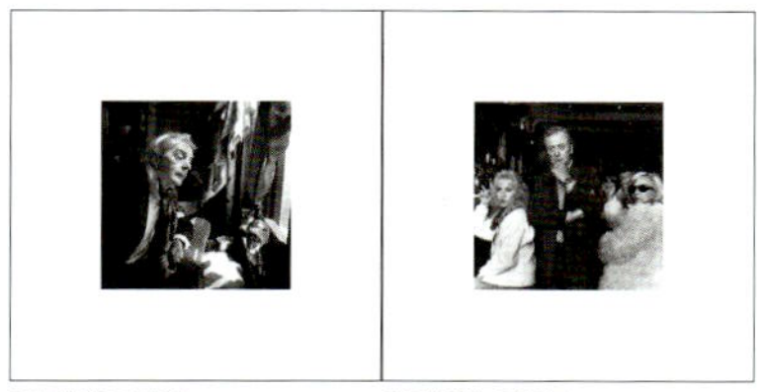

QUENTIN CRISP
1990, QUENTIN'S HOME,
NEW YORK CITY

MICHAEL CAINE
1997, MICHAEL'S
RESTAURANT, SOUTH BEACH,
MIAMI, FLORIDA

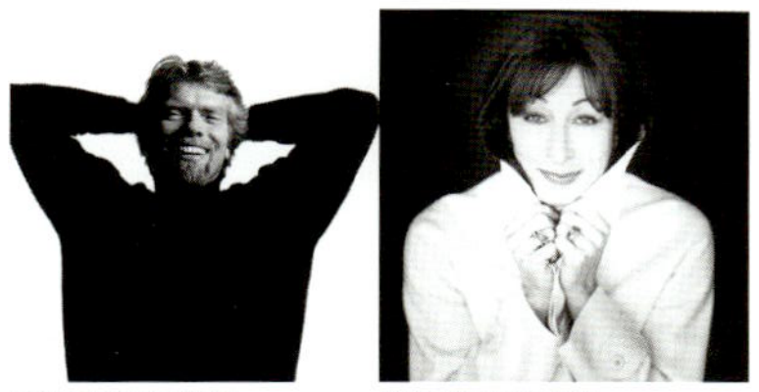

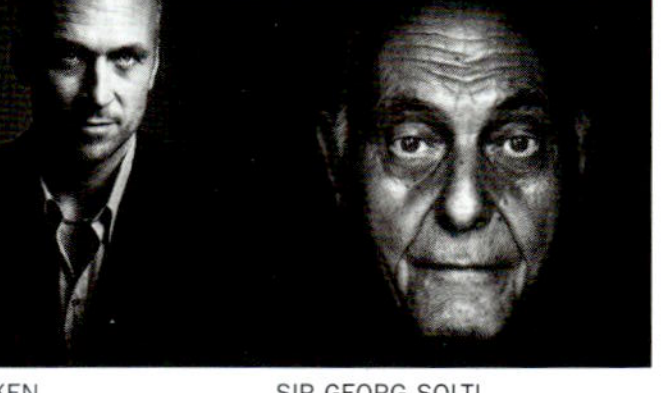

RICHARD BRANSON
1996, SMASHBOX STUDIOS,
LOS ANGELES

ANJELICA HUSTON
1999, SMASHBOX STUDIOS,
LOS ANGELES

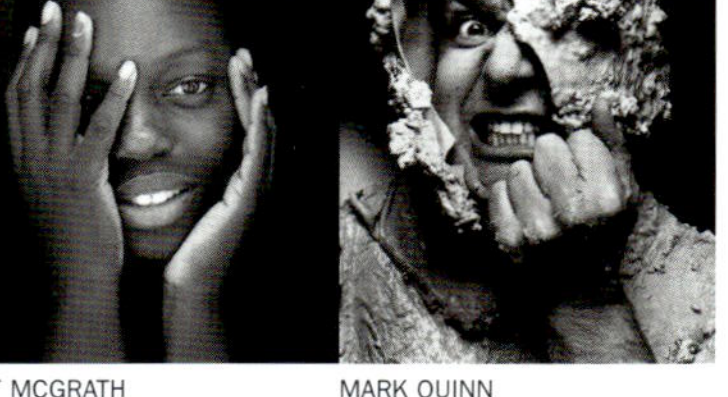

JEFFREY MACDONALD
1998, OREGON STATE
PENITENTIARY, OREGON

ALEC BALDWIN
1997, HOLLYWOOD HILLS,
CALIFORNIA

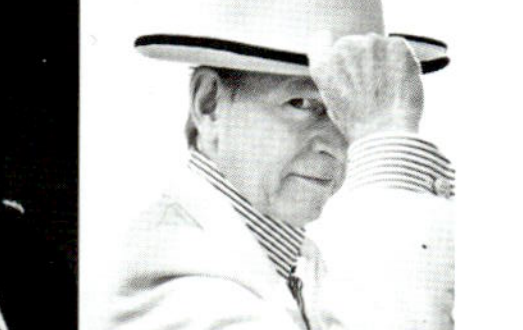
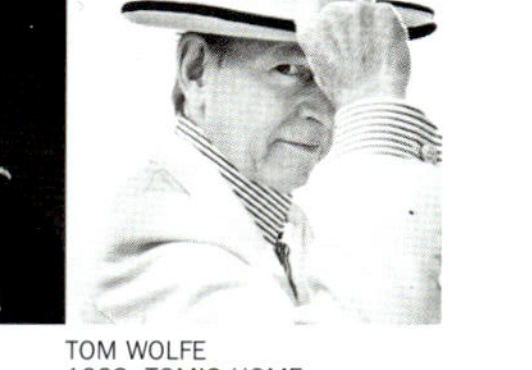

ALLEN GINSBERG
1994, BOULDER,
COLORADO

ALFRED EISENSTAEDT
1994, THE TIME-LIFE BUILDING,
NEW YORK CITY

THEY'RE ALWAYS
TRYING TO CENSOR
ME... LET'S DO IT
LIKE THIS!

PEDRO ALMODOVAR

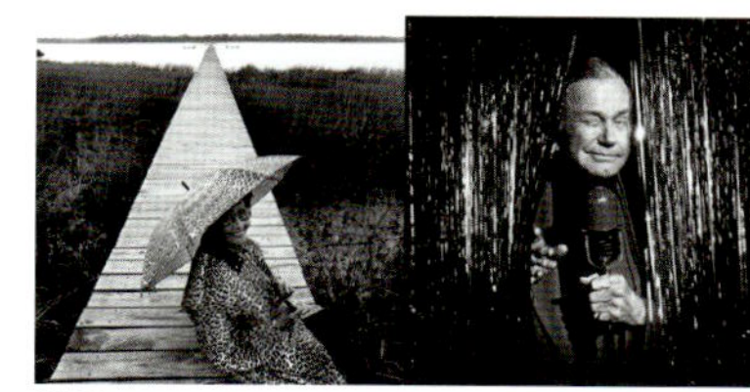

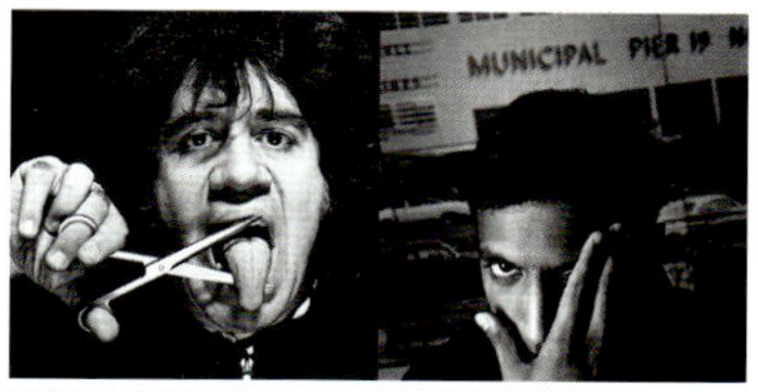

PEDRO ALMODOVAR
1994, THE BERKLEY
SQUARE HOTEL, LONDON

M. NIGHT SHYAMALAN
2000, PHILADELPHIA,
PENNSYLVANIA

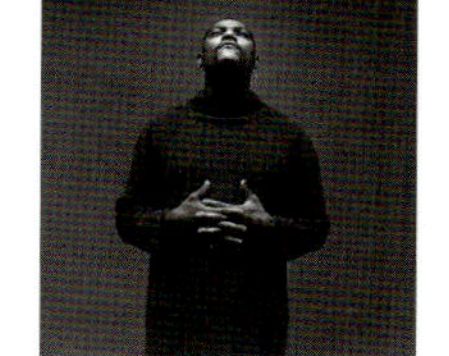
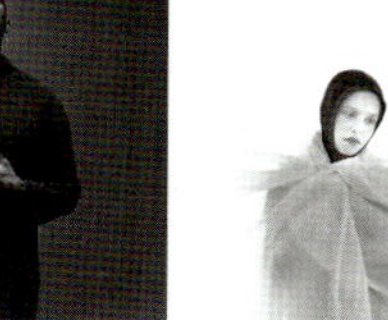

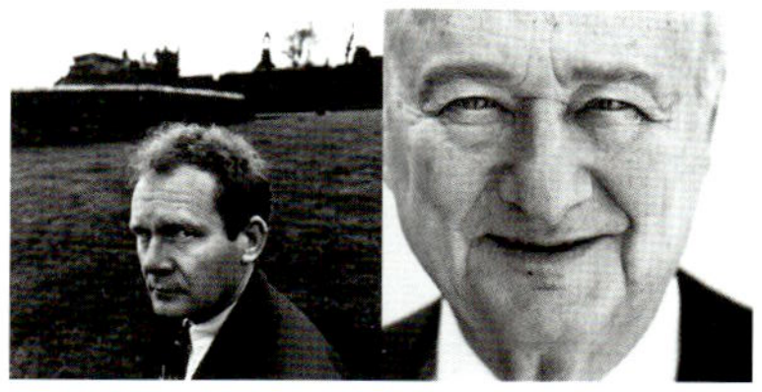

MARTIN MCGUINNESS
1995, DERRY,
NORTHERN IRELAND

ED KOCH
1998, INDUSTRIA
SUPERSTUDIO,
NEW YORK CITY

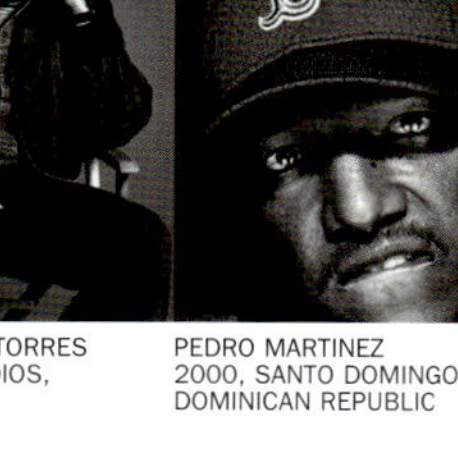

FRANCESCO CLEMENTE
1997, NEW YORK CITY

JEFFREY WIGAND
1995, LOUISVILLE,
KENTUCKY

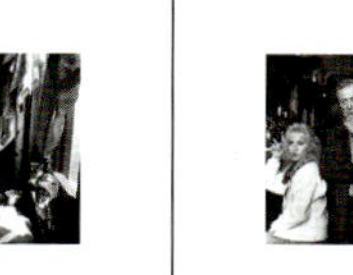

PETER BERG
2000, NEW YORK CITY

THE COEN BROTHERS
1996, INDUSTRIA
SUPERSTUDIO,
NEW YORK CITY

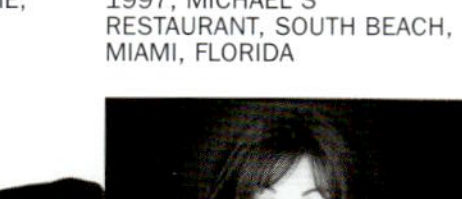

CAL RIPKEN
1997, BALTIMORE,
MARYLAND

SIR GEORG SOLTI
1992, SALZBURG,
AUSTRIA

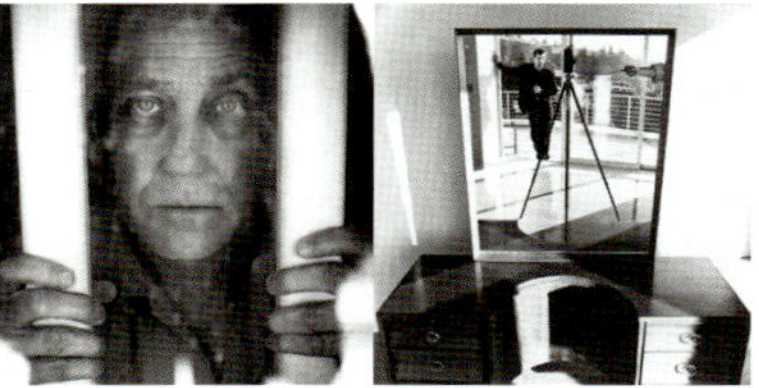

PAT MCGRATH
1999, INDUSTRIA
SUPERSTUDIO,
NEW YORK CITY

MARK QUINN
1995, CLAPHAM,
LONDON

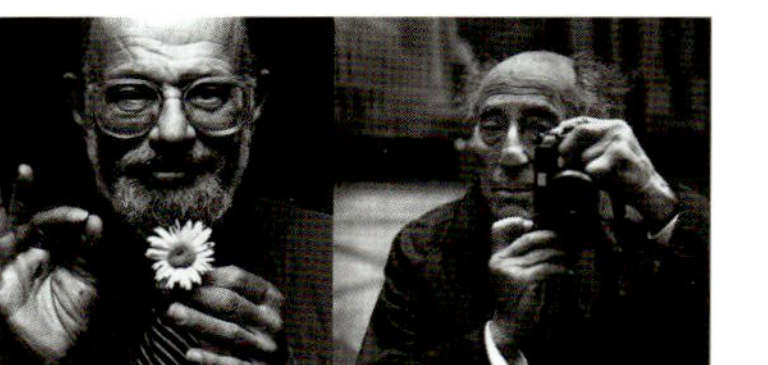

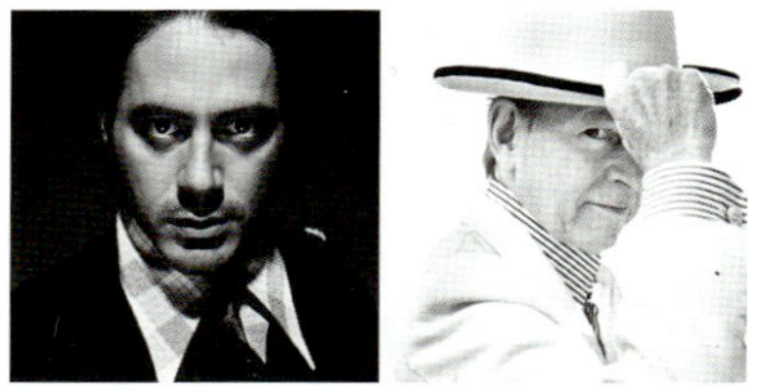

ROBERT DOWNEY, JR.
1994, METRO STUDIOS,
LONDON

TOM WOLFE
1998, TOM'S HOME,
NEW YORK CITY

A WORD TO ALL OF YOU WHO MADE THIS
BOOK POSSIBLE – FOR YOUR ENCOURAGEMENT,
ENTHUSIASM, AND ABOVE ALL, PATIENCE
(GOODNESS KNOWS, YOU ALL NEEDED IT!) –

THANK YOU

ESPECIALLY TO:

MELANIE

SHEILA, EMMA & JACK

GEOFF & PAM

JUSTUS AND BERNHARD AT PENTAGRAM

**DANNY & LISA, MARY, TANJYA, HUGO, MIKE, DARWISSA,
AND EVERYONE AT** CPI

STEVE AND ALL AT KATZ PICTURES

DANIEL & CRAIG, AND EVERYONE AT POWERHOUSE BOOKS

**DEBRA, GREGG, LOR, CHRISTINA, JENNIFER, KAREN, SHARON, AND ALL THE
OTHER ABUSED (VERBALLY AND OTHERWISE) PHOTO-ASSISTANTS**

**JENNIFER, KIM, CLAIRE, MARION, MELISSA, LEA, JIM, JULIE, AND ALL THE
OTHER WONDERFUL STYLISTS**

**ASSUMPTA, REGINE, JEANNIE, AMY, KATRINA, GITA, GUNN, AND EVERYONE
ELSE WHO'S DONE MY MAKEUP AND HAIR**

ANNE, AND ALL THE OTHERS WHO GENEROUSLY DONATE THEIR IDEAS

PATRICK, DENNIS, EDDIE, AND ALL AT *W*

GRAYDON, DAVID, SUSAN, LISA, AND ALL AT *VANITY FAIR*

KATHY, JODY, SARAH AND ALL AT *THE NEW YORK TIMES MAGAZINE*

CHRIS AT *NEW YORK*

BOB, JACK & KEVIN, AND ALL AT *GEAR*

SARAH & RICHARD AND ALL AT *ENTERTAINMENT WEEKLY*

FRED & ANTONIA, AND EVERYONE AT *MADISON*

AIDAN AT THE *SUNDAY TIMES MAGAZINE*

GQ, *VOGUE, ESQUIRE, ESPN, HARPER'S BAZAAR, LIFE, LA, NEWSWEEK*, TIME,
AVENUE, US, GEORGE

**BARBARA GRIFFIN, ROBIN HARVEY, MICHAEL RAND, SUZANNE HODGART,
COLIN JACOBSON, CAROLINE METCALF, NIGEL SKELSEY, JUNE STANIER,
AND ALL THOSE WHO SUPPORTED ME (AND STILL DO!)**

MATTHEW AND CAROLINE EVANS, TONY MACINTOSH, AND EVERYONE AT
THE GROUCHO CLUB

ALINA & PAGE, MIKE & CHRIS, AND EVERYONE AT INDUSTRIA

EDEN & ANTHONY, AND EVERYONE AT SMASHBOX

**LIAM, AND ALL OTHERS WHO ALLOWED ME THE HONOR OF
PHOTOGRAPHING THEM**

ACKNOWLEDGMENTS

MUM – THANKS FOR MY FIRST CAMERA

I LOVE IT...
I LOVE IT!

I LOVE IT...

WHAT I SAY WHEN THE SHOOT GETS
GOING REAL GOOD...
(YOU DON'T WANT TO HEAR WHAT I
SAY WHEN IT DOESN'T).

Published in the United States by powerHouse Books,
a division of powerHouse Cultural Entertainment, Inc.
180 Varick Street, Suite 1302, New York, NY 10014-4606
telephone 212 604 9074, fax 212 366 5247
e-mail: info@powerHouseBooks.com
website: www.powerHouseBooks.com

First edition, 2000

Library of Congress Cataloging-in-Publication Data:

Parry, Nigel.
    Sharp / Photographs by Nigel Parry ; introduction by Liam Neeson.
        p. cm.
    ISBN 1-57687-088-X
    1. Portrait photography. 2. Celebrities–Portraits. I. Title.

TR681.F3 P38 2000
779'.2'092–dc21
                                                00-055784

Hardcover ISBN 1-57687-088-X

Separations and printing by Arti Grafiche Amilcare Pizzi S.p.A.

A complete catalog of powerHouse Books and Limited Editions is available upon request;
please call, write, or cut to our website.

10 9 8 7 6 5 4 3 2 1

A slipcased, limited edition of this book with a signed and numbered artwork by the artist is available upon inquiry;
please contact the publisher.

Designed by Justus Oehler / Pentagram, London

Printed and bound in Italy